A Commodious Yard

The history of

WILLIAM THOMAS & SONS

SHIPBUILDERS, SHIPOWNERS AND MANAGERS

OF

AMLWCH

ISLE OF ANGLESEY

1858 – 1920

Bryan D. Hope

First published 2005

© Text: and photographs: Author

ISBN (soft-back): 1-84527-021-5
ISBN (hard-back): 1-84527-022-3

Published in Wales by
Gwasg Carreg Gwalch,
12 Iard yr Orsaf, Llanrwst, Wales, LL26 0EH.
Tel: 01492 642031   Fax: 01492 641502
e-mail: llyfrau@carreg-gwalch.co.uk
www.carreg-gwalch.co.uk

Printed and published in Wales.

This books is dedicated to the memory of my late son in law
Mitch Baines
and to my five marvelous grandchildren:
Jack and Josh
Lewis
Kira
Adam
and their equally wonderful parents,
as well as to my very best friends – you know who you are.

Iard Newydd as it was in 1872 – illustration taken from William Thomas's headed notepaper of that year.

Mae Capten Tomos Amlwch
Newydd fildio llong.
Mae'n lansio ar ddydd Gwener
A hynny yn ddi siom.
Morthwylion yn eu dwylo, a'r wejis yn eu lle;
Miss Jenni'n taro'r botel
Ac off â hi, awé!

Di enw

Captain Thomas, Amlwch
Has newly built a ship
He's launching on a Friday
And that without a slip
Hammers in their hands and wedges in their place
Miss Jenny strikes the bottle
And off she goes apace.

Anon.

AMLWCH

Location of Amlwch, Isle of Anglesey, Wales.

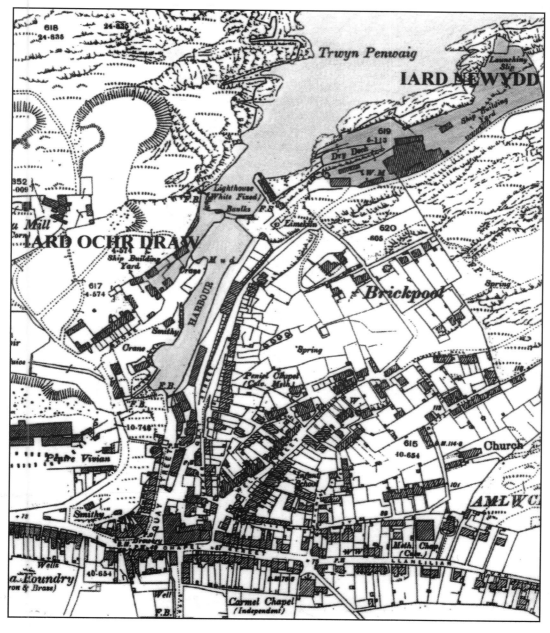

Map showing the location and extent of Iard Newydd

FOREWORD

Professor John Armstrong may think himself a little young to be saddled with the title of 'doyen', but for over twenty years he has been preaching the message that the history of the British coastwise trade has been seriously neglected as a result of maritime historians being seduced by the histories of the great passenger and cargo lines, be they Blue Funnel, Cunard or whoever.

In north west Wales, a remarkable little circle of maritime historians grew up in the 1960s and '70s, of whom the best-known, because the most-published, were Aled Eames and Lewis Lloyd, neither, sadly, still with us. But they were not alone; there were enough others, both as authors and subscribers, to sustain the publication of that much under-rated journal *Maritime Wales*, which continues to this day. They not only recognised the importance of the coasting trade in general terms; but also concentrated on the almost forgotten ports of north west Wales, their ships, their cargoes and their trades. Some, like the slate trade, were of fairly obvious importance, and because they were often associated with great land-holders' estates which had reasonably systematic archives, comparatively easy to research. What was less easy was the analysis of patterns of ship ownership, for here there were neither estate archives, nor those company archives in which the researchers of such as Harrisons or Elder Dempster had a comparatively easy time. But it was done, often from mind-bending amounts of effort expended in dragging forth a bit here or a bit there from the local newspapers. Of course, such source material can provide outsiders' views of companies, sometimes even giving us insights into the personalities of the people involved.

Some ten years ago, the editor of an international journal asked if I would review Bryan Hope's earlier (1994) work, *A Curious Place: the Industrial History of Amlwch (1550-1950)*. I had been a student of John Harris, with whose masterly history of *The Copper King* I was well familiar, and I suppose that after the passage of ten years I can confess that what I expected to read was just an up-date or a dissemination of Harris' work. What an agreeable surprise it was (for I had not then met the author) to realise that here was a true scholar pursuing the history of what was indeed a very 'Curious Place'.

To the modern visitor, turning up in his family car to have a nose around the old port of Amlwch, it seems impossible that the inner harbour could have accommodated anything much bigger than a sailing dinghy. In reality, it shipped quantities of copper ore which changed the face of the British copper industry: but it might seem even more improbable that to the seaward side there could be a significant shipbuilding and repairing yard.

There are many hundreds of places around the British coast where coastal sailing vessels were built, their raw materials being wood, the practical and entrepreneurial skills of a maritime community; but not a lot else. Very few of them have left us much in the way of recorded material. Finding out what the ships were like from fragmentary photographic evidence, the odd lines plan or hull block model that escaped the liquidation bonfire, is difficult enough. In this respect Amlwch is not merely a curious place, but a quite exceptional one.

This book is based on archive material of a quality and quantity which surpasses that surviving from many of the famous shipbuilding yards of the Clyde or the Tees. But it goes much further than that, for in such a small place as Amlwch, the local shipbuilder was a 'one stop shop' involved not just in building and repairing, but in shipping operation and ship-brokerage as well. In the remarkable records of William Thomas, his firm and his family, we should be able to expect to easily find a complete account of an undertaking of some of the unsung heroes of British maritime supremacy in the late nineteenth and early twentieth centuries: but can we?

No, we can't. The archival material employed includes an estimated 33,000 copies of' letters out', and that is by no means all through which Bryan Hope has ground his patient way in writing this book. It is a huge amount of toil, without which the archival material would remain to almost all of us readers, totally unassimilable. He has rendered maritime history a huge service, initially by doing all the boring work of collating and analysing the raw data, and then by presenting the fruits of this labour of many years in a highly readable book.

I will admit to having a bit of a soft spot for the shipping of north west Wales. Perhaps it's because I'm part-Welsh myself (my father was Welsh enough to serve as an adjudicator at more than one National Eisteddfod) but it's more likely because I am a Liverpudlian: show me a pre-1914 building in Liverpool and I will show you which bits of it left a hole somewhere in North Wales. I have an office in a former merchant's house in the School of History at the University of Liverpool. The bricks are local, but the slates of its roof and the limestone for its mortar came from Wales, carried in ships such as those whose building and operation is both graphically described and painstakingly analysed in this book.

I have not seen the printing specification for the book, but I hope it includes the use of acid-free paper, because its content is a contribution to maritime history which deserves to last a long time.

Adrian Jarvis,
Co-Director, Center for Port & Maritime History
University of Liverpool.

PROLOGUE

In many respects, it is a comparatively straightforward, but not necessarily a simple undertaking to chronicle the achievements of a small 19th century family shipping firm such as William Thomas & Sons in terms of its business policies, and the operational histories of the vessels it built, owned and managed. More difficult however, is the task of revealing the nature of the principal characters involved, an essential ingredient in any good narrative.

In this respect, my task was made very much easier when I was given access to the firm's business letters and financial ledgers, detailing much of the firm's activities over 60 or more years. For this privilege, I have to thank the late Elwyn Williams of Holyhead, and his son Robyn, the founder's great grandson, who has been nothing less than supportive. Apart from her personal recollections of some of the people involved, several artifacts relating to the firm, were lent to me for recording purposes by the late Gertrude Thomas, Captain William Thomas's last surviving granddaughter; to whom I shall always be indebted.

It is highly unlikely however, that were it not for the introduction of *Copy Letter Books*, a system widely used to record business correspondence during the late 19th century, very few of the firm's letters would have survived, and many historians, as a result, would have been much the poorer for it. Despite its many advantages however, the system did not always guarantee that all copies were readable, and many pages in the surviving Thomas letter books, some of which are probably pivotal to the fuller understanding of the firm's history, are for one reason or another, completely illegible.

Twenty-two of the firm's copy letter books spanning a period of over 50 years have survived, out of an estimated total of thirty-nine. It is thought that in the early years of the firm's existence, one letter book would probably have been sufficient to record a full year's correspondence, and on this premise, the eight books preceding the first surviving one, are missing. These would have recorded the formative, and possibly the most exciting period in the firm's history. Of those which have survived however, only one, that from August 1888 to October 1889, coincides with the founder's lifetime. The few surviving letters known to have been penned by Captain William Thomas, give a brief insight into his character and business methods, albeit when his health was deteriorating, and his most eventful achievements well behind him.

Each book contains a token number of 1000 pages: but as a great number record two outgoing letters, it is 'guesstimated' that each contains something in the order of 1,500 letters. Based on this assumption, approximately 33,0000 letters have survived; all of which I have read as far as I was able, and many thousands of which I have noted by way of researching what has turned out to be a most fascinating subject. The resulting wealth of information, recorded in over 700 pages of notes, has been sufficiently daunting to delay until now, any attempt on my part to collate and present it in a coherent and hopefully, interesting manner. My main difficulty however, has been not so much in having to decide what to include in the work, but more significantly, what to leave out; particularly as I realise that every part of it is relevant to someone, somewhere!

Very few incoming business letters have survived, but despite that, it is not too difficult a task to deduce their content from the replies they elicited. Taken as a whole however, the correspondence shows that management issues changed very little over the firm's lifetime, inasmuch that one year's business was much like any other, and apart from the fact that the names of the captains and their vessels changed over time, the problems which attended them, and their subsequent solution, remained very much the same.

Amongst the private letters recorded in the books, there are several which are either addressed to Captain Thomas's recalcitrant son, John, or relate directly to him. It is difficult to understand why such trenchant and highly personal letters needed to have been recorded at all, let alone amongst the firm's business correspondence. Although the principal characters have long since passed away, the question had to be addressed as to whether or not it was proper to reveal the contents of the letters in this work, or indeed, if they even added anything of worth to the narrative. Following discussions with Robyn Williams however, it was agreed that since the events happened a century or so ago, there was little point in withholding information which could possibly add colour to the story by shedding light on the nature of the personalities involved; but of equal importance perhaps, by illuminating some of the personal problems which attended the family's business lives.

By way of adding further flavour to the story, I have quoted directly from the letter books in those many instances where the original correspondence seemed to me to convey far more by way of subtleties, written as they were in the style of the time, than if the same information were to be related in the form of a précis. Similarly, I have quoted directly from letters containing technical information, as any attempt at summarising these would without doubt, lose much of worth in re-telling.

In those instances where there are gaps in the firm's letter books, I have had to rely partly on the firm's ledgers which detail expenditures incurred on various vessels, but also on more conventional sources of information, much of it being primary source material held in archives and libraries elsewhere. Where such annals have been quoted, I have, as far as my own disorderly records permit, indicated their source; and further researchers into the activities of William Thomas & Sons, particularly students of economic history, should note that almost all of the relevant material is now lodged with the Anglesey Records Office in Llangefni.

In customary fashion, I sincerely wish to acknowledge the help given me by many friends in the preparation of this book, in particular Dr Adrian Jarvis, Secretary-General of the International Commission for Maritime History, who kindly gave me his expert views on the almost completed work, all of which I have addressed and subsequently embodied in it. The fact that he later agreed to write the foreword to the book only adds to my great indebtedness to him. Very high on the list of people I have to thank is Elspeth Wagstaff, who undertook the daunting task of proofreading the completed work as subsequent galley proofs were received from the publishers. For this and the combined practical interest which she and her husband Dave have shown in my work over the years, I can only express my deep appreciation. Many others also, too numerous to mention by name, have assisted me in my long drawn out efforts to make sense of it all. Some have waded through early scripts, and made constructive observations which I very much value; whilst others like Terry Belt of Winchester, and Peter Newcombe of Exeter, have freely allowed me to use photographs and information from their private archives in order to better illustrate the work.

In particular however, I have to thank Robyn Williams and his family, not only for allowing me to borrow their valuable family documents for more years than I or they care to remember, but more especially, for subsequently committing them to the care of Anglesey Records Office for all to use.

My thanks must also go to The Isle of Anglesey Council for financially supporting the publication of this book, and in particular to John Rees Thomas of the Council's Education and Heritage Department for his abiding interest in my work. Because of their sheer volume and breadth, these papers have to be unique in their power to reveal an extremely important facet of the mercantile maritime history of Britain in the late 19th and early 20th centuries, hitherto difficult to discover in such detail. More especially however, they provide a clearer insight into the quite extraordinary and invaluable contribution made by the Welsh nation to the maritime history of the British Isles; a contribution which has rightly been described elsewhere as being quite disproportionate to the modest size of its population. In that respect, if some small measure of justice has been done to these extremely important documents by way of this work, I shall consider the effort to have been worthwhile.

Penultimately, I have to sincerely thank my wife Anne, not only for her patience and encouragement in the face of my prolonged sessions over many years in front of what in my own defence, I can only describe as a diabolically hypnotic computer screen: but more especially for reading and commenting on the outcome in a sympathetic and constructive manner.

Finally however, I wish to acknowledge, not only the help given me by my late son-in-law, Mitch Baines, who responded with patience and good grace (more often than not) to my unending pleas for help in restoring my long suffering computer to working order after unenlightened meddling on my part; but more so, for his ambitious plans to publish this work when it was completed – we almost made it.

Bryan Hope
Moelfre, Ynys Môn.
February 2005

CHAPTER 1
THE BEGINNINGS OF THE AMLWCH SHIPBUILDING INDUSTRY
"...men came swarming, as in a gold fever..."

Amlwch, on the craggy, windswept northern coastline of the Welsh island of Anglesey, was once described as being little more than: *a fishing village, consisting of a parish church, and a few small, thatched cottages of the most primitive shape and construction.* A remarkable mining discovery made in the second half of the 18th century changed all of that; and in common with very many other parts of Wales, Amlwch now bears the scars of a mining industry which in its heyday dominated the life of the community.

Present-day visitors approaching Amlwch by road from the west, can hardly fail to notice the dark, humped outline of *Mynydd Parys* (Parys Mountain), topped by the shell of a dilapidated windmill, rising gently from the surrounding green fields ahead of them. Despite its name however, the mountain is in reality, little more than a long, low hill, the highest point of which barely reaches 200 metres above sea level. Its northern heather-covered slopes reveal little of its former history: but when seen from the south however, its scarred, multicoloured landscape, in which stands a derelict, but easily recognisable Cornish engine house, clearly points to an industrial past.

Few visitors to the area are aware that what they are seeing are the remains of what was once the greatest copper mine in the world. Such is its present-day significance however, that in 1998, the landscape was included in the Register of Landscapes of Outstanding Historical Importance in Wales. Subsequently, following submissions by the Amlwch Industrial Heritage Trust, the combined industrial landscapes of Mynydd Parys and nearby Porth Amlwch through which the mountain's ore was shipped, were designated an 'Anchor Point', the most prestigious category for sites on the 'European Route of Industrial Heritage'.

From being a small fishing village, Amlwch became a boom town, when after many years of limited scale mining ventures, vast reserves of copper ore were discovered by one Rolant Pugh on the 2nd of March 1768. He was then working under the able direction of Jonathan Roose, a Derbyshire miner brought to Amlwch by Roe and Company, who had a mining lease on the mountain granted to it by Nicholas Bayly, forebear of the present Marquess of Anglesey.

This opportune finding has since become known as the "Great Discovery", and such was its importance that:

men came swarming, as in a gold fever; houses of good class were built; a harbour was excavated from the rock; and vessels were built and bought to such an extent that the port became one of the most important in Wales.

Evidence that the mines had been worked in earlier times was regularly uncovered during later operations, and at that time, this was attributed to the Romans although the methods used could hardly be described as being typically Roman. It has since been established by the radiocarbon dating of charcoal discovered both above and below ground in the company of mauls or hammer stones, themselves good indicators of very early mining activities, that the mountain's mining history began in the early Bronze Age, some 2000 years BC.

The discovery on Mynydd Parys, and elsewhere on Anglesey, of several crude copper bun ingots bearing Roman inscriptions, confirms that the mines were later worked during the occupation of Britain in the first century AD. Because evidence of much of what went on then was destroyed by later activities at the mine, it has hitherto been impossible to determine precisely where on the mountain the Romans actually worked. Following their departure however, copper mining in the British Isles declined to such an extent that the essential technology was lost.

This was not helped by the fact that copper is invariably found in the company of gold and silver, and as the British Crown laid claim to both metals, they prohibited its exploitation. During the reign of Elizabeth the First however, demand for copper needed for the manufacture of brass and bronze armaments, led to a re-vitalisation of the British copper industry led by The Crown. This resulted in the establishment of the 'Mines Royal' and the 'Mineral and Battery' Companies, both of which relied heavily on German finance and expertise. The former company was charged with the development of metalliferous mining, and the latter, with the exploitation of the metals produced.

Several documents which relate to Mynydd Parys during this early period of resurgence still exist ; but only one so far discovered, relates specifically to Porth Amlwch. A time-ravaged map discovered amongst the *State Papers Supplementary* in the Public Records Office, notes the existence of the havens of 'Amlewhye' and nearby Dulas. Crudely drawn, it shows the distances of the two havens from the Parys mines; and its title: *A plotte of the woorkes and havens n(ow) fitt for that purpose*, implies that work had been undertaken at both sites, no doubt with the intention of facilitating the exportation of copper ore to the Crown-owned smelters at Swansea. It should be noted however, that the provision of a second haven at Dulas had probably more to do with the need for a safe alternative to Amlwch, which was inherently dangerous when subjected to onshore winds, than with the quantities of ore then being exported.

Adaptations to the narrow creek at Amlwch were almost certainly carried out on the haven's western side where the topography was far more conducive to the loading of vessels. Even so, such changes were unlikely to have been extensive, and a site which the author believes to be that of the original Elizabethan quay has been identified, but which can not be confirmed as such until vital archaeological excavations have been completed.

It is interesting to note that the Elizabethan map depicts the creek occupied by a small sloop whilst a larger, three-masted vessel is shown anchored in the bay. This could be interpreted as meaning that the harbour was then unsuitable for large vessels, which it almost certainly was, and that smaller ships or lighters were used to transport the ore to those anchored offshore.

So successful were the Parys mines under the later, inspired direction of Thomas Williams, following the 'Great Discovery', that for a time they came to dominate the world price of copper. Williams, an Anglesey-born lawyer who became nationally known as the 'Copper King', but who was better known to the Parys miners as *Twm Chwareu Têg* (Tom Fair Play), became an undisputed giant of the world's first ever Industrial Revolution. Because of his single-minded and what might fairly be described as quite ruthless business methods, he succeeded in undercutting the Cornish copper trade, making powerful enemies along the way. There can be no doubt however that he was held in absolute awe, to the point of being feared, by far better known industrial contemporaries such as Wedgwood, Boulton, Watt, and the steel producing Wilkinson brothers.

The crucial part played by Amlwch-produced copper in the success of the world's first industrial revolution is widely recognised: but few people are aware of Williams' own contribution to maritime history, when he created international markets for high tensile bronze bolts for fastening ships' hulls, and copper sheathing plates for the protection of wooden vessels against the feared Teredo worm. At that time, Williams claimed that his Liverpool-based organisation alone, had supplied sufficient plates in 12 months to sheath no fewer than 150 vessels; and the Parys Company was contracted to provide no fewer than 25,000 bolts per week, some of which could be as long as 20 feet (6m approx). Such was the efficiency of Thomas Williams' Greenfield Valley rolling mills in Flintshire however, that he was able to deliver as many as 40,000 in the same period .

In addition to its power to protect vessels from the Teredo worm, the copper sheathing inhibited marine growth on the underside of the vessels' hulls, and it has since been recognised that Williams' copper plates used to sheath Nelson's world famous flagship *HMS Victory*, and other contemporary ships of the line, gave them extra speed and manoeuverability; factors which have since been claimed as having been instrumental in Nelson's renowned victory in the battle of the Nile.

By the early 1790s, the number of ships sailing into Porth Amlwch had increased to such an extent that delays caused by congestion and unsuitable berths became wholly unacceptable, and for that reason, an Act of Parliament was enacted in 1793 which resulted in the enlargement, deepening, cleansing, and regulation of the harbour.

By far the most ambitious part of the project was the quarrying back of the steeply sloping rock face on the eastern side of the harbour, in order to create a wide, modern quay. On this were built warehouses and large bins for the storage of ore, coal and scrap iron; all of which were then being shipped through the port in prodigious amounts.

As a result of the much needed improvement, the western side of the harbour was more or less abandoned and left free for shipbuilding, an industry which, until then, had been denied serious consideration due to the lack of space.

It is probably true to say however, that a combination of factors such as the great number of vessels using the port, the heavy nature of their cargoes, and the rigours of the Irish Sea, were such that some form of basic ship-repairing facilities must have been available at the port, long before the passing of the 1793 Act. It is difficult to be certain as to where such repair work would have been carried out, for space on the western side of the port was very much at a premium. There was however, one area at the port's landward end, where the ground slopes gently upwards from the harbour floor, which would have been suitable for such an undertaking, and where disruption to the port's facilities would have been minimised. This location would also have provided an ideal place for a gridiron, a platform standing above the natural floor of the harbour, onto which vessels could be floated at high water whenever they needed to have their hulls cleaned or repaired.

Following the exhaustion of the more easily worked bodies of ore, mainly using techniques more akin to quarrying than mining *per se*, the mines at Mynydd Parys fell into steep decline. This stemmed from a lack of local expertise in deep mining technology, and as it was confidently believed that considerable reserves still existed at deeper levels under the northern slope of the hill, that facet of operations became of vital importance to the survival of the mines as a profitable venture.

By way of overcoming this problem, the mineowners entered into an agreement with the Vivians, a well-known Cornish family which had extensive interests in, as well as intimate knowledge of, copper mining, banking and smelting. Yet again, it is evident that the local copper industry was to benefit from a combination of wealth and expertise brought in from elsewhere.

One expert brought in by the Vivians was another Cornishman by the name of James Treweek, who arrived in Amlwch in 1811 to take up his duties as Mine Captain. It was due to his undoubted expertise that the mines' fortunes were restored, albeit not to their former glory. Despite his supposed penury on arrival in the town, it is evident that by 1822, he had accumulated sufficient capital to enable him to establish his sons Nicholas and Francis in business as coal merchants in Porth Amlwch – much to the annoyance of their already established competitors, who still regarded the Treweeks as *pobl dwad* (incomers).

Their business premises were situated on the western side of the harbour known locally as *Ochr Draw* (the far side), which had been vacated when commercial activities transferred to the newly constructed quay on the eastern side following the Act of 1793. The compound and its associated buildings were eminently suitable for conversion into a much needed shipyard, and it was this factor, perhaps more than any other, that changed the course of the brothers' careers – they were in the right place at the right time. James Treweek himself had a financial interest in the business, and not only were his sons assisted by his investment, they undoubtedly benefited greatly from his later to be revealed business acumen as well.

The fact that the brothers had initially elected to become coal merchants in what was an already well serviced market, suggests that neither one had skills in his own right. For that reason, it is evident that from the very start they would have had to employ suitably skilled local artisans to carry out the work involved in the yard. It is probably true to say that the new venture began life as a ship-repairing business, which would have needed far less capital, and that over a shorter period of time, than would have been necessary had the brothers decided to embark on shipbuilding from the very outset. This is especially true since it is a recognised fact that shipyards in those times only undertook the building of new vessels by way of keeping skilled craftsmen occupied when repair work was hard to come by.

Thus was established the town's first recorded shipyard, known locally as *Iard Ochr Draw* (the yard on the far side), from which in 1825 was launched its first vessel, the 68 ton sloop *Unity*. She was followed by a further 14 vessels over a period of 19 years, all of which, with the exception of the 130 ton brigantine *James and Jane*, named in honour of the brothers' parents, were smaller than the *Unity*. The partnership ended when, despite receiving the best medical treatment available, Francis died in 1832 of an undisclosed illness – he was then 21 years of age.

Nicholas Treweek's business enterprise went from strength to strength during the first twenty or so years of its existence, and he went on to extend his financial interests by becoming a shipowner, absorbing several vessels he had built at Amlwch into his own fleet. One of the vessels he then owned was the 97 ton Canadian built schooner *Red*, the command of which in September 1841, he entrusted to William Thomas, a 19-year-old Amlwch man – it was young Thomas's first known command.

In the period 1845-1855, Nicholas Treweek had a financial interest in no fewer than 48 vessels, amongst which were 3 full rigged ships, 7 barques, 6 brigs, 5 brigantines, 12 schooners, 3 snows, 9 sloops, 3 smacks and a galliot.

Although he had a thriving business of his own to manage in Amlwch, he unaccountably accepted a post as the Liverpool broker for the Parys mining interests which were then employing his father as their principal agent. His main task in the city was the management of copper shipments from Amlwch, which were then forwarded to Birmingham and elsewhere by rail and canal.

For what are thought to have been health reasons, Treweek resigned his post in July 1854, the year of the Crimean war. What his state of mind was at that time is difficult to comprehend, for he went on to dispose of many of the shares he owned in a great number of vessels amongst members of his immediate family. Despite his strange behaviour, he continued to take an interest of sorts in the affairs of his Amlwch shipyard; for his stay in Liverpool had brought him into close contact with progressive maritime technology. As a result of this, he became acutely aware of the growing importance of iron in the construction of seagoing vessels; whilst at the same time, he saw for himself the benefits enjoyed by shipyards possessing a dry dock.

The possibility of building ships of iron had been pursued in the early years of the 19th century when there was much prejudice against the idea of using a material that did not itself float, which it was argued, was contrary to nature. Because of its inherent strength however, there were immediate gains to be had from its use. Unlike wooden vessels, iron ships were not limited in size as was demonstrated when in 1848, Brunel launched the mighty *Great Eastern*, a vessel five times the size of any previous ship afloat; not that this factor had any significance at Amlwch where the size of vessel produced was governed more by topographical and physical limitations than for any other reason. In addition, the smaller dimensions of the frames of iron vessels allowed a greater carrying capacity than that of their wooden counterparts, giving them greater earning power e.g. in the case of a wooden vessel, the weight of the hull and equipment amounted to about 40% of its displacement, whereas in an iron vessel, this was reduced to 30%, a significant difference.

When Treweek returned to the island with these ideas foremost in his mind, he was determined to modernise his yard. Such was the confined nature of the land on which it stood however, it was evident that he could neither expand his operations nor create a dry dock with ease, and he was compelled to look elsewhere for a site more suited to his needs.

He found a location that answered his requirements, immediately outside the entrance to, but on the opposite side of the harbour to his own yard, access to which had been improved when the new eastern quay was constructed. Apart from having sufficient space in which to expand, the land included a narrow inlet, which, according to a map of the port drawn in 1828, was known as *Porth Cwch y Brenin*.

Running into the rock in a roughly north-easterly direction, the inlet was sheltered from the worst effects of an onshore wind. More important for the owner however, was the fact that it could be enlarged with comparative ease to form a dry dock capable of accommodating relatively large vessels. This, he proceeded to do, blasting the rock to create a regularly shaped dock which was closed off with a pair of stout, outwardly opening wooden gates, and as the floor of the dock was above mean low water, it dried out naturally on ordinary tides, obviating the need for pumping.

The transfer of shipbuilding activities to *Iard Newydd* (the New Yard) as it was to become known locally, was completed some time in 1857, fully equipped to build both wooden and iron vessels. A map drawn by Algeo in 1869 of Nicholas Treweek's entire Bodednyfed estate, shows that the yard consisted of several large buildings and a slipway extending in a westerly direction across the entrance to the harbour; but it would appear that the dry dock had not been completed by that time.

The old yard, *Iard Ochr Draw*, had by this time been sold to William Cox Paynter, yet another Cornishman, who went on to build a number of superb, and very well known vessels, such as the *Jane Gray*, the *Camborne*, and the *Donald and Doris*.

The Treweek/Cox-Paynter yard known locally as Iard Ochr Draw, *as it was in the 1920s. The schooner* Kate *is seen tied up alongside the eastern quay.*

William Cox-Paynter's 3-masted schooner Camborne *built in* Iard Ochr Draw *in 1884. This is one of a pair of paintings by Reuben Chappell depiciting the vessel in 'fair' and 'foul' weather.*

CHAPTER 2
WILLIAM THOMAS – THE EARLY YEARS (Part 1)

"the port throbbed with activity in the days of my childhood"

William Thomas was born in June 1822 at *Cae Pant*, a smallholding less than a mile distant from Porth Amlwch. He was the second of three children born to Elinor and Lewis Thomas, who is described as having been both a yeoman and a miner. This was not an unusual combination of occupations in Amlwch at that time, where miners at the nearby copper mines of Mynydd Parys often had smallholdings to provide them and their families with a supplementary income, and fresh food. Because of the long hours worked by the miners however, such arrangements meant that the holdings had to be worked collectively by family members, and by the age of 12, William was expected to shoulder his responsibilities on the farm. Whatever the ambitions of his parents may have been for him, it is evident that his own sights were firmly set on becoming a sailor.

A resurgence in the fortunes of the mines brought about principally by James Treweek's extensive mining expertise, gave Amlwch at that time, an air of the prosperous place it had once been. In his reminiscences of the town when he was a child, TG Walker, a local historian, recalled how:

The constant cavalcade of carts on Madyn Hill always held my attention in those early days. I could watch the procession of horse-drawn carts from the garden, the loaded ones bearing copper ore to the smelter or to the quay, having an easy passage downhill all the way from the mines to the harbour, and the empty carts travelling uphill without overstraining the brawny Shires that drew them. The cart wheels and the heavy iron-shod hooves pounded the metalling on the road into powder; and in March a rollicking south-westerly wind would blow, driving before it immense clouds of dust down Madyn Hill and away to the harbour, and beyond, to the sea ...

... another grand sight was presented every evening when work was done, for all the horses freed from harness were led to their pasture, between fifty and sixty of them. One man rode bare back at the head of the pack, the rest trotting in his wake and jamming the streets with their bulk. There would be the thunder of their shod hooves on the metalling, there would be a flurry of flying manes and tails, and great snorting and neighing as they crunched past the shaking houses, with dust swirling at the rear and a smell of equine sweat and manure behind them. Thus they raced up Wesley Street to the Square, and then to the fields on Bull Bay Road. At the first sound of their approach, people scattered for safety lest they be trampled or crushed: but this sort of stampede was a regular feature of the township and was accepted without protest. Indeed now, Amlwch in its heyday was a match for the Wild West!

... Saturday nights were notoriously noisy and riotous, the taverns were numerous and crowded, and quarrelsome miners and sailors fought in the streets. Fists, feet and heads were used in the brawls, but never knives or pistols. As a result, there would be black eyes and smashed noses and cut cheeks to be seen on Sundays, and once a broken jaw. Once, also, a fight between a father and his son ended in the death of one of the participants. Women also fought.

Describing the port, Walker said:

> *It throbbed with activity in the days of my childhood: it was dusty, dirty, smelly, smoky and noisy. The sweetest noise was produced by a battery of caulking mallets wielded by the gang who were packing oakum into the seams between the planking of ships on the slipways. From a distance, this pleasant tattoo sounded quite musical to my boyish years, for it had a certain ring to it.*
>
> *Three youths of my acquaintance worked in shifts to keep the fire going under the huge cauldron of melted pitch which was poured over the oakum to seal the seams. I can see one of them now, Enoch by name, nearly as black as the pitch itself with smoke and grime, sitting on his haunches in a canvas-covered shelter, and shaping the hull of a model ship with his pocket knife to while away the long hours.*
>
> *Boys of my age stole on board the vessels at every opportunity, making for the cook's galley, or the crews' quarters in the cramped forecastle. A few of the more daring lads would scale the rigging and accept a challenge to place their caps on the truck of the mainmast, a feat beyond my capability: but, I was capable of eating the occasional ship's biscuit that a generous cook would dole out, a hard and tasteless confection needing a strong set of teeth to crack it. As a rule, the sailors dipped it into their tea or into their stew.*

This was, without doubt, the port with which William Thomas would have been extremely familiar as he was growing up, and there can be little doubt either, that the nearness of his home to the bustling little harbour meant that he and his friends spent much of their time there, despite what would surely have been, their parents' dire warnings against doing so. To someone who later revealed a remarkable degree of imagination, the milieu of the port must have invoked in him a tantalizing vision of an adventure-filled life at sea.

Knowing full well that his parents' consent would not be forthcoming, William took matters into his own hands, and ran away from home. As he was then but 12 years of age, it is unlikely that a ship's master trading regularly to and from Porth Amlwch would have knowingly taken the boy on without his parents' consent: and consequently, it is reasonable to assume that he managed to stow away on one of the many small coasters plying between Amlwch and the Mersey, with the intention of finding a berth on one of the great number of deep-sea vessels working out of Liverpool at that time.

When they realised that he was missing, his anxious parents immediately guessed what had happened, before asking local seafarers to keep an eye open for him. After many years during which they knew nothing of his whereabouts, they came to the agonizing conclusion that he must somehow, somewhere, have lost his life, which unfortunately, was all too often the case at that time. After suffering many years of uncertainty followed by despair, it is easy to imagine their initial disbelief, and the utter joy they must have experienced, when some 7 years later, he turned up fit, well, and full of confidence.

If, as there is every reason to believe, he was in the north Atlantic trade during that time, there would have been many occasions on which he could easily have returned to the comfort of his home. The ties with his family were evidently close, and one compelling reason why he chose not to visit his family would probably have had more to do with his belief that he would not have been allowed to return to follow his chosen career, than with not wishing to be with them.

A leather-bound textbook on the principles of maritime navigation, discovered recently amongst his granddaughter's effects, states on the flyleaf in William Thomas's own handwriting, that it was bought by him in America in 1839, when he was 17 years of age. This fully supports the theory that his seafaring career began in ships sailing between Liverpool and America; where someone in authority had seen his potential, and had coached him in his endeavours to further his seagoing career. The book's flyleaf also records the death of his mother Elinor.

Bearing in mind his subsequent colourful and highly successful business life, it is thought somewhat curious that details of this, and other highly significant aspects of his early life at sea, have not filtered down to his descendants. This may have resulted from his innate diffidence, as there is evidence to indicate that he was somewhat reserved, and could well have been reluctant to discuss his experiences and achievements. The circumstances under which he returned home will always remain a mystery: but it is known that within a short while of doing so, he married Jane, two years his senior. Their first child Ellen, was born in 1848.

An early photograph of Captain William Thomas.

Further notes written in William Thomas's hand on the textbook's flyleaf, record that in September 1841, when he was 19 years of age, he took command of the schooner *Red*, at Amlwch. The Canadian-built vessel was one of several owned by Nicholas Treweek, who was sufficiently impressed by the young man's maturity, knowledge and experience, to entrust him with the command of his vessel, at what was even in those days, an early age for such weighty responsibility. Time however, was to prove that the faith Treweek displayed in the young man was absolutely justified; and in this way began an association which was to influence, probably more than any other, the course of William Thomas's subsequent career.

In addition, the flyleaf of the book bears a list of vessels, with the dates on which he took command of them. In December 1848, he become master and part owner, with his father and a man called William Lewis, of the *Clyde*, a 123 ton brig, built in Nova Scotia two years earlier. He remained her master until February 1850 when he joined the *Red Rover* at Barrow; command of the *Clyde* being handed over to a Captain John Thomas, who was almost certainly his younger brother, and who is thought to have previously served him as mate on the same vessel. William remained with the *Red Rover* for nine months only, before taking over command of the schooner *Superb*.

June 1849 saw the repeal of the greater part of the restrictive 'Navigation Laws', the last remnants of which were taken off the Statute Book some 4 years later. This had the welcome result of opening up the coastal trade to all comers, thereby sharpening competition between shipowners, Captain Thomas amongst them. He had by then bought shares in, before becoming Master of, Nicholas Treweek's 85 ton schooner *Kendal Castle*, with which he remained until 1854, when he again relinquished command in favour of Captain John Thomas. Good fortune had obviously attended his endeavours, for during this time he also acquired shares in the schooners *County of Cork* and *Clarence*.

The schooner Kendal Castle *off the Smalls 1855 (Captain John Thomas)*

In 1853, the Captain became a father for the second time with the birth of his son Lewis. As his family was growing in size, so were his shipping interests, and in the same year, he became the owner and master of the 99 ton schooner *Anglesea Lass*, built to his specification in a Welsh yard on the River Dee. His records show that he joined the vessel on the 30th of July 1854: but as it was not launched until the 21st of November of that year, it is probably true to say that he personally supervised the last four months of her construction. The vessel made her maiden voyage from Bangor to London under his command on 9th January 1855. Later the same year, he acquired an interest in the schooner *Mona's Isle*, built by Ishmael Jones at Cemaes, a little harbour located some 6 miles west of Amlwch.

A local newspaper at the time, described Porth Amlwch as:

thriving and full of bustle, being crowded with shipping, discharging and receiving cargoes, and the shipbuilding yard of Mr Treweek busily occupied with a fine schooner in wood nearly completed, and another in iron – the first of that material ever constructed in North Wales.

The yard referred to in the newspaper report was Iard Newydd, and the wooden vessel was the 93 ton wooden schooner *Alliance*. According to her new owners, she was named in recognition of the union which existed between the towns of Amlwch and Holyhead. At a dinner held in the Dinorben Hotel to celebrate the launch, a toast was proposed to the new building yard of Messrs Treweek, Sons and Company; a clear indication that the new venture was not an exclusively Treweek affair as had been supposed; but was from its inception, a wider-based venture. The fact that Captain William Thomas's young daughter Ellen was asked to perform the prestigious christening ceremony, and that it was he who responded to the toast on behalf of the builders, indicates that he was a significant figure in the undertaking.

The iron vessel described as being under construction in the report, was the 77 ton schooner *Mary Catherine*, which was launched in 1858. Curiously enough, Treweek's name is absent from the Port of Beaumaris registers relating to the vessel, which record that she was built by Hughes, Thomas and Co., for Amlwch buyers. This apparent anomaly can be readily explained however, for those commissioning the construction of a new vessel at that time, frequently assumed the title of shipbuilders.

The launch of the new vessel was an auspicious occasion, as was reported in the local newspaper:

On Friday there was launched from the building yard of Messrs Hughes, Thomas and Co., at Amlwch, a beautifully modelled iron schooner named the 'Mary Catherine', of about 160 tons, to be commanded by Captain John German, late of the schooner 'John Morgan'. The builders were warmly congratulated on this their first successful attempt at iron shipbuilding, and on the noble appearance of the ship on the water, which looked a perfect yacht. In the afternoon the builders and the owners, with a few friends, celebrated the event by partaking of a substantial dinner at Parry's vaults. All the workmen in their employ were also entertained to a dinner at the Britannia Inn.

The all iron *Mary Catherine* was built as a topsail schooner, but was later re-rigged as a ketch. Her two bulkheads gave her tremendous strength, and she went on to serve her owners well, calling at many of the principal home and continental ports over a period of some 58 years. In 1916 she was converted into a barge at Iard Newydd, and sold to a Liverpool firm; an unfitting end no doubt for a vessel once described as being of a noble appearance. Her active life ended in her 82nd year when she was broken up for scrap.

There is no evidence to suggest that Treweek or any of his known associates at the time of the *Mary Catherine's* construction, possessed the expertise to design and build iron ships, and for that reason, the yard would necessarily have had to employ an experienced manager who could undertake such demanding work on a professional basis. Similarly, a high percentage of the skilled workmen required to build Amlwch's first iron vessel would clearly have had to have been recruited elsewhere, most probably either in Liverpool or Deeside, where the art of iron shipbuilding was by then, firmly established.

One example of a Deeside-built iron vessel associated with Anglesey, was the steam clipper *Royal Charter*, which had been constructed expressly for the Australian emigrant service. She was described as a vessel of the highest order, and her owners confidently offered regular passages between Liverpool and Melbourne in under 60 days. This was not as remarkable as it may seem, for the sailing clipper *Thermopylae* had also made the voyage in the same time. The difference however, was that she was subject to the vagaries of the wind, which often added substantially to her passage time. As the *Royal Charter* was returning to her home port in October 1859, laden with gold, she was overtaken by a hurricane, which drove her on to the rocks at Moelfre, some 6 miles south-east of Amlwch (see appendix 24). The loss of over four hundred of her passengers and crew, many of whom were returning with their hard-won wealth from the Australian goldfields, was described at the time as one of the greatest peacetime maritime disasters to have ever befallen a British vessel. Two of the crew were from Amlwch – quartermaster Thomas Griffith was fortunate enough to survive the ordeal, but William Hughes was drowned, as was Isaac Griffiths, another crew member, who tragically died within sight of his home in Moelfre.

Part of a flyer advertising passages between Liverpool and Australia on board the Royal Charter.

A local newspaper reporting the effects of the storm, stated that the waves at Porth Amlwch on that day were so powerful that few vessels in the port were left undamaged. Many which had broken free of their moorings in the surging waves, were swept down to the landward end of the harbour with such force, that they toppled an iron bridge at the bottom of the inclined plane off its abutments and into the sea. Indeed, so high were the seas running into the harbour, that not only did they damage vessels, they also demolished a landing stage and a warehouse belonging to the Amlwch Steamship Company, sweeping its entire contents into the sea.

The same newspaper also reported that a vessel nearing completion at the port had been swept off its blocks and completely destroyed. No further details were given; but the fact that a new vessel was launched from Iard Newydd later in the month suggests that the stricken vessel was under construction at Cox-Paynter's Iard Ochr Draw, which had little or nothing by way of protection from the destructive effects of an onshore wind.

So lengthy was the list of losses to shipping all around the coast of Britain by what subsequently became known as the 'Royal Charter Storm', that the local newspaper saw fit to give no more than two lines to reporting the total loss of the Kendal Castle and its master.

A month or so after the storm, a two-masted schooner named Grace Evans, was launched from Iard Newydd. The fact that both Nicholas Treweek and William Thomas each owned a quarter share in her, highlights not only the successful business partnership that had developed between them, but also the latter's burgeoning wealth.

In that same year, the Captain also became the sole owner of the 69 ton wooden schooner Lord Willoughby, built at Preston some 19 years earlier; whilst at the same time acquiring shares in the 88 ton wooden schooner Pride of Anglesea, newly built at Barnstaple. Between 1860 and 1865 the Captain became the owner, or part owner of the vessel Jane Pringle, of which he took command on the 4th of March 1860, as well as the Sea Queen; Albion; Coila; Lord Mostyn; Cymro, Woodman; William & Jane; Euphemia, and the Thomas Blythe. The Sea Queen and the Cymro had both been built at Amlwch, the first in Treweek's old yard in 1844, and the second in the new yard in 1861, which, by that time, was giving employment to no fewer than thirty-seven craftsmen and eight boys.

By this time, Captain Thomas and others had established a business in Porth Amlwch, the headed notepaper of which described them as being Sail Makers as well as dealers in canvas, twine, bolt rope, bunting etc. It is believed that although the Captain was the major shareholder, giving his name to the enterprise, the sail making was in the capable hands of a craftsman named William Morris, formerly employed by Nicholas Treweek. Although supported by many local businessmen, such blatant poaching of local talent did little to endear Thomas to others who opposed the initiative.

Local legends surrounding the manner in which the Captain acquired the wealth by which to expand his shipping interests, abounded. One, a fascinating account written by a descendant many years after the Captain's death, relates how having supposedly arrived in an American port during the time of the American Civil War (1861-1865), he rendered some form of highly secret service of great significance to one or other of the opposing sides in the conflict. The account claims that by way of reward, he was given a tract of land which subsequently became the site of the Anglo American oilfield, which he sold at enormous profit.

A second, not entirely dissimilar story, appears in Enwogion Môn, an anthology of the biographies of the notable men of Anglesey. It relates amongst other things, how Captain

Thomas had supposedly sailed into an American port at the time of the Civil War, where he was pressed into service on board an American warship. (see Appendix 1) Improbable as this may seem, records show that numerous seamen from north-west Wales did sail voluntarily as mercenaries in warships belonging to the Confederate States Navy. One such mariner was 'Captain' Sam Roberts of Groeslon in Caernarfonshire, who is known to have served on board the *CSS Alabama*, which herself had a fascinating connection with the Isle of Anglesey. What William Thomas is supposed to have done, or where he was supposed to have sailed to, are not recorded.

Bearing in mind the known facts, it is highly unlikely that Thomas could have taken part in the American Civil War, either on American soil or on board an American warship, for at that time he was far too busy extending his business empire at home. His family as well as his maritime interests were increasing as he became progressively wealthier. A year before the start of the Civil War, his wife bore him a second son, John; who was followed 2 years later by William, known fondly to his family as Willie. Willie was to become the predominant figure in the later annals of William Thomas & Sons.

On the premise that there is no smoke without fire however, the distinct similarities in the two accounts suggest that each may well contain an element of truth, and that the Captain was somehow involved in the American conflict, albeit covertly. Surprising as it may seem, Anglesey did have a part to play in the American Civil War, not that its island inhabitants were aware of it at the time, for the operations that took place there were wholly clandestine.

Faced with the Union blockade of their ports at a time when they desperately needed to maintain cotton exports to pay for the war, the Confederate States were anxious to procure ships that could be used as blockade-runners and marauders. With that in mind, Captain J.D. Bulloch of the Confederate States Navy was sent to Liverpool in June 1861, with orders to purchase and commission suitable vessels. Through his efforts, which included an inspection at Holyhead of two redundant vessels belonging to the London and North Western Railway Company, the Confederates acquired the cross-channel steamers *Cambria* and *Scotia*. The vessels were surplus to the railway company's requirements following its failure to win the lucrative Irish mail contract, which had been awarded to the City of Dublin Steam Packet Company.

It is unlikely that Captain Thomas was involved in that particular venture either: but his intimate knowledge of the coastline of Anglesey together with his many contacts in Liverpool, could have been of immense value to the southern States in their efforts to turn the war around in their favour.

The British Government had before that time, declared its neutrality in the conflict; but because of their strong commercial ties with the cotton-producing southern states, many Liverpool businessmen and Lancashire mill owners in particular, were firmly on the side of the Confederates. Amongst these was the well-known Merseyside shipbuilding family of John Laird and Sons, who had made their name as builders of superb iron ships, with whom Bulloch placed an order for a new warship based on a proven British naval design.

Known only by its yard number *290*, the vessel took shape under the eyes of the United States Consul in Liverpool, who reported each stage of her construction to the US Ambassador in London. Although a flimsy cover story had been concocted locally to disguise her true purpose, there could have been very few people on Merseyside who were unaware of what she was, and who she belonged to. Protests by the American Ambassador to the British Government went unheeded, probably because of intense pressure by members of the Laird family, one of whom, John, was then a member of Parliament.

The *290* was duly launched and prepared for sea trials. Fearing that the vessel would be impounded on her return to the Mersey following those trials, arrangements were made to take on board many influential local business people, including two of the Laird brothers, for what was ostensibly to be a proving voyage along the North Wales coast. As a supposed precaution against engine failure however, provision was made for the vessel to be accompanied on her voyage by the steam tug *Hercules*.

Following successful trial runs off Amlwch, the *290* was renamed *Enrica* whilst anchored in Moelfre Roads where her acceptance checks were completed. Whilst there, the warship's passengers, who until then, had probably been unaware of the part they were playing in the subterfuge, were transferred to the *Hercules* for their return passage to Liverpool. When the tug returned alone to the Mersey with the warship's passengers on board, the US Consul realised that he had been duped, and immediate arrangements were made for the *USS Tuscarora* which was then cruising off the south coast of England, to intercept the *Enrica*, and sink her.

In the meantime, arrangements had been made by Bullock with an unnamed collaborator, for a scratch crew to be taken out to the *Enrica* as she rode at anchor in Red Wharf Bay off the eastern coastline of the island. After spending a night anchored offshore, the vessel's captain, having anticipated the US Ambassador's reaction, sailed north from Anglesey, and made his escape around the north Irish coast, before sailing directly to the Azores, where the ship was renamed the *CSS Alabama*. She went on to become one of the Confederate Navy's most successful and feared raiders before she was eventually sunk by the USS *Kearsage* outside Cherbourg harbour on June 19th 1864.

The Confederate warship Alabama.

An international arbitration court before which the matter was placed, found in the United States' favour, to whom they awarded £3,299,166 (equivalent to £170,478,000 in year 2002, see Appendix 25) in compensation for the British Government's failure to use due diligence in the discharge of its neutral obligations. A refusal to pay the award would have meant that Britain faced the real possibility of a war with the United States, and as this would almost certainly have resulted in the loss of the Canadian territories, the matter was settled, if not amicably, then certainly to the reasonable satisfaction of the Americans.

Who recruited the men and arranged for them to gather on the east coast of Anglesey, ready to board the *Enrica* will perhaps never be known: but because of his many associations with Merseyside, either through Nicholas Treweek's many friends in Liverpool or his own many contacts in the city, Captain Thomas would have been well placed, and well able to provide such a service.

The question as to whether or not he was involved in the Confederacy's secret war must clearly remain the subject of conjecture; but if he were involved, he was indeed wise to keep that involvement a well-guarded secret, bearing in mind the result of the litigation which followed, into which he could so easily have been drawn.

Between 1865 and 1868, Captain Thomas further expanded his maritime interests by investing in the vessels: *Albion; Clara Louisa, Amanda, Ocean Belle,* and *Sarah Jane.* His involvement was not confined to the coastal trade however, for in 1869, he and another Anglesey man, also named William Thomas, acquired the Jersey built *William Melhuish,* a 680 ton fully rigged ship. By a strange coincidence, the captain appointed to the vessel was a third native of Anglesey named William Thomas!

The 680 ton fully rigged ship William Melhuish.

Legend has it, that the vessel made a profit on her first voyage, amounting to five times her original cost: but in the light of new evidence, this has been shown to be grossly exaggerated. Her operational success was significant nevertheless, and the name Melhuish continues to appear amongst members of the respective families who profited by her.

The vessel's prime owners went on to invest the money they had made in other shipping ventures, some of it in joint enterprises. William Thomas (Liverpool) for example, was able to expand his own considerable fleet of ships, before becoming a highly respected Merseyside figure, and Mayor of Bootle.

Captain Thomas subsequently went on to build the 99 ton wooden schooner *Welsh Girl* in March 1869; and in June 1870, the 79 ton schooner *Lewis and Mary*, which he named in honour of two of his children. The fact that the *Lewis and Mary* left Amlwch with a cargo of ochre for Runcorn within 6 days of her launching, suggests that she had been launched fully rigged.

As Captain Thomas did not then possess a yard of his own, exactly where the 2 vessels were built in the port, is a mystery: but as there had been a gap of 3 years since the launch of the *Perseverance*, the last known vessel to leave Iard Newydd, the possibility that they were built there is strong. If that were the case, the absence of Treweek's name from the records could well be explained by reasons similar to those discussed earlier as they applied to the building of the *Mary Catherine*.

CHAPTER 2
THE EARLY YEARS (Part 2)
"I shall be ready to build any size of vessel that I may get orders for."

The discovery in 1850, of a rich deposit of iron ore at Hodbarrow Point on the Duddon estuary in what was then known as Cumberland, led to the formation of the Hodbarrow Mining Company. The two principals involved in the concern were Nathaniel Caine, a Liverpool metal merchant, living in Coniston; and John Barratt, who coincidentally hailed from the same Cornish parish of Gwennap as did James Treweek.

Early difficulties encountered at the mine had been overcome by the 1860s, and a vast quantity of haematite, remarkably free from impurities and containing something close to 60% of metallic iron, was subsequently being raised. Apart from the fact that overland facilities for the transportation of ores from the mine were wholly inadequate, rail freight was unable to compete with seaborne freight charges then being asked, and almost all of the mine's output was exported by ship, mainly to smelters in South Wales, and some via the Mersey and the Dee, to Coalbrookdale and the Midlands. Indeed, Caine was later to say that he and Barratt were induced to re-open the mine by the natural advantages presented for shipping at a small cost.

The first regular shipments of ore began in 1862, and such did the extent of the seaborne trade become, that no fewer than 1,400 ships are recorded as having passed through the port in 1867. This was despite the treacherous nature of the Duddon estuary itself, which was notorious amongst the shipping fraternity for its extremely dangerous and constantly shifting waterways, and the all too frequent long 'stems' or delays, associated with the port itself. In Duddon's case, the latter resulted directly from the woeful inadequacies in the port's management structure, which was minimal.

Adding considerably to this combination of hazard and delay, was the extraordinary degree of wear and tear which vessels' structures suffered as a result of the punishing ore cargoes they carried. Not surprisingly therefore, owners and captains alike tended to avoid the Duddon trade whenever other freights were in the offing, even those which were less remunerative.

Such did the demand for high quality haematite become, mainly in order to satisfy the increasing use being made of the Bessemer Process, that an insufficient number of ships were available to the mineowners for its transportation. Greatly worried by the situation he found himself in, Nathaniel Caine, the younger of the two partners, held several meetings with shipowners in Liverpool and ports along the Welsh coast, in a desperate effort to induce more of them to enter the Duddon iron trade. To them, he offered guaranteed regular cargoes, as well as high rates of freight and generous demurrage by way of compensation for any delays suffered whilst in port.

Captain Thomas, who had by then become a shipowner of some standing, was one of several owners approached by Caine, and persuaded to enter his vessels in the trade. A copy of a 12-month agreement dated 1st March 1870 between him and the mining company shows that he was guaranteed cargoes of no less than 500 tons every week, all the year round. It is evident however, that this was a renewal of at least two earlier contracts; for in a letter to Caine dated 3rd October 1870, Thomas referred to the Captain of the *Thomas Pearson*, who:

> *... is an Amlwch man, and if you look in the books, he was with me in the first contract, and the second. It was through my influence that he went first in trade.*

The schooner Thomas Pearson *(foreground) at Amlwch.*

On the assumption that contracts were of 12 months' duration, it is clear that Thomas's association with Duddon began as early as March 1868. There can be little doubt that he was totally committed to the trade, for 22 vessels described as 'Captain Thomas's Ships' passed through the port of Amlwch between January 1870 and December 1872 , and of these, *Elizabeth Martha; Albion; Mary Ann Jane; Lord Mostyn; Jane Pringle, Ocean Belle; Sarah; Jane Elizabeth; Mountain Maid; Crystal Palace; Euphemia; Lewis and Mary; Mary Ann;* and the *Eleanor and Grace*, were recorded as having sailed either to or from Duddon (see Appendix 4).

It is clear to see that Captain Thomas had by then formed an excellent business relationship with Nathaniel Caine, who turned to him for advice concerning the management of the port. As a result of their discussions, Captain William Morgan, an Amlwch man, was appointed as Duddon's first Harbourmaster on Thomas's recommendation. He was undoubtedly the same William Morgan who had commanded the *Clara Louisa* until November 1868, the command of which he obviously relinquished in order to take up his new appointment ashore. Morgan turned out to be precisely the kind of overseer the mining company and the port so desperately needed; and as might have been expected following Captain Thomas's recommendation, he turned out to be a very capable and conscientious servant, loyal in every respect to his new employers.

The friendship which had developed between Captain Thomas and Caine provided the means whereby the former was able to realise his long held ambition to establish a shipbuilding yard of his own. In much the same way as Nicholas Treweek had capitalised on his perceived need for a ship repairing yard at Amlwch, so Captain Thomas saw a comparable need at Duddon, where there were few if any, facilities for the day to day maintenance of vessels engaged in the arduous iron ore trade. Helped by Caine and his fellow directors, the Captain was permitted to lease land belonging to the Earl of Lonsdale on the sandy shore of Crab Marsh, on which to build his own shipbuilding yard; taking William Postlethwaite, who was then secretary to the mining company, into a one third partnership.

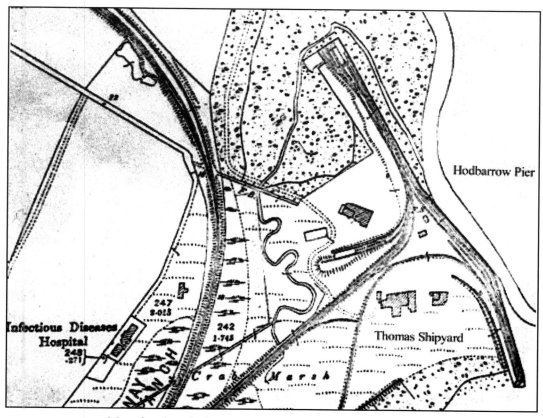

Map showing the location of the Thomas shipyard at Millom.

33

Quite apart from the capital required to establish the yard, Captain Thomas needed an efficient and skilled workforce to work it, and as the town was relatively close to well established shipyards at Barrow, Ulverston and Whitehaven, he would have had no difficulty in recruiting his men locally. Instead, he chose to appoint Hugh Jones, a 29-year-old Amlwch man as shipwright and yard overseer. In his new role, Jones was not only expected to undertake repairs to vessels, he was also required to design and build new ones, and it is highly unlikely that Thomas would have appointed him without sure knowledge of his capabilities. It is reasonable to suppose therefore that Hugh Jones had previously been employed by Captain Thomas to design and build both the *Welsh Girl* launched in March 1869, and the *Lewis & Mary*, launched in June 1870. It is also thought highly likely that Jones would have remained to oversee the launch of the latter vessel before leaving for Duddon.

Accompanying Hugh Jones to his new life were his 15-year-old brother Micah, described as an apprentice ship's carpenter; 22-year-old ship's carpenter John Morris, and 20-year-old Hugh Owens, a blacksmith. Their address at Millom, according to the 1871 census, was given as Crab Marsh, and as there were no houses on Crab Marsh at that time, it is thought that they first took up residence in a hulk which had been cast up on the shore, which later became the known home to some of the yard's workmen.

In a letter addressed to Nathaniel Caine, dated the 3rd of October 1870, William Thomas alluded to the new yard which was then under construction:

When the gridiron will be completed and the smithy completed, I shall be ready to build any size of vessel that I may get orders for. I shall be very happy to submit you a model for a schooner suitable for the Bristol Channel trade, and to draw a light draft with a cargo of about 150 or 160 tons, and to sail without ballast. Such vessel will answer for the Bristol Channel or Mersey or Dee as the wind blow, and can build her as cheap as anyone and will if required, take a share in her myself as this plan will establish Duddon.

The terms on which I shall build you a schooner it depend on what class vessel you required. If I was to suggest to you, it would be a suitable vessel it would be as follows. Length of keel 75 feet; 20ft beam by about 8 to 9ft hold. The frame to be of English oak with large dimensions for heavy trade. Planking, bottom A(merican) Elm, Bilge to Wales Pitch Pine, and binding strakes hardwood E(nglish Oak) or Teak, Ceiling Hackmatack or Red Pine. Fit out to be as customary and to class 8 years that the vessels they generally build in that neighbourhood.

I could build a vessel to carry 150 tons, 8 years Class with extra strong frame completed for sea for 1700, as can agree for and will guarantee the vessel to be a first class rate one entirely for the trade as Capt. Morgan (the new Harbourmaster) can look after the building of her.

Postlethwaite's interest in the new venture was private inasmuch that it was in no way associated with his duties as secretary to the mining company. Although Captain Thomas would obviously have kept a watching brief over the practicalities of the venture, probably commuting on a regular basis between Amlwch and Duddon by sea, it is believed that Postlethwaite had general oversight over the day to day office management of the yard during the formative years.

The construction of the yard had been completed by January 19th 1871, and in his capacity as secretary to the mine company, Postlethwaite placed an order with Captain Thomas for 2 vessels:

I now beg to hand you specifications of a new schooner which we offer you to build at the rate of

£12-5-0 (twelve Pounds five shillings) per ton, builders measurement. We would give you two to build at that price, one to be built at Amlwch in six months, and one at Duddon in 12 months from time of signing agreement. If you agree to it, please make out agreement, sign and send to me and we will send you ours as well.

A copy of the agreement dated January 24th 1871, relating to the building of the Amlwch vessel, reads as follows:

Memorandum of Agreement made between William Postlethwaite, Holborn Hill, Cumberland of the one part and William Thomas, Ship Builder, Amlwch of the other part. That is to say, the said William Thomas agrees to build a new schooner of about 180 tons Builders Measurement. The vessel to be built to Class A1 for 12 years at Lloyds and to be of the sizes named in the specification received from William Postlethwaite. The said William Thomas to build the vessel in 6 months from date of agreement and complete her ready for sea according to the specification. In consideration to build such a vessel the said William Postlethwaite to pay the sum of £12.10.0per ton Builders Measurement. Payments as follows viz. When Keel Stem Stern post and floors laid down a payment of say £200. When vessel in frame complete the sum of two hundred Pounds. When beamed and planked Four Hundred Pounds. When ready for sea, the remainder according to measurement.
Signed by William Postlethwaite Witnessed by Robert Johnson
William Thomas Witnessed by Evan Evans

In anticipation of being given the order, Captain Thomas had sought the permission of the Amlwch Harbour Trustees to build a vessel on land they controlled, as was recorded in the Minutes of their meeting held on 25th July 1870:

Mr William Thomas Shipbuilder, having made application to be allowed to lay and build a vessel at the upper end of the Harbour to the extent of 100 feet for her keel ordered that permission be given him on payment of Two Guineas to the Trust, for the use of such place, he agreeing to pay such sum and to take every risk upon himself, and not place any encumbrance or cause any obstruction to the Harbour, and not to occupy such room longer than 18 months from this date otherwise a payment of 2 Guineas will be enforced for every month beyond that time.

The end of the harbour referred to is clearly the narrow, landward end, where the topography was eminently suitable, and where the least inconvenience would be caused to other users of the port, a factor that clearly exercised the Harbour Trustees. One possible reason why the same location had not previously been used for shipbuilding, is that it could quite possibly have been the site on which stood the warehouse belonging to the Amlwch Steamship Company, which was demolished in the 'Royal Charter' Storm' 11 years previously.

Captain Thomas evidently wasted no time in drawing up the contract for the Duddon vessel with the mining company, because, 11 days later, on 30th January 1871, Postlethwaite wrote back accepting the offer to build the vessel at the specified price, and advising the Captain that the agreement would be attended to in a day or two, adding that he should begin work on the vessel in the meantime.

Despite his obvious commitment to the Millom yard, the Captain was still extremely keen to develop shipbuilding facilities of his own at Amlwch, and encouraged by the Harbour Trustees' agreement to allow him to build a ship on their land, he made yet another application to them, as the Minutes of their meeting held on the 1st of May 1871, record:

> *Mr William Thomas, Shipbuilder made an application to place a strong gate near the mouth of the cove at the upper end of the harbour for the purpose of constructing a graving dock. The same was taken into consideration and it was decided that the proposal could not be entertained.*

Undaunted by the Trustees' decision, he carried on with the new vessel which was eventually launched on the 9th of March 1872. The 119 ton, two-masted topsail schooner *Holy Wath*, had taken 13 months to complete, over twice the time stipulated by the contract, and a somewhat longer time than that stipulated by the Harbour Trust.

The schooner Holy Wath, *built 1872.*

In the 3 years from 1879 to 1881, the vessel is known to have spent her time exclusively in the Irish Sea trade, carrying ore, coal, timber, rails, clay and iron; earning for her shareholders a total of more than £714 in dividends, a very fair return indeed on their investment.

Although disappointed by the Harbour Trustees' decision to refuse him permission to build a graving (dry) dock, the Captain nevertheless continued to explore any avenue which could eventually lead him to the fulfilment of his ambition to establish his own yard at Amlwch, and it was clearly with great pride and satisfaction that in May 1872, he was able to announce to his business friends that he had purchased Mr Nicholas Treweek's extensive and commodious shipbuilding yard and dry dock. It should be noted that in the announcement William Thomas refers not only to Duddon, but to shipbuilding yards in the Principality, which seemingly included his yard at the end of the harbour leased to him by the Harbour Trust.

AMLWCH PORT, ANGLESEA

NORTH WALES.

WILLIAM THOMAS,

SHIP BUILDER, &c.,

Begs most respectfully to inform his Friends and the Public generally, that he has lately purchased Mr. NICHOLAS TREWEEK'S Extensive and Commodious SHIP-BUILDING YARD and DRY DOCK, and that he is now in a position to execute any work entrusted to his care, with the greatest promptitude, and upon the most reasonable terms.

He employs a most efficient Staff of Workmen, including Carpenters, Joiners, Smiths, Sailmakers, Block-makers and others. He, also, begs to intimate that he keeps all sorts of SHIP CHANDLERY STORES, &c., and has constantly on hand a Large Stock of BUILDING MATERIALS; such as Boards, Bricks, Chimney Tops, Laths, Nails (in great variety), Ridge and other Tiles, Slabs, Slates, Timber, &c., &c.

W. T. begs to state that his Ship Building Yards are very conveniently situated, and are some of the most extensive in the Principality.

He has, also, a large Grid Iron Yard at Duddon, in Cumberland.

MAY, 1872.

Captain Thomas's flyer announcing his purchase of Iard Newydd in 1872.

There are no clues as to why Nicholas Treweek came to sell his yard. His curious behaviour when he had earlier disposed of his shipping interests to his family, together with his evident lack of interest in the working of Iard Newydd, suggest that he was far from well, and as Captain Thomas seemed to have some interest in the yard already, he was clearly in a good position to benefit from Treweek's decision to pull out. The final instalment on the yard, the total cost of which amounted to £1515-19-5, was paid to Treweek on the 5th of May 1874 (see Appendix 3).

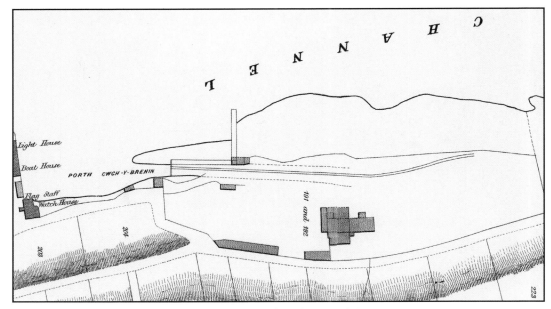

Algeo's plan of Iard Newydd.

Captain Thomas's joy at proclaiming his purchase of Iard Newydd was marred when, within a few days of writing a letter to William Postlethwaite, requesting a stage payment due to him on the vessel being built at Duddon, he received the following reply:

As to giving you instalments on the new vessel now building here I don't think the Company will, as there is no agreement whatever. Nevertheless the Company may take shares in her when completed and ready for sea.

Quite understandably bewildered, and dismayed by this latest turn of events, the Captain continued over a number of weeks to press his case in correspondence with Postlethwaite, but without receiving any assurance whatsoever regarding reimbursement for what had clearly been a costly investment on his part. In desperation, and at Postlethwaite's suggestion, he wrote directly to Nathaniel Caine. The contents of his letter reveal much about his character, in particular the moderate manner in which he approached what was clearly for him, a very serious problem indeed:

Some weeks ago when I called upon Mr Postlethwaite for the first instalment of the new vessel now being built at Duddon, he wrote back and said that the Company had not agreed for her, and that he could not move in the matter himself, suggesting that I write to you on the subject.

You will no doubt remember that I made an agreement with Mr Postlethwaite, on behalf of the Company to build two vessels, one in Amlwch and the other at Duddon, the former having been completed, & I hope to the perfect satisfaction of yourself and the Co.

Another one now being built at Duddon is ready for planking according to the specification. Had I thought for a moment that there would be any dispute about her or refusal – I would not have gone to such expense with her for I cannot make my money out of her in the market as she is built expressly for your trade with so much more strength than would be required for a vessel of ordinary dimensions.

I beg to enclose for your inspection and return 3 letters from Mr Postlethwaite to me on the subject, (on behalf of the Company) and I shall be glad to hear from you at your very earliest convenience, for if you will not take the vessel I shall indeed be greatly disappointed, and the loss to me will be very great. But I should hope that you would kindly contribute toward it and not suffer me to be the loser.

*But I cannot understand the reason why you don't take her after **agreeing to do so**. However I hope that this will be settled to our mutual satisfaction when you move in the matter for you will no doubt **remember** having spoken to me **yourself** about this identical vessel, cautioning me against putting any inferior timber in her &c. &c.*

I shall have no objection to take a share in her if you will allow me to suggest a good Captain – for your approval – for her. After Mr Postlethwaite refused the vessel I suggested to him to plank her with pitch pine – and to Capt. Morgan also – and class her 10 or 11 years and allow the difference if you approve of it.

*I shall be **much obliged** of an early reply as I cannot keep this an open question any longer.*

Unless the purchasers were in some form of unforeseen financial difficulty, it is difficult to understand why they should have wished to back out of half of their agreement with the Captain, particularly as there had been no apparent difficulty regarding payments for the recently completed *Holy Wath*.

Despite Captain Thomas's confusion and dismay, his confidence in Nathaniel Caine's integrity was unimpaired, and this was clearly demonstrated when he enclosed for the latter's perusal, the three letters which were the only concrete evidence he possessed of an agreement between them. In a situation which could readily have led to litigation, crucial documents such as the letters could so easily have been 'accidentally lost'; but the Captain's faith in his friend's probity was not misplaced, and the matter was eventually resolved to everyone's satisfaction.

Because of the vast amount of repairs being undertaken at the Duddon yard, work on the Duddon vessel proceeded rather more slowly than had been anticipated when Postlethwaite wrote to Captain Thomas in January 1871. It is known that repair work was far more profitable than shipbuilding, and there can be little doubt that Postlethwaite's reluctance to push for the completion of the new vessel was due to the fact that he owned a substantial share in the yard. By the time the vessel was launched, it had been on the stocks for four years.

Known as the *Nellie Bywater*, the new two-masted topsail schooner was launched on the 20th December 1873, by Mary, wife of William Morgan, the Harbourmaster. Although the customary celebrations which followed the launch had a distinctive Welsh flavour about them, Captain Thomas was not present for some reason, and it was Postlethwaite who replied to the toast to the vessel, on behalf of the builders. Aware of the local criticism

The schooner Nellie Bywater *at Liverpool.*

regarding the inordinate time taken to build her, he claimed that she had been nothing but a sideshow which was only worked on when the yard had little else to do.

The vessel's first master was Captain Richard Morgan, an Amlwch man who was probably William Morgan the Harbourmaster's brother. He however, was succeeded in 1878 by yet another Amlwch man, Captain Solomon Ellis who later went on to command deep-sea vessels.

The *Nellie Bywater* traded mainly in home waters, and she remained in the Duddon trade for about 40 years before being sold. During the Second World War she was requisitioned by the Admiralty as a supply and refuelling vessel, and when she came off charter at the end of hostilities, she was refitted and later bought by Captain Richard England, who had served his time 'before the mast' in schooners.

In his book *Schoonerman*, Captain England describes how, before buying the 73-year-old vessel, he inspected her in a Belfast dry dock, where he spent several hours:

thoroughly examining the bottom of the schooner, which was bone dry and scraped to the bare wood. Keel, garboards and skin planking were in excellent condition and all she needed was the renewal of a few trunnels and a bit of recaulking and hardening up of seams. I was amazed at the skill of her builders in constructing such a fine run to the schooner with scarcely any stealers and it was obvious she was the work of superb craftsmen.

Hugh Jones could not have wished for a better epitaph. The *Nellie Bywater* which featured in the film *The Elusive Pimpernel*, eventually became the last working topsail schooner on Lloyd's British Register. Unable to find paying work for his vessel at home however, Captain England decided in 1951 to sail with his family and others to the West Indies where he hoped to find employment trading between the islands. When the schooner was south-west of Ireland en route to the Caribbean, she was overtaken by a fearful storm which made world news when it claimed the modern, 6,700 ton *Flying Enterprise*, captained by Kurt Carlsen.

A total of 14 persons were aboard the schooner when she was several times blown off course by winds which reached 97 miles per hour at their height. Continuously battered by 30 foot high waves, she began to take on water. Although one ship's member was reported as having been on the pumps for over 30 hours, the crew failed in their efforts to stop her flooding. The vessel heeled over, and the captain of the tug *Careful* which was standing by, reported seeing those on board stepping over the side into the sea. The tragic incident cost two lives, those of Captain England's 17-year-old daughter, and the ship's carpenter.

The second vessel to leave the Millom yard was the wooden schooner *Countess of Lonsdale*, which after four and a half years on the stocks, was eventually launched in September 1878. Built as a speculation, she was registered in the joint names of Thomas and Postlethwaite: but the Captain bought her outright some 2 years later. Command of the schooner was given to Lewis Hughes of Amlwch, and he is known to have continued as her master until 1889, some 2 years before she was run down and sunk by the steamer *Sherbro*, fortunately without loss of life.

On the 20th March 1874, the three-masted barquentine *Cumberland Lassie* was launched from Iard Newydd. Built for William Postlethwaite, she was felted and yellow metalled for foreign trade, and was the largest vessel to have been built at Porth Amlwch up to that time.

The schooner Cumberland Lassie *which became one of Kent's best known colliers.*

Following her delivery voyage to Duddon, the vessel sailed under the managing ownership of William Postlethwaite. Her first commercial voyage was to Cardiff in April 1874, from where she went on to Madeira, and then Pomoron; returning to Garston at the end of the same year. In June 1875 she sailed from Barrow to East London, before she went on to Mauritius, then to Adelaide, Algoa Bay, Chittagong and Cochin. From Cochin she sailed to False Point, and then back again to Cochin, returning to London in September 1877, a very busy life indeed.

Captain Thomas, by his own reckoning, was by this time an extremely wealthy man. He wholly or partly owned no fewer than 25 vessels, and his own assessment of his worth, which included real estate, amounted to no less than £22,000, which would be equivalent to well over £1 million at 2002 values!

On the 3rd of December 1888 the *Cumberland Lassie* made one of her infrequent visits to Amlwch with a cargo of sulphur from Huelva in Spain for Hills' chemical works, which was by then having to depend on imports rather than the locally generated product from the mines. After an eventful life sailing the high seas, the vessel finished her days as one of the best known colliers working between the north-east of England and Kent. Her life ended however when having left Gravesend on a voyage to Newcastle on Tyne, with a cargo of burnt ore, the vessel ran aground 1 mile south of the Martello Tower, Aldeburgh on the morning of 16th January 1918. By 11 o'clock, she had broken up, leaving very little of her structure to salvage. Three members of the crew were saved, but the Master and a lad were drowned.

Porth Amlwch had been the station for Liverpool pilot boats since well before 1748 when Lewis Morris, the coast surveyor, described it as the place where:

vessels load Corn, Butter, Cheese etc., and here the Liverpoole (sic) *Pilot Boats lie afloat, to be ready to meet any vessels in the offing*

As well as using Amlwch for berthing purposes, masters of Liverpool Pilot Boats frequently made use of the port's facilities in order to maintain and clean their vessels' hulls, and it may well have been as a result of this, that Captain Thomas discovered in 1874 that the pilotage service required a new vessel. Anxious to find work for his new yard, Thomas decided to tender: but before doing so, he went to the trouble and expense of familiarising himself with the construction and layout of several boats already working in the service. The resulting specification (see Appendix 5) for what was to prove to be the largest wooden schooner ever built for the Liverpool service, shows that she was constructed and appointed to a very high standard indeed.

With his tender, Captain Thomas submitted a half model of the proposed vessel, which is now in the ownership of the Amlwch Industrial Heritage Trust. Built by the shipwright whose task it would be to build the new vessel, the model was intended to show the prospective buyer the hull form of the vessel he was being offered. Often the buyer, if he was seriously contemplating placing an order, would request changes to the vessel's final shape to satisfy his own requirements; and unless the shipwright had serious reservations about the proposed changes, he would modify the model accordingly.

By way of simplifying matters, only one half of the hull was built, that is, representing the ship as if it had been cut lengthwise along its centreline from stem to stern. Such a model had two purposes: the first, to convey the information required by the potential customer; and secondly to assist the shipwright when he came to lay out the full size sections of the finished vessel.

In the early days, a shipwright's skills were almost entirely of the practical kind, invariably hard won after many years as an apprentice and journeyman; much of which was of the 'rule of thumb' kind. As such, it is highly unlikely that he could develop ship lines on paper, and had to rely on the half model, the dimensions of which he could scale up to determine the finished ship's dimensions. In order to do this, he fashioned the model from a number of layers of hardwood screwed together, which could easily be taken apart.

The original half model of the Mersey, *Liverpool Pilot Boat Nº 11, 1875.*

In many cases, the wood layers were alternately made of light and dark coloured wood, but in the case of the *Mersey,* as she would be known, the layers are all of prime mahogany which have been very accurately planed to an uniform thickness of half an inch (¹/₂"). Each layer represents a 'lift' of 1 foot (12") in the depth of the finished vessel, thus making the model of one twenty-fourths scale i.e each ¹/₂ inch representing 12 inches.

For conservation reasons, no attempt has been made to dismantle the *Mersey* half model: but if it were to be done, it is expected that each of the vessel's frames would have been marked on the layers in such a way that the scale distance from the ship's centreline to the outside of its hull at any particular frame, could be measured. This would be done at each layer, representing one foot above or below a given datum, for each frame station along the ship's length. Each measurement thus taken would then be multiplied by a scale factor of 24, in order to arrive at the actual, full scale dimension. These dimensions would then have been transferred to the loft floor, and a full sized frame of the exact shape of the vessel's profile arrived at. This in turn would be used to guide the sawyers whose job it was to saw the timbers of which the frame was to be constructed.

A photograph of the *Mersey,* which became *Liverpool Pilot Boat 11,* newly painted on the stocks prior to her launch in 1875 is the earliest known photograph taken in Iard Newydd, if not in Amlwch.

The boat was most unlucky inasmuch that 2 years after her launch, she was in collision with the ss *Menelaus,* and sunk, fortunately without loss of life. Raised, she then served until 1885 when she was run down again by yet another steamship, the *Landana,* and finally sunk. On that occasion, the Master lost his life.

Although he was clearly receiving a substantial income from his coasting operations, and other investments such as the *Rhyd Talog* Mineral Water Works, established close to his family home, much of William Thomas's wealth resulted from his investment in deep-sea vessels such as the Jersey built *William Melhuish*; the 483 ton wooden bark *Yuca,* built in

The Liverpool Pilot Boat Mersey, *on the stocks at Iard Newydd 1875. This is believed to be the earliest known photograph relating to Porth Amlwch.*

1860 by Lamport of Workington; the 498 ton *John Bright*, built in 1869 in Dumbarton, and the 689 ton wooden bark *Toronto*, built in 1872 by Anger of Quebec.

Building work at Iard Newydd continued apace, and the wooden barquentine *Baron Hill*, the 6th vessel to leave the yard, was launched in June 1876. The vessel was named after the seat of the wealthy Bulkeley family in Beaumaris, on the shore of the Menai Strait. Like the *Cumberland Lassie*, she too was built for William Postlethwaite, and as the two vessels' tonnages were near enough identical, it is probably true to say that they were built to the same model.

In November 1876, William Thomas launched the much smaller, 89 ton wooden schooner *Lady Neave*, named after a member of the landed Dinorben family, who were joint owners with the Marquess of Anglesey, of the copper mines at Mynydd Parys; and one of whose country estates was in nearby Llys Dulas. The fact that two successive vessels had names associated with the local aristocracy may have been coincidental; but it could also have meant that both William Thomas and William Postlethwaite were by then beginning to move in more esoteric circles.

No doubt aware of the difficulties he had experienced from his own lack of formal education, Captain Thomas was determined that his children should receive the best schooling he could afford. Although a National School had been established in Amlwch in 1821, followed by the British School in 1863, his daughter Mary, and her brothers John and

Willie, were placed in a private school known as Sellars Amlwch Academy between 1869 and 1873.

There is no record of eldest son Lewis's formal education, but the command of both the English and Welsh languages displayed in his letters, as well as his clear handwriting, show that it had been of a high standard. The fact that he followed in his father's footsteps by becoming a Master Mariner suggests that his education was undertaken locally; quite possibly in the School of Navigation run by William Francis, a retired sea captain, and his gifted daughter Mary, who herself became a legendary teacher of navigation in Caernarfon following her father's death.

. EDUCATION.

WILLIAM FRANCIS proposes to open a School at Amlwch, in the county of Anglesey, on Monday the 10th day of January, 1814, wherein he intends to instruct a limited number of Pupils, in the following branches of Literature, according to the most approved methods; and with the strictest care and attention to the scholars morals and progress.

TERMS PER QUARTER.			Ent.	
	£.	s. d.	s.	d.
Spelling, reading, and writing English,	0	7 6	2	6
English grammar, arithmetic, mensuration, book-keeping,&c.	0	10 0	2	6
Mensurations universally; land-surveying, geography, and astronomy, the use of maps, charts, terrestrial and celestial globes, drawing in oil and water colours, &c.	0	15 0	5	0
The elements of geometry, plain and spherical trigonometry, algebra, theoretical navigation, &c.	1	0 0	5	0
Practical navigation, with the use and construction of sea-charts, keeping a journal at sea, &c.	2	0 0		
Theoretical and practical navigation, the use of globes, quadrants and sextants, double altitudes and lunar observations, complete, &c.	3	0 0		

Parents and others that may intend to honor him with the tuition of their children, are requested to enter their names immediately, as he is determined to limit the number of his scholars, to what he may be able to teach and attend with due and just assiduity.

N. B. Seamen and others may be accommodated with Board and Lodging on very moderate terms in the neighbourhood.

Captain William Francis' flyer advertising his School of Navigation at Amlwch.

45

In November 1876 , the Captain's second son John, who was then 16 years old, was known to be lodging in Liverpool. It is evident that he had received a good education before his arrival, and there can be no doubt that he was there to undergo some form of vocational training. In view of his later, somewhat turbulent career, it is reasonable to suppose that his father had placed him as a pupil in a ship broker's office where he underwent training designed to fit him for eventual employment in the family business.

His younger brother Willie was a boarding pupil at Wesley College in Sheffield between January 1877 and November 1879. The College, which opened in 1841 to provide education on Wesleyan principles, was affiliated to the University of London: but the likelihood is that Willie was a pupil in what was then known as the B Division, which was intended to provide training for business rather than academic careers. When he left the college in November 1879, he too went to Liverpool, but his stay in the city was a relatively short one, for he returned to Amlwch some time in the summer of 1880 to take up duties in his father's yard.

By January 1880, when payments for his Liverpool lodgings ceased, John who was by then 20 years of age, was considered by his father to be sufficiently prepared, but more importantly perhaps, had the ability to take over the management of the Duddon yard. As the supervision of the yard's side was still in Hugh Jones's very capable hands, it is thought that the remainder of the firm's day to day business, which had by then been established some 10 years, was unlikely to have been particularly onerous. The first ledger entry referring to John in his new position, is the transfer to him at Duddon of £100, on 21st April 1880.

It is obvious however, that he must have gone there immediately he left Liverpool, for Louisa, daughter of Captain Thomas Rich, an official of the Hodbarrow Mine, whom he later married, gave birth to their first son, in November of that year. The marriage of members of two well-respected local celebrities, seemed to promise much: but unfortunately was blighted from the start, for John was by then nurturing a drink problem. The Census of February 1881 records, that he was then lodging in Millom, as Duddon had become known; and in due course, Louisa gave birth to their second son, Norman.

During John's time at Millom, the yard turned out the wooden steamer *Lady Kate*, bought whilst still under construction for the Lady Kate Steamship Company. She was launched on the 1st February 1881 with John being appointed as her manager. Powered by engines fitted by De Winton of Caernarfon, she survived until her break up in 1948 still with her original 67-year-old machinery on board!

On the 18th of June 1882, 16 months after the launch of the *Lady Kate*, the yard launched the *Lady Louisa*, a screw steamer powered by J.T. Young of Ayr, which, like her sister ship was destined for the Lady Kate Steamship Company. Her first manager was William Postlethwaite and not John as might have been expected. Whether or not this reflected the beginning of serious problems with his behaviour, can only be guessed at.

As his evident success as a shipbuilder and manager became more widely known, Captain Thomas found little difficulty in finding partners to join him in more progressive shipping ventures, and one such was the purchase of the 1082 ton iron bark *Barbara*, built to his order in 1877 by the highly respected yard of William Doxford & Sons of Sunderland at a cost of £15,000 (£699,150 in 2002) (see Appendix 6). Command of the vessel was given to Richard Hugh Roberts, an Amlwch man, who had earlier been the master of the Thomas-owned vessel *Toronto*.

Multi ownership of small vessels was usually in divisions of 64 shares, 4 of which taken together were referred to as an ounce, each ounce representing 6.25% of the vessel's value. The *Barbara* was owned by a total of 14 investors, amongst whom were James Treweek, Charles Henry Hills of the Amlwch Chemical Works, and Captain Roberts, her Master: William Thomas, however, was the major shareholder, owning 24/64ths, or 37.5% of the vessel's shares. During her working lifetime, the vessel paid her owners well, but her eventual loss, described elsewhere in this work, was to cause a major rift between Captain Thomas and the Amlwch Maritime Mutual Insurance Company her insurers, which he had been instrumental in establishing.

In a flurry of building activity, Iard Newydd launched no fewer than 7 vessels between August 1877 and October 1881: the first being the 103 ton wooden schooner *Nantglyn* (see Appendix 7), which was followed by her sister ship, the 104 ton *Nesta*, both of which were destined for Captain Thomas's own fleet. Two further vessels were launched in 1878, the 98.7 ton wooden schooner *Eilian Hill,* and the much smaller 16 ton wooden smack *Glyndwr.*

The schooner Eilian Hill *1878, Iard Newydd Nº 10*

November 1879 saw the launch of the 72 ton wooden schooner *Margaret,* which possessed what was known as an *Irish Sea* stern, which was elliptical, unlike the *Cumberland Lassie* for example, which had a square transom. She was 76 feet long and carried 140 tons, and Captain Thomas was pleased to appoint Lewis his eldest son as her master. It is known that both Lewis and Willie possessed considerable artistic skills, and it is thought that the illustration of the *Margaret* passing an unknown lightship was painted by the former when

The schooner Margaret 1879, *(Captain Lewis Thomas), Iard Newydd N⁰ 12.*

he was her Master. Because of its similarity to the painting of the *Eilian Hill* it is possible that that too was painted by him.

Iard Newydd was then busy with the 100 ton wooden schooner *Pearl* which was launched in September 1880; followed by the smaller, 48 ton schooner *President Garfield* which was launched a year later in September 1881. It is significant that the latter was named in honour of the 20th President of the United States who had been assassinated in Washington DC's railway station a few weeks earlier. It is quite evident from his choice of name for the new vessel, that Captain Thomas had a close affinity with the American people, which could well support the author's theory that he had served his seagoing apprenticeship on board an American vessel, and not a British one as had been automatically assumed. This hypothesis might also explain the legends associating him with America at the time of the Civil War.

About this time, William Thomas acquired shares in the *Countess of Kintore*, a 783 ton wooden ship built by Duthie in Aberdeen.

It is evident that some time during 1882, the Captain and William Postlethwaite were minded to float the Millom business as a limited company, but apart from drawing out a prospectus for a company with a share capital of £10,000 (£533,400 in 2002), the matter proceeded no further (see Appendix 8).

The very first steamship to be built in Iard Newydd was the 74 ton, iron-built, screw-propelled dandy, called the *W.S. Caine*, named in honour of teetotaller William Sproston

Caine, brother of Thomas's great friend, Nathaniel. An account in the local newspaper, of the launch which took place on the 7th of April, 1883, is worthy of recalling for a number of reasons, not least of which, being the style in which the event was reported:

A very successful launch of the ss W.S. Caine was effected at 10 o'clock last Saturday morning from the shipbuilding yard of Captain Wm Thomas at this port. The launch was performed under exceedingly favourable conditions in respect of weather and tide, the christening having been entrusted to Mrs Fanning Evans of Mona Lodge (wife of the Sheriff of the County), who executed her onerous duties in a graceful and efficient manner, and amidst the hearty cheers of the vast assemblage present.

The W.S. Caine took to the water as naturally as the honourable gentleman whose good name she bears, and who, through teetotalism enables him to vie with the gallant vessel in the love of the limpid element. The W.S. Caine is built of iron, being the first iron steamer ever built in Amlwch, is of about 200 tons deadweight capacity, classed A.1 for 100 years at Lloyds, and it is designed for the coasting trade.

She will immediately be filled with splendid boilers and engines by Messrs De Winton & Co., engineers, Caernarvon.

Great credit is due to Capt. Thomas for his successful efforts to establish such an excellent shipbuilding yard in Amlwch. The vessel is only the first in a line of steamers which our enterprising fellow countryman contemplates building. Another vessel twice as large has just been started, and with his splendid machinery and efficient staff and appliances will very quickly be modelled into shape. The recent addition to his premises is an acquisition of incalculable benefit to facilitate the turning out of heavy tonnage.

In order to put this in its historical context however, it should be noted that Robert Fulton had built the steamer *Clermont* in Charles Brown's yard in New York some 76 years earlier. Powered by an engine designed and built by Boulton and Watt, both of whom had visited, and had close associations with Amlwch in the copper mines' heyday, the 133 feet long vessel was running an extended schedule long before a comparable service had been inaugurated in the United Kingdom.

Five weeks after the *W. S. Caine's* launch, the same newspaper carried the following report:

On Thursday last week this new vessel, under the command of Captain L. Thomas, left the Port of Caernarvon (sic) for a trial trip round the island of Anglesey, and to Llandudno, and back to Amlwch. This ship was launched five weeks ago from the extensive shipbuilding yard of our enterprising fellow countryman – Captain William Thomas; being the first iron steamer to be built in North Wales, but is to be quickly succeeded by several others of much heavier tonnage.

The W.S. Caine is 122 feet long between perpendiculars, beam 21 feet, depth of hold 8 feet, and capable of carrying about 200 tons on 8 feet of water, being thus practically of the most suitable dimensions for the coasting trade.

Shortly after the launch she was towed to Caernarvon to have her new boiler and engines fitted at the foundry of Messrs De Winton and Co. Her engines are of the compound surface condensing type of fifty nominal horse power, and upon the most recently improved pattern, the cylinders being 14 inches and 27 inches respectively by twenty one inches stroke, and her trial runs were most satisfactory.

A start was made from Caernarvon between nine and ten a.m. reaching Holyhead by twelve, where the vessel was inspected by several gentlemen, and a cruise of about two hours was made. At three p.m. a course for Amlwch was steered, and the distance of twenty miles covered in one hour and twenty minutes.

At Amlwch a numerous and distinguished party of ladies and gentlemen joined those who had previously embarked, and a prompt start for Llandudno was made... At five o'clock tea was served all round, and the weather being very fine, and the rich sea coast scenery, a most enjoyable trip was had. The party landed for two hours at Llandudno, and having viewed that fashionable watering place, re-embarked for the homeward trip at nine p.m.

The W.S. Caine behaved admirably, and will prove a very fast cargo boat. Her pretty model, fine lines, and other appurtenances are all worked by steam, and the steam winch is sufficiently strong to discharge a full cargo in five hours.

The *W.S. Caine*, valued at £5,000 (£262,050 in 2002), was put up for sale in 250 share lots of £20 each, by William Thomas & Co., Captain Thomas's Liverpool-based partner in the highly profitable *William Melhuish* venture.

Continuing with its policy of producing wooden, screw-driven steamships, the Millom yard turned out the *Lady Bessie*, which was launched on the 24th of June 1884. In common with her predecessor, she too was powered by De Winton machinery, and destined for the Lady Kate Steamship Company. John Thomas's role as her manager did not last long, as she was very early on in her career, sold to George Farren of Caernarfon, who had earlier acquired the *Lady Kate*. From this, one can only conclude that his choice was based on his complete satisfaction with the *Lady Kate*.

The wooden steamship Lady Bessie, *Millom Yard Nº 5 – machinery by De Winton, Caernarfon.*

On the 20th February 1884, Captain Thomas launched the *Eilian*, a 292 ton iron, screw-driven steamer, at Amlwch. It was an auspicious occasion inasmuch that the vessel was the largest built in Iard Newydd up to that time, and it was the first occasion that use was made of a new slipway built at the north-eastern end of the yard. Such was the steepness of the new slip however, that many of the yard's workforce were convinced that it was inherently dangerous, and for that reason, refused to join the traditional volunteer crew on board the vessel as she slid into the water. Under the circumstances, many more people than usual gathered to witness the launch, no doubt expecting a mishap to take place, and in one sense they were not disappointed, as a contemporary newspaper report testifies:

> Only Captain Lewis Thomas (Lloyd's Agent), and a youth in the employ of the firm ventured on board. However, gaily and gracefully this new born daughter of the ocean glided into her precarious future. The ceremony of christening was performed by Miss Lallie Evans of Mona Lodge, and hundreds assembled to witness the interesting spectacle.
>
> An exciting incident occurred. Like a self willed steed the Eilian broke loose from the little steamer which was engaged to bring her into port, and went off at full speed with the tide in the direction of Cemaes when a tug sighted her and towed her into desired waters.
>
> Amlwch is likely to be a great shipbuilding station. We understand that Captain Thomas has a new Manager who has had great experience in the construction of iron vessels.

As there is no record of Willie Thomas having ever received any form of training as a shipwright before taking up employment at Amlwch, it can only be concluded that he was trained in his profession by a qualified naval architect employed in the yard; and for that reason, it is thought more than likely that the manager referred to in the newspaper report, was his mentor.

On the 23rd of March 1884, three weeks after her launching, the *Eilian* was towed by the steam flat *Temple* to Caernarfon where she was to have her boiler and machinery fitted by De Winton.

Seven weeks later, the Harbourmaster recorded the fact that the steamer *Express*, having a captain of the same name as that of the recently launched *Eilian*, came into Amlwch on her trial trip from Caernarfon, carrying a cargo of slates and timber. The vessel's name had been changed, more than likely because it belonged to another vessel, but as she was a little later to be known as the *Exchange*, and not the *Express*, it has to be assumed either that the Harbourmaster had got her name wrong, or that there had been a double change of name, which is the more likely of the two interpretations.

Another, smaller steamer, the 149 ton *Anglesea* (see Appendix 11), jointly owned by the Captain and his two sons Lewis and William, was launched from the yard in November 1884. This probably reflected the fact that Captain Thomas had taken his two sons, Lewis and William into partnership on the 1st of July, although the agreement between them was not signed until some 6 months later. The lengthy partnership agreement between them shows that the yard remained in the Captain's ownership, for which he was paid an annual rent. The operational side however, was in three equal holdings; and the schedule of the yard's assets appended to the agreement not only

The steam flat **Temple** *(alongside), believed to be at Mostyn on the Dee,
then known as the Chester River*

Captain Lewis Thomas

William Thomas Junior (Willie)

gives an indication of its worth, but also, of its then engineering capacity (see Appendix 10).

The fact that John was not made a partner, suggests that matters between father and son were beyond redemption; but this may not have been strictly true, as Captain Thomas, despite his obvious frustration, clearly had particularly strong feelings towards his wayward son. Precisely what occurred and when, to finally ostracise John from the strongly Welsh community in Millom is not known; but according to Cumbrian maritime historian Trevor Morgan, John left the town under a cloud, having besmirched his family name to such a degree that his father felt compelled to sever his connection with the town by selling his interest in the business to Hugh Jones and his brother.

This may well have been the case; but it should nevertheless be remembered that Captain Thomas was by then 65 years of age. Despite the fact that he had taken Lewis and William into partnership, his other shipping interests continued to be wide and demanding. His yard at Amlwch was flourishing in a way that Millom had never been able to match; and in this respect, it is interesting to note that between December 1873 and October 1886, the Millom yard built only 6 vessels against the 15 produced at Amlwch. Furthermore, John's failure to shoulder the responsibilities involved in looking after the Millom yard would have meant that had the Captain wished to continue his business there, either Lewis or Willie would have had to take John's place, both of whom had very taxing responsibilities of their own in Iard Newydd by then, and could clearly not be spared.

After the transfer of ownership, Captain Thomas was anxious to have his son at Amlwch, where he could exercise some parental control over him, but John in turn, clearly wanted none of it. Information relating to his subsequent whereabouts comes in a letter written and signed by him in April 1887, addressed to Thomas Fanning Evans of Amlwch, regarding the vessel *President Garfield*. The letter was written on headed notepaper bearing John's name, which described him as being a ship and insurance broker, sail maker and general commission agent of 12, Baltic Buildings in Liverpool. For this reason, there can be little doubt that he had received professional training as a ship broker; and there can be little doubt either, that it was his father who had set him up in business. Having already assisted him in this way, would also account for the fact that the Captain was disinclined to take him into partnership.

The last vessel to leave the Millom yard whilst it was still in Thomas ownership, was the three-masted topsail schooner *Greyhound*, launched in October 1886.

Laid down as yet another steamer for the Lady Kate Steamship Company, the prospective owners of the *Greyhound* unfortunately went into liquidation before her building was complete and she was absorbed into the Thomas fleet, the strongly built vessel spent part of her life in the Brazilian hide trade.

10th March, 1887, saw the launch from Iard Newydd, of the 222 ton iron schooner *Gelert*; which, like the *Anglesea*, had been built as a joint venture by Captain Thomas and his two sons. The vessel, which was to be the forerunner of a line of superb schooners, was well known locally for her unusual figurehead in the form of a dog which represented Prince Llewelyn's faithful wolfhound of that name.

According to the Harbourmaster's logbook for that day, the *President Garfield* came in from Liverpool, and there were 20 vessels in the harbour, a number of which belonged to

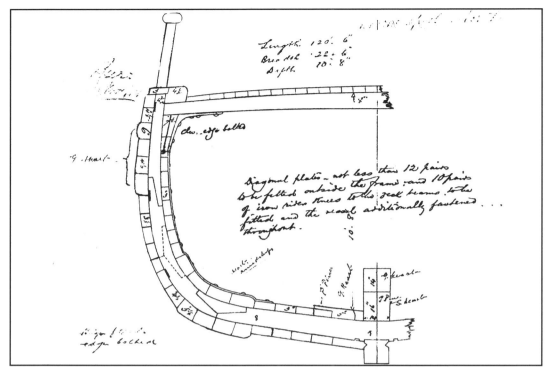

Cross section of the Greyhound's *hull indicating its innate strength.*

the Thomas family. *The Lady Louisa, Lord Mostyn, Anglesea* and the *Thomas* were loading; whilst *Zelinda* and *Kate* were lying idle, and the *Ocean Belle* was undergoing repairs. The *Gelert* sailed light for Liverpool a week later.

The Kate *neaped at Abersoch.*

In the very same month as John had written to Fanning Evans of Amlwch regarding the *President Garfield*, Willie sent him another concerning the *Ocean Belle*. The second however, was written on Millom headed notepaper and signed by William Thomas Junior, and the only construction that can be put on his presence there, is that he had been asked by his father to tie up loose ends before his side of the business was transferred to the Jones brothers. A photograph taken to mark the occasion shows Willie sitting in front of a group of yard workers with Hugh Jones standing somewhat self effacingly, in the back row, wearing the traditional bowler hat of a yard overseer. William Postlethwaite retained his interest in the yard for several years before he too sold out to the Jones brothers. Although Captain Thomas and Postlethwaite continued to share a few business enterprises, the Duddon venture had been all but forgotten by 1888.

William Thomas Junior with the Millom workforce, probably taken at the time of the sale of the yard to Hugh Jones and his brother.

The brothers' duties at the Amlwch yard overlapped to a certain degree; but it would appear that Captain Lewis Thomas, the elder of the two, and already appointed Lloyd's agent for the locality, was given control of the yard, whilst William, who was probably the better suited of the two to office work, looked after the Counting House and the Design Office.

Between them, the two wrote practically all of the letters recorded in the first available letter book: but a few however, are written in the Captain's own hand, and although perfectly readable, their contents sometimes reflect the limitations of his early education, as well as the fact that English was not his first language. The letters nevertheless show quite clearly that he continued to be a potent driving force behind the enterprise he had so assiduously established, and which had by then made him exceedingly wealthy. His letters, always businesslike, sometimes painfully blunt, reveal a compassionate and often vulnerable side to his nature, allowing the reader a fleeting insight into his somewhat larger than life character.

As might be expected, much of the correspondence is between the firm and its captains, and in the late summer of 1888, two Thomas vessels, the *Greyhound* (Captain William Williams) and the *Thomas Boustead* (Captain. Owen Jones), which were then engaged in the South American hide trade, were together at Rio Grande do Sol. The latter vessel had suffered damage to its rigging at the port, and in two letters from Amlwch, Captain Jones was advised to have temporary repairs carried out, to tide him over until such time as he was home, when proper repairs could be effected. After working the South American coast over the winter months, the *Greyhound* arrived in Plymouth on the 7th of May 1889, after making the passage from Rio Grande in 50 days, which was considered to be a very smart passage indeed. From Plymouth, the vessel was ordered to St Petersburg, where, having discharged her cargo, she was to load another for home waters. The *Greyhound* was eventually sold to a South African owner in 1891, spending the next 20 years trading along the east African coast. Bought by a Mauritian owner in March 1912 for the island guano trade, she lasted but 15 months in his ownership, before she was lost sailing between Albatross and Raphael Islands (see Appendix 21).

The master of the *Thomas Boustead* sailed on shares, and on the 19th of November 1888, when the vessel was in the Mersey, Captain Jones was asked where he wanted to go on his next voyage, and what he needed done to his vessel. He was advised that 45 shillings freight had been offered to the Rio Grande, *but as freights are rapidly improving, even more could be expected.* The following day however, the owners had to advise their shareholders that the vessel was neaped on a mud bank at Weston Point, and making water. After she had been lightened she was refloated and taken into dry dock. In a letter to R.J. Francis & Co., the owners required them to ensure that payment was received for the vessel's cargo before the lighters were discharged, and reminding them that the buyers were to pay their portion of the cost of discharging the vessel in the river. They then went on to offer the *Thomas Boustead* for sale through the offices of the brokers, for £1,800 nett cash after repairs had been effected, subject to the shareholders' consent.

No doubt remembering his own early days at sea, Captain Thomas wrote to Captain Lewis Hughes of the *Countess of Lonsdale*, enquiring if the latter would take with him on his next voyage: *a very nice lad of about 15 years of age… he is highly respectable, and would go for trifle wages,* before suggesting that a wage of ten shillings a month would suffice, and then adding: *we should prefer him joining you than any other of our captains, knowing that he would not be ill-treated.* Two days later Captain William Thomas wrote again to Captain Hughes, in which he proposed:

> to put a rolling chock in the bilges of the Countess (of Lonsdale), about 30 feet long and 8 inches wide, which in our opinion would be a very great improvement as she is such a laboursome vessel. We are doing this to a new steamer that we are building, and it answers the purpose very well, and if we don't sell the Countess, it may be wise to do it. If the vessel were to be sold, we could build you a steel barquentine similar to the Gelert, to carry 400 tons cargo on $10^1/_2$ to 11 feet (draft) for the Rio Grande trade, and if such a vessel were to be built, and to be a clipper, she would be the best investment going – what would be your wish to have such a vessel? We think a Barquentine rig will be best for long passages.

Less than a week after writing to Captain Hughes, regarding the possibility of his taking a lad with him on his next trip, Captain Thomas wrote another to him at his berth in Ipswich where he was loading for Guadeloupe, introducing Albert Roberts; *the lad whom we wrote to you about… trusting that you will take care of him, and teach him as much as you can.*

On 21st of March 1889, there was a violent storm at Amlwch, and in his capacity as Lloyd's Agent, Lewis Thomas advised the Liverpool Underwriters, that several portions of wreck had been seen floating within a short distance of Porth Amlwch, and naming the following vessels as having been damaged that day: *Renown; Martha; Success; Alnwick; Mary Ann; British Queen; Emperor* and *Ellen Elizabeth*, the last 2 being total wrecks.

It is evident that Captain William Williams of the *Greyhound* was salaried, for on the 14th of August 1889, an agreement was drawn up between himself and Wm Thomas & Sons, by which he would henceforth 'sail by the shares'. This was an honour bestowed on their best captains, and one which allowed masters to profit from their own diligence. This brought William Williams on a par with Owen Jones, who was already benefiting from the same arrangement. The agreement reads as follows:

It is this day mutually agreed between William Thomas of Amlwch Port on the one part, and William Williams, Master Mariner of Amlwch Port on the other part. That is to say that the first named party William Thomas engages the said William Williams as his servant who has and is at present in command of the 3 masted schooner Greyhound, now at Leith, Scotland, on the following terms and understanding viz. That is to say the said William Williams agrees to pay all crew's wages and victualling, also half of all port charges whether in a foreign or British port, and agrees to remit half of all freights earned, demurrage gratuities etc., after deducting port charges, towages etc. The said William Williams further agrees to deposit with the said William Thomas the sum of £100 in consideration that if the said William Williams should at any time not remit in accordance with what he should do that the same or any other debt incurred on his part is to be deducted from the ,£100 advanced as security. Three months notice to be given by William Williams for the withdrawal of the money, and should William Williams have cause to leave the said vessel he is to give at least one month's notice and agrees to deliver the vessel in a safe port in England or Wales as instructed. Interest to be paid for the money advanced at 2¹/₂% per annum.

A letter sent to Captain Williams three days later, noted that he was about to put his vessel into dry dock, at the same time expressing the hope that: *you will do all that is required exactly as if the vessel was your own.* This emphasises the profound change in attitude which resulted from such an agreement, another facet of which had been demonstrated earlier, when the owners asked Captain Owen Jones where he wanted to go next. On the other hand, relationships with captains in the coastal trade were generally more direct, and often less than courteous.

In addition to their other duties whilst in home waters, all captains were expected to write to the owners every other day whilst they were in port, in order to keep them abreast of the vessel's business. In a reply dated 8th August 1888, to one such letter from Captain William Hughes of the schooner *President Garfield*, William Thomas and Sons expressed their surprise that he had gone to Bray contrary to company orders which forbade masters from taking cargo to and from open beaches, because of the danger involved. By way of emphasising their dismay, they threatened to transfer command of the vessel to a captain who would obey instructions. Two weeks later, they wrote again, informing Captain Hughes of their concern about the lack of profit made by his vessel in the preceding 6 months, and expressing the hope that there would be no need to write in such a vein again, *otherwise changes would be made!*

Matters could not have improved significantly however, for in April of the following year, the vessel which carried about 100 tons on a draft of around 8 feet was offered for sale, priced at £600.

An extremely acrimonious letter dated 25th August 1888, penned by Lewis Thomas, but clearly prompted by his father, was addressed to Captain Thomas of the schooner *Margaret,* which was then berthed at Glasson Dock. The letter was in reply to his answer to their query regarding his acceptance of an inordinately low freight :

We are in receipt of yours, and note contents. The explanation you offer for the reduction in your freight is but a very faint one, and are surprised that you should have accepted it at such rate. We do not care to trouble ourselves further in the matter, nor do we want your assistance to refer us to anyone, and please understand that we are not supposed to consult you whom we are to make our enquiries from, and further, that we look for nothing from you nor any of our captains but what is right, and failing to get this we must make a change, and when writing to us again bear in mind that you do so in a business manner and not as if we were your servants, but that you are ours.

As might have been expected, John's ship brokerage business failed, and after its collapse, he briefly returned to Amlwch in the spring of 1888. For some reason, undoubtedly brought about by his inability to co-exist with his father, he eventually found his way back to Liverpool, where he was given employment in the highly successful ship brokerage business of R.J. Francis and Company. This arrangement reflects Captain Thomas's close association with the firm, with whom he conducted a great deal of business, and with whom he may well have placed John several years previously, to undergo his professional training.

In a letter written in November 1888, addressed to John at Francis's business address, his brother William informed him that the captains of the family-owned vessels *Pride of Anglesea* and *Margaret* had, despite being instructed to transfer their ships' business to R.J. Francis & Co., continued to patronise their former brokers, Messrs Thomas Bros & Company. Whether or not the transfer of business was part of the price exacted by R.J. Francis for employing John, will probably never be known, but it might well have been so.

Matters between John and his new employers soon took a bad turn however, for some three months later, R.J. Francis wrote to Captain Thomas complaining about his son's behaviour, and in his reply, Captain Thomas apologised on John's behalf, adding that he would not:

pay any more for him if he is not looking after your business properly. I feel thankful to you, and am sorry you receive such annoyance from him.

The reference to payment suggests that the Captain was supplementing John's salary in some way. Matters were destined not to improve however, for within two months, John was sacked, and the Captain was compelled to offer him employment in Iard Newydd at a salary of 28 shillings a week, with the added inducement that he could rent one of his several properties for £6 per annum. The offer was rejected, and matters came to a head when Captain Thomas wrote an angry letter to his son reprimanding him severely for his behaviour, and counselling him to either find himself another job, or emigrate to America where he could seek his fortune. Whatever course of action John may have decided upon, he was told in clear terms that he was under no circumstances, to return to Amlwch.

It must have added considerably to Captain Thomas's anguish at this time to receive a letter from his old friend Captain William Morgan the Millom Harbourmaster, for whom he had done so much in the past, and whose shipping business he continued to manage, informing him that Morgan had appointed another person to look after his interests – the person referred to was almost certainly William Postlethwaite.   Whether or not this was a means whereby Morgan wished to be seen to distance himself from Captain Thomas will never be known: for Louisa, unable to continue living with John, had about that time, returned with her children to her parents home in Steel Green, Millom. Understandably distressed by this turn of events, her father, Captain Rich, wrote to Captain Thomas expressing his concern at the way his daughter and her offspring had been treated. In his reply dated the 30th of April 1889, Captain Thomas said:

> I should be only too glad to have John with me, but I am sorry to say that I cannot think of doing this until such time as I find he has altered in his behaviour: but I am quite prepared to contribute towards the maintenance of his little family, for whom I very much feel. As you are no doubt well aware, that I have given John hundreds (of Pounds), and shall be only too glad to assist him again when I find that he is to be depended upon: but as for allowing him to come here, I am satisfied that he and I could not agree together, and he had much better be with strangers.

The Captain, clearly very worried by this latest turn of events, wrote to his son yet again, offering this time, to sell him the original family home at Cae Pant as well as employing him in the yard, both of which taken together would he argued, have afforded him a comfortable living. This offer too was refused; but true to his word, Captain Thomas wrote to Louisa in May 1889, expressing the hope that she and the little ones were well, and enclosing a gift of £2.

It is evident that John's predicament worsened, and as an indication of his father's increasing unwillingness to accept further responsibility for his behaviour, he replied to a letter seeking repayment of £20 owed by John to a firm of Liverpool engineers, expressing his regrets, and informing them that his son was by then employed in some capacity at Canada Dock.

In a letter dated August 1888, addressed to Captain Hugh Thomas of the schooner *Elizabeth Ann*, the owners admonished him for failing to write to them oftener than he did, at the same time suggesting that he would be better suited if he were in command of a smaller vessel. Whether or not he agreed to their proposal is not known, but in a further letter dated 18th August 1888, the owners required him to transfer command of the vessel to Captain Jones, a Bangor man. Having done that, he was to come to Amlwch Port to see them in order to discuss their proposal to give him command of a smaller vessel.

As if to satisfy themselves that all was well with the *Elizabeth Ann*, they wrote to Captain Jones a day or so later, enquiring as to the state in which he had found the vessel when he took over her command. An offer of £400 made by Dawson & Son of Sunderland for the vessel, prompted a close look at her trading figures, and the offer was met by the reply that the owners had found to their horror, that she was in the company's debt to the tune of £1,400 , which probably represented the difference between their outlay on her and the amount she had earned – a figure which was clearly far above her worth. To further add to the owners' problems, the vessel sprang a leak, and on the 6th of September 1888, Captain Jones was advised to bring her to Amlwch to have it attended to. This was not done for some reason, and on the 20th of October, the Captain was advised to put his vessel on a gridiron in order to find the leak which they considered to be a *private one*, as she appeared to admit water in so light a trim. He was further advised to secure a cargo for either Amlwch or the Isle of Man, so that she could be placed in their own dry dock for examination.

Unfortunately however, Captain Jones's difficulties did not end with the leak, and in a further letter to the owners, he advised them that following an accident which had befallen his vessel, he had been forced to put into Milford Haven. Realising from the tone of the unfortunate man's letter that the saga of events was worrying him unduly, Captain Thomas showed a high degree of compassion and understanding when he replied saying:

We have been sorry to hear that you have been so unfortunate, still these things cannot be helped, and we must not break our hearts as long as we are doing our duty.

From this example it is clear that Captain Thomas was sympathetic and very tolerant of genuine misfortune, but even when faced by what at best, could be described as neglect, he could be equally understanding: as was demonstrated in the case of Captain Hugh Thomas, former master of the *Elizabeth Ann*.

Given command of the smaller *Euphemia*, John was apparently still unable to cope, and in a letter dated 27th December 1888, addressed to him at his mooring on the Menai Strait,

The 2-masted schooner Euphemia.

the owner informed him quite explicitly that he had been relieved of his command owing to his carelessness and neglect. Having slept on the matter however, Captain Thomas wrote to him again on the following day, explaining that his reason for 'threatening' to replace him was because other vessels which had left the Mersey after him, had gone to the Isle of Man, and had arrived back at the Strait and loaded again before him, adding that, unless he could move faster than he had done in the past, it would be better to place another man on her.

The *Euphemia* was later to be run into by a tug whilst in the Thames, and William Junior was sent by his father to London in order to assess the damage she had sustained, and to try and reach some agreement regarding compensation with the tug's owners. The firm had by then begun to build the steamer, *Prince Ja Ja*, and were about to tender for the building of 2 iron lighters. Captain Thomas saw his son's visit as an opportunity to learn how one of the best known yards on the Thames went about its business, and in a letter to him, he was told to try and find out:

> How many rivets a day will they put in at London, say $^3/_4$ins or $^7/_8$ins… it may be that we are finding too much fault with our men as they seem to be at it very hard, and to get more out of them is very hard… get information on turning frames, plating, iron plate fittings, keelsons, stringers and all work in common with hulls. Hope this damage will pay you well in special information about iron ship building, hope you will put things down in your book so that you may not lose them.

Captain Thomas continued at this time to have some business connections with William Postlethwaite; and the *Baron Hill*, although managed by the latter, was jointly owned by the two of them, the greater part of the shares being held by Captain Thomas. A sharp exchange of letters between them took place in September 1888 when Postlethwaite took her into the Millom yard for classing, and despite having previously agreed that the vessel's new sails would be made at Amlwch, Postlethwaite gave the work to his own sailmakers. In a letter to him, the Captain said:

> I think it too bad of you grasping all. It is unpleasant that we will have to fight for our rights after all the long years of friendship – be manly and a gentleman, and do towards me as you would wish me to do to you.

In his usual autocratic style, Postlethwaite ignored the complaint, and in reply, accused William Thomas of wanting all of the work himself.

The reasons for altering the name of the steamship *Eilian*, to *Exchange* within a matter of weeks of her launch in 1884 are a matter of conjecture; but Captain Thomas was, to his undoubted satisfaction, able some 5 years later, to lay claim to the name, with which to christen a 116 ton wooden schooner he had built for the family fleet.

The appended table (see Appendix 19) showing the prime cost of building the vessel is interesting for several reasons, foremost amongst which is the fact that it shows the ratio of the costs into which the various elements in her construction were divided; and also the ratio of profit against her actual, or prime cost, which was of the order of 10%, a margin which by today's standards, seems somewhat modest. What is really interesting however, is the fact that the vessel was partly built of second-hand timber costing almost one fifth of her total cost. What exactly the timbers were used for, and where they came from, may never be known: but the practice was apparently not uncommon, for it will be recalled that

The 3-masted schooner Eilian.

An artist's impression of the 3-masted schooner Eilian.
Compare with photograph above.

Nathaniel Caine warned Captain Thomas against such usage when the building of the *Nellie Bywater* was being negotiated.

Continuing a policy which probably resulted more from a perception of the then current trends in shipbuilding, rather than from a true affinity with steam power, Captain Thomas having built the *Prince Ja Ja* in 1890, went on to build the steamships *Prince George* built specifically for the developing tourist industry centred on Llandudno, and the only paddle steamer turned out by the firm, and finally, the *Cygnus* in 1891, the yard's very last steamship.

Prince George *on Afon Conwy. This was the only paddle steamer built by William Thomas & Sons.*

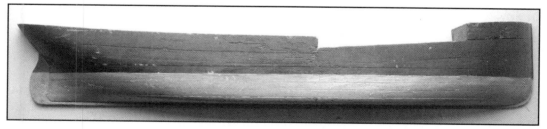

Original half model of the steamship Cygnus.

Problems were later to occur with the *Cygnus's* machinery, and in correspondence with Messrs De Winton, the makers, William Thomas stated:

> *we very much regret to be continually in receipt of complaints about the machinery of the ss Cygnus, and we now beg to enclose a letter received from Messrs Francis and Co., referring to a very serious breakdown which occurred lately… it is very annoying that these accidents should arise so often, and these no doubt do your reputation and ours, a deal of harm.*

The 3-masted steel schooner Detlef Wagner *on the stocks prior to launching in September 1891.*

The 3-masted steel schooner Maggie Williams *on her launch day in March 1892.*

This sort of complaint may have hardened Captain Thomas's views on the question of sail versus steam. Balanced against the obvious advantage possessed by steamships: primarily their superior ability to deliver cargoes on time, regardless more often than not, of inclement wind and weather, there were many who still clung to the notion that the traditional power of sail had other equally cogent benefits. This belief was based on the argument that steamships relied on expensive coal for motive power, whereas wind power was free. Similarly, the carrying capacity of steamers was severely curtailed by their need to have space for boilers, machinery and coal bunkering, thereby seriously reducing the volume of profitable cargo they could carry; and of importance, restricting them to ports which had coal bunkering facilities.

Although they remained open to orders for steamships, the family decided that henceforth they would, for their own purposes at least, concentrate on building sailing vessels. The policy resulted in the launching of the iron barquentine *Detlef Wagner* in 1891, and the iron schooner *Maggie Williams* in 1892, both of which were built to the same model as the *Gelert*.

In his daily visits to the yard, Captain Thomas must have watched the building of what became known as the *Cymric* with an immense amount of pride and growing satisfaction, knowing that she had been designed by his son. Unfortunately however, he did not survive to witness her launching, for he died some two weeks earlier, on the 3rd of March 1893, aged 71.

The following newspaper account of the Captain's funeral gives some indication of the high esteem in which he was held:

Amlwch was on Wednesday in mourning on the occasion of the funeral of a great public benefactor of the place in the person of Captain W. Thomas, the head of the firm of Captain Thomas and Sons, ship-builders.

Captain Thomas died on Sunday last after being ailing more or less for some years, but latterly he seemed to have improved with the fine weather, and during the last few days he had rallied so considerably that he was able to attend to his business in the yard. He was particularly bright and cheerful on Thursday, but on Friday morning, when getting up, he had a stroke of apoplexy from which he did not once rally, and passed peace-fully away on Sunday morning in the presence of all his children.

He went to sea when 12 years of age and quickly made his mark, coming up in the front rank of the late Mr Treweek's numerous fleet of vessels. Having made a substantial fortune at sea, he came ashore and started business as ship-chandler and ship-builder at Amlwch. He commenced in the face of considerable difficulties and some opposition, but his indomitable courage and exceptional abilities (were) equal to all obstacles. He soon became the pioneer ship-owner and ship-builder of Amlwch, and later on , the whole of north Wales. Latterly he had taken his two sons into partnership, and undoubtedly they are well qualified to undertake the duties that will now devolve upon them in carrying on the business. Besides being an extensive employer of labour, he was also a large landed proprietor, and owned some pretty tenement in his native district of Llaneilian. He was of a very charitable disposition, and his loss will be keenly felt by the poor and needy of the district. His eldest daughter (Ellen, wife of Capt. John Hughes of the Barkentine Baron Hill) died about 14 years ago, and his only remaining daughter (Mary) is the wife of Mr Lewis Hughes, the representative of the district on the Anglesey County Council. Captain Thomas leaves a widow to mourn his loss, and she has been a faithful nurse to him during his failing health. He had sought relief from the creeping paralysis which was gaining upon him at the most renowned watering places and had had the best medical attendance. The funeral procession was the largest that is remembered to have taken place in the neighbourhood.

No fewer than nine Ministers of Religion took part in the interment, and prominent amongst the very long list of mourners were: William Thomas (Liverpool), who was by then Mayor of Bootle; Colonel Owen Thomas, representing De Winton & Co. of Caernarfon, and Captains Morgan (Millom?); Parry; T. Hughes; R. Jones; W. Pritchard; Ishmael Williams and Hugh Jones. The last named, although not a captain as described, was in all probability, none other than Hugh Jones, the highly competent master shipwright of Millom.

The anguish which had attended Captain Thomas's fraught relationship with his son John was apparently never resolved, for although the newspaper account of his funeral states that he died in the presence of all of his children, John's name was absent from the list of family mourners, which named both Lewis and William, and every one of their siblings.

CHAPTER 3
THE END OF THE 19th CENTURY
"His body having been found afterwards entangled in the rigging."

Although Captain Thomas continued right up to his death to take a great interest in the yard, Lewis and William had over the years they had been partners, taken an increasingly heavier share of the burden inherent in its running. They had also become more influential in matters affecting the management of the family fleet of vessels, and were without question, fully conversant with every aspect of the business. Their brother John on the other hand, was disinclined to work, and freed from the constraints imposed by his father, became even more persistent in his demands for money.

Following on from the *Cymric*, William Thomas continued to refine his highly successful schooner design based on that of the *Gelert*, by producing the truly beautiful vessels *Celtic* and *Gaelic*.

The schooner Cymric *showing her deck layout.*

The steel schooner Gaelic *on her launch day March 1898.*

Designed primarily for the Brazilian hide trade, both vessels had a draft which allowed them to negotiate the sandbar of the Rio Grande, and then on to either Pelotas or Porto Alegre via Lagoa dos Patos. Depending on the time of the year, the 'round' most favoured by William Thomas was to have his vessels take coal either from the Mersey or south Wales to Gibraltar which was an extremely busy coaling station. Having discharged their cargoes there, the schooners were then towed to Cadiz where they loaded sea salt which had been cheaply produced by the simple expedient of allowing sea water collected in shallow lakes to evaporate in the heat of the sun. The salt was then conveyed to Rio Grande where it was used to pack cowhides for the return voyage to Europe. It was customary for the returning vessels to call in at Falmouth for orders, which almost invariably required them to sail on to St Petersburg in Russia, where having discharged, they loaded timber for delivery either to Liverpool or Conwy.

On the 17th of November 1893, the brothers were informed by letter, of the loss of the schooner *Eliza Bell*, in Drummore Bay, near the Mull of Galloway. The vessel, carrying a cargo of coal from the Point of Ayr in Flintshire to Douglas in the Isle of Man, was owned by Mrs Edwards of Llaneilian Road, Porth Amlwch. Following the death of her husband John, Mrs Edwards had wisely placed the vessel's management in the hands of William Thomas & Sons, and it was they who dealt with the consequences of the vessel's tragic loss.

There were only three people on board the *Eliza Bell* when she was wrecked: Captain John Griffiths; his wife Grace, and the Mate, John Roberts; all of whom were from Amlwch, and all of whom lost their lives in the accident. It was not unusual at that time for wives,

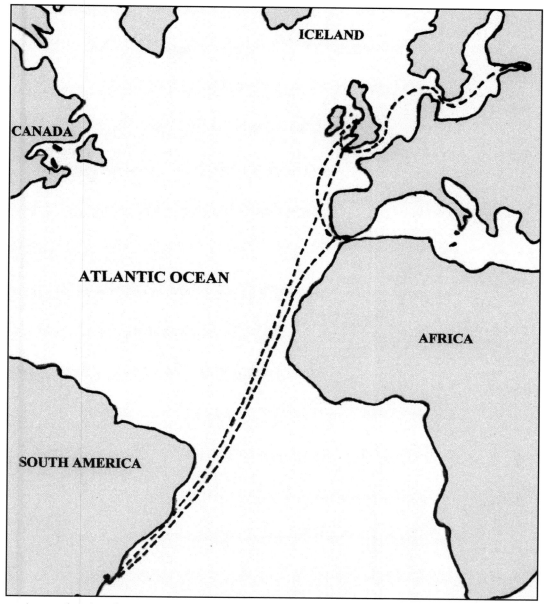

A map showing the routes taken by Thomas vessels plying in the South American hide trade:
The Mersey or south Wales, to Gibraltar with coal.
Gibraltar to Cadiz, light.
Cadiz to the Rio Grande (Pelotas or Porto Alegre), with salt.
Rio Grande to Europe with hides, (usullay calling at Falmouth for orders).
Falmouth to the Baltic – usually St Petersburg.
The Baltic, to Conwy or the Mersey with timber.

and even their children to accompany masters on such voyages; but this trip however, was a very special one for the Griffiths family, inasmuch that it was 35-year-old John Griffiths' first trip as captain, following many years service as a mate.

The *Eliza Bell* would under normal circumstances, have had a complement of no fewer than four able-bodied men on board, and the question as to why Captain Griffiths was sailing so desperately shorthanded, particularly as he had the safety of his wife to consider, will perhaps never be answered.

Drummore, on the Scottish coastline, is some 45 miles to the north of Douglas, and it must be assumed that either Captain Griffiths was lost, or had run up to Luce Bay to seek shelter. In view of his long experience as a Mate however, the second option seems to be the more likely. Lewis Thomas, who knew the bereaved family well, imparted the dreadful news to the young woman's mother, who lived at nearby *Tyddyn Sara*, which was one of several smallholdings Captain Thomas owned in his home parish of Llaneilian.

Anxious for further news, the brothers wrote to Mr McCulloch, the Lloyd's agent at Drummore, asking if any bodies had been found, before adding, that if any effects were to be recovered, that they would expect him to see to their safe custody; and if of any value, he was to send them on to William Thomas & Sons at Amlwch as managers, so that they could be passed on to the bereaved families.

All the bodies from the wreck were recovered, and in a later communication addressed to Mr R. McVie, of the Drapery Warehouse in Drummore, who was probably the local undertaker, the Thomas's thanked him for his thoughtfulness in sending locks of hair from the bodies, which they had passed on to the respective families. William, later went on to ask if McVie could recommend a local stonemason who would make a small headstone for what appears to have been a common grave, before stating that he would personally accept responsibility for all costs incurred.

Not having received any information by the 5th of January 1894, Thomas wrote to the Procurator Fiscal at Stranraer, enquiring as to when they might expect to receive the effects of those on board the ill-fated vessel. Five days later, he was to write to him again, acknowledging the receipt of a ring and watch found on the bodies of John and Grace Griffiths.

A letter addressed to a Mr Hutchinson of Portlogan, who had according to one newspaper, witnessed the foundering of the vessel, had been written by William Thomas, but signed by the Captain's father. It contained a very unusual enquiry:

We find by the papers that on the 17th of November last that you saw a man clinging to the top of one of the masts of the wreck of the Eliza Bell. There were only 2 men aboard, one, the captain, of about 35 years of age, and the other about 60 years. Could you please state whether the person whom you saw was the former?

The father had a very practical reason for seeking this specific information, for in a later letter, written in reply to Hutchinson's answer, he went on to explain:

The age of the person you saw clinging to the mast is not very distinctly given (in your reply); but I presume you considered him about 40 years of age. His body having been found afterwards entangled in the rigging tends to show that he was the Captain. Perhaps you will be good enough to let me know if in your opinion, he was the younger of the two men whose bodies were found. I want this (information) on account of there being some money which will be paid me if my son, the Captain, was seen alive after his wife. If not, I lose the money.

It is evident that everyone assumed that the wife and one of the two men on board had already drowned when the last man was seen clinging to the rigging, and if the Captain's father was to benefit from his son's estate, he had somehow to prove that it was he who had survived the longest. Unfortunately, the outcome of his enquiry was not recorded.

In most cases following a shipwreck, there is at best, very little of the ship or its cargo to salvage; or at worst, absolutely nothing. It will be recalled that the *Thomas Pearson*, was one of the first vessels to be employed in the revitalised Duddon iron ore trade, and her loss on Dulas Island, some 6 miles to the south east of Amlwch, in January 1896 resulted in the Thomas brothers writing to her owners, John Walton & Co., of Barrow, asking if they would be good enough to appoint them in their capacity as the local agents for Lloyd's, to look after their interests. As if to underline their efficiency, the owners were advised that they would have been contacted on the very same day as the shipwreck, had the telegraph wires not have been 'blocked'; which presumably, was a reference to the overloading of the local communications system. As the weather continued to be extremely wild, neither of the brothers was able to get on to the island to survey the wreck, but they told Walton & Co. that they were endeavouring to dispose of the remainder of the hull, and would investigate a report that a number of her spars had already been taken to Moelfro (now Moelfre).

In a letter written a few days later, they suggested to the vessel's owners that they should persuade the owners of the vessel's cargo, to agree to its disposal with the hull itself, pointing out that otherwise, there would be little or no chance of selling the hull on its own, before adding that the best way of doing that was by public auction in Moelfro – *you may rely that we will do all we can for you, as though the vessel and cargo was our own.*

It is evident that local seamen were active in their efforts to salvage whatever they could from the stricken vessel, and in a further letter to her owners, the Thomas brothers wrote:

We got the labourers to accept £12 for their services, including use of boats etc., ...some of the men are not satisfied with the amount; but having so much experience with wrecks, we gave them to understand that no salvage would be paid but 5/- (shillings) a day for ten men, for 4 days, and £2 for the use of the boats... as for floating the vessel off, this can be done provided the weather is favourable – she is so much damaged that we consider, if she was taken off and repaired, that she would cost much more than she would be worth.

A few days later, they received an enquiry, and wrote to the owners asking them what value they placed on the vessel and her cargo of 169 tons of coal as they stood. The utmost they were offered for the vessel and her cargo was £14, the next best offer being £11. They declined both, and it was only when Captain Jones of Moelfro, the highest bidder, increased his offer to £20, that they accepted.

About this time, William Thomas wrote to E.T. Brown & Co, of London, offering the *Hodbarrow Miner* for sale through their brokerage business, the asking price being £860. If a buyer could not be found however, it was suggested that they should try to dispose either of the *Cymric*, which had left the Rio Grande and was expected in the Mersey in March, or even the *Celtic* which was then under construction. Thomas was later to claim that the *Cymric* was a smart vessel, having made the fastest passage on record to Rio Grande for a commercial sailing vessel, a record which it is believed, remains unbroken to this day.

Following in his father's footsteps, William Thomas was forever on the look-out for work for the yard which was then having a very lean time, and a good opportunity arose when the Spanish sailing vessel *Dos Hermeanos* sustained a great deal of damage when she grounded on Holyhead's Penrhos beach, some 10 miles west of Amlwch. This followed the parting of her anchors in what was described at the time as a terrifying storm. The local Welsh language newspaper noted that when she first grounded, the vessel was in great danger of breaking up, but after strenuous efforts on the part of many local people, she was successfully refloated, and taken into dry dock for inspection and repair.

In a letter to O.H. Parry, the Spanish Consul in Holyhead, William Thomas thanked him for his kind promise of assistance, which he assured him would not be overlooked! In a subsequent letter to the Consul, he asked if his foreman Richard Williams could be allowed to inspect the vessel, with a view to the firm tendering for the necessary repair work. On the same day, he wrote to the firm of Griffiths and Williams, in Liverpool, seeking a quotation for 3 bower anchors of 11 cwt (hundredweight) each, 1 stream anchor of 5cwt, 1 kedge anchor of 3 cwt, and 240 fathoms of $1^1/_4$ inch cable, complete with connecting shackles, all to be delivered to Holyhead.

Realising that the work needed more craftsmen than he could spare from their work in the Amlwch yard, William Thomas wrote to friends at Caernarfon, Portmadoc and Port Dinorwic, enquiring if there were local carpenters willing to take on 4 to 6 weeks' work at Holyhead, where he had a large repairing job. Whatever response may have resulted from his enquiries, it is evident that it fell short of his requirements, and he was forced to write to the Consul again, this time advising him that as he had been unable to secure the services of the necessary number of carpenters, he was seeking his permission to take the vessel to Amlwch for repair, adding by way of inducement:

we consider ourselves greatly indebted to you, and we shall at the first opportunity reciprocate the great kindness you have shown us.

Such a move must have been denied him however, for no record can be found of work carried out on a vessel of that name in Porth Amlwch at that time.

On the 17th of January 1894, William Thomas wrote to Captain Andrew Kinsella of Wicklow, informing him that on his recommendation, he was prepared to allow his brother Thomas Kinsella, to take command of the vessel *Thomas* without any form of security, despite describing this as being contrary to the firm's custom and regular rule.

Notwithstanding his brother's recommendation, and William Thomas's indulgence regarding a deposit, Thomas Kinsella was to prove to be something less than an ideal captain. In March, he wrote to the owners requesting them to supply charts for his vessel, which prompted the swift response that masters were expected to provide their own, which they could take with them should they at any time decide to leave the ship. It can only be surmised that during the 2 months he had been in command of the vessel, Kinsella must have sailed without the benefit of any chart whatsoever; probably relying entirely on his experience to see him through. In addition to charts, captains were also expected to provide their own nautical instruments, as well as cooking utensils for all the crew.

In August of that year, a very uncompromising letter was sent to Captain Kinsella, whose vessel was then at Wicklow, requiring him to send his accounts for the previous six months to the vessel's owners by return of post, at the same time reminding him that he had failed to honour his signed agreement to remit each share as it was earned. The fact that he had allowed the matter to go on for so long suggests that William Thomas was far less strict in such matters than was his father, who did not hesitate to write quite forcefully to any captain failing to send in a financial account at the end of each voyage. Similarly, if he thought that a master was in some way falling short of his duties, Captain Thomas would write confidentially to one of the many friends he had at various ports, enquiring as to the Master's behaviour and sobriety.

In a similar way, his son William wrote in reply to a letter received from a Captain Conway in Wicklow informing him that the firm had no vacancies for captains at the time, adding that he:

would esteem it a favour if you would kindly let us know if our schooner Thomas is at your port, and what condition the captain is in, as we have not heard from him for a long time. Assuring you that whatever you communicate to us will be kept strictly private.

Later that month, a letter was sent to John Edwards who was William Thomas & Sons' agent in Liverpool, as well as a cousin, informing him that the captain of the *Thomas* had asked the company to send someone to take charge of the vessel. It was suggested to Edwards that he should enquire if Robert Thomas, mate of the *Eliza Jane* was prepared to deposit £10 as security for his good behaviour in order to take command.

On the same day, a letter was sent to Captain Kinsella acknowledging his letter and telegram, adding:

You will know of your stamped agreement with us, also your behaviour towards us. We wish to know at once when you intend paying what you owe us, being money lent to you when here and short remittances. We need hardly point out that you have appropriated our money for your own use, and the consequences of having done so. We do not wish to have the matter pressed against you, but unless you come forward and pay, we shall have no alternative but to bring you to justice without delay as we consider that you have treated us shamefully, which we do not deserve.

In a further letter to Captain James Conway, he was advised that the company had no vessel other than the *Thomas* to offer him, and that would be on the same terms as those applying to his brother when he took command of their vessel *Albion*. He was assured however that he would be transferred to a better vessel as and when the opportunity arose. His reply must have been immediate, for on the following day, the firm wrote to John Edwards asking him to arrange to have work done on the *Thomas* as required by the Liverpool Port Sanitary Authority, and advising him that James Conway would be taking charge of her.

Following the death of his father, who had left him an annuity in his will, John continued to cause his brothers a great deal of anguish by his constant demands for more money than he was entitled to, and on the 26th of May 1894, they must surely have been happy to confirm a booking they had made for him on the *Laurentian*, sailing on the 31st of that month for Montreal.

Eight months later John was apparently staying in the YMCA in Dominion Square of that city, from where he wrote a letter to his brothers pleading with them to send him money. An earlier letter he had written had seemingly been ignored, and he went on to describe how he had met a young mining engineer on the *Laurentian*, whose brother was the manger of a mine in Nelson, British Columbia, where he had offered John a job. John's agonising letter continues:

I am willing to do anything at all, even working in the mines, but how can I get out there. As I told you before, I am stranded and have not a cent. I have not got anything to do, and its useless looking for anything to do here, business is very dull, and since the snow and cold weather has set in, business is almost entirely suspended. I do hope and trust that you will send the money I asked you, viz. £25 to enable me to get out to B.C. and do something for myself. I have left no stone unturned to try and get something here, but it is simply impossible to get anything, even if you gave your services free. I am simply sick of Montreal, and once I get away from here I would not return in a hurry. You have no idea what hardships I am suffering here and if you do not send me the money, God only knows what will become of me, but I have every faith that after giving my case your consideration, you will remit to enable me to get out to B.C. as I stated in my last (letter). *I would be willing to (forgo?) 1 year's annuity for the advance. My face and arms are all covered with scales after the boils that broke out (all?) over. I am a pitiful sight, and last week I had one of my ears frost bitten with the cold, the pain is intense, I never experienced anything like it before. If you knew half of the sufferings I have endured here, I am sure you would never tolerate it. It will cost nearly £20 to go out to Nelson, and if you send £25, I will have a little in my pocket for meals on the train, as you know I would have to buy my own meals, and it takes 8 days to get out there. I do hope you will remit as soon as you get this, unless you have already done so. My fond love to all, your loving brother, John*

Whether he eventually got to British Columbia is not known; but what is known, is that he was back home again in Amlwch some 2 years later.

At this time, the *Celtic*, described by William Thomas, as having the most modern appliances, teak deck fittings, and fitted out in a first class style; was offered for sale in Germany through Thomas's agents, Renck und Hessenmuller of Harburg, on the Elbe, now a suburb of Hamburg. As an inducement, the agents were offered £50 by way of commission; and in an effort to negotiate a quick sale, William Thomas & Sons stated that they were prepared to sell her for £3,300.

A broker friend in Port Dinorwic was also approached regarding her sale, and in the event of his being disinterested, he was asked if he could fix her with a cargo of slates for the Elbe, where she could be inspected by Renck und Hessenmuller, in what was clearly a greater effort to interest potential German buyers.

A problem arose however, inasmuch that there was some disagreement with the Surveyor's office of the Board of Trade in Liverpool regarding their calculations of her net tonnage.

In comparing these with the tonnage of the Cymric, we find the sail room and boatswain's store, less, whereas the actual measurements are more; and we also thought that the forecastle of this one would measure a little more. The size of the Master's room we also make a little larger, the others are what we thought they would be. We would esteem it a favour if you would kindly look over the measurements of those we have mentioned, and if possible, get her down to 175 net tons.

The *Celtic* was eventually launched at 9 am on the 27th of October, 1894, and announcements of her launching were placed with the *Shipping World*, the *Engineer's Gazette*, and *Fairplay*. After her launching, the *Celtic* was immediately put into dry dock to have her bottom coated; and on the 2nd of November 1894, William Thomas advised the

Thames and Mersey Insurance Company of Liverpool that:

> *the new vessel Celtic is in every respect a duplicate of the Cymric, launched by us early last year. She is intended principally for the Rio Grande do Sul trade, and we desire her covered for 12 months. She will be commanded by Captain Ishmael Williams, late Master of the Sudbrook, and former master of the Annie Park of Barrow. He has had 12 to 14 years experience in the trade and has always been very fortunate not having met with a single accident during the whole of that period.*

The master chosen to be the captain of the *Celtic* as Robert Griffiths of Amlwch. The following letter written by him to the owners as he set out from Liverpool in May 1895, gives an idea of his delight with the way she handled:

Amlwch Bay, May 5, 1895

Gentlemen,

Just a few lines to let you know that the Celtic is steering like a little boat. But the wind was light: but she seems to cut the water like a yacht, with the least of air, and everything is working so far, and hope this good wind will keep blowing for a few days so that we will get into the trade wind.

I have had some small things from Messrs M. Hutchinson; 30 fathoms of ratling, 20 fathoms $1^1/_2$ of Manilla, and a few balls of Marlin spunyarn and a few things from John Mathews which you forgot to put down in the specification, what we could not do without. I have given Mr Edwards (John Edwards & Co.) the Abstract of Log of the Eilian to post last night, so I hope the good ship is going out to make money.

Trusting we will get a remarkable passage.

With kind regards

Your obedient servant

R.Griffiths
Celtic
ps
Father got ashore at Point Lynas where I trust he has safely landed with 200 of the best cigars, and 2lbs of Cavendish between you.
R.G.

Captain Thomas of Aberporth, who having told William Thomas & Sons that he had no interest in the *Celtic*, was offered the *Pride of Anglesea* instead, which was then in their dry dock undergoing repairs. He was informed that the latter carried 140 tons deadweight on 10ft aft, and was an exceptionally strong vessel, which would be sold cheaply. As he showed little or no interest in her, she was then offered to Betson and Company of Dublin for £400. Their counter offer of £300 was refused, but they were advised that the owners would accept £350 for her. The following month, William Thomas offered to sell the *Pride* to W. Parkes & Co. of Liverpool, informing them that she had undergone an extensive overhaul, and was a splendid little craft, of oak throughout. The new work consisted of replacing timber strakes, 13 inch wide by 5 inch thick, well bolted through floors with 1 inch diameter bolts; the bilge and side stringers as well as all iron knee bolts had been replaced; her keelson had been fastened with 1 inch bolts, and she had been caulked all over.

Having heard that the *Pride* was undergoing repairs, Captain Richard Thomas of the *Eliza Jane*, then berthed at Bangor, wrote to the firm in their capacity as managers, offering his immediate services as her master. In a response that displayed an understanding of shipowners' problems, he was advised that since his own vessel had already been fixed with a cargo, such a move would put her owners in rather an awkward position if they failed to get another master. The best plan, he was advised, would be to try to make the round as quickly as possible, by which time the *Pride of Anglesea* would have completed her repairs, and he would have first refusal regarding her captaincy.

William Thomas & Sons were also minded to sell the *Eilian*, which on the 19th of May 1894, was berthed in Harburg. In a letter to her Master, the owners said:

> We should be very pleased if you could manage to sell the Eilian there. We have been asking £1,600, but try to obtain us a good firm offer, and if you are successful in selling, we should be pleased to treat with you for the new vessel… What is the utmost you could invest to take command of the new vessel. We are prepared to fulfill our promise to you when here.

A few days later they wrote in reply to a letter received from him by return of post:

> We regret to learn that the highest offer you have had for the Eilian is £1,000. When we named £1,600, we hardly expected to get it. As far as we are concerned, if you get £1,200 or £1,300 for her, we would be inclined to sell… With regard to the new vessel, we are sorry to find the amount you can invest is considerably reduced as you told us when you were here that you could muster at least £700 apart from your interest in Eilian, and upon this we have been working all along; and are prepared to redeem our pledge on these bases. We do not think we are guilty of the conduct you attribute us in the last portion of your letter. We have not put anyone in command of the Cymric over your head. As you know, she was intended for the foreign trade, and at the time she was launched, you had no certificate. Had you then been in the position you are now in, things would have been different.

Later, William Thomas & Sons were to claim the following passage times for the *Cymric* on her first 5 voyages to South America:

First voyage	Liverpool to Rio Grande	April 15th to June 14th 1893	59 days
	Rio Grande to Liverpool	Jan 22nd to April 15th 1894	83 days
Second voyage	Cardiff to Rio Grande	July 6th to August 27th 1894	52 days
	Rio Grande to Liverpool	August 1st to Sept. 8th 1895	69 days
Third voyage	Liverpool to Rio Grande	Jan 8th to Feb 19th 1896?	42 days
	Was dismasted on her homeward passage		
Fourth voyage	Cardiff to Rio Grande	Nov 22nd to Jan 10th 1898	49 days
	Rio Grande to Falmouth	Mar 25th to June 10th 1898	77 days
Fifth voyage	Cadiz to Rio Grande	Jan 2nd to Feb 17th 1899	46 days
	Rio Grande to Falmouth	May 9th to July 25th 1899	77 days

These were, by the standard of the times, remarkable passages indeed.

Matters in the industry had been at a low ebb for quite some time, and little or no work was being carried out on the *Celtic*, the builders preferring to wait until they had a firm buyer in sight. They had tried to interest William Postlethwaite in the new vessel, either as an outright buyer, or as a major shareholder. He, however, was clearly less than enthusiastic, and in a letter to him on the 18th of June 1894, William Thomas wrote:

> *... as you say, shipping is in a very bad state, but everyone appears to agree that we have now touched the bottom, therefore any change that will take place will be for the best, that now is the time to secure at a low figure, property which, when the first improvement sets in, advances in value, besides, a few vessels like this one will make up for the losses of the other vessels. We understand that Captain Ishmael Williams has been in communication with you about this vessel, and is prepared to take up a fair numbers of shares in her. He has also informed us that if we do not sell her to you, that he will invest the same amount with us, conditionally of course, that he shall have command of her: but we did not care to treat with him until you had first of all declined to purchase, and as she is now all but completed, we are anxious to know your decision, as we cannot afford to keep her idle... As already stated, we shall be pleased to give you every reasonable accommodation in the payment.*

In his reply, Postlethwaite told William Thomas that he was thinking of going in for a steamer; and not being one to pass up an opportunity, the latter asked that he should be given the chance to quote for her building, as he felt that his yard could do as well as anyone else. He went on to add that he would be prepared to take up shares in the vessel himself if he was allowed to build her.

Matters in the industry did not improve as William Thomas expected, and in a letter penned the following month, he stated that business had been so bad over the past year that the firm had been forced to discharge all of its employees with the exception of foremen and apprentices. He continued to press Postlethwaite to buy the *Celtic*, even though he was by then busily trying to fix her in the South American trade. He had discovered that Hugh Jones of the Millom yard, was at that time visiting relatives at Amlwch, and it was suggested to Postlethwaite that he might wish to instruct Jones to inspect the *Celtic*, with a view to purchasing her. Conversely, and by way of making doubly sure, Hugh Jones was asked by William Thomas to try to influence Postlethwaite's thinking regarding the vessel on his return to Millom.

It is not known how the firm came to discover that all was not well with their schooner *Ocean Belle*, but in a letter dated 5th of September 1894, addressed to Captain Hugh Thomas of the ketch *Renown*, a well-known Amlwch vessel which was then in an Irish port; William Thomas enquired if the *Ocean Belle* had by then left for Whitehaven. He went on to say that he would esteem it a favour if he could be advised how her captain had behaved whilst he was in port, adding that any information he supplied would be kept a perfect secret.

The reply must have shocked William Thomas, for a day or so later, he wrote to Thomas Wilson & Co., of Whitehaven, informing them that the bearer, Captain O. Pritchard had been appointed to take charge of the schooner *Ocean Belle*. Two days later, he wrote to Captain Pritchard, telling him that he regretted:

> *to learn that there is as much wages due to the crew, it turns out to be a lie that the Captain had stated that he only shipped them on the 16th of August. I however, enclose you a cheque for £16-*

18-4 to pay them off, and you can tell the late Captain that I will spare no expense in having him punished for his bad work and lies.

On the same day, he wrote to David Williams, Ship Broker of Port Dinorwic, informing him that Captain Morris Elias, presumably the former master of the *Ocean Belle*:

had behaved most scandalous (sic) and caused us great loss. Will you kindly inform me if he has any property or any asset that I could sue upon.

Realising that selling the *Celtic* at a fair price was going to be an almost impossible task, the brothers decided to add her to the family fleet. For that reason, they needed minority shareholders which would ease the burden of the cost of her building; but at the same time, allowing them to control her future operations. Having run out of likely subscribers in what was still a very deeply depressed market, they turned their attention to their business suppliers, by offering them shares in the new vessel.

Their proposals did not bring in the expected replies however, and in what was clearly a fit of pique, they wrote to two of the firms that had declined to cooperate. With what can only be described as a mild form of blackmail clearly in mind, they wrote firstly to P. Morris and Company of Birkenhead, saying that they regretted:

... to learn that you do not see your way clear to assist us by taking a small interest in our new vessel, especially considering that we have for a good number of years, patronised you with orders for your supplies, and even paying you higher prices than we were offered by others, so that we trust that you will reconsider your decision, but in the event of you not doing so, you cannot reasonably expect our custom any further.

Their letter to M. Hutchinson & Co., of Liverpool, was in a similar vein, but worded a little differently: In that too, they regretted:

to learn that you do not see your way clear to assist us by taking an interest in our new vessel especially considering that we have abandoned our old friends and given you our orders even at higher figures than we could buy elsewhere. We hope therefore you will reconsider the matter as it will be unreasonable to continue our business relations when others are prepared to assist us, at the same time we do not need to press you unduly as other friends in the trade will gladly assist.

In view of the firm's practice of soliciting quotes from as many as six suppliers in their efforts to find the cheapest product, the claim that they had passed other suppliers by, in order to patronise them especially, would seem to be contradictory to say the least. Nevertheless, as prices were more or less stable, suppliers with whom they had previously dealt, and who were considered to be trustworthy, were often favoured with orders without the benefit of an enquiry regarding the likely cost. Where suppliers did take shares in their vessels however, as was the case with D. Corsar and Sons of Liverpool, they undertook to patronise them:

We are extremely obliged to you for your kind promise to take one eighth share of the Gaelic. In return, we undertake to use your sail cloth in preference to all others. Of course, you will understand that occasionally, some people insist upon a certain cloth, but where this is not specifically stated, we shall use your cloth.

Corsar and Sons must have been highly satisfied with their investment when they were sent a cheque for £20-10-00 as their portion of the profit made by the *Gaelic* on her round voyage to the Rio Grande.

As has been illustrated, William Thomas & Sons were very direct, to the point of being blunt, in their dealings with suppliers; and if they thought for one moment that they were being asked to pay anything other than a fair price for goods, they would invariably write to them suggesting quite politely, that obviously, a mistake had been made in their calculations, and asking them to go over their figures again with a view to making a *liberal reduction in the bill!* In those instances where the suppliers did not agree, as was the case involving Messrs Hitchen and Squire of Liverpool, the latter were advised that as they had been extremely sharp in their demands, William Thomas & Sons would instruct their captains to keep away from their shop in future.

Not only were invoices carefully scrutinised; but also the number and quality of the items supplied were also checked on delivery. It is difficult to comprehend how any self respecting firm, knowing the harsh conditions encountered at sea, where lives were constantly at risk, could supply items which were not just known to be inferior; but had been 'doctored' in an attempt to hide that very fact. Such was the case however, when 'deadeyes' supplied to the Amlwch shipyard by a Scottish firm were found to be seriously defective:

> We regret to find that the last lot of deadeyes you sent us are of very inferior wood, a bad heart running right through them – each had been filled with dust to escape detection – we shall return these.

Similarly, they were always on the lookout for what they considered to be sharp practices, and in a letter to a timber supplier in Caernarfon, they noted:

> that you have charged the pitch pine log as $16\,^1/_2$ ins just, and the spars $9^1/_2$ ins, whereas you told the writer on Thursday that the gut of the log was $16\,^1/_4$ ins, and the 4 spars 9ins, and presume that you have made an error in charging them as you have done; however when they arrive we shall measure them carefully.

The following day, they wrote confirming receipt of the log and spars, which as the suppliers had been forewarned, were carefully measured on receipt, before adding:

> we find as we stated yesterday that the gut of the log is $16\,^1/_4$ and not $16^1/_2$, and you have also charged $^1/_2$ ins too much in the just of each spar.

Two days later, having received a denial from the supplier, they wrote again:

> We regret any difference between us respecting the measurements of the pitch pine log and spars. We have carefully measured them again (by 3 independent persons) and find that the measurements are as we stated. Perhaps you would like to re-measure them, in which case, please send a person over here so that you may satisfy yourself.

The difference in the dimensions quoted may appear to be insignificant, and hardly worth pursuing: but it is evident however, that the wood was being purchased by volume, and a comparatively small difference in the diameter of the timber could, particularly if the pieces were long, have had a significant effect on the calculated volume, and hence the price.

In another instance a letter addressed to John Stanley and Sons of Redditch, requested them to:

Send us 50 sail sewing needles, number 14 short, square heads. Please endeavour to send good ones, as the last we had were of rather inferior quality.

In what was probably a reply to a demand for payment, Messrs J.O. Jones of Cardiff were told that:

The Captain of the Cymric writes us complaining very much that the paints which you supplied him last time were mere rubbish, not worth the labour of applying, to say nothing of their first costs. We therefore hope you can see your way clear to make a liberal deduction, as we have been put to the expense of buying other stuff.

What would now be referred to as cash flow problems, occurred periodically in the business life of William Thomas & Sons, and in a letter addressed to a cable works in Staffordshire, they regretted having:

kept you without a remittance, but we have been rather pressed for ready cash of late having some heavy accounts out, so we hope you will bear with us for a little while longer.

In his private life William Thomas was at that time looking around for a home of his own, and an offer by his stepmother, with whom he had found it somewhat difficult to get on, to sell him her house following the death of Captain Thomas, was politely turned down:

Since our conversation on Thursday evening, I have carefully considered the matter of taking Bryn Eilian, and whilst sincerely thanking you for the offer, I very much regret to say that I cannot afford to pay the figure you ask, nor indeed would I be justified in renewing the offer which I then made you without having considered the matter, as I have since done. Therefore I must abandon the idea, as my present circumstances will not permit me to contract anything beyond what is absolutely necessary. Again, thanking you for the offer, and with best love. Yours affectionately, Willie.

Mrs Thomas died on the 19th December 1894, leaving Bryn Eilian to him.

Despite being busy in Iard Newydd, matters in the shipping industry generally, were still depressed in January1895. In reply to a cablegram received from Captain Robert Jones of the *Cymric* which was then in Montevideo, and about to sail to Pernambuco, informed him that shipping matters in England were in a very depressed state, with freights being scarce and low.

William Postlethwaite too, appears to have had cash flow problems, for in response to an application by William Thomas & Sons to have long overdue dividends paid to them regarding vessels in which they had shares, and which he managed, Postlethwaite tried to deduct £20 (£1,300 by 2002 standards) owed to him by their brother John. In their reply, they stated quite rightly, that the matter was not theirs to resolve. Dissatisfied with their response, Postlethwaite later suggested that the money could be deducted from John's annuity left to him by his father and in reply, they said that if John agreed, they would arrange to do so.

Postlethwaite was a short while later sent a small final account for the building of the schooner *Maggie Williams*, built for him some 3 years previously. By way of avoiding the full payment, he wrote back arguing that the vessel had not been completed as per specification, and in their reply, William wrote:

> We are surprised that now, three years after the vessel has been working, you say that she was not finished according to specification. If such was the case, why did you not advise us before accepting delivery as you had the Captain (William Morgan?) here during the whole time she was under construction superintending her building, and you ought then to have advised us of anything wrong: but we assure you, there was nothing, or certainly he would have noted it as he did other matters.
>
> We have gone carefully through the specification, but cannot find any mention that the bulwarks were to be the same as the Gelert's. The only mention of that vessel was that the Maggie (Williams) was to be built on the same model as her, and which we have done, and if you will please refer to your specification, you will find that this is so. We have nothing whatever in the account rendered you except what is to be, so we shall be pleased to receive your cheque.
>
> We shall be pleased to raise the bulwarks of the Maggie Williams if you determine to do so, but of course we shall expect to be paid for doing so, and in addition to the account rendered you. We hardly think you are serious when you say the vessel cannot be loaded to her marks in account of her bulwarks as this has nothing whatever to do with her buoyancy, and is never reckoned in the Assignment of Freeboard.

This correspondence continued into March 1895, when still not having received payment, a letter was sent to Postlethwaite:

> We are both disappointed and surprised at not receiving your cheque in settlement of our account against the Maggie Williams, after the explanation tendered... permit us to assure you that no reasonable complaint whatsoever (can be made) against the vessel, and we quite see that you are being misled on the matter of facts. We should extremely regret that the long friendship which has existed between us should be so abruptly terminated, especially through the interference and mis-statements of untried persons.

In his reply, Postlethwaite again brought up the matter of the money owed to him by their brother John, to which they replied:

> to show that we are anxious to continue the good relationship which has existed between us for so long, we are prepared to sacrifice £10 off our account (This of course is made without prejudice to our case), and we think you will agree with us that this is a handsome sum to allow off such a small amount which is strictly and honestly owed to us. With regard to John's debt, we are as powerless as yourself to do anything in this matter otherwise we would gladly do so, and we therefore trust that you will not attribute to us that which we have no control over.

It would appear that Postlethwaite was still not satisfied with anything less than the £20 owed him by John, and he continued to press his case. In a final attempt to reach an agreement, the brothers wrote:

> we regret to find that you do not attempt to settle our account after the handsome offer we made you, and you know very well that if extreme measures had to be resorted to, we can recover the whole amount; but as we have already stated, we should be extremely sorry to have to take such course with an old friend like you, at the same time we cannot afford to accept any kind of settlement and to show you how anxious we are to have the matter settled in a friendly spirit, we will accept £30 and not a penny less, this offer we make you without prejudice, and if you

should decline this, it will not be our fault if you compel us to recover the whole amount.

Having taken the brothers to the absolute limit of their tolerance, William Postlethwaite seemingly paid up.

The general depression in the shipbuilding industry around 1896, when firms were desperately seeking any advantage to keep their yards going, was underlined in the letter regarding the steamship *W.S. Caine,* sent to William Thomas & Sons (Liverpool), her managers, with whom relations had been both cordial and profitable during Captain Thomas's lifetime:

we are both disappointed and surprised to learn that you have decided to repair this vessel at Liverpool, especially after your promise of the 12th inst. when the writer asked you to give us the refusal of the work at 15% less than the lowest tender received... and considering that we own nearly all of the vessel, we think we were at least entitled to this especially as it benefited the whole shareholders.

During his lifetime, Captain Thomas was renowned for his charitable acts towards the poor, particularly if they were former mariners. Apart from gaining admission for sick people to hospitals through the offices of subscriber friends, he also arranged at Christmastime, to supply all of the needy people of Amlwch, as well as its outlying districts, with large loaves of bread which were baked in the local bakery belonging to Josiah Griffiths. The letter, written to him in Welsh, is appended below, together with its English translation:

Annwyl Gyfaill,

Mae'r Nadolig eto'n agoshau a gwenau rhagluniaeth yn garedig wrthym fel nas gallwn rwystro ein teimladau i gyfranu eleni i'r tlodion. Byddwch mor garedig a pharatoi torthau da fel arferol ar ei cyfer, a bydd yn bleser gennym dalu am danynt.

Cofion caredig atoch fel teulu.

Yr eiddoch yn gywir,

L. a Wm Thomas.

Translation:

Dear Friend,

Christmas is again approaching, and as providence has once again smiled kindly upon us, we cannot ignore our predisposition to contribute to the poor again this year. Be so kind therefore, as to prepare your customary good loaves on their behalf, and it will be our pleasure to pay for them.

Kind remembrances to you as a family.

Yours truly,

L. and Wm Thomas.

Irrespective of how this act of largesse might be viewed today, there should be no doubt that it was a magnanimous, and indeed, a very welcome act of compassion at the time. The charity of the Thomas family extended as far as to provide an unofficial pension for one man at least, regarding whom, nothing else is known. In a letter to his son Henry Williams of Holyhead, the Thomas brothers, with a characteristic veiled threat, wrote:

You are no doubt aware that we allow your father 5/- (shillings) a week as charity. We do not care to see him seeking Parish relief, and especially when you and your brother are in good situations. It is our intention to give him 5/- weekly provided you pay his house rent, £2-5-0 per year, which is past due. Failing this, we will make the usual Parish application, and you will of course have to contribute towards his maintenance.

Following a letter of enquiry by Shenker, Walford & Co., of London, William Thomas advised them that they would be very pleased to build them a vessel capable of carrying 600 tons; but that the specified draft of 9 feet was too little for the quantity of cargo they had named, particularly if it was intended that the vessel should be ocean going. A day later they wrote to them again:

we enclose you an account of the working of one of our vessels, by which you will have a good idea of the monthly cost. We fit all of our vessels with the most modern appliances for the economical working of both ship and cargo, and as you will observe, they only carry 6 hands all told. We have placed the victualling at 9 pence to 10 pence per man, but if the owners care to do the victualling themselves they could save a good deal on that, as in one instance, we were able to provide at 8 pence per hand when we tried it as an experiment, but a certain sum is generally allowed the Captain in order to give him some encouragement.

The account referred to was not included with the copy letter, which is unfortunate, as this would have clarified the impression given in the letter that crew members could be adequately fed for as little as 9 to 10 pence each per month, which would have been a ludicrous and an impossibly low figure by any standard. As this was at a time when a prospective purchaser was advised that the firm's captains sailed by the shares, but that William Thomas & Sons, as owners, would rather engage them on a fixed salary of £10 a month, it is reasonable to conclude that the figures quoted were the daily cost of feeding one man. In this respect, the rations provided for the crew of the *Kate* before she was absorbed into the Thomas fleet, gives an idea of the quantities of food provided each day (see Appendix 22).

In August 1896, the brothers received the sad news that John's son Herbert had been thrown off a horse, and killed. They advised Captain Rich, to whom they had been sending regular payments for the maintenance of John's children according to Captain Thomas's will, that John was then at Amlwch, and would undoubtedly be attending the funeral. The following day however, they wrote again, stating that John would not be going to the funeral, adding: *perhaps it is just as well that he should not attend.* The fact that John could not face returning to Millom, even to attend his own son's funeral, would clearly support Trevor Morgan's claim that he had left Millom under dire circumstances.

John had by this time made his way back to Liverpool, and still restless, he continued to make further demands for money, one for the fare out to Africa where he intended to settle, which prompted the following reply:

we enclose you another Postal Order for 20 shillings. We can ill afford to give you the money you ask to go out to Africa, besides you have been abroad, and every time to no good, only losing time and spending money.

This seems to suggest that he had been somewhere other than Canada; but there is no indication as to where. Despite being sent regular substantial amounts of money, his demands became more insistent, and failing to persuade his brothers, he approached his cousin John Edwards, who was in business as a ship broker in the city, seeking a loan of £3-5-0 with which to buy himself a new suit. Edwards told his cousins of this, and they agreed to the sum mentioned in his letter, adding a further 10 shillings, because John had claimed to have been out of work that week. Two weeks later they sent him an additional cheque for £3 so that he could go and see his little boy, adding that it was high time he did something for himself and his child.

In response to his brothers' suggestion that he should try and do something to better himself, John wrote to them seeking money to go into business with a named partner. In their reply, the brothers wrote:

we should be only too pleased to assist you provided we were satisfied that such assistance would have any lasting benefit, but we must confess that we have many strong misgivings as to the scheme you suggest; but rather than put any obstacles in your way, we are making careful enquiries through one or two sources respecting the gentleman you name, and his business, and provided the result of those enquiries are favourable, we will advance you the £10 you mention; but beforehand, we must have your undertaking not to trouble us for any further sum of money for at least another year.

As they had correctly guessed, it was another calculated attempt by John, to relieve them of their money; for the business address he had furnished was that of a public house, where the person he had named was unknown.

Undaunted, John wrote again a few weeks later, seeking his brothers' assistance in getting him a passage to the Klondike, where he intended to mine for gold. This too was refused, but his brothers agreed to send him a further £5 so that he could buy himself yet another suit. His later proposal to return home to Amlwch was rebuffed when he was refused further finance, and told not to waste his money on the fare as he would be most unwelcome.

Inventive as ever, John wrote yet again to his brothers, informing them that his wife was dangerously ill, and was not expected to recover, and that her mother too was bedridden. By way of ascertaining the facts, Lewis wrote to his son Owen, asking if he could substantiate his uncle's claim. It was eventually discovered that John's wife was not ill, and the brothers steadfastly refused to send him any more money. They later relented, and sent him £5!

John became seriously concerned about the hardening of his brothers' attitude in refusing to send him any more money, and he consulted the Thomas family firm of solicitors, Messrs Forshaw and Hawkins of Liverpool. In reply to a letter received from Mr F.J. Hawkins, William enclosed letters they had received from John over the years, by way of giving him an idea of their brother's past lifestyle, and the money they had given him.

From this point on, all warmth seems to have disappeared from the brothers' letters to John, and they adopted a very formal attitude towards him. In the face of whatever advice he may have been given by Mr Hawkins, and despite having been sent a cheque for £25 some 3 days earlier by his brothers, John continued to pester them for even more money, eventually eliciting the following reply:

We are astonished at the contents of your letter of yesterday, and take this opportunity of denying having either directly or indirectly, ever promised to continue your annuity, or to be in any way bound to pay you any sum whatever. We made it perfectly clear to you that if we should at any time feel disposed to assist you, it would be (as a result of) our good will only, and not because you have any claim upon us. You must understand that if you bother us with such letters as the last two or three we have received from you, we shall cease to have any communication with you.
Yours faithfully,

L and W. Thomas.

Some time in 1900, John took out a High Court summons against his brothers, claiming that they should invest a sufficiently large sum of money to guarantee the ten shillings annuity left to him by his father. Unfortunately, the outcome of his action is not known.

CHAPTER 4
THE AMLWCH HARBOURMASTER'S LOG
"A rough hardy seaman, unus'd to shore ways,
Knew little of ladies, but much of lay days"!
'Captain Cuttle'

As the Thomas yard was an integral, and highly significant part of the life of Porth Amlwch, the following references to it, or to vessels associated with it (marked with an asterisk) which are recorded in the Harbourmaster's log, will be of interest. Included too, are references to incidents which, often humorous, sometimes grave, give an insight into the workings of a small port in the late 19th century. In many instances, the log was accompanied by a rough outline of the port showing the position of each vessel on that particular day.

1875
January 7th
Eliza Jane came in against the rules of the harbour. Port full and the ball and flag up.
8th
Put the chain across the harbour.
10th
Juno came in contrary to the rules of the harbour.

Note: The Rules of the Harbour, which were drawn up by the Harbour Trustees, permitted the closure of the port for either one of two reasons:
1. The harbour was full – something in the order of 24 vessels, depending on size could be safely accommodated. An elderly resident of Porth Amlwch once recalled how as a child, he and his friends used to frequently cross the harbour by stepping from one closely packed vessel to another.
2. The balks were down – balks (baulks) were massive lengths of timber 35 feet long and about 18 inches square in section, laid one on top of the other across the harbour, in order to create a breakwater. This was intended to ameliorate the effect of waves driven into the narrow inlet by onshore winds. The harbourmaster was empowered to require captains of vessels in the port to provide two thirds of their crews to assist with the lowering and raising of the baulks; and in the event of a vessel's crew having been 'paid off', the harbourmaster would employ others, usually 'hobblers' , to carry out the work at the expense of the vessel's captain. As a warning to captains that the port was closed, a pole erected on the nearby headland of Llam Carw, displayed a flag and a ball; and at night, a red light was displayed in the small lighthouse at the port's entrance. On such occasions, it was usual to sling a restraining chain or rope across the harbour entrance between the watchhouse pier and the opposite, western side, to prevent vessels entering the outer basin.

February 5th

The Victoria came in contrary to the rules of the harbour, the balks were down, and the chain was slung across the mouth of the harbour, as the harbour was full of vessels of the time, and the ball and flag were up at Llam Carw. The said vessel had to lay outside all that night.

The schooner Victoria *of Liverpool,*

March 9th

A general meeting of the Trustees was held at the Harbour Office to take legal proceedings against the Eliza Jane, the Victoria, the Breeze, and the Charles*, for coming in contrary to the rules of harbour.

16th

Several vessels allowed in -- previously waiting at Holyhead to come in.

May 8th

No 11 Pilot Boat* came out of dock at 3 pm.

Note: *The Mersey,* Liverpool Pilot Boat Number 11, had been launched from Captain William Thomas's yard on 6th April 1875.

29th

Commences with a moderate breeze from north east, fine and clear. At 4am the schooner Breeze broke her moorings and got a little damage -- balks down. At 3.35 got the balks up.

Note: It was the custom for captains of the period to begin their day's sea log by saying: "Began...", or "Commenced the day ...", followed by a comment on the prevailing weather conditions. This entry is a good indication that the harbourmaster, whose name is not known, was himself a sea captain who had evidently come ashore, or in maritime parlance, "swallowed the anchor".

31st
Wind easterly, fine and clear. Gave Captain Thomas notes not to have any more rubbish in the mouth of harbour.

Note: There are several recorded complaints by the Harbourmaster concerning the rubbish from Captain Thomas's shipyard accumulating at the entrance to the harbour!

June 16th
Wind sw, strong with rain at 10.35. No 11 Pilot Boat* went out.
29th
Samson loading copper.

Note: As the Amlwch copper smelters had closed by then, this entry should have read either 'copper ore', which was still being mined in small quantities at Mynydd Parys;

The Harbourmaster's Mud Flat, used to clear the harbour of detritus.

or, to copper precipitate from the Dyffryn Adda precipitation ponds. (See the entry for 10th August 1875)

July 6th
Took one load off the bar with the Mud Flat.

Note: The 'Mud Flat' was a flat-bottomed vessel into which mud and other accumulated detritus from the harbour floor could be loaded for dumping at sea.

August 10th
Symmetry discharging old iron.

Note: 'Old iron' was imported in vast quantities through Amlwch Port, for use in the precipitation ponds at Dyffryn Adda and elsewhere on Mynydd Parys. The iron was deposited in shallow ponds containing acidic copper sulphate solution which flowed from the mines. There, by way of a simple chemical exchange, the iron was turned into a copper rich precipitate, which was exported in large quantities through the port. The depleted water was then allowed to oxidise naturally to form ochre, used as a pigment. This process continued in Amlwch until well after the end of the Second World War.

24th
Ann and Mary came in having carried away her mast.

Note: The terms, 'carried away her mast' and 'carried away her sails', meant that a vessel had either been dismasted or had lost her sails.

25th
The steam tug Tartar came in from Cemaes and laid at the watchhouse pier to take some timber onboard to take to the wreck at Cemaes. Commenced to shift vessels and while doing so, Captain Lewis of the Martha came up and asked me if I would haul the Flat Ellen astern so as to enable him to bring his vessel into a position where he could take in a cargo through his after hatch. By so doing, he would occupy the length of two vessels, and consequently would hinder any vessel which might at any time arrive, from working at the crane. I told Captain Lewis that I could not do it, but that he could either haul his vessel with his main hatch opposite the (illegible) *where the cargo was, or haul him to another berth where he could load with cants. But despite every explanation and opposition, he insisted on bringing his vessel to the berth preferred by him, which was against the rules of the harbour, and the consequence was, that he stayed there.*

Note: 'Cants' were sloping open funnels down which certain cargoes could be slid into the ship's hold from the quayside.

September 4th
The master of the Ann and Mary of Chester refused to move his vessel, causing an inconvenience in the harbour.
22nd
Captain Thomas "droing" (drawing?) *timber.*

The Corby Castle *at Cemaes*

Note: It is known that Captain Thomas occasionally had rafts of timber towed from Conwy to his yard at Amlwch, and it is thought that this is a reference to one such occasion.

October 16th
The Mona and the Ada went out. Put the Eliza Jane in the basin to load, and put the Corby Castle* under the crane. Lying in the harbour are 13 vessels.

Note: There were 3 cranes at Porth Amlwch, 1 steam powered on the eastern quay, and the other 2 constructed of wood, on the western side.

November 1st
Mary Elizabeth and Lord Mostyn* went into the graving dock.

Note: The graving dock was another name for Captain Thomas's dry dock, which had been quarried out of the living rock, and left without the benefit of dressed and stepped stone walls. For these reasons, it is thought that the Amlwch dry dock is unique.

14th
Strong gale from north by east with rain, when one of the balks broke: and some of the vessels broke loose in the harbour. The Jane Pringle* got some damage by the Charlotte.

December 10th
Moderate breeze from north, the Eliza Jane, Ocean Belle*, Jane Pringle* and Mary Ann towed by the steam tug Osprey on the bar to take on ballast.

Note: The 'bar' was the hard sill on which the lowest of the baulks rested. At this time, all ballast was loaded from the western side of the harbour.

1876
January 12th
21 vessels in the harbour.

13th
One of the chains fastening the balks broke, causing a little run in the harbour.

Note: High seas funnelling into the harbour as a result of onshore winds, was known as a 'run'.

17th
Harbour full of vessels.

26th
James and Maria, and the Mary Ann Jane, both from Liverpool, warped into harbour.

Note: Warping was a means of moving vessels using ropes attached to buoys or fixed objects ashore.

February 16th
Marmion received damage taking the ground (berthed to discharge coals).

Note: The term 'taking the ground' indicates that the vessel had settled on the harbour floor at low water. The fact that she sustained damage by doing so suggests that she had settled on a large stone or other projection, in which case the owners would have had good reason to claim against the Harbour Trustees.

18th
The Brig. Lord Lidsborough was towed in by the steam tug Iron King, and had to go out again – not sufficient water for her to get in safely.

23rd
New Bylaws where put up at the harbour office, and the church door.

Note: Copies of important public notices were invariably nailed to the door of the parish church.

25th
The Marmion was put on the block to be repaired. Mary Elizabeth came out of the graving dock.

Note: The 'block', or 'gridiron' as it was also known, was a structure on to which a vessel could be floated at high water, thereby allowing better and longer access to the underwater part of the vessel's hull. The block at Amlwch was at its top, or landward end.

March 10th
Schooner Isabella from Bangor ran aground in the entrance of the harbour when the balks were down. Fresh breeze from north west by north. I refused to get the balks up for him as there was much run in the harbour.

May 20th
Light breeze from the north. Fine and clear. 11 am Zelinda* warped out to the bay.

21st
Rain cleared up in "halff a hower"

23rd
Joseph* and the Earl of Zetland* came in from the graving dock.

24th
Gwen and E(leanor) Grace went into the graving dock.

26th
Welsh Boy put into crane berth to take in a water tank.

June 9th
Baron Hill* towed out by the steam Flat Minnie Jane.

Note: 'Mersey Flats' as they were known, were flat-bottomed single-masted vessels suitable for use on rivers such as the Mersey and the Weaver. Their use however, was not confined to rivers, and many are known to have worked the north Wales coastline as far as the Llŷn Peninsula. Many were later adapted to steam power, of which, the *Minnie Jane* and the *Temple*, both frequent visitors to Amlwch, were examples.

13th
Minnie Jane loading copper ore, and the Eliza Jane loading Sulphur for Antwerp.

Note: Sulphur, a by-product of an ore betterment process known as calcining, was exported from Amlwch in vast quantities for the manufacture of sulphuric acid, a vital element in many chemical processes. Another use of sulphur at that time was for the fumigation of ships' holds to rid them of vermin.

July 6th
The Ann was turned away from the quay as her laying days was up.

Note: Lay Days – the time allowed for shipping or discharging a cargo, and if not done within the term, fair weather permitting, the vessel comes on demurrage.

August 24th
The Jessie was hauled to top of harbour to be repaired.

Note: Probably on the blocks.

September 15th
The Jessie commenced to load sulphur for Antwerp.

28th
The Port Penrhyn came in when the balks were down and the ball up on the pole at Llam Carw. At 3 pm the balks were got up for her, as it was too much risk to leave her outside.

October 3rd
Euphemia* and Nellie Bywater* went out.

7th

About 12.30 pm, the Charles* was put under the crane. At about 2 pm the Florence Miriam hauled from her berth without my orders and knowledge, and in trying to get between the Charles* and the Velocipede*, got so jammed that it was impossible to get them loose, as the 'C' and the 'V' were lying alongside of the quay on the east side, the other on the west. The 'FM' listed on the 'C' and has done the latter vessel some damage.

November 11th

At 4.30 pm the Mary Elizabeth ran in and broke four of the balks. In about 10 minutes after, the Victoria ran in and was checked by the checking ropes. Both vessels entered the harbour contrary to the Rules of the Harbour. The two vessels had to lay outside in the outer basin for the night.

The Baulks Pier with the massive wooden baulks lying ready for lowering across the entrance to the harbour.

12th

The balks were got up as they could not be secured on account of those that were broken. I had to employ seven carpenters to get four new balks made, and they were all put down at 2 pm, and the two vessels got into safety inside the harbour.

24th
I had to employ two carpenters to repair the winch on the east side as the barres (sic) was broken.

25th
Nothing in the harbour.

31st
25 vessels in the harbour.

1877
January 5th
Harbour full of vessels -- 26 vessels in.

Note: This is the highest officially recorded number of vessels in Porth Amlwch at any one time, although legend has it, that it once accommodated 27.

February 20th
Begins with a strong gale from north north west. Some time in the morning after four o'clock, the Fanny broke adrift from her moorings and went against the Martha's stern, and did some damage to her. Had there been somebody aboard of the Fanny at such time, the damage would not have been done, or if she had been moored properly.

March 13th
The Corby Castle* was put alongside of the quay in the ballast berth on the west side. All the vessels took the ground properly that tide.

14th
At 9 am commenced to make a general shift of the vessels in the harbour. The Charlotte Maull was placed under the crane, and the Martha put in berth to load. At 11 am while in the act of shifting the vessels, the Jessie came into the bay. I sent the boat at once with two of the hobblers to inform the captain that I could not let him in because I could not leave the vessels at that time to have the balks got up that tide, and I did not consider it safe for him to enter the outer basin to take the ground. Contrary to the rules of the harbour Captain German, the owner of the Jessie took the harbour boat without my permission, and went into the bay and brought the Jessie into the outer basin where she laid and took the ground until the next tide. At 5:30 pm the balks were got up and she was let in.

April 23rd
Mersey put into berth to load. Red light put up in the Watchhouse as it was intended to put the balks down if it continued to blow, but at 10 pm it moderated and then the light was turned white.

24th
The Edith Morgan* took the ground before getting into her berth and blocked the passage up. At 11 am the Upton ran in and took the ground in the entrance of the inner basin, and the ball was hoisted up at Llam Carw because the Upton was in the entrance. At 8 pm the white light was

lighted and the ball taken down.

May 2nd
The Savant* took the ground at the entrance to the pierhead.

10th
The Brig. George Reynolds of London came into the harbour in tow by a steam tug contrary to the bylaws. After she came to the pierhead I asked the captain of the Brig why he had brought his vessel in without receiving orders to do so. He made no reply. She was let in at 6.35.

11th
Mary Ann Mandel came into the bay. I sent the boat out to inform the captain that I could not admit him as I was afraid I could not get enough men to lift the balks up.

June 13th
Alice Anna went out to the wreck.

21st
At 6 am, the Marmion went out to the wreck and came back in the evening.

25th
Sampson loaded a cargo of crates from the Marmion.

July 12th
The Rob Roy came in from Porth Gwichiad with wreckage.

24th
The Marmion went out, but she had to come back as it was blowing too hard for the Noah to tow her to the wreck.

August 10th
Marmion came in with a cargo of crates and coal from the wreck.

October 7th
Coila* ran in and broke the checking ropes, but no damage to herself nor any other vessel.

25th
The Ocean Belle* was towed in from Liverpool – her main rigging carried away and fore top mast broken.

30th
Holy Wath* was put alongside of the quay on the east side to take in some chains to go to Duddon.

Note: The Holy Wath, built for the Duddon iron ore trade, was the 3rd vessel to be built by William Thomas at Amlwch.

1878

January 4th
At 9 pm the Sarah Pringle* came in from Swansea and went on the rocks at Porth Offeiriad before coming into the harbour.

18th
The Marmion went out to the wreck of the Mersey.

March 5th
County of Cork* and the Sarah Lloyd into graving dock.

April 8th
The Pride of Anglesea* ran in in distress and failed to get the checking warp on board, and did some damage to the Hannah and Joseph and herself.

June 1st
County of Cork* and Eliza Jane towed out by the Noah.

22nd
Marmion out to the wreck and came back the same day.

24th
Marmion out to the wreck but loaded nothing.

26th
The Noah came in with part cargo of copper from the wreck.

July 10th
The Mud Boat sank under the cargo in the harbour and was put to rights the next tide.

August 1st
At 12 pm the Eilian Hill* was launched.

Note: The Eilian Hill was the 10th vessel to be launched from William Thomas's Iard Newydd at Amlwch.

2nd
At 12 pm the Parys Lodge was launched.

Note: The schooner *Parys Lodge*, named after the residence of the Mine Captain in Amlwch, had been built by Cox Paynter in Iard Ochr Draw.

28th
Eilian Hill* out of graving dock to take on ballast.

September 15th
Five vessels laying up and under repairs.

November 10th
Strong north west by north breeze. Captain of schooner Emerald* given orders to have his vessel tight in her moorings so as to keep her steady in her berth and also to get more ropes out. Captain said he had no crew as he had paid them off. At 11.15 the Emerald broke adrift and parted her moorings from the quay.

December 16th
Steam Flat Minnie Jane came in from Mostyn with coal.

24th
Eliza Bell* out from graving dock.

28th
23 vessels laying in the harbour -- no room for more.

1879
January 6th
Four vessels waiting their turn to come in at Bull Bay, Cemaes and Holyhead. Corby Castle* came in contrary to the rules… told to go out, but refused. Laid in outer basin throughout night. Twenty-two vessels in the harbour.

7th
Corby Castle* hauled inside the harbour without permission.

22nd
Corby Castle* put in berth to discharge.

26th
Caroline* into dry dock.

March 8th
Savant* into graving dock.

April 4th
No 10 Pilot Boat came in to clean her bottom – went out 8 pm.

May 1st
Moderate breeze from east north east. At 7 pm the Juanita* was towed out by the tug Iron King.

5th
Schooner Triumph of Chester towed in leaking by tug Iron King. The vessel struck on the coal rock and was in a sinking condition when towed in.

15th
Winch rope broke twice when putting down the balks.

16th
Winch broke and blacksmith got at once to repair it.

20th
Mud Boat sank under her cargo having sprung a leak and had to be discharged again.

June 4th
Savant* and Kate* out from graving dock.

9th
Jane Pringle* into graving dock.

30th
Marmion went out and came back in the evening with iron.

September 3rd
Joseph* into graving dock.

16th
Sampson went out to Cemlyn to load gravel for Liverpool.

17th
Number 12 Pilot Boat came in to have her bottom cleaned.

20th
Hodbarrow Miner* into graving dock.

October 6th
Charles* went out to Liverpool with a cargo of purple slime.

Note: Purple slime was a type of copper ore.

November 14th
Hodbarrow Miner* out of graving dock. The Margaret* was launched.

Note: The *Margaret* was the 12th vessel to leave William Thomas's Iard Newydd.

15th
Holy Wath* into graving dock.

20th
Victoria (Captain Owen Roberts) ran in contrary to the rules, and broke 8 balks. Captain Roberts when coming in to "lore" (sic) down his sales (sic) and let go his "ancor" (sic), but

nothing was done. But the jib was taking off her and a few links of the chaine (sic) *cable slackened this and that by the watchhouse pier. The heaving line was heve* (sic) *on board but no one tried to get the checking rope on board.*

December 3rd
Winch broke and balks put down with tackle.

1880
February 5th
Fresh breeze from south south west. At 3 am the Ann Mulvey came into the bay and the boat went out to her, and by towing, the boat was sunk and was lost. The men were taken to Holyhead by the vessel.

Note: The boat referred to was the rowing boat used by the hobblers to tow vessels in and out of the harbour.

March 19th
Steam Flat Trader came in windbound from the wreck in Church Bay.

April 9th
Lady Fielding and the Puffin towed out by the Noah.

10th
Anne Mulvey towed out by the Noah.

12th
Parys Lodge towed out by the Noah.

14th
Marmion went out to Dulas Island and brought back the part cargo of coal.

Note: This would without doubt have been salvaged from a wrecked vessel.

May 27th
Marmion went out to the Dakota*.

Note: The steamship *Dakota*, a transatlantic liner, ran aground close to the harbour entrance as a result of what was then claimed to have been a misunderstanding resulting from an 'opposite helm command'. This was a vestige of an early procedure when in order to turn the vessel to starboard, the helmsman was ordered to put the tiller to port.

August 23rd
Marmion and the Noah went to the Skerries.

September 6th
The Bowes came in from Quebec with a cargo of timber for Mr W.C. Paynter.

Note: W. C. Paynter was the then proprietor of Iard Ochr Draw, the shipyard he had bought from Nicholas Treweek in the late 1860s. He was also a joint owner with his brother, of a water-driven sawmill located at the landward end of the harbour, and a grain windmill on its western side which became a landmark for mariners.

21st
The Brig Bowes went out in ballast for Maryport.

October 16th
The Glyndwr came in from Bull Bay with a cargo of slates from the Eliza Catherine which ran into Bull Bay in distress of weather on the 5th of October and received some damage.

Note: The term 'distress of weather', meant that the vessel was unable to make headway, and was either confined to port, or had to return to the safety of a port. The term was frequently abbreviated to 'stress of weather'.

18th
The Eliza Catherine in from Bull Bay.

28th
Wind east, a strong Gale -- three of the balks broken by the sea. Two replacements from W. C. Paynter and one from Captain Thomas.

November 2nd
Eliza Catherine into graving dock.

December 2nd
Priscilla* towed in by the Lord Stanley from Liverpool and was put in berth to discharge.

1881
March 5th
East south east moderate breeze. The balks down and too much sea coming in to lift them up

July 12th
Pride of Anglesea* out of graving dock.

August 13th
Had to employ five to put the balks down.

24th
The Dart was towed in from Moelfre, which vessel went ashore at Moelfre having sprung a leak and was brought into Amlwch to be discharged and repaired.

31st
Lady Neave* towed out by the Noah.

September 10th
Dart towed out by the Noah – she was bound for Wexford in ballast.

October 7th
The President Garfield* was launched at 9 am.

22nd
The schooner Robert was sold by "octon" (auction) *and was bought by Captain Morgan.*

November 10th
President Garfield* went out for West Bank with a cargo of copper ore.

1882
March 12th
Eliza came in with a cargo of limestone from Moelfre.

April 7th
At about 11 am the Noah was blown up in the Bay by towing the Victoria out. Owen Pritchard, N. Peters and E. Jones of Holyhead were lost.

Note: The small, 35 ton steamship *Noah* was, because of its motive power, often used as a tug serving Porth Amlwch; but was better known as a 'wrecker', because it was mainly used to salvage cargoes or any other recoverable material from wrecked vessels. It is evident that both the *Marmion* and the *Noah* were at the time, working on the wreck of the *Mersey* which had foundered on the Skerries, a tightly-knit group of rocky islands off the north-western corner of Anglesey.

The *Noah*, once owned by Captain Thomas, had a tragic end however. She had returned to Porth Amlwch following a spell of work on another wreck, that of the *Welsh Girl* which, it will be recalled, had been built as Captain Thomas's first solo venture at Porth Amlwch some 13 years earlier, and which had been wrecked at nearby Cemlyn. On his arrival at Amlwch, the skipper of the *Noah* was asked to tow the sloop *Victoria* out of the port, and as the small tug was returning having cast off the tow rope, her boiler blew up, killing all three of her crew outright, one of whom was Edward Hughes, a young newly-married diver from Holyhead. During the subsequent enquiry, it was revealed that the *Noah's* boiler had in fact been salvaged from the wreck of the *Dakota*, which had run aground close to the entrance to Porth Amlwch a few months earlier. The possibility exists that in order to save coal, the safety valve on the *Noah's* boiler had been 'screwed down', allowing the pressure to build up beyond its safe limit. In a compound surface condensing engine for example, at 60 pounds per square inch boiler pressure, the coal consumption would have been about $3^1/_2$ lb/HP/hr, and at 200 pounds per square inch, it would have been less than a half of that figure.

May 14th
The Flat Glance sank ¹/₂ mile northwest by west off Point Lynas at about 2 am.

June 22nd
The steamer Enterprise came in.

Note: The *Enterprise/Enterprize* was a wooden vessel, known locally as *Y Stemar Fach* – the little steamer.

30th
The Syren came in from Lisbon for Mr Hills.

July 8th
The Jane and the Eliza went out to the sound and brought some iron in.

9th
The wreckers went out.

10th
The wreckers went out and brought some copper in.

20th
Mud boat towed out by the Enterprise.

September 29th
The balks were got up for the purpose of taking the Jane Louise to the outer basin to remove a piece of iron which was laying there.

Note: This was clearly one of those instances when the Harbourmaster was acting to prevent damage to a vessel which might settle on it as the tide receded. See the entry for the 16th February 1876 which refers to such damage.

October 2nd
The Euphemia* came in -- she was in distress.

December 6th
Strong breeze from North East. In the evening a gale from north east with snow. The balks down but hard work to hold the vessels and the harbour.

18th
Moderate breeze from the east. At about 3 pm the Holy Wath* came into the bay bound for Amlwch. The boat was sent to her and gave her permission to come in. The vessel came in and let go his stern anchor and also his bow anchor. The harbour rope was given to the vessel but that broke, and the vessel went up against the balks and broke three of them.

1883

March 10th

The Fanny came in windbound -- had been ashore on the West Mouse.

Note: The West Mouse, close to the Skerries, is one of three rocky islands off the northern coastline of Anglesey, the other two being the East Mouse, very close to the entrance to Porth Amlwch, and the Middle Mouse, off Cemaes.

April 7th

The new steamer W.S. Caine* was launched from Captain Thomas's new yard.

Note: The W.S.Caine was the 15th vessel to leave the Thomas yard in Amlwch.

8th

W.S. Caine* went out to Caernarvon, towed out by the Lady Kate* steamship.

Note: Bought on the stocks by the Lady Kate Steamship Company, the *Lady Kate* was the 3rd vessel to be launched from Thomas's Millom Yard.

1884

May 14th

The steamer Express* came in from Caernarvon on her trial trip with a cargo of slates and timber.

Note: This vessel was launched as the *Eilian* on 28th of February 1884 from Iard Newydd. She was subsequently known as the *Exchange* however, and unless there had been a double change of name within a matter of a few weeks, it is thought that the Harbourmaster had recorded her name incorrectly.

July 20th

The Pleiades came in with a cargo of herring from Port St Mary.

August 24th

The Jane Pringle* came in from France to be repaired.

November 5th

The new ss Anglesea* was launched from Captain Thomas's yard, and was towed to Caernarvon by the steam tug Wellington.

Note: The ss *Anglesea* was the 17th vessel to leave the Thomas yard. It is quite possible that the steam tug referred to was originally the sailing flat *Wellington* which had been at the centre of the Amlwch riots in 1817. Her rudder was removed and hidden in a nearby churchyard by rioters in order to prevent her sailing with a cargo of locally grown oats at a time when due to a very poor harvest, a great famine was predicted in the town.

December 20th
William Foulkes, master of the Smack Sisters, died on board his vessel at about 10.30 am.

1885
February 28th
The ss Anglesea* came in at 9 pm.

March 3rd
The ss Anglesea* went out bound for Wexford.

9th
The ss Anglesea* came in from Wexford.

10th
The ss Anglesea* was neaped.

Note: A vessel is neaped when within a bar harbour, it is left aground on a spring tide in such a way that it cannot, unless lightened, be floated off until the next spring tide. Spring tides occur when the sun and moon act in conjunction with each other to create higher and lower tides than usual.

April 3rd
The Anglesea* towed the wreck Rossendale from Holyhead.

May 3rd
The ss Lady Louisa* came in from Liverpool with a cargo of timber for Captain Thomas.

8th
The Sarah Ellen went out in ballast for Bangor. She was the first vessel that took in ballast from the east side of the harbour.

September 10th
At about 1130 am the Elizabeth Peers* was launched.

November 6th
Hodbarrow Miner* came in from the graving dock.

1886
February 5th
At about 12 midnight the Mary Catherine* came to the bay and in coming in too close to the east side, went ashore but floated off the next tide.

September 20th
At 3 am the Hodbarrow Miner* and the Priscilla were towed out by the steam yacht Falcon.

26th

The President Garfield* ran into contrary to the rules. The balks were got up and the vessel was let in as her draft was only four feet.

1889

January 24th

About 3 am the signal pole at Llam Carw was shot down with Dynamite by some persons unknown.

Note: It was widely believed locally that the perpetrator was Thomas Fanning Evans, who owned the land on which the pole stood, and for which he was paid a nominal rent of one shilling per annum. What prompted such extreme action on his part, will perhaps never be known. On the following day, the Harbour Trust erected a replacement, but no sooner had it been put up that it was cut down on Fanning Evans's orders.

Four days later, the weather made it necessary to lower the baulks, a fact which could not be communicated to the master of a vessel wishing to enter the port, until it was too late. The unnecessary danger this put the vessels and their crews, angered the local community to such an extent that on the afternoon of the 30th the Harbour Trust's foreman was accompanied by no fewer than thirty men when he went to replace the pole for a second time. The message was not lost on Fanning Evans, and there were no further incidents relating to it.

March 20th

At sunrise moderate breezy from NW. Misty with shower of rain. At 9 am put the balks down, 15 in number, 14 being the usual complement. At 10 am wind north strong breeze. Misty with rain. Martha discharging and British Queen repairing. Noon wind NE. Strong breeze with showers of rain. At 3 pm fresh gale. Cloudy at about 3.30 pm. I sent Edward Griffith and Wm Hughes (Hobblers) to warn the Masters of the vessels in the harbour to have them well moored as the weather was threatening. At 5 pm wind NE blowing right into the harbour. Strong gale and misty. At 6 pm had the balks well secured, heavy sea and furious run coming up to the outer basin which continued to increase. At about 10.45 pm it was found that some of the lower balks had been broken by the force of the heavy sea, and run which broke over the pier heads. The tide being the highest spring of the year, between this and midnight, the vessels in the harbour parted from there (sic) moorings causing a deal of damage to themselves and the harbour. Everything that could be done by the harbour officials to secure the safety of the vessels inside had been done, further service could not be rendered owing to the seas breaking over the Pier head.

21st

NE whole gale and heavy sea. Misty at about 1.30 am. The schooner Emperor (of Beaumaris) broke adrift from Captain's (Thomas) graving dock and came in contact with the watch house pier and caused damage to the lighthouse and buildings attached. The vessel became a total wreck at about 2.45 am. The remaining balk got loose from the groove owing to the fall of the tide. Wind NE strong gale about 4 am. Got carpenters to make new balks. At 6 am employed the steam crane to raise the balks out of the harbour and employed about two dozen men to have the balks replaced.

Noon, wind NE moderate gale. New balks secured and had the vessels put in their proper berths and got men employed putting chains across the entrance of the harbour to keep the wreck of the schooner Emperor from coming in contact with the balks.

Note: An almost identical accident was to befall the steamer *Black Rock* some 24 years later.

22nd
Sun rise, wind NW fresh breeze and misty. The wreck of the schooner Emperor layed across the entrance of the harbour. At noon, wind WNW moderate breeze. At about 5 pm the Pliadias (Pleiades) came into the bay but could not come in as the wrick (sic) lay across the mouth of the harbour and too much Ebb tide for her to float over her. At 6 pm the wind WNW moderate breeze and continued. Employed G. Williams, John Hughes and G. Williams to clear wreckage in harbour.

23rd
Sunrise wind WSW strong breeze, misty and rain. 2 men employed in clearing wreckage inside of the harbour. Vessels working Martha discharging and repairing, also British Queen repairing. Balks down, the wrick (sic) still laying across the entrance of the harbour.

25th
Wind WNW Strong breeze. At about 8 am the 'Pliadias' (Pleiades) came into the entrance to the harbour and had to wait until the next tide, that being about 2 pm. The chance (chains) which were across the harbour were lord (lowered) down. She came in and was loaded and went out. At 3 pm fresh breeze and misty. Employed R. Jones, J. Hughes, J. Williams, Thomas Williams, W. Pritchard, W. Hughes, W. Thomas, G. Williams, Robert Jarret, W. Hughes, G. Williams to shift the wrick of the schooner Empror (sic) from the entrance. She was shifted about 20 feet to the eastward. The balks were still down.

26th
Sunrise wind NNW Strong breeze. Had 17 min (sic) employed in shifting the wrick (wreck), and got her in the evenings tide at the back of the watch house pier, and got her chained there to the wrocks (rocks).

29th
Sunrise wind WNW 'modrate' (sic) breeze. Vessels working, Martha and the Jane discharging, ss Enterprise and the Renown loading. Arrived the Prissila (sic) in ballast from Belfast. Saled (sic) the ss Enterprise for Llanhairn (Llanaelhaiarn) with a cargo of guano. At 6 pm wind WNW light air. Got the wreck of the 'Empror' (sic) in side the harbour with the Mud Flat.

Note: It is evident from the spelling mistakes that the regular Harbourmaster was not on duty between the 22nd and the 29th of March!

1894
July 31st
At about 11 am when the master of the Jessie of Fleetwood came down I ordered him to move his

vessel to another berth higher up the harbour to make room for the Flat Providence to come into her berth as she was going to load ochre, that berth being more convenient, but Captain R. Jones refused to move his vessel, saying that he didn't care a damn for me or anyone else, and threatened to throw John Parry, one of the hobblers, over the quay if he casted (sic) his ropes adrift. Fearing a fight to take place and the tide ebbing, I ordered Captain Robert Jones to come down the next tide, to shift his vessel, but he neglected, so I had to put men on board to shift her. The Jessie laid in the same berth without being shifted from the 5th of July until the 31st. She commenced discharging on the 7th and finished on the 16th. Laid idle in berth after discharging 15 days.

The importance of having a conscientious and dependable harbourmaster to oversee the efficient running of a small port was clearly illustrated when Captain William Morgan transformed the port of Duddon from one which was notorious for its long delays, to becoming an exemplar, efficiently handling thousands of ships annually.

The name of the unfortunate man so employed at Amlwch during this time is unknown; but it is fairly evident that he too was a retired sea captain, and his occasional difficulty with written English suggests that it was not his first language, and that he too was a Welshman. His job at Amlwch was not a particularly easy one for several reasons, the most obvious being the confined nature of the port itself, which presented serious problems resulting in congestion and delays.

Apart from his office in the little stone-built Watch-house which gave him a commanding view over the harbour and out to sea, he had few if any luxuries. Apart from a badge of authority in the shape of a bowler hat perhaps, he was unlikely to have been issued with any sort of uniform such as his contemporaries in the great ports were privileged to wear. Not for him either was the luxury of dealing with relatively sophisticated ships' officers, for he was more accustomed to contend with hard-nosed captains who had learnt their trade in small ships, and whose very livelihood depended on spending as little time as possible in port.

CHAPTER 5
MARITIME INSURANCE
"no vessel shall sail to Norway after the first day of November"

The sea always has been, and will undoubtedly continue to be, a most hazardous place in which to conduct business: but perils faced by seafarers were probably never as grave as they were in the 18th century, when ship losses brought about by natural causes were commonplace. Indeed, so frequent were the shipping losses in St. George's Channel, that the Lords of the Admiralty were prompted in the mid 18th century, to commission Anglesey-born Lewis Morris, to conduct a survey aimed at identifying those havens along the Welsh coastline between Pembroke and Great Orme's Head, which could safely be used as harbours of refuge for vessels in distress.

His evaluation of Amlwch as a possible nominee, was such that he did not even consider the place worthy of a plan, because it was to his mind, little more than a cove between two steep rocks, in which a vessel could barely turn; and as if to add insult to injury, he went on to state that the entrance to it was nothing short of difficult to find at the best of times.

The danger, particularly to sailing vessels, became even more acute with the coming of steamships, when collisions brought about by excessive speed and poor watch keeping were all too frequent occurrences. Several examples of such tragedies have been highlighted elsewhere in this work; but in this respect, perhaps the unluckiest vessel associated with Amlwch was the Liverpool Pilot Boat, *Mersey*, which was collided with, and sunk twice by steamers, in what was an inordinately short lifespan of 10 years.

The history of marine insurance, in which 'Lloyd's became pre-eminent, is well documented; and in that august company's wake, many smaller companies specialising in maritime protection sprang up in most of the country's leading ports. Despite the fierce competition for business however, their premiums were often excessive because of the losses then being encountered, so much so, that many shipowners were forced to operate either with inadequate cover, or as was all too often the case, with no security whatsoever.

By way of reconciling the heavy premiums imposed by insurance companies with the need to make a living, many maritime communities in Wales, and indeed, elsewhere in the United Kingdom, established what were known as 'Maritime Protection Clubs'. These were non-profit-making federations of ship-owners which agreed to underwrite losses sustained by their fellow subscribers in the ratio of the ship tonnages they themselves had registered with the club as a percentage of the total tonnage involved.

Protection clubs, usually governed by a board of directors, and managed by a secretary, subsequently became the means whereby many small shipowners were able to survive in a highly competitive and precarious business milieu. One such, was the 'Amlwch Maritime Mutual Insurance Co. Ltd' (A.M.M.I.C.), of which Captain Thomas was a founder member and director.

It is probably true to say that in the early years, maritime insurance clubs were mostly confined to the protection of vessels associated with their immediate locality; but in time, membership was opened up to owners from further afield, simply as a means of ameliorating the severity of calls upon their founder members.

Much of a club's business success depended on trust and goodwill; and inasmuch as the club depended on its members' integrity for its own survival, the converse was also true, for the insured depended on the probity of his club for his own continued existence. This unfortunately, was not always the case.

Protection clubs were closely bound by their rules, and managers were always on the lookout for those of their members who appeared to them to be by some means or other, unfairly manipulating the system to their own advantage.

It was common practice for clubs to accept only part of the full risk on a vessel, referred to colloquially as 'a line'. This was a legitimate means whereby the burden of responsibility for what might otherwise have been a crippling claim against a small club, was spread amongst many. Conversely, shipowners were safeguarded from the consequences of protection club insolvency, which was not an unknown occurrence.

Usually, hulls and machinery were protected by one set of insurers, and cargoes with others; and in order to prevent fraud within the system, it was universally required that the total value of all insurances was not to exceed the true value of the vessel and its cargo.

In the case of William Thomas & Sons, their vessels' hulls and machinery were almost invariably insured for 12 months, usually with protection clubs: but insurances on cargoes, particularly those involving deep-sea voyages, were negotiated on a single or return voyage basis if the return cargo and port of delivery were known beforehand. This business was usually done through specialist cargo insurance companies.

Although Captain William Thomas was a director and founder member of the Amlwch club, his dealings with it were subject to the same close scrutiny by the club's secretary, as would apply to any other member; a situation which led to him becoming the plaintiff in a legal action commenced against the club following the loss of the *Barbara* on the 22nd of November 1881.

The vessel was returning to Britain with a cargo of rice from Rangoon, and on arrival in Queenstown (Cobh) for orders, her master was directed to the port of Liverpool. Whilst on passage up St George's Channel however, his vessel became a total loss near Milford Haven where he had sought shelter in the Sound.

Difficulties arose when the claim against the A.M.M.I.C., put forward by Captain Thomas in his role as the vessel's managing owner, was rejected by the club's secretary. This, as might well be expected, was hotly disputed by the Captain whose immediate reaction was to instigate legal proceedings against the club. It is interesting to note that in an estimate of his assets written in December 1877, Captain Thomas placed a value of £2,220 on his personal share of the 8-month-old vessel, which at year 2002 values, would have been in the region of £113,555.

Stating his reason for rejecting the claim, Thomas Morgan, secretary of the club, told a meeting of the directors held on the 30th of December 1881, at which Captain Thomas was present, that the *Barbara* had been overvalued by the owners when they made their application for cover, and consequently were over insured within the meaning of the club's Byelaw 12. He then declared that the claim was null and void, and that all that was required of the club under the rules, was to repay the original premium.

As was the usual practice at the time, the hull of *Barbara* had been insured with more than one protection club, to a total value of £12,000. The figure arrived at was, according to Captain Thomas, based on the ship's original cost, less an annual depreciation of 5% per annum. Genuinely believing that a mistake had been made, and clearly fearful of his good name being tarnished, Captain Thomas argued that if the ship had indeed been overvalued, then the blame should not lie with him personally, but with his chief clerk, whose job it had been to calculate that figure.

Given that the 5% per annum depreciation was correct, and it should be borne in mind that this was a perfectly realistic figure where iron vessels of the quality of the *Barbara* were concerned, the vessel at the time of her entry in the Amlwch club was indeed overvalued by something in the order of £380.

Captain Thomas went on to remind those present at the meeting that the valuation of the vessel had not been questioned at the time she was entered in their club, and that the premium he had paid, was based on that valuation. The club's surveyor would have been required to verify the figure at the time of entry; but clearly, he too must have made the same mistake as William Thomas's clerk. Evidently, there was fault on both sides.

Unfortunately, there is no information available regarding the final outcome of the dispute: but as the Captain continued to patronise the club, and had no fewer than 28 vessels entered in it in 1882, it would appear that the matter was resolved to the satisfaction of both sides.

In the same year, Captain Thomas had lines on 19 vessels with the Bangor & North Wales Mutual Marine Protection Association Ltd., of Plas Llwyd, Bangor; managed by R. Hughes. Mr Hughes was at the time also manager of the City of Bangor Mutual Marine Protection Association Ltd, which was registered at the same address.

These two clubs could well have devolved from the Bangor Mutual Ship Insurance Society which was first registered in 1853, and which had its office at Plas Llwyd also. The then secretary was Samuel Roberts, and two of its Directors were John H. Treweek and T. D. Griffiths, who were recorded as being Amlwch shipowners. The remaining directors were described as shipowners, shipbuilders and coal merchants.

Under the Society's Rule 66, the Board of Directors:

have discretionary powers to receive into the Society any vessel either wholly or in part registered at , or belonging to, someone of the ports of Conway (Conwy); Bangor; Carnarvon (Caernarfon); Nevin (Nefyn); Holyhead; Amlwch, or Beaumaris; or, of which not less than one eighth belongs to any person or persons residing within ten miles of any of the said seven ports.

Under Rule 67 introduced in March 1854, and amended 2 years later, the Directors had the final word concerning where the vessels it protected could sail to. Unless specifically agreed to beforehand, the voyages were confined to the British Isles:

including the islands of Guernsey, Jersey, Alderney, Sark and Man; and to any safe port of the Continent of Europe, between and including Onega to the north, and Gibraltar to the south, and also to the Baltic and Mediterranean Seas.

The Insurers could also stipulate the times of the year during which vessels trading to foreign ports outside those limits, could do so:

all vessels sailing to the lower ports of British America, sail on or before the first day of September; and, sailing to Quebec, shall sail on or before the twentieth day of August; and that no vessel shall sail to Norway after the first day of November; or to the White Sea, before the first of May, or after the twentieth of August; or to any part of the Baltic after the first of September; or to Alburg, Randers, Hamburg, or the River Wezer (sic), or to any port in Holland or Belgium, after the first of November, or before the first of February. Provided also, that all vessels allowed by making applications to the Directors to proceed beyond the limits by paying an extra premium, are warranted not to sail to or from any ports of the Spanish Main, Jamaica, St Domingo, Cuba, or any of the West India Islands and Colonies, between the first day of August and the 12th day of January; nor to the Black or White Seas, between the 1st day of October and the 1st day of April. And the times of the clearing at the Custom House, shall be deemed the time of sailing, provided the vessel is then all loaded or ballasted, and ready for sea. Any vessel insured in this Society and trading to the Azores, shall forfeit all claim upon the Society.

The regulations were clearly put in place to minimise danger and damage to the insured vessels by reason of climatic exigencies. Additionally, under Rule 68:

... in time of war the Board shall have power to require the Owner or Owners of any vessel which, or any share which is insured by the Society, to furnish and carry such arms and ammunition as they think necessary; and if the Owner, or Owners shall neglect to furnish and carry such arms and ammunition, after being so required, he or they shall have no claim on the Society in respect of the Insurance upon such vessel or share, if such vessel shall be captured...

Before a vessel could be accepted by the club, it had first to undergo a survey by a competent surveyor, who would need to be satisfied that her hull was seaworthy, that she was sufficiently manned, and that she was well found and fitted with boats etc., all of which had to be of the size, length or quantity and quality stipulated by Lloyds Rules. Any defects found would have had to be made good before the vessel could be accepted for insurance. The Surveyor would then place a value on the vessel, before placing her in either one of two classes; vessels which were most eligible for insurance were designated as being First Class, and those less so, in the Second. The main difference between the two in terms of insurance, was that First Class vessels were not insured beyond three quarters of their value, and those in the Second Class, not beyond a third. The club would then record the value and give notice to the owner of that valuation, allowing him 3 days in which to dispute the figure in writing. Had this example been followed by the Amlwch club in the case of the *Barbara*, there would have been no grounds to dispute Captain Thomas's claim. In addition, and probably by way of ensuring that owners did not over insure their vessels, the Bangor club's directors stipulated that vessels insured by them could in no wise be insured by any other Society or Company. In such cases, claims against the club would be automatically invalidated, and the owner expelled.

Bearing in mind that William Thomas was but 19 years of age when he was given command of Treweek's schooner *Red*, the Bangor club refused to insure a vessel commanded by a person younger than 21 years of age, unless the previous consent of the Board had been obtained, and the facts entered into the books of the Society. Similarly, the master of every vessel insured by them, who has not previously commanded a ship or vessel for a period of 12 months, had to appear before the directors, or before two competent and experienced mariners named by them, to be examined as to his competency. As an alternative, the Board were prepared to consider, without examination, applications supported by satisfactory testimonials as to the applicant's competency.

Patronising several protection clubs as he did, it is difficult to fathom exactly why on 1st of January 1886, Captain Thomas should wish to launch and trade as the Eilian (Private) Mutual Marine Insurance Co., of which he had appointed himself Manager. The inclusion of the word 'Private' in the company's name indicates that it had been formed primarily to service his own vessels, with the inclusion of some of those he managed. The insurance account ledger begins with entries for 23 ships; all of which with the exception of one, were either wholly or partly owned by him (see Appendix 16).

The last entry in William Thomas's insurance ledger which relates to the Eilian M.M.I.C., appears in February 1889, after the expiry of which, the private club was presumably wound up. It has not been possible to discover the reasons why this happened: but there can be little doubt that the highly professional and competitive efficiency of other societies, like the Dee and Mersey Protection Club under the most able direction of Walter Reney, was a major factor.

It became obvious to Captain Thomas that the Bangor club was not being run as efficiently as it should, for on the 27th of August 1888, he had occasion to write a letter to the Mr Hughes the Secretary, complaining that he had still not received a reply to his claims involving the *Countess of Lonsdale* and the *Yuca*, adding that his co-owners were urging him to take proceedings for the recovery of the money.

Matters clearly had not been attended to by the 11th October, when the Captain again wrote to Hughes stating that he was:

> in receipt of your circular of this morning, but cannot for the life of me understand what this has to do with my claims on your other Society, when I have requested you to deduct the calls of our Society from my claims on a different Society, is separate, and yet you are using this circular to try and blindfold me from your inexcusable delay in settling my claims... I intend pursuing my claims through a solicitor.

Clearly, Hughes had made a vain attempt to muddy the waters; but with someone as acutely aware as Captain Thomas, who was far and away beyond the average small shipowner in terms of business acumen, it was to no avail. Whether or not this ploy was to conceal Hughes's inefficiency, or an effort to hide something far more serious, is a matter for conjecture.

Problems with the Bangor club continued, for on the 8th of October 1896, the Amlwch firm wrote again to its Secretary informing him that:

> We must again ask you to send us receipts for the cheque sent you on the 19th ult.,and we cannot understand why you have not done so long before this. You are the only one who treats us in this manner. Don't let us quarrel over this, but attend to the matter at once, and get done with it.

A club simply referred to as the Bangor Club in William Thomas's correspondence, which could have meant either or both of the established Bangor clubs, crashed in 1896. The first intimation that something was seriously wrong, appears in a letter sent by William Thomas to Mr Hughes, the secretary, on the 12th of November 1895, advising him to:

> take notice that on and after the present year, we desire to withdraw all our vessels entered in the Bangor and North Wales M.M. Protection Association Ltd., as well as the two vessels entered in The City of Bangor M.M. Protection Association Ltd.

On the same day (12th November 1895), William Thomas wrote to Walter Reney, secretary of the Dee and Mersey Shipowners Mutual Insurance Association Ltd, at Connah's Quay in Flintshire, enclosing a proposal form bearing the names and tonnages of eleven of their vessels which were then available for entry into that Association. Those were the: *Albion; County of Cork; Euphemia, Hodbarrow Miner; Jane Pringle; Lady Neave; Mary Catherine; Ocean Belle; President Garfield; Pride of Anglesea,* and the *Thomas.* The total value of the vessels amounted to £12,225, (worth £624, 760 in 2002), a significant sum for any protection club to have entered on its books by a single owner at that time.

It is quite evident that by this time, William Thomas had discussed the Bangor club's problems with at least one of his friends, because a fortnight later he wrote a letter to the club on behalf of Robert Griffiths of Porth Amlwch, stating that he too wished to discontinue the cover provided by the club for his vessel, the *Dinorwic.*

Matters clearly came to a head quite rapidly, for in a letter to Walter Reney, dated the 15th of September, Thomas informed him that a meeting regarding the proposed winding up of the Bangor Protection Club, was to be held at Rowlands' Temperance Hotel in the city on Wednesday 21st of September. There can be no doubt that great interest had been aroused locally in the misfortunes of the club, but as the meeting was essentially a private one involving only its members, its deliberations and outcome went unreported in the local press.

The proposal to wind up the Bangor club was agreed to, and in further correspondence with Reney, the Amlwch firm informed him that several of the club's members had received a call amounting to 1% of their involvement, in order to pay the estimated costs of the club's liquidation. Although the percentage was seemingly small, the actual sum due from the Thomas family was £122, (£6234 in 2002) which was a heavy charge indeed. Quite understandably, they added that they relied on their solicitors to see that their objections were lodged with the Court before the expiry date. In their letter, they also expressed a wish to examine a detailed breakdown of the sums involved, in order to see how the figure had been arrived at, and to see if items which had been included in the calculations were valid.

Informing Reney that his circular had been received that morning, William Thomas & Sons wrote to him on the 24th of October, outlining their objections to the calls being made upon them by the Liquidator:

> *... we have paid all the calls made upon us by the late Secretary; but since the company has gone into liquidation, we have received demands for the outstanding calls which the Liquidator states were made prior to the Winding Up Order. Our reasons for declining to pay these calls are that we paid calls in 1894 and 1895 for claims which the club never paid, and which were not claims against the Protection Club. We therefore claim that we have overpaid more than the present calls made upon us, and instead of calls due from us, we maintain that we are entitled to the amounts we overpaid in 1894 and 1895.*

On the 5th of November, William Thomas & Sons wrote again to Reney, saying:

> *We cannot imagine why Directors and Surveyors were appointed to the Committee of Inspection, unless these gentlemen who are claiming against the Society are the only ones who would have proposed calling in the 1% on the capital. Our reasons for objecting to the calls made upon us was because in 1894,5,6, we overpaid calls for claims which were never paid to the owners of the vessels on whose behalf the calls were made.*

If William Thomas & Sons were typical of their contemporaries, the shipping community was by one means or another, extremely well informed regarding each others' fortunes and misfortunes, and it is almost impossible to comprehend how the club secretary could have made a succession of false calls on his members without being detected, particularly as his accounts are known to have been audited annually.

It is evident from the correspondence that the matter although very serious, was at no time considered by Thomas to be criminally motivated; and for that reason, the problem probably arose as a result of poor book-keeping on Hughes's part. In order to hide what was evidently an embarrassing mistake, the club resorted to the simple expediency of misdirecting funds obtained against a later call, in order to settle earlier claims. An ongoing situation of this nature where Peter was constantly being robbed to pay Paul, would not necessarily have been readily apparent to the auditors; and Thomas's assertion that specific monies were not paid to the owners of the vessels on whose behalf the calls were made, was strictly speaking, absolutely correct.

For example, Captain Griffiths, whose vessel the *Dinorwic*, was first entered in the Bangor Protection Club in January 1893, received and paid calls in 1894 and 1895 for losses which had occurred in 1891, two years before he even became involved with the club! Similarly, the Thomas-owned vessel *Mary Catherine* was first entered with the Bangor club in 1890, but in 1893, the year of Captain Thomas's death, the firm was charged and paid for, losses which had occurred in 1889! This suggests that William Thomas & Sons, who were constantly on the lookout for even the slightest hint of sharp practice in their day to day business affairs, were uncharacteristically lax in their financial dealings with the Bangor club.

What this account undoubtedly illustrates, is the great degree of trust the firm must have originally had in the integrity of the club, and which in all probability, was reflected in their business dealings with other protection clubs they dealt with elsewhere.

Following the Bangor club's collapse however, William Thomas & Sons, were, by the tone of their later letters, much more circumspect, and undoubtedly a great deal more candid, in their business relationships with protection clubs generally, a list of which is appended (see Appendix 9).

CHAPTER 6
THE YACHTS *SAUCY ARETHUSA* AND *KATHLEEN*
"you will find that she is not a bit worse than new"

Following the death of Captain William Thomas in March 1893, his sons Lewis and William were appointed his executors. As they had no use of their own for his steam yacht, the *Saucy Arethusa*, they decided to sell her. She was then laid up in their dry dock where she took up valuable space and was very much in the way. The yacht was built by Rawston of Freckleton, near Preston in 1882, for John L. Birley of Mill Bank, Kirkham; and it was he who sold her to Captain Thomas in August 1890.

In December 1893, she was offered for sale through the offices of the Secretary to the Yacht Owners' Association, who suggested that she could well be hired out for private use. The idea did not appeal to the brothers at that time, and they declined his offer; offering instead, to sell her for £750 (£50,830 in 2002), and describing her as being a splendid sea boat with good accommodation, and in good order.

With no results forthcoming from their efforts to sell her through the Y.O.A., the vessel was offered some 2 months later, to Clement G. Morris and Co., shipbrokers of Liverpool, advising them that:

> She has been used for yachting purposes, and that for but a short period. She is practically new. She has the usual complement of sails which are new. Rigging etc. in perfect order. In fact she only requires steam up and provision to go to sea. She is now in our dry dock where she can be inspected… she could be fitted for cargo at a very small outlay. The fore cabin is 19^1/$_2$ feet long, could be made into a hold, as could also part of the after cabin which is 12^1/$_2$ feet long. Our price for this splendid yacht is £800.

The price was considered excessive by the Morris Company, but in their reply, William Thomas & Sons argued that the price was not unreasonable, and that when their client saw her, he would undoubtedly be of the same opinion. In a further letter, the owners agreed to the brokers' demand for a 2^1/$_2$% commission on the sale, on condition that the figure offered by their clients was close to the asking price. A subsequent offer, which came a few days later, was refused out of hand, as the amount offered would, the owners claimed, have resulted in them receiving a net amount of only £437-10 -00 for the yacht, for which sum they argued, they could sell her over and over again with little or no effort.

Disillusioned by the offer they had received, and realising perhaps that the vessel may not have been as sound as they had at first presumed, the brothers approached Mr Alfred Lotinga, who was Morris and Company's client, directly. For them to have taken this unusual, and somewhat unethical course of action, can only mean that they harboured serious reservations about Morris and Company's business integrity, and were determined to go to the fountainhead themselves.

It is evident that Mr Lotinga, whose home was in Italy, was minded to sail the yacht which had originally been built for service in cold waters, to the Mediterranean. In their letter to him, they offered to adapt her to his needs, by sheathing her as a precaution against the Teredo worm, a warm water predator which could cripple a small wooden vessel such as the *Arethusa*, in a matter of days. Their offer was to:

> *caulk her from keel to gunwales, also the whole of the deck. Sheet her over felt and 9 inch boards with 16 oz yellow metal one foot above light water mark and extend the $^3/_4$ inch wood sheathing to load waterline. Make and supply one squaresail boom and one squaresail, for the sum of £830.*

The brothers advised Morris and Company that Mr Lotinga had been written to, and at the same time they confirmed their willingness to pay them a commission of $2^1/_2$% on the price of the vessel, but went on to deliberately exclude the additional work specified in their letter to their client. As a result, Mr Lotinga offered them £500 for the vessel, which was flatly refused as they argued that later on in the season, they could expect to sell her for more.

The brokers were very unhappy with the latest development, and strongly argued that their commission should rightly include the additional work; which prompted the following unequivocal response:

> *we beg to say now, once and for all, that if we have to keep the boat for 20 years, we shall not allow you a single cent (more, by way of) commission.*

Believing perhaps that Mr Lotinga was unaware of what was happening, William Thomas wrote to him detailing the history of the offers and counter offers which had been made, and offering him the vessel as she stood in their dry dock, for the sum of £675 cash. This offer was made on condition that his agents gave them the refusal of the work to caulk and copper her at a reasonable price.

Undeterred by the sharp letter they had been sent, Clement Morris and Co. wrote back offering £500 for the yacht, and adding that they would have no difficulty in having a boat similar in specification to that of the *Saucy Arethusa*, built for £900. In the brothers' reply, they were told in no uncertain terms that they were talking nonsense, as the prime cost of the *Arethusa's* hull alone had exceeded £1000, which was an awesome price to pay for a private yacht at that time!

Knowing when he bought her, that the *Saucy Arethusa* would be lying idle for long periods of time, captain Thomas decided that she could quite easily earn her keep as a tug. More often than not, Captains of sailing vessels arriving or leaving Porth Amlwch had either to rely on hobblers towing their vessels in and out, or on the services of visiting steam flats such as the *Temple*, which was a frequent visitor to the port. To enable her to act as a tugboat, the *Arethusa* was supplied with additional two-bladed propellers in place of her usual three-bladed ones, needed for normal use. The yacht's inventory shows that she was equipped with a mainsail, one fore and aft foresail, one stay foresail and one jib.

By the 20th of March, Mr Lotinga had given up all hope of driving down the price of the yacht, and he wrote to the brothers, advising them that he was no longer interested, as he had set his sights on another. By way of not leaving any stone unturned however, they wrote back to him offering to sell him the latest vessel on their stocks which they described as being in every respect, a most beautiful craft; well worthy of the attention of anyone requiring such. Mr Lotinga however, was not interested. On her launch day on the 27th of October 1894, the three-masted iron schooner was christened the *Celtic*.

Having noted that several small craft had recently been bought for use on the Manchester Ship Canal, the brothers wrote to their cousin John Edwards the Liverpool shipbroker, in an effort to persuade him to try and sell the *Saucy Arethusa* on their behalf. Four days later, on the 7th of April, they advised H.E. Moss & Co., also of Liverpool, that their asking price for the yacht was £670. Despite that, and in a last ditch attempt to sell the yacht to Mr Lotinga, who had made another bid for her, they wrote to tell him that they were not disposed to sell the craft for less than £560!

In reply to an enquiry by the Secretary of the Liverpool Underwriters Association on the 12th of April 1894, William Thomas stated that they had no salvage steamers, except for a small yacht of their own which was suitable for towing purposes. They went on to add by way of information, that they possessed everything necessary for diving purposes as well as a dry dock measuring 180 feet by 30 feet in width, with just over $13^1/_2$ feet of water on the sill at high tides.

On the 19th of April, they wrote to thank William Jones of Blucher Street, Liverpool for his enquiry concerning the work he needed doing on his yacht *Miranda*, and offering:

to sheathe the yacht Miranda with your metal, nails, paper etc., including dock dues, caulking labour, pitch and oakum, for one shilling a sheet with forty shillings additional for docking and undocking. The whole cost in connection with the ballast to be paid by you, also the cost of one man to punch the sheets, unless they are already punched. If you decide to bring her here, we should be pleased if you would arrange to bring her at once. We should then dock her without loss of time leaving another vessel we now have in harbour until she would be completed.

When, after a week had elapsed without hearing from him, they realised perhaps that their quoted price had been somewhat steep, and they wrote again to Mr Jones on the pretext that they wanted to know the number of yellow metal sheets he intended to fix on to the *Miranda*, adding that if he had not arranged to have the work placed elsewhere, they would be pleased to re-consider the matter of price! It would appear that Mr Jones had indeed found another yard to carry out the work, for there was no further communication from him which needed a reply.

Negotiations relating to the *Saucy Arethusa*, then took a quite different turn, inasmuch that the brothers had decided that if they could not sell the vessel for a fair and acceptable price, they would hire her out on a time charter. On the 5th of June, they advised Messrs Sampson and Payne of London that they were prepared to entertain a charter for the yacht at £110 per month. A counter offer of £70 a month was dismissed perfunctorily as the owners had already been offered £100 a month for a 2-month-time charter less 5% commission by another broker, but were holding out for £120 a month, with a minimum charter period of 3 months.

On the 28th of August, the yacht was offered to H.E. Moss & Co for £600. This offer was not taken up, and the Thomas brothers went on to re-offer the vessel to their cousin John Edwards; but this time, rigged as a fore and aft schooner, complete with one set of sails, delivered in Liverpool, for £950. It was estimated that, modified in this way, the vessel would be able to carry 60 to 65 tons on a draft of $6^1/_2$ feet.

William Thomas advised James Waugh of Glasgow on the 29th of October, that the *Saucy Arethusa* could be inspected in their graving dock at any time convenient to himself, and although they were asking £650 for her, they would certainly be happy to consider any reasonable counter offer he would wish to make.

In reply to an enquiry, by Jones, Price & Co., of London, about the vessel a month or so later, they were told that the yacht, although in dry dock, was not undergoing repairs, but merely laid up: and that from time to time, the yard required the room she occupied in order to dock vessels undergoing repairs.

Early in 1895, the yacht was offered to Borthwick and Company of Glasgow for £700, and on the 14th of April, she was offered to John Edwards for £750. Why they should have added the extra £50 when dealing with their own cousin is difficult to understand.

On the off chance that business might result, William Thomas wrote to Mr H. Clegg of Plas Llanfair, Anglesey:

> We notice that you have a small steam yacht for sale, and have one ourselves, somewhat larger. Dimensions 72'x12'x7'. It has just struck us that we may bargain, taking yours in part payment… full particulars of which you will find in Lloyd's Yacht Register, and although built in 1882, she has not been in actual service more than six months during the whole time, and if you decide to inspect, you will find that she is not a bit worse than new. She has twin screws, and consequently is very handy to handle… although she was built regardless of cost for her late owner (Mr Birley), we are prepared to dispose of her for a reasonable sum.

Mr Clegg did inspect the vessel, was suitably impressed; but more importantly, was prepared to come to terms. In a further communication with him, William Thomas & Sons said that:

> Subject to approval on inspection of the Kathleen, and a slight modification of the other conditions you name, we will agree to your terms. The boiler to be tested to 130 lbs (pounds per square inch) and not 200 lbs, and as Messrs De Winton and Co., do all our engineering work, we presume that you will have no objection to us employing 'their man' in the presence of your engineer.

There are reasons to believe that 'their man', was none other than the author's great uncle, William Hope, who was then De Winton's foreman boiler maker, and who later bought out the firm in order to establish himself as an engineer in his own right. He and his immediate family went on to provide a high quality engineering service to the north Wales slate quarrying industry; at the same time designing and constructing numerous buoys for use in the Menai Strait by the Caernarfon Harbour Trust.

Arrangements were made at Amlwch to carry out routine maintenance work on the yacht in anticipation of the sale. This involved painting the hull with anti-fouling, and the replacement of a broken windlass casting and chain pipe cover. This done, the brothers wrote to Clegg, advising him that they accepted his yacht in part payment for the *Saucy Arethusa*, the balance of £700 to be paid to them in cash. Gaining £50 more than their lowest asking price, as well as receiving another yacht valued by themselves at £300 in exchange, was beyond their most sanguine expectations, and in their letter to Clegg in Reddish, Stockport, the brothers enclosed the boiler's 'Certificate of Testing', adding that it had been subjected to no fewer than four severe tests during the course of the day, when not a single leak was found.

On the 1st of June 1895, the firm informed Clegg that his vessel would leave their yard as arranged, and that they had insured her for £1000 for the passage from Amlwch to the Menai Strait. Later, acknowledging receipt of his cheque for £700, the brothers noted his adverse comments regarding the *Arethusa's* engines, adding:

> … of course, it must be borne in mind that she has been lying idle for some time, therefore it cannot be expected that the engines would be in the same condition as if constantly under the charge of an engineer, as you had the Kathleen.

Mr Clegg however, continued to be dissatisfied with the *Arethusa's* engines, and was certainly not placated by her former owners' assurances that given time, all would be well. Indeed, he went as far as to have the engines professionally examined by a qualified engineer whose report he sent on to them. This resulted in William Thomas & Sons' reply confessing their surprise:

> at the report upon the engines of the Arethusa, especially the starboard engine, as we always considered this the best of the two, and worked the smoothest. Of course, we did not consider them perfectly modern engines, but thought that in a season or two, your engineer would have them in a fairly perfect condition; but not at anything like the expense the report leads us to believe. We have been considering what might have caused the defect, and can only imagine that when she broke her propeller in the harbour, that possibly her shaft might be slightly bent: but again, if this was so, it would not account for the condition stated in the report, and we cannot but think that the engineer who examined her has overstated the case. If we had any idea that there was anything wrong with her engines, we would in common honesty have informed you before selling. The last time we had her out, both engines worked without a hitch except that in the port engine, there was a slight escape of steam... we extremely regret that the report made is so unfavourable, but trust you do not for a moment think that we in any way attempted to pass her off our hands knowing this.

It would appear that Mr Clegg fully accepted the brothers' contention that they knew nothing of the *Arethusa's* latent problems, for it would appear that no further correspondence passed between them regarding the matter. By way of redressing the balance a little however, the brothers informed Clegg that:

> We propose paying the necessary fee into the Custom House here to get the Board of Trade Surveyor down to measure her, and this of course will be at our expense as we cannot expect you to pay these fees for what should have been previously done.
> P.S. When overhauling the Kathleen, part of her garboard strake, which we think had been put in not very long ago, fell clean out. We mention this as a warning when next having repairs executed, to have them done either by proper men, or look after them carefully, as if it had happened to come off at sea, she could not possibly float many minutes, and probably someone would lose their lives.

The friendship between the brothers and Mr Clegg was not to end there, for on the 6th of May, 1896, confident in their ongoing relationship, they wrote to him regarding another matter entirely:

> A mariner of this port has lately returned home suffering from a severe attack of Rheumatic Fever and other complications, and as he does not appear to be deriving any benefit from the local treatment, he is very anxious to get to the Bangor Infirmary, and as I understand, you are a Subscriber to the Infirmary, I would esteem it a favour if you could send me an order if you have one to spare.

Clegg must have responded immediately, for a week later, they thanked him for his kind assistance on behalf of the 'invalid mariner', and a day later, informed him that the person who had undertaken to pay 2 shillings and 6 pence towards the mariner's treatment was *a highly respected person, being a retired Master Mariner of good means.*

Through the offices of a Mr D. Morris, enquiries were received on behalf of a Mr

Dunlop, who was the manager of the Oakley Slate Quarries in Merionethshire, regarding the possible purchase of the *Saucy Arethusa*. Having advised him of her recent sale, the brothers tried to interest him in the *Kathleen* instead: but he was not in the least interested in her; neither were Messrs De Winton, who had been offered the opportunity to try her under steam before they decided.

In the reply to an enquiry by St Clare Byrne of Liverpool regarding the possible purchase of the yacht, William Thomas & Sons informed him that:

> *Since we purchased this yacht from Mr Clegg, we had her thoroughly overhauled, and spent a large sum in placing her in first class condition, having refurbished her from keel to gunwales. Our price for her as she now stands is £325, less your commission of 5%. Her dimensions are as follows, 46 'x 8' 2" x 5' 6" depth. Engines equal to new, high pressure having 2 cylinders x 14" stroke. Boiler very large, made by Messrs De Winton, Caernarfon, and we think, in 1885 or 1886, but was rebuilt last year... her draught of water is 5 ft aft and about 3¹/₂ ft forwards, and speeds 8 to 9 knots on a very small consumption (of coal). Once steam is up, we have to keep the damper on regularly... the cabin is about 7' 6" with a portable table.*

One further attempt was made to sell the *Kathleen*, and that to Mr Lotinga at an address in London. In their letter, they described the yacht as being in the very best of condition, adding that she had been built expressly for the Marquess of Anglesey. There the story stops unfortunately, for records of further correspondence regarding this matter have not survived.

Having spent a great deal of money in purchasing the *Saucy Arethusa*, Captain Thomas made little or no use of it, which most probably reflected the fact that he was not by then in the best of health. His sons were extremely anxious to rid themselves of the vessel for two reasons, the first and probably the most important, being to free valuable space which it took up in their dry dock, and secondly to liquidise the capital tied up in it which had been lying idle for some considerable time. Although they went on to negotiate what was to prove to be an advantageous deal in the process, thereby realising their second objective, they were nevertheless frustrated in their attempts to free up space in the dry dock until the *Kathleen* was eventually disposed of.

CHAPTER 7
THE 'FIXING' OF THE *CYMRIC*, 1898
"Can you offer us a freight for any safe port at a reasonable rate and on fair terms?"

The Cymric *(background) unlodading barrels of wine in Jersey.*

The process of 'fixing' a commercial vessel embraced all that was necessary to achieve a legally binding agreement relating to the taking up of a cargo at one port and delivering it at another.

Without the benefit of the firm's early letter books it is impossible to determine what use if any, Captain Thomas made of brokers in the early years of his operations. It would appear however, that he more often than not elected to trade between ports where there were regular 'freights in the offing' which were relatively stable, and upon which he could depend. Once there, he used his own judgement to agree any variations on the spot with the consignee, seemingly without the need of a broker. His later strategy of employing dependable, 'pushing' captains who sailed 'by the shares' in the home trade, extended this philosophy by ensuring that each one was highly motivated, and able to conduct the ship's business efficiently, thus ensuring the best for himself as well as the vessel's owner.

The British postal service in the 19th century was clearly very efficient as were businesses themselves, for replies to the great majority of Thomas letters were usually received by return of post. There are several recorded occasions when this ease of communication within the British Isles particularly, was exploited by Willie Thomas when he wrote to Harbourmasters at various small ports, seeking their help and advice concerning cargoes available 'in their neighbourhood', their destination, and the freights then prevailing. Such information was probably freely given at one time; but as similar enquiries multiplied in number as they surely would have, it is thought unlikely that later officials would have been altruistic enough to assist without some thought of recompense – probably making them brokers of a kind in the process.

Conditions in the larger ports such as London and Liverpool with their many independent docks, were a vastly different proposition however, and there, consignees had little choice but to employ specialist brokers to negotiate the lowest freight possible for their cargoes. Services of this nature were probably available in Edward Lloyd's London coffee house towards the end of the 18th century, alongside the shipping intelligence he provided; for such middlemen were aware of who sailed where and when, thereby knowing whom to approach by way of business. Conversely, shipowners would offer their vessels through the same intermediaries.

In his later years, Captain Thomas was certainly making use of R.J. Francis & Co., shipbrokers of Liverpool, whilst his sons Lewis and William appointed brokers in Porto Alegre, Brazil and in Harburg on the Elbe, to conduct their business at those ports for them. Communication with these was frequently by letter, but when business was particularly urgent they would use the international telegraph service.

In a business strategy first instituted by their father, the brothers continued to allow their captains to conduct business on their behalf at various ports of call; but even then, and particularly if communication with those ports was good, they would still telegraph helpful advice to them regarding advancing freight rates, whilst at other times issuing warnings of potential pitfalls.

The fixing of the *Cymric* in the autumn of 1898, some 5 years after Captain Thomas's death, was a very lengthy process indeed, involving over one hundred letters and telegraphic communications with numerous brokers countrywide over a two month period. This was clearly a progression from the original procedure whereby very few people indeed were involved in such negotiations, to one which allowed shipowners to negotiate on a much wider scale in an open market, to their obvious advantage. All of this reflected the greater use then being made of national and international business communication systems, brought about by its steadily falling cost.

From the contents of the letters, mainly written by Willie Thomas, it is very evident that he understood his business thoroughly, and it will be seen that he was prepared to wait in order to achieve an agreement which he considered to be of best advantage to his business; but nevertheless fair to all concerned.

So that the reader can better appreciate the work that went in to a successful 'fixing', and the lengthy sequence of events which led up to it, extracts from each of Thomas's outgoing letters relating to the procedure are recorded below in date order.

The correspondence began on the 26th of August 1898, with a letter to his cousin John Edwards, the Liverpool ship broker:

We are daily expecting this vessel's arrival on the Conway, have you anything to offer her for the Mersey?

29th August to Morgan Richards & Co., 110 Fenchurch Street, London:

Your favour of the 29th inst. to hand, and we note contents. We do not however feel inclined to offer this vessel at the rate you mention, as we hope to secure something better than 25/- for coal. This vessel is now at Holyhead awaiting water to get to Conway.

2nd September to John I. Jacobs & Co., 14 St Mary Axe, London:

This vessel has now arrived at Conway, but have not yet fixed her outwards, so pleased to know if you can offer her a paying freight.

2nd September to Morgan Richards & Co:

We shall be pleased to know the best you can now offer this vessel.

2nd September to H. Richards, Lloyds Agent, Caernarvon:

This vessel has arrived at Conway. Can you offer her an outward freight cargo?

5th September to J. I. Jacobs:

We thank you for your favour of the 3rd inst., but we do not think there is any chance of us coming to business with the Gallegos round on the Terms of Charter furnished us, as we should want alterations which we fear your friends would not agree to. Principally, we should require the cargo to be taken to and from alongside, free, and a number of days stipulated for discharging and loading alongside. The stowing to be done by Shippers with the assistance of the crew. Neither would we agree to a cancelling date for the homeward cargo. Can you not offer us another round charter on fair terms and rate? Is there nothing offering to Maracaibo and home, or Nickerie with sugar home. If you can offer us anything like this, we shall be pleased to hear from you.

5th September to H. Richards:

Replying to your favour of the 3rd inst., we beg to state that this vessel carries 370/380 tons on 11 ft (draft), and should be very pleased if you could offer us a suitable cargo of slates from the Straits (sic), to the Elbe preferably, but of course, we are not tied to this. Even Stettin at a fair rate, we would entertain. If you cannot secure her a cargo for one port, you might arrange to discharge at two ports.

5th September to Morgan Richards & Co:

We thank you for your telegram of this day, but we do not care to fix for Rio Grande just now as it is rather a bad time of the year to secure a freight homewards. With regard to Goalzacoalcos, this has been offered to us some time ago by your neighbours, but our Policy of Insurance prohibits us from going there. Can you not offer us a freight to the West Indies? We once took a cargo to Nickerie and back to London, and if a fair rate was obtainable, we would entertain this, or say, a round cargo to Maracaibo?

5th September to Matthews and Luff, 52, Leadenhall Street, London:

This vessel has arrived at Conway. Can you offer us a freight for any safe port at a reasonable rate and on fair terms. We should not care to send her to Rio Grande just now as it is rather early in the season for our purpose. Can you offer us a round freight to Nickerie or Maracaibo?

6th September to H. Richards:

We confirm wires exchange between us this day. We consider 15/- a ton for Gibraltar at this time of the year to be not a fair rate as the wear and tear would be considerable.

6th September to R. Owen, Harbour Office, Caernarvon (sic):

Can you offer this vessel a cargo for Hamburg or other safe port?

7th September to J. I. Jacobs:

We thank you for your favour of yesterday, and note all you write. We should be pleased if we could agree about the Gallegos freight, but we fear there is no chance whatever upon the terms of the Charter you sent us, as according to that, the vessel might be kept there for six months or more. If your friends would agree to insert a clause that the cargoes are to be taken to and from alongside free, and a reasonable number of days for loading and discharging, then we have no doubt but we could come to terms.

8th September to Morgan Richards & Co:

We thank you for your favour of yesterday which crossed ours of same date. With regard to the Port Gallegos freight, this has been offered us some time ago by your neighbours, but the conditions of the Charter are such that we would not entertain it for a moment.

9th September to Matthews and Luff:

We thank you for your telegram of this day offering a freight of 9/- for this vessel from Cardiff to Tangiers (sic) and 3/6 p/qr from Larochel (sic). We cannot however, make out where this place is, therefore we do not know what kind of place it is, we therefore await your news in the morning, as it may be an error in the transmission of the telegram. In any event, we don't much care to go to Cardiff to load outwards and should like to know if you could arrange Mersey loading.

9th September to Jones, Price & Co., 1, Church Court, Clement's Lane, London:

We thank you for your favour of yesterday. Our idea was to take out a cargo either to Cadiz direct or some adjacent port, whichever would be most suitable. The rate of freight however which you offer to Rio Grande is less than we have already been offered.

9th September to John Edwards & Co:

We thank you for your wire of this day. The rate of 7/- p. ton for pitch Garston to Cadiz is out of the question, as we will not entertain it at anything like the rate. The rate to Gibraltar is also very low considering the season of the year when strong weather may at any time set in. We thought you might get 9/6 for Gib.

10th September to Matthews and Luff:

Your favour of yesterday to hand. As stated in ours of yesterday, our Underwriters will not allow us to go to St Johns at this time of the year, so this business must be considered off. We wait to hear whether you can arrange to load the Tangier cargo at Garston or Liverpool, as we do not like the idea of going light to Cardiff.

10th September to J. I. Jacobs & Co:

We thank you for your favour of yesterday. We prefer to lose the Gallegos freight than accept the terms of the Charter sent us. Would you care to charter this vessel by the month for this round at a fair rate?

10th September to H. Richards:

If you have not already written respecting the Gibraltar freight, will you please wire us first thing on Monday morning whether she is accepted or not, as we are offered another freight which we fear to lose.

10th September to Jones, Price & Co:

Your wire to hand. We hope to see the Captain of this vessel on Monday, and will consult him about the freight offered, as he sails the vessel by shares.

12th September to J. I. Jacobs:

We thank you for your wired reply to our offer of this vessel at £125 per month, but your counter offer is out of the question altogether as we can secure much better employment than you propose, and if you cannot improve considerably on your offer, it is only a waste of time to correspond. We thought that in naming £125 that we had named a very reasonable figure as this is under her average earnings since she is out. You must bear in mind that crew's wages and victualling alone, runs over £50 per month. To this has to be added the insurance, so you will see that we would not get very much towards wear and tear, and profit. The very best we could do is £120 less 2% chartering commission or £125 less 5%, Charterers to pay all charges home and abroad except as stated; crews wages, victuals etc. Less than this we will not take.
The vessel is now at Conway already discharged with ballast on board, so if your friends cannot see their way clear to accept the above terms by 1 pm tomorrow, we shall fix her for another cargo which is offering.

13th September to Jones, Price & Co:

Your favour of yesterday to hand. We regret not being able to make you an offer for the Cadiz – Rio Grande business, but we hope to write to you definitely in a post or two. We notice the coal freights Cardiff to Rio Grande or Pelotas have advanced 2/- per ton, and presume the Cadiz freights will be in proportion.

13th September to H. Richards:

We thank you for your favour of yesterday, but regret that we did not hear from you by wire today. We have however kept the other freight offered us in hand until we have your reply which we hope to receive tomorrow.

13th September to Matthews and Luff:

Your favour of yesterday to hand. The rate you offer from the Mersey to Gibraltar is a very low one considering the time of the year to cross the Bay of Biscay. Apart from either the Tangiers (sic) or the Gibraltar freight, what is the outside rate you could offer for Larochel (sic). We may be able to secure a better outward freight than you quote.

14th September to J. I. Jacobs:

Your favour of yesterday to hand, and after careful calculation, we wired you that £115 per month nett is absolutely the lowest we could accept for this vessel, as anything below this figure would mean that we should have no return on capital. The last general cargo she had on board was 467 tons W&M. Her D.W . is 370/380 tons.

15th Sept to Matthews and Luff:

We were absent when your wire was received yesterday. We are negotiating for a cargo of slates for this vessel, and if it comes through, we will let you know. We cannot accept the Huelva round, as we should be compelled to go to the expense of fitting her with a platform, which would not pay us.

15th September to Jones, Price & Co:

It being a general holiday here yesterday, we were absent from the office, and we did not get your wire of yesterday until it was too late to reply. Our idea of rate for the Cadiz freight are so wide apart that we did not consider it worthwhile wiring you today. You are offering much less than other brokers, besides we can secure 27/- from Cardiff with coal, as this has been offered us firm, and declined, and we consider 27/- with coal much better than the same rate with salt. However, we are negotiating for a cargo for Gibraltar, back with grain from the coast of Morocco, and we think that this will pay us as good as anything.

15th September to J. I. Jacobs:

We thank you for your favour of yesterday, and telegram of this day; but we do not see the slightest chance of coming to terms for the Gallegos round on the Conditions of Charter you sent us, as we will not on any account take the risk to land and ship your cargo, as this is an unusual thing for a ship to do. If charterers would agree to the insertion of a clause that the cargo is to be brought and taken from alongside at Merchant's risk and expense, and in the event of it being more than 9 months on the voyage, they will pay £115 per month, then we might come to terms, but otherwise there is not the slightest chance. We know what she will earn on her regular trade, and we wont accept risks which charterers ought to bear. Our own risk is sufficient for us.

15th September to John Edwards & Co:

We thank you for your wire of today asking for the offer of this vessel Garston to Gibraltar at 9/- and 63/- gratuity , but we regret that we cannot at the moment make you an offer, as we are negotiating for a cargo of slates. If this falls through, and we find any inducement by going to Gibraltar, we will advise you.

15th September to H. Richards:

We thank you for your postcard of yesterday, and hope to hear from you tomorrow with a final reply respecting the Gibraltar cargo.

16th September to Coppack, Carter & Co., Ship Brokers, Connah's Quay:

This vessel is still unfixed, but we do not care for any of the freights you quote. The Copenhagen one is the most likely, but it is rather too late in the season to go there. Have you nothing offering for the Elbe or a French port, with a good rate?

16th September to H. Richards:

We thank you for your wire of this day, and note that the freight to Gibraltar has fallen through. If you have any other suitable freight to offer, we shall be pleased to hear from you.

16th September to John Vickers, Ship Broker, Connah's Quay:

We confirm wire sent to you this afternoon, and now await your reply whether you can work the Dunkirk freight quoted in your p/card of yesterday, up to 11/6 per ton. The vessel is now at Conway, ready to leave for yours at once.

!6th September to John Edwards & Co:

We thank you for your wire reply to ours respecting the Gibraltar freight. We expect Captain Jones to call here tomorrow morning, and will consult him respecting the rate advised you.

17th September to John Edwards & Co:

We confirm wire sent you this morning as per enclosed copy, and hope to hear from you that your friends have cabled the offer of this vessel @ 9/3 and 63/- gratuity.

17th September to Jones, Price & Co:

We are arranging to load the Cymric for Gibraltar, but before finally closing for the homeward cargo from the coast of Morocco we wired you this morning offering to accept 28/- Cadiz to Rio Grande or Pelotas with usual gratuity, and subject to approval of Charter. We hope to receive your reply by noon on Monday, as we cannot keep her open indefinitely for fear of losing both.

19th September to Jones, Price & Co:

We thank you for your favour of the 17th inst., and now beg to offer you this vessel on terms of enclosed Charter, which we think you will consider fair for both parties. In fact, they are the same conditions as we obtained with coal from Cardiff for both this vessel and the Celtic, and we have just received a telegraphic offer to take her up again on the same conditions, but with an advance of 6d per ton on freight. This is firm, and can be fixed off at once. Kindly advise us as early as possible if accepted. Will you please say what you will pay us if we sent her out direct in ballast?

19th September to E. Jones & Co., Mount Stuart Square, Cardiff:

We thank you for your telegram of this day. We cannot offer you this vessel for the Rio Grande freight, as we are in negotiation for another cargo. Can you offer us a cargo from one of the Bristol Channel ports to either Cadiz or Gibraltar at a fair rate?

19th September to John Edwards & Co.,

We confirm wires passed between us this day, and now await to hear whether she is accepted at 7/6 and £5-5-0 gratuity for the pitch cargo Garston to Cadiz. This is a very low rate considering the cargo to be carried and the season of the year. If this is unobtainable, or an increase in the Gib freight, we shall see what can be got from the Bristol Channel, but trust you will be able to secure this 7/6 freight. We shall of course have to approve the Charter before closing, as we must be protected against war and other dues.

22nd September to Jones, Price & Co:

Your favour of yesterday to hand and note contents. We were in hopes that as you were Charters' Agents, that we might obtain full benefit of a freight and conditions, but it now appears that you can do neither, and for your information, we may mention that we have positively declined 27/6 Cadiz to Pelotas and good terms of charter, further a vessel was fixed yesterday with coals from Cardiff at 26/6 with £5-5-0 gratuity. We asked for no special terms except the commission which we would allow as usual, but other conditions we have had before, and which we know through experience should be inserted, and which are only fair for both sides. If you will take her up on terms of enclosed Charter, please wire us tomorrow. We are invited to offer Cardiff to Rio Grand or Pelotas at 127/- and 35-5-0 gratuity.

22nd September to Matthews and Luff:

We were away from home yesterday, otherwise we should have acknowledged receipt of your telegram offering us the Cadiz Pelotas freight. The rate you offer to go out in ballast is too low, if you could offer us say 31/6 we might entertain it, though we should prefer 28/- with liberty to take cargo to say Cadiz directly.

22nd September to John Edwards & Co:

We were absent from home yesterday, otherwise your telegram would have been acknowledged last evening. The rate you offer is much lower than we have been offered, and declined, but we are in hopes of securing even a higher figure. What about the pitch freight to Cadiz; have you not induced merchants to improve upon their late offer?

22nd September E. Jones & Co:

Your favour of yesterday to hand. If any London brokers have offered this vessel for the coal freight, they have done so without our authority, as we have only offered her for the Cadiz / Pelotas cargo, which we regret to say has fallen through, but we do not care for the idea of going light to Cardiff.

23rd September to J. I. Jacobs:

We thank you for your favour of yesterday. There is not the remotest chance of coming to business for the Gallegos round freight except on one of two conditions. Either that Charterers agree to insert a clause that the cargo is to be brought to and taken from alongside at their risk and expense; or that they will charter her by the month at the rate quoted, which we consider a very reasonable rate, but to meet you we will allow you the usual chartering commission from the £115 stated, which could reduce it to £111-6-6, below which we shall not for a moment entertain. We may state that we are in close treaty for a cargo to Rio Grande, so above offer is made subject to being unfixed on receipt of your acceptance.

23rd September to E. Jones & Co:

We are in due receipt of your telegram of this day, but we regret we cannot offer you this vessel for the Tangier cargo as we have already declined 11/- for the same port, and this solely because we do not want to go to Cardiff to load. Of course, if we fail to get anything suitable, we shall be glad to fall back upon the Bristol Channel. The rate of 25/6 with coal is out of the question as the 'Maggie Williams' has been fixed at 26/6 and we were in hopes that freights were advancing instead of declining. Can the Rio Grande coal cargo be loaded at any other Bristol Channel port besides Cardiff, say Swansea, as we may be able to secure a cargo for this port.

23rd September to Matthews and Luff:

Your letter of yesterday to hand, crossing ours of same date which will explain why your communications were not replied to earlier. The slate cargo to Gibraltar has unfortunately fallen through, but if anyone has offered this vessel for the Cardiff / Rio Grande business, they have done so on their own responsibility without our authority. With reference to your wire, the lowest we will accept for Cadiz to Rio Grande or Pelotas is 28/-, free lighterage, and with liberty to take cargo on the way out. The salt business has been offered us first of all by your neighbours who are old friends of ours, and until they fail to secure this rate, we should not leave them.

23rd September to Coppack, Carter & Co:

We thank you for your favour of yesterday, but we regret we cannot offer you this vessel at present, as we are in close treaty for another freight. Should we however, be open later on, we shall not fail to communicate with you.

24th September to R. Owen:

We thank you for your P/C to hand this morning, but 270 tons is much too small a quantity for this vessel. If you can increase it to 350/360 tons, we would entertain.

26th September to Coppack, Carter & Co:

If you can offer us a cargo from yours to Cardiff, we shall be pleased to hear from you. We presume you do ship pitch to Cardiff as well as Swansea.

26th September to Matthews and Luff:

Your favour dated 23rd inst. only came to hand this morning. If you can obtain 28/- and 105/- gratuity Cadiz to Pelotas, we shall be pleased to hear from you as early as possible, as there is every chance of securing a cargo direct to Cadiz from the Mersey. This would be quite as quick as going out in ballast.

27th September to E. Jones & Co:

We thank you for your telegram of this day, but very much regret to state that we had just previous to its receipt, offered this vessel for a cargo of salt from Cadiz. Should this fall through, we will communicate with you at once.

27th September to Matthews and Luff:

We confirm telegrams passed between us this day. We now await yours in the morning with copy of Charter for our approval.

27th September to John Edwards & Co:

We confirm our wire of this day, offering you this vessel for the Garston / Cadiz cargo at 7/3 per ton subject to approval of Charter, when we hope, business will result.

28th September to E. Jones & Co:

We are much obliged for your favour of yesterday. As already advised you, this vessel is under offer to proceed to Cadiz to load salt for Pelotas, but we have every reason to fear that the Charterers will not give us the terms we are asking, although they have agreed on the rate. We are trying to secure a cargo for Cardiff in anticipation of the Cadiz business falling through, but we very much fear we shall not succeed in securing a cargo for your port, but we can fix right off for Swansea. Could you not secure us the same rate and conditions from Swansea as the 'Maggie Williams' got from Newport. That is if we fail to induce merchants to take her up for Cardiff. We shall know definitely at noon tomorrow whether Charterers accept our terms for the Cadiz business.

28th September to Coppack, Carter & Co:

We thank you for your favour of yesterday, and note that you are trying to work this vessel for Cardiff and hope to hear that you have succeeded, but in the event of you failing to do so, could you offer her a cargo for Cadiz at a fair rate? We should of course prefer Cardiff, and we know that a great quantify of pitch is shipped to that port.

28th September to Matthews and Luff:

Your favour of yesterday with 'pro forma' charter to hand. We did not wire you as we would not on any account accept the proposed terms. In yours of the 23rd inst., you state that it was to be free lighterage, but it was not down in your Charter. We return the Charter with alterations in red ink, which are the terms we will accept, and if unobtainable, we prefer to lose the business. We may however state that the conditions inserted are the same as we fixed the last two cargoes, and we shall be pleased to receive confirmation if they are accepted on our terms.

28th September to John Edwards & Co:

We thank you for your telegram of this day, but regret that there is no cargo to go to Cadiz. At the moment we cannot offer for the Gibraltar freight as we are awaiting a reply respecting another freight.

29th September to Matthews and Luff:

We are in receipt of your telegram stating that Charterers have agreed to some of our additions, and we now await your letter in the morning to know what these are. We do not consider that we inserted anything but was fair to both sides, and they are conditions we have already had.

30th September to Matthews and Luff:

Your long letter of yesterday to hand. We altered the form of Charter you sent us in the full expectation that Charterers would have agreed to them, as we inserted nothing but what was fair to them and us, and we know from experience that they are necessary, otherwise we should not ask them, and if Charterers mean what they say, what objection can they have to insertion in the Charter. However, as they will not agree, they must look out for some other vessel to take their cargo, as we will not.

30th September to Coppack, Carter & Co:

We are negotiating an outward freight from Swansea for this vessel, and in the event of fixing, can you secure us the pitch cargo from yours to Swansea?

PS. Can you fix for the Swan sea cargo subject to us securing an outward freight from Swansea?

30th September to Jones, Price & Co:

In reply to your favour of yesterday, we beg to say that Charterers agreed to pay us 27/6 but we could not agree on conditions. We are therefore in close treaty for another cargo.

1st October to E. Jones & Co:

We thank you for your favour of yesterday, contents of which we note, and hope to hear from you on Monday that this vessel has been accepted, and with a view of closing the business as soon as a reply is received, we return the pro forma Charter with three slight alterations viz; Draft altered to 10³/₄ ft Mean Draught, and balance of freight to be paid at Bank Rate instead of Current Rate. The Cancelling Clause we have altered to give the vessel liberty to take a cargo to Swansea direct. This will give her a better chance of making a passage and we hope Charterers will agree to these slight alterations.

3rd October to E. Jones & Co:

We are in due receipt of your favour of Saturday and telegram of this day, by which we regret to learn that no reply has yet been received respecting the Swansea / Pelotas freight altho' we presume it is not definitely off. We will therefore wait until tomorrow to see if a reply comes, as we do not see our way clear to send her in ballast to Cardiff, and so far we have failed to get a cargo for this port, and very little prospects either of getting one, but for Swansea we can fix right off. If you can possibly arrange to load the Rio Grande cargo at Swansea, we shall be pleased to hear from you. If not, and nothing comes of it, we have a salt freight in view.

3rd October to Coppack, Carter & Co:

If there is any prospect of securing a cargo for Cardiff or Cadiz, will you please pass us a wire tomorrow?

4th October to Morgan Richards & Co:

We shall be pleased to know whether you can offer us a freight from Garston to Rio Grande for this vessel, at a fair price?

4th October to E. Jones & Co:

We thank you for your favour of yesterday and telegram of today. The rate you offer from Swansea is altogether out of the question. If you had succeeded in getting 25/-, we might have come to business. It will be better for us to accept this figure from the Mersey, and failing the Pelotas freight coming through, we shall to try and secure something else.

PS. Can you not induce your friends to Cablegram Pelotas?

4th October to Jones, Price & Co:

We thank you for your favour, but we do not at present feel inclined to offer you this vessel at the rate and conditions you offer.

5th October to Matthews and Luff:

Your favour of yesterday to hand. The 10 feet lighterage is no value to us, as the vessel only draws fully laden about 10 ft 9 ins mean. We have just received your telegram, but we will not go out in ballast without more inducement than you offer. Can you not offer us a cargo from the Mersey or a cargo for Aracaju from the Bristol Channel?

5th October to E. Jones & Co:

Your favour of yesterday to hand. As stated in ours of yesterday, we are not prepared top accept 23/- from Swansea. We hope to hear that you have got your friends to repeat the cable to Pelotas. Can you offer us anything for Aracaju?

6th October to Jones, Price & Co:

We thank you for your favour of yesterday, the contents of which we note. As far as we are concerned, steamers are quite welcome to the Cadiz – Rio Grande business, but we are certain that they must have better despatch than any sailing vessel ever got, besides they cannot go to Pelotas without lightening almost the whole of their cargo. You do not offer as good a rate as the Maggie Williams got for Pelotas (26/-), and we can fix at the same rate from Cardiff, but we don't like the idea of going there in ballast. Will you pay 27/- for Rio Grande direct, without the option of Pelotas, and allow us to take a cargo out on our way?

6th October to Morgan Richards & Co:

We thank you for your favour of yesterday with pro forma Charter Garston / Rio Grande which we return herewith with slight alterations, the principle of which is the clause relating to Pelotas. If however, the Merchants do not care to remove this, we are quite prepared to go to Pelotas provided they will agree to lighten the vessel at San Jose do Norte instead of Rio Grande, and this at their risk and expense. Under the wording of the Charter, they would have the power to send her to Rio Grande to discharge a portion, and then order her to Pelotas to finish. We have known this to happen. They no doubt know which of the two places the cargo is for, but if not, we are quite agreeable to a clause as follows: Vessel to proceed to San Jose do Norte for orders, which are to be given within 24 hours, to discharge at Rio Grande or Pelotas, one port only. All lighterage necessary to enable vessel to proceed to Pelotas, to be done at San Jose at Merchants' risk and expense, and time occupied in lightening to count as lay days, but not the time consumed in shifting. The above are what we have obtained in the last two Charters from (undecipherable) We shall be pleased of a wire tomorrow, if entertained on these terms.

6th October to E. Jones & Co:

We thank you for your favour to hand this morning. As you cannot arrange Swansea loading, we are trying to secure a freight from the Mersey, as the expense of shifting in ballast to Cardiff is very heavy.

7th October to E. Jones & Co:

We thank you for your favour of yesterday, and note all you state. We cannot entertain the Mogador freight as our insurance policies prohibit us going to the coast of Morocco this season of the year, further we would have to go to your port in ballast, and this is what we wish to avoid.

7th October to Matthews and Luff:

Your favour of yesterday and telegram of this day to hand, but we regret that we cannot entertain the Mogador freight as we are prohibited by our insurance policies from the coast of Morocco during this season of the year. We may state that this freight had been offered us from Cardiff before we got your telegram.

7th October to W. H. Stott & Co, 17 Fenwick Street, Liverpool:

We thank you for your favour of yesterday, but 27/- for general cargo is a very low rate considering the heavy expense attached to it. Therefore we prefer trying something else, but we don't care to go to Cardiff in ballast.

8th October to Jones, Price & Co:

We thank you for your favour of yesterday, contents of which we note. If you think there is any prospect of business resulting, we should be pleased if you would cable on Monday to your Principals, offering this vessel at 27/- with £5-5-0 gratuity from Cadiz to Rio Grande direct, as we are now offered a general cargo from the Mersey. The only clause we should require altering in your Charter, in the event of her acceptance for this port direct, would be 25 running days for discharging, instead of working days, and you will agree that we are allowing ample time for doing the work. We think we can secure a cargo on our way to Cadiz, so we would want this liberty inserted in the Charter. Kindly write us on Monday if you decide to cable, so that we may not treat for anything else.

PS Even if you wanted to go to Pelotas, it would pay you to give her 2/- a ton more freight than ordinary vessels, as she only draws loaded about $10^3/_4$ feet mean, so the expense of lighterage would only be small comparatively.

8th October to John Edwards & Co:

We thank you for your telegram of this day. We are already in negotiation about a freight from Cadiz, tho' we are not bound to any offer, still we do not like to cast those who have gone to so much trouble and expense on one side until they have had a fair trial and failed. With regard to the general cargo, we would not entertain it on any account at the rate quoted, as they are paying 26/6 with coals from Cardiff, and we are offered this morning 25/- from Garston to Rio Grande or Pelotas. If your friends would pay £650 lump sum for Rio Grande direct with £70 extra Porto Alegre, we would accept, though we are not over anxious for it. If we secure our rate and terms for Cadiz, we hope you will be able to secure us a freight from the Mersey to either Cardiff direct, or Gib.

8th October to E. Jones & Co:

We beg to own receipt of your favour of the 7th inst. As the freight from Swansea to Rio Grande is not yet ripe, we will wait until it is more so.

8th October to Morgan Richards:

We thank you for your favour of yesterday, but regret that your friends can not arrange lighterage at San Jose, to go to Rio Grande or Pelotas means double expense and loss of time, so we prefer losing the business than accept these terms. With regard to the Cadiz / Pelotas freight, we have already been in treaty for this business, but failed to agree on terms of Charter.

10th October to W. H. Stott & Co:

We thank you for your favour of the 8th inst. And telegram of today. This vessel is under offer since Saturday last, so we cannot say anything with regard to the outward cargo. We prefer taking the risk of an improvement in homeward freights in preference to accepting 26/- for hides, as this rate is very low. If however 32/6 was available, we would close, provided the quantity would not be less than 11,000 heavy Ox hides.

10th October to Matthews and Luff:

Your favour of the 8th inst. to hand. This vessel is now under offer for Rio Grande direct.

10th October to Jones, Price & Co:

We thank you for your telegram of this day, and hope to hear from you in the morning that this vessel is accepted for Rio Grande direct.

11th October to E. Jones & Co:

We confirm messages passed between us this day, and regret that Merchants will not pay 25/- Swansea to Pelotas, and for less, we are not prepared to accept.

11th October to Jones, Price & Co:

We have your wire, and regret Merchants will not accept our terms, in which case we must look for something more suitable for this vessel.

14th October to Coppack, Carter & Co:

Can you fix this vessel from Connah's Quay to Swansea. If so, please wire us in the morning as we are closely treating for an outward cargo from Swansea.

14th October to E. Jones & Co:

We have yours of yesterday and observe. We are trying to secure this vessel a cargo for Swansea, and if fixed, will let you know later on.

18th October to E. Brown & Co., 22 Great St Helen's, London:

The offer your client makes for this vessel is quite out of the question, having already refused a considerably higher figure. Perhaps your friends are not aware that this is an extra built craft.

19th October to W. H. Stott & Co:

We confirm wires passed between us this day, and hope to hear from you in the morning that this vessel is accepted @ 29/6 Cadiz to Rio Grande or Pelotas, with free lighterage and usual gratuity, and with liberty to take out a cargo on our way. We note you quote 8/- for Gibraltar, but 9/- and 63/- gratuity has been mentioned to us, and we presume you will be able to secure this in the event of the salt cargo being secured.

19th October to Matthews and Luff:

Your wire of this morning to hand, but we will not accept 25/6 from Cardiff to Rio Grande as our offer was at 26/- with £5-5-0 gratuity. As this offer has not been accepted, we consider that we are free.

21st October to Matthews and Luff:

When you failed to get the 26/- for coal Cardiff to Rio Grande direct, we were offered a good rate for salt from Cadiz to Pelotas, and that is still under consideration, so we cannot at the moment offer her to you.

21st October to W. H. Stott & Co:

As we have not heard from you by wire today, we conclude that you have not had any news from your friends. You, of course, understand that we are not bound to our offer any longer, so that if any other suitable freight turns out, we are at liberty to accept. If you have any news tomorrow, we shall be pleased to hear from you.

22nd October to W. H. Stott & Co:

We now confirm telegram sent you this morning offering to accept 28/6 for this vessel Cadiz to Rio Grande or Pelotas, free lighterage and with liberty to take a cargo on our way out. To send her in ballast this time of the year, would mean a much longer time to make her passage than if loaded, as she is such a shallow vessel she would make very little to windward with contrary winds. We cannot agree to be bound down to time for leaving the Mersey, but for our own sakes, we would naturally push her on as much as possible. It is quite possible we may secure a cargo for Cadiz direct. Can you not offer us a cargo of pitch for there as we understand that this is shipped very frequently from the Mersey. Please wire us on Monday if she is accepted on the above terms.

22nd October to Matthews and Luff:

We are in due receipt of your telegram of this morning, but regret we could not wire you the offer of this vessel as she was in other hands at an advanced rate

24th October to W. H. Stott & Co

We confirm wires passed between us this day, and now await Charter for our approval. You may depend that if the vessel is fixed, we shall do our utmost to despatch her away as soon as possible.

24th October to Jones, Price & Co:

We beg to own receipt of your letter of the 22nd inst., and to state that this vessel is now under offer with every prospect of coming through.

25th October to W. H. Stott & Co:

We are in receipt of your favour of yesterday, and two wires of today, and note that you are posting Charter tonight.

26th October to W. H. Stott & Co:

Your favour of yesterday to hand with pro forma Charter. After perusing same, we wired you that we insisted on free lighterage clauses, and now confirm wires passed between us in the course of the day.

We return the Charter with alterations and additions we require before accepting Charter, and we are sure you will agree that we are not asking anything but what is fair and reasonable. For the Charterers to say that they mean all these things is not sufficient for us, they must be inserted, and if they do mean them, they can have no objection to their insertion. We have only inserted what we know through experience are required in the trade. Will you kindly wire us tomorrow morning if they agree to our terms. In any event, you may offer her Garston to Gibraltar at 10/- per ton with £3-3-0 gratuity subject to our approval of Charter, and shall be pleased to hear the result as early as possible.

26th October to Jones, Price & Co:

In reply to your favour of yesterday, we beg to state that we are sending this vessel to Gibraltar with coal from the Mersey, and if we fail to secure a suitable freight from Cadiz to Rio Grande or Pelotas, we can obtain a cargo from the coast of Morocco home, but we are now offered 28/6 firm for the salt business, but we have an idea by the time she is ready to leave Gib., that higher rates will be paid.

26th October to E. Jones & Co:

We intend sending this vessel to Gibraltar from the Mersey in the hope that by the time she arrives out, that we shall secure a good freight from Cadiz.

26th October to Matthews and Luff:

As this vessel is now under a firm offer, we cannot do anything until we know the result.

27th October to W. H. Stott & Co:

We regret to learn from your wires that the Charters will not agree to any of the alterations we made in the Charter, we can only therefore repeat what we stated in our telegram, that if they will not, we prefer to lose the business. We have asked for nothing unreasonable, and further, they are terms which we have had in coal Charters from Cardiff for both Cymric and Celtic. We cannot understand why they decline the insertion of what they say they mean, it leads us to think that they do not mean what they say . However, if they do not agree to the insertion of the clause, we will let the matter drop, but if 10/- is obtainable in terms of enclosed Charter for Gibraltar, we will accept it, so trust you will succeed in getting it tho' in this case also. We have only struck out clauses to make it similar to our last Charters to Gib.

28th October to W. H. Stott & Co:

We very much regret to find by your telegram, that Charterers are insisting upon unusual conditions in the Gibraltar Charter. To meet these they ought to increase their freight. We are not very particular whether we receive this freight or not, as we can secure 12/6 for Tangiers (sic) from Cardiff, but if your friends will pay a reasonable rate to meet the conditions of their Charter, we shall be pleased to accept it, otherwise we are quite agreeable for a steamer to have it, tho' we feel confident that they will have to pay a much higher rate for a steamer to go to (undecipherable – probably Biscay) Bay. Would Charterers not agree to 9/6 per ton if we allowed the 2% address commission and the $^1/_4$d p. reg ton for every day the vessel would be at the Gas Co's wharf discharging?

29th October to W. H. Stott & Co:

We beg to own receipt of your favour of yesterday, contents of which we carefully note. We are pleased to learn from your last telegram of today that our conditions for the Cadiz to Rio Grande cargo has been accepted, and we hope to hear from you on Monday that you have succeeded in inducing your friends to pay 9/- for the Gib. Cargo from High Level.

31st October to W. H. Stott & Co:

We are very pleased to learn by your telegram of this morning that this vessel is fixed for the Gib cargo at 9/- from Liverpool, and we notice you stipulate 2¹/₂% address commission instead of 2% as originally required. This, we presume is an error, and we rely that you will put this in order. We shall now push on as much as possible to get the vessel loaded. For this purpose we shall be very pleased if you will wire us tomorrow the lowest rate you can get a tug to tow her from Conway to Liverpool as she will have to dock for cleaning and painting. We shall exercise the option of Liverpool loading. Will you kindly furnish us with a name and address of firms who undertake this kind of work to enable us to communicate with them without loss of time. We shall also be glad if you will be good enough to make enquiries at what price you can dispose of 40 to 80 tons of fresh water sand ballast which is on board. We return the salt Charter duly signed. The Cocks tugs have generally done our towage, and we find that they have been the cheapest as a rule. After arranging the rate, the Captain will wire you when to send the tug down. Kindly send us copies of Charters and oblige, Yours truly, Wm Thomas & Sons.

CHAPTER 8
THE *MARY ASHBURNER* – A DETECTIVE STORY
"we have no news whatever of this vessel since she sailed"

The correspondence brought about by the loss within a few weeks of each other, of the 2 schooners *Mary Ashburner* and *Harvest Home*, reveals a great deal about the personality of William Thomas, who had shares in both.

His thoroughness and tenacity in pursuing, in almost classic detective fashion, the loss with all hands of the former, are revealed in his letters; as is his undisputable knowledge of the many aspects of his profession. Also demonstrated in the case of the latter vessel, is his compassion towards a Master who had lost his ship through what could well be construed as bad seamanship: a similar spark of compassion and understanding as had been shown by his father towards the Master of the *Elizabeth Anne* some 20 years earlier when he told him that he should not fear the consequences of any misfortune which befell him, provided that he was conscientiously carrying out his duties at the time.

The circumstances under which the 2 vessels were lost could hardly have been different, inasmuch that a great deal of mystery surrounded the loss of the *Mary Ashburner*, simply because both vessel and crew vanished without trace: a matter which did not arise in the case of the *Harvest Home*, the crew of which fortunately survived the ordeal.

The schooner Mary Ashburner

The 106 ton, two-masted schooner *Mary Ashburner*, was built regardless of cost by William Ashburner at his Barrow-in-Furness yard in 1887, for his own use. Constructed mainly of hardwood to Lloyd's Special Survey standards, she represented all that was best in contemporary wooden shipbuilding.

Her ageing owner had in many ways neglected her maintenance over the last few years she was in his ownership, and when she was bought by William Thomas at an auction held in Connah's Quay on the 13th of November, 1908, her condition was far below that in which he maintained his own vessels. He was, as might be expected, a remarkably shrewd buyer when it came to ships, and the fact that having already paid £1190 for what was a relatively old vessel, he went on to spend a further £593 in bringing her up to his own exacting standards, spoke volumes about the quality of her construction.

The vessel's new owner was constantly on the lookout for ships which were basically sound, but in need of a refit, which he could undertake very efficiently and profitably in his own yard. In this respect, his considerable knowledge of vessels in the British coastal trade, sometimes gained through having had them in his yard for repairs, was invaluable when they came up for sale.

Ship sales were widely advertised and well attended; but his interest in the *Mary Ashburner* may originally have been kindled by her Captain, John Hughes, an Amlwch man, who had been her Captain for all but one of her 32 years. He had a hard-won reputation as a diligent and efficient Master, a view clearly shared by William Thomas, who allowed him to retain command of the vessel when he bought her.

The 79 ton schooner, owned in equal shares by William Thomas and his nephew John, was managed by the former for an annual fee of £6. Under his expert supervision, the vessel was mainly employed in the china-clay trade, taking coal and general cargo from the Mersey to several West Country ports, and returning to Runcorn with clay from Cornwall.

It was from the Cornish port of Charlestown that she sailed in the late afternoon of 25th November 1913, with a total of five crew members aboard, bound for the Mersey. She appeared to have left port in good trim; and was not below her marks, for she had an ample freeboard of 1 foot 7$\frac{1}{2}$ inches.

William Thomas made it a point to know the whereabouts of his vessels at all times, and when no reports were received of the *Mary Ashburner's* expected arrival at Runcorn within a few days of her departure, he wrote to Sage & Co., the vessel's insurers, informing them that she had:

> *sailed from Charlestown, Cornwall for the Mersey with a cargo of clay, and although other vessels which left Falmouth and the neighbouring ports have arrived at their destination, we regret to say that we have no news whatever of this vessel since she sailed. We cannot understand what has happened to her as the weather was fine, and we are forced to the conclusion that she must have got into collision with some other vessel.*

On the 12th of December, William Thomas wrote to Kellway and Co., of Milford Haven telling them that he had received a letter that morning from the Receiver of Wrecks at their port, informing him that the *Mary Ashburner's* boat had been picked up, overturned, some 4 miles east of Lundy, and eliciting whatever further information he could furnish.

The boat had been picked up by Skipper Nicholas of the *Queen Alexandra* of Milford, and William Thomas was forced to admit that:

There is now no doubt but that she has been run into in the fog in the neighbourhood of Land's End. We can only hope that the crew has been picked up and in safety, and that the vessel which ran into her will be discovered, as we feel confident that the mishap did not occur through the fault of Captain Hughes, as he was a most careful man who had been in command for over 36 years, during the whole time without a mishap of any consequence.

By the middle of December, there was still no news regarding the vessel, and he again wrote to the insurers suggesting:

that a reward should be offered to anyone giving such evidence as will prove which vessel collided with and sunk the Mary Ashburner, as there is no doubt in our minds that she has been lost as a result of a collision. We are writing to the shippers of the cargo of clay at Charlestown, enquiring if they will join in the cost of tracing the colliding vessel. We find that the ss Leonatus which sailed from Barry on the 25th November for St Nazaire is reported in Saturday's Gazette as being at Nantes on the 13th inst., with her fore peak tank leaking, and as she would, according to our calculations, have been just in the track of the Mary Ashburner it might be well if some enquiries regarding the cause of the leakage, and the vessel kept under observation until her arrival in the U.K. when the crew could be interviewed. We are keeping a strict lookout for all accounts of dockages of vessels which sailed out about the date that the accident might have happened.

He went on to say that he had heard from the Receiver of Wrecks at Milford Haven, who had said that the lost vessel's boat was damaged on one side, and that there was no evidence that it had been occupied by any of the crew.

Despite the mounting evidence, the owner still clung to the hope that the crew were safe, preferring to believe that they had been picked up either by the vessel they had collided with, or by another outward bound vessel, which had yet to arrive at a port where the accident would be reported. He was nevertheless forced to admit that a long time had elapsed since they had heard anything of them.

In a further letter to Sage & Co., William Thomas revealed his intimate knowledge of coastal seafaring when he enclosed a diagram he had made, showing the probable course the vessel had taken once it had left Charlestown. He had calculated that as the wind on the day was light, the Master would have steered for the Smalls with the wind on her quarter. On the diagram, he had marked two blue crosses where he thought the accident could have occurred, and in red, the course along which the ship's boat would have drifted after the collision. He admitted that the *Mary Ashburner* could equally well have been struck by an inward bound vessel as one that was outward bound, and he told them that he was pleased that the insurers were making enquiries about those recently docked in the Bristol Channel area. He added that although the *Leonatus* was reported as having been damaged when she struck the pier at St Nazaire, he did not think that too much reliance should be placed on its veracity.

It is evident that William Thomas had even gone as far as asking some of his many friends on Merseyside to advise him of any incoming vessel bearing signs of damage, and as a result, he was able to inform the insurers that the Greek vessel *Giorgios Antippa* had arrived in the Mersey about the beginning of the month with her bows stoved in. In the same letter, he confirmed his telegram to them suggesting that they should withdraw their offer of a reward for information relating to the accident, as they had not stipulated that the informant should if necessary, be prepared to give evidence in court.

In a letter dated 23rd of December, he informed Sage & Co., quite emphatically that the vessel they were seeking was the Ellerman Line steamship *Castilian*, which had sailed from Liverpool on the 26th of November for Constantinople, calling at Tangier on the way. Although he had told them that his informant was E.O. Roberts, a great personal friend and owner of the schooner *Elizabeth Roberts*, built for him by William Thomas in 1904, they were asked to keep his identity absolutely secret.

Writing to Roberts on the following day, William Thomas expressed his surprise on being told that morning that Sage & Co., had already been in touch with Ellerman regarding the accident. He confessed however, that he was at a loss to know how they came by their information, and he supposed that it might have resulted from their offer of a reward. He was nevertheless clearly not in favour of the action they had taken, for he considered it premature, and he went on to say that:

If I had conduct of the case, I certainly would not have approached the owners of any vessel under the circumstances which we are in, as the longer they delay informing the Board of Trade, the more difficult it will be for them to defend any action.

He made no reference to his feelings when he wrote to Sage & Co., on Christmas Eve however, informing them that the *Castilian* had been on passage to Constantinople, and had called at Tangier, where the Captain had cabled news of the accident to Ellerman's Liverpool office. Under the provisions of the Merchant Shipping Act, it would have been incumbent on Ellerman to have made such information known immediately, even had they genuinely believed that the accident was of a minor nature as they claimed in the subsequent Board of Trade enquiry into the loss of the *Mary Ashburner*. Somewhat airily, William Thomas closed his letter by saying:

we have no doubt that our friend will be able to obtain further information regarding the circumstances of the collision.

The insurers were clearly anxious to find out how "our friend Roberts" had come by his information, presumably for reasons associated with the payment of a reward; but all that Thomas would say was that:

We venture to state that no person from - - - - - (indecipherable) or other outpost could have furnished the information we sent you, as this was obtained from a very reliable source, and a very private one, so we trust you will acknowledge the one that deserves the acknowledgement.

It is fairly evident that William Thomas's insistence on absolute secrecy arose from the fact that the person from whom E.O. Roberts had obtained such sensitive information must have been employed in Ellerman's head office.

In the absence of independent witnesses to the accident, Sage & Co., wrote to William Thomas suggesting that between them should insure the *Castilian's* safe return to the U.K., where its crew could be questioned about the collision. Although he did not wish to add to the mounting cost of the loss in the beginning, he did eventually agree to contribute towards the premium which, as it happened, turned out to be relatively modest.

Writing to Sage & Co., on the 2nd of January, William Thomas informed them that:

the Castilian sailed from Alexandria on the 28th ult., so we trust that you are making all arrangements to interview the crew on their arrival. In the meantime, we are doing all we can to glean some information which will be of assistance to us.

He wrote to them again a week or so later to say that he had:

> received your favour of the 6th on my return from Liverpool where I had been trying to obtain further information in connection with this collision. I intend, if possible, to attend the meeting on the 14th inst., and we can discuss the best means to adopt on the Castilian's arrival home. We notice she left Jaffa on the 2nd, and passed Malta on the 5th, therefore she ought to reach Liverpool at the end of next week.

The *Castilian* arrived in Liverpool on the 19th of January, when the company admitted that she had been involved in a collision at 7.15 pm on the 27th of November about 9 miles south west of the Smalls, thereby confirming William Thomas's uncannily accurate appraisal of the situation when he first learnt of the finding of the *Mary Ashburner's* boat.

In a later letter to Sage & Co., William Thomas told them that he had just returned from Liverpool:

> where I had been trying to gather some information from the crew of the Castilian, but I regret that did not succeed much better than Messrs Weightman, Pedder & Co. (Solicitors), except that I was told that the spar and sail which fell on the steamer's deck, was thrown overboard on the same night as the collision occurred; but my informant would not state by whose orders, although he admitted he knows. From what I could gather from one of the firemen, there was a great commotion on board at the time, and in the excitement, a rush was made for the lifeboats as they thought their vessel was in a bad way, and it took about ten minutes before they gathered their wits about them. They all agreed that no boat was launched, but some lights were placed on the side, but nothing could be discovered whether these lights were for the purpose of ascertaining the object they had collided with.
>
> The men were most reluctant to give any further information, and no doubt they had been warned not to do so. There was one man whom I understand was on watch at the time of the collision that I was anxious to see, but it appears that he had left on the ss Lisbon, another vessel belonging to the same owners which sailed last Tuesday for Alexandria. This may be a very convenient way of keeping him out of reach. I was on board the steamer, but the strange thing is, there were hardly any signs that she had been in a collision, except that a plate on the starboard side at a distance of about 15 feet from the stem had been bulged inwards, and about two dozen rivets had been renewed on her arrival in Liverpool. I could not see the port side, but one of the boilermakers told me that he had put in a similar number on that side also. In the absence of greater damage to the steamer, I could only conclude that she struck the M.A. right stem on, as the paint on the face of the stem was rubbed off in that part… Do you think the Board of Trade will hold an enquiry, as it would save a great deal of expense if they did so, and they would no doubt get a correct account from the crew.

In a further letter passing between them, William Thomas thanked them for sending him copies of the depositions and Official Log of the *Castilian*, regarding which, he made the following comments:

> If the story of the white light is a correct one, I can only assume that it was a flare from the M.A. which they saw, and I can quite understand that this was so, as it is the usual practice to exhibit such a light when steamers appear to approach too dangerously, and this proves that there was not a proper lookout on the steamer. The Captain of the schooner had evidently seen the steamer coming in their direction, and had tried to attract their attention to their position. This proves that the steamer's lights were seen from the schooner, so evidently they were on the lookout, and

the steamer ought to have seen the schooner's lights because it is not likely that when they were so careful to observe the steamer's lights that they would neglect their own lights, if only for their own safety. I notice that the direction of the wind was from the NW, whereas the Masters of the other vessels which were in the neighbourhood at the time stated that it was WNW; but assuming that it was NW as they state, it is quite evident that the M.A. was struck on the lee side, that is, her starboard side, in proof of this, the gaff and sail were on the starboard side of the steamer. If the steamer had struck her on the weather side, no spar or sail would have dropped on the steamer's deck. I am now more convinced than ever that the blow was a 'stem on' one. I enclose a rough sketch showing how in my opinion the collision took place, and if I am correct, you will observe that the steamer by porting her helm did more mischief than good. If she kept on her course she would probably have gone clear.

I am taking it that the M.A. was on a northerly course which is the usual one for these vessels to take from the Longships whenever the weather is not clear, as the general rule is to set a course for the Tuskar in order to be certain of avoiding the dangerous Hats and Barrels, and to make this course, I am taking the wind to be from the WSW, this you can verify from the report which I understand you have received from the Smalls Lighthouse.

Unless there was some deviation in the steamer's compass, I do not see how she could clear the Longships on a S 16 (?) course, let alone the Scilly which is SW by S from the Smalls, but this of course does not affect us so much as their admission that the vessel was going at full speed up to the time of the collision, and at the time which they state was dark with misty showers.

The fireman whom I interviewed told me that it was thick, and he could not see a couple of feet distance. The Captains of the Frances, Buela (Beulah?), Eilian, and Camborne all say that it was thick fog at the time in that neighbourhood, in fact it was so thick at 3 o'clock on that afternoon, he (the Captain of the Camborne?) took in some sails as a precaution. You will recollect that the vessel left Falmouth on the morning of Wednesday 26th November at 10 am, and from all calculations, he must have been close to the M.A. at the time of the collision, as he sighted the Smalls at about 9o'c on Thursday night 27th, bearing about E, and at midnight the Smalls were abeam bearing about SE, so he must have been close to the spot of collision. The Captain states that the weather was very moderate, and nothing like the heavy breeze which the depositions lead one to assume. I notice that the Depositions were not made before the 20th inst., four days after her arrival in port. This would allow sufficient time to consult their solicitors, and it struck me that both tales were very well balanced.

I should say that the steamer had a Spar Deck, and on this were a number of threshing machines etc. Unless the lookout was on the upper bridge, these would have obstructed the view ahead. It is very strange that an accident should have happened to the Official Log on this particular voyage. To say the least, it appears suspicious on the face of it.

Although the underwriters were disposed to join the owners in some kind of action against Ellerman, they were not prepared to enter into expensive litigation, which reflected William Thomas's own feelings, for he foresaw the difficulty in proving that the steamer owners were negligent without the benefit of a witness to refute their version of events, and he assumed that a Court would be bound to accept their sworn testimony, unless it could be proved otherwise. Better he thought, for them to make an application for a Board of Trade enquiry into the accident, as this would save them the expense of a trial which was bound to be great, whatever its outcome. He was not surprised at this time to hear that Ellerman's solicitors had repudiated all liability for the accident, but he was pleased to hear that the lookout man on the *Castilian* had admitted that the steamer was in dense fog at the time of the accident, as this would make it difficult for its Captain to justify his going at full speed.

Now that the *Castilian's* Captain had admitted to sinking a sailing vessel, the next most important thing to be done was to show that the victim was indeed the *Mary Ashburner*, and in the belief that without an independent witness to the accident, proving that point would be extremely difficult. For that reason, William Thomas wrote to the Harbour Master at Penzance asking if he could make enquiries regarding a ketch of that port which had spoken to the *Camborne* when off the Lizard at about the time of the accident, telling them that she had earlier passed a schooner.

On the 31st January 1914, William Thomas & Sons were informed, much to their satisfaction, that the Board of Trade intended to hold an enquiry into the loss of the *Mary Ashburner,* and in a letter to their London solicitors they sought verification that the legal steps they were taking against the *Castilian's* owners would be suspended until the Board's findings were made known.

Board of Trade officials had already begun their enquiries by the middle of February, and were anxious to know if the Master of the *Mary Ashburner* had sufficient oil on board for his navigation lamps. As a result of their enquiry, William Thomas wrote to Messrs Couch and Son of St Austell, enquiring if Captain Hughes had bought paraffin for his vessel whilst at Charlestown; and whether he had paid his crew their wages, as it was his custom to pay his men after they had discharged the vessel's cargo at the end of each voyage.

During the Board of Trade enquiry into the accident, held at Liverpool on 19th March 1914, it was agreed that of a list of the reports received by the Board of Trade of collisions between vessels on the west coast of England, none of the cases could have any bearing on the loss of the *Mary Ashburner* except for that which occurred between the British steamship *Castilian* and an unknown sailing vessel on the 27th of November in Lat. 51.22 N: Long. 6.6 W, about 25 miles off the Smalls.

In his evidence to the Board of Enquiry into the loss of the schooner, Captain Gomes, Master of the *Castilian*, described how he had been on the vessel's bridge until 7 o'clock on the evening of the collision, when he had gone below to have dinner, leaving the chief officer in charge of the bridge. At 7.15 when the collision occurred, he was in his cabin, and having realised that something unusual had taken place, went immediately to the bridge where he asked the Chief Officer what had happened. In his reply, the officer affirmed that there had been a slight collision with a sailing vessel, whose lights had been seen momentarily immediately before the collision when he had ordered the helm to be put 'hard-a-port', and the engines stopped.

Nothing was seen of the other vessel however, and after two hours in the vicinity of the collision he assumed that it had sailed away into the night, without lights, and unharmed. This was despite the fact that the other vessel's gaff was found lying on the rail outside the *Castilian's* fore rigging. Captain Gomes admitted that a few days later, he and another threw the gaff into the sea, as he maintained that it was a danger to navigation inasmuch that it might be washed overboard where it could easily foul the steamer's propeller. The possibility that as a result, the gaff might just as easily have fouled the propeller of another vessel seems to have escaped him.

It would appear that the ship's original log book was not produced as evidence in the

Enquiry, for in his testimony, Captain Gomes stated that the one offered as evidence was a replacement given to him by the British Consul in Alexandria because the original was dirty. It was claimed that this had happened when eight Moors who were deck passengers, were sheltered in the chart room during a spell of heavy weather. He then admitted that as a result, the account of the collision placed before the enquiry was written up from memory on the following day, and the entries countersigned by his officers.

From the available evidence, it could easily be construed that a very clumsy attempt had been made by officers on board the *Castilian* to hide the true facts relating to the collision. Firstly, the fact that evidence in the form of the gaff, from which the other vessel might possibly have been identified, was on the Captain's own admission, disposed of without examination, and for what was clearly a very ambivalent reason. Secondly, the fact that the accident was reported directly to Ellerman's head office and not to the Consul in Tangier, the vessel's first port of call, as might have been expected, also appears to be somewhat suspect; and thirdly, even if the original log book was indeed as dirty as was claimed, any self respecting captain would have known that in spite of its condition it constituted a primary source of evidence relating to the incident, and for that reason should have been preserved for any enquiry that was likely to follow.

At the hearing which began in Liverpool on March 19th, the Board found that the *Castilian* had indeed run into and sunk the *Mary Ashburner* with the loss of the whole of her crew, and blamed the accident on excessive speed in foggy conditions.

William Thomas & Sons expressed sorrow when they later learned that despite the finding, Ellerman were going to contest their claim for compensation; but this they thought, was little more than a ploy aimed at forcing a compromise, and they harboured no doubts whatsoever that they would eventually have to back down and admit their liability.

In a letter to their solicitors regarding their action against Ellerman, William Thomas expressed his satisfaction on learning that the latter were now making overtures regarding a settlement. He made it clear however, that there was no possibility whatsoever of the owners accepting the 65% settlement then being offered to them, preferring instead to go to trial rather than agree to anything less than the full value of their claim which amounted to:

Value of vessel, outfit and stores at the time of her loss	£1,350 - 00 - 00
Freight	£38 - 03 - 03
Extra insurance when vessel was overdue	£21 - 00 - 03
Loss of management of vessel	£100 - 00 - 00
Insurance premium on *Castilian*	16 - 06
Provisions and other consumable stores	£6 - 00 - 00
Charts, cooking utensils etc.	£5 - 00 - 00
Telegrams of enquiry when vessel was overdue	£1 - 15 - 00
Travelling expenses to Liverpool inspecting *Castilian* and interviewing crew 3 times	£4 - 08 - 06
Sailmakers time attending enquiry	£2 - 01 - 04
TOTAL	£1,529 - 06 - 10

Captain John Hughes, Master of the *Mary Ashburner* was succeeded by his 37-year-old son and 35-year-old daughter. His son, Thomas Hughes, had suffered for many years following a fall from aloft on to the deck of a ship, which had left him permanently impaired and unable to do little other than very light work. The daughter too had suffered from ill health for many years, and she and her brother were entirely dependent on their father for financial support. Their faith in their father's employers was undiminished, and both had expressed a wish that their claim for compensation should be dealt with by William Thomas & Sons' own solicitors. The family of the Mate and his brother had decided otherwise, and had consulted a firm of solicitors in Liverpool. In a letter to his own solicitors, William Thomas told them that:

> Personally , I am not sorry that the others are taking their own course, as they expect to recover a great deal more than they are likely to, and if they failed, both you and us would be blamed for it.

Immersed as he was in the problems attending the loss of the *Mary Ashburner*, little did William Thomas imagine that they would be further compounded by the loss of the *Harvest Home*, the ownership of which he shared with E.O. Roberts who had earlier advised him of the *Castilian*'s involvement in the loss of the *Mary Ashburner*. Writing to Roberts, he said:

> I cannot express my surprise and grief on learning of the loss of the Harvest Home... whilst I recognise that the loss is great to you, we are unfortunately worse off still, as we have not so much insurance on our share as you have... we have wired for Hansen (the Captain) to come here so that he can explain how he got into the position he did, and until we have his report, we do not want to express an opinion; but it does appear strange that he should be inside the Sound at all.

Until such time as he had received Hansen's report, William Thomas delayed writing to Sage & Co., with whom the vessel was partly insured. When this had been received, he informed them that:

> They left Fishguard at 1.30 pm on Monday last, wind about NW. At 9.30 pm that night, they passed Bardsey at a distance of 7 or 8 miles, the wind at that time increasing, and the sea becoming rougher; but they continued on their course until about 11.30 pm, until the South Stack light bore about NE by N at a distance of about 20 miles. At this time the tide was just commencing to ebb, and the sea on his beam, he concluded that he could not weather the Stack, so he determined to run back towards St Tudwal's Roads, and whilst doing so the Fore sheet carried away whilst the men were securing the foresail. They had by this time arrived close to the entrance to the Sound. The vessel took a sudden sheer towards the island. He immediately put his helm down and trimmed the sails to get her head out and succeeded in doing so; but the ebb tide was so strong that she was carried broadside on to the rock known as Maen Bugail where she thumped heavily several times, but eventually she drifted off the rocks and they tried to run the vessel for either Aberdaron beach or Pwllheli as she was making so much water that it was not safe to remain on board, so they got the boat out and into it as they stood, without saving anything, and they then remained close by the vessel until about 3 am when suddenly they lost her starboard light and they concluded that she had gone down.
>
> The vessel had drifted to the southward of Bardsey Island, and was about 3 miles away when they lost her. The crew then rowed for St Tudwal's Roads and there got on board a small fishing vessel which took them to Portmadoc.

From the above account, there is very little hope that has kept afloat and been picked up, altho' there was a steamer not very far away at the time.

In further letters to E.O. Roberts regarding the loss of the *Harvest Home*, William Thomas, despite his other problems and considerable financial loss, displayed his compassionate nature and great understanding of the perils attending those whose lives were bound up with the sea, when he informed him that:

I had already gathered from what Hansen told me, that you were not overpleased with his explanations, but however unsatisfactory his statement may be, it is you and I who will have to suffer for the mishap and nothing which either of us can do will now improve matters. I must confess that I had a much better opinion of Hansen's courage and seamanship than he had displayed lately, whether it was bad luck or what, he certainly has been most unfortunate since his accident at Seaham last February.

I quite agree with you that his (Hansen) *reference to the Gracie is simply to justify his action in attempting to go through Bardsey Sound at night time; but with all his faults, I must confess that I do not think he is guilty of losing time through drink, as I have met several Captains who have been in his company, but I have never heard that he was fond of drink.*

Despite his apparent anger with Captain Hansen, E.O. Roberts was evidently a compassionate man also. This was acknowledged by William Thomas when he wrote to him. In his letter, he told Roberts that it had been extremely kind of him to assist Captain Hansen, who had left all of his personal belongings behind when he abandoned ship, by buying him a new outfit, adding that: *after all, he is only a human being!*

CHAPTER 9
MANAGING THE BARQUENTINE *BALDER*
"we shall look after the vessel as tho' she belonged entirely to ourselves"

A specification dated 2nd July 1890, drawn up by William Thomas & Sons, of a three-masted, iron schooner, which was launched a year later from their Amlwch yard as the *Detlef Wagner*, was used as the model for a similar steel barquentine, to be built, if accepted, for Dr Macartney of Pelotas, Rio Grande do Sul, Brazil. The alterations to the original specification, annotated in red ink on the original, show that the length of the new vessel was to be 120 feet, its breadth 24 feet 9 inches, and its moulded depth 12 feet 3 inches. Although no agreement was entered into, it is evident that the failure to do business did little to harm the relationship between William Thomas and Dr Macartney.

Three almost identical letters referring to the barquentine *Balder* of Liverpool, owned by Dr Macartney, were sent on the 29th of September 1913, by William Thomas & Sons, to Lloyds agents at Queenstown (Cóbh), Falmouth, and Plymouth, stating that:

> It is quite possible that this vessel which is on passage from Rio Grand do Sul with a cargo of hides, may call at your port for orders; in which case, we shall be pleased if you will kindly wire her arrival as promptly as possible... please do not advance the Captain any money without our authority.

The former Norwegian-owned vessel, code letters JCWG, was allocated the code letters HTVB on the day she became a British registered ship. Managed by the Animal Products Co. Ltd of 24, Benson Street, Liverpool, the *Balder* was engaged in the same Brazilian hide trade as were William Thomas's own vessels *Cymric* and *Gaelic*, and there can be little doubt that the friendly business association between the two owners sprang initially from their common business interest. There is some evidence to suggest that a protection ring existed in the South American trade in which owners had bonded together with the intention of securing 'fair' freights by reducing unrestricted competition. Whether or not William Thomas and Dr Macartney had met through being members of such a cartel is a matter for conjecture, but there is nothing in their correspondence to support this view.

In a letter dated 29th of October 1913, addressed to Dr Macartney in Pelotas, William Thomas acknowledged receipt of the doctor's letters, including nine envelopes containing various documents relating to the *Balder*, before going on to say that:

> We have also received the Power of Attorney from Rio Grande which we are forwarding to Liverpool to be officially translated.
>
> The letter addressed to the Animal Products Co. Ltd, we are forwarding to its destination by Registered Post, and will follow this up by a formal request to transfer the vessel, and all documents thereto to us, and we shall then know what attitude these gentlemen intend to take up, upon which we shall decide what course to take to protect your interests, as it is quite evident that up to the present, these have not had much consideration. In the meantime we are applying to the Customs Officials at Liverpool for a copy of the Ship's Register, to find whether she has been encumbered.
>
> As you correctly state, there will undoubtedly be a great deal of trouble in getting this matter

settled, and unfortunately, it will also involve some expense, but you may rest assured that we shall spare no pains to attain that end as economically as possible.

With regard to the general accounts, we cannot trust ourselves to express our opinion of some of the items charged therein. For instance, we find that no less than £347-2-4 has been charged you for commission alone, quite apart from those paid to the regular brokers for doing the ship's business, and a further sum of £92-11-11 has been charged as interest, making a total of £439-14-3, so there is no wonder that you have been called upon so repeatedly for money. Apart from the excessive rate, we find that interest has been charged upon interest and commission upon commission, and in the latter case, upon sums which have never been disbursed by those that claim it.

It is quite evident that proper supervision has not been exercised over the heavy expenditure made by the Captain, and in our opinion, this is gross negligence on the part of those who were entrusted with, and who were paid for protecting your interests, consequently these people are legally responsible for such dereliction of duty.

We quite agree with you that it is not prudent to enter rashly into the expense and worry of a lawsuit, but at the same time, there are occasions when it is cheaper to adopt this course rather than submit to exorbitant charges such as appear in this case. However you may rely that we shall not attempt anything without good prospects of succeeding in our objective. In any event it will be absolutely necessary to engage the services of a Solicitor if only for the purpose of showing our determination of enforcing what is right and fair. Further, we doubt whether the Animal Products Co., would run the risk of their accounts being scrutinised in a court of law.

We are very pleased to observe that you have declined to be coerced to pay the demand for £372-5-1, as we are perfectly satisfied that this amount is neither morally nor legally due to them, and if they had faithfully carried out their duties, and had been satisfied with a reasonable sum for their services, such a sum would not have been due to them. As matters stand, it will be our aim and duty to recover as much as we can of the overcharges.

We cannot understand why these people should in the first instance have undertaken the duties of managing the vessel, as it is quite evident that they had no previous experience of such work, and this is practically admitted in one of their letters to the Saladero Products Co., a copy of which was enclosed in the documents you sent us.

It is most unfortunate that the vessel is registered in their name at the Customs House, as this gives them the whip hand over us to a great degree. Had it been otherwise, we would have declined to pay them a single penny piece, and would have allowed them to adopt any means they chose to recover: now, if they decline to transfer the vessel and policies of insurance etc., the onus falls upon us to compel them, so we can only hope that after we have had an interview with them and discussed the several charges, they will see the wisdom of settling amicably.

We understand that you are prepared to suffer a reasonable loss, and submit to some of the charges rather than enter into a lawsuit, as we ourselves always advocate such a course, provided of course, that it is anywhere within the bounds of reason.

There is not, in our opinion, any reason why the first settlement of £914-18-7 should not be reopened if it can be proved that there were any errors or overcharging in it, and we do not think there would be much difficulty in doing this. At the same time, there are some items which we are precluded from attacking, as you have practically agreed to them by such a settlement, which otherwise should have been disputed as being unreasonable. However, all these matters shall have our careful consideration when going fully through the accounts, as we have only been hurriedly through the vouchers in the short time since their receipt.

The letter which you enclosed, and addressed to Captain Potter, we are withholding until his arrival on this side, when it will be handed to him. In the meantime, we are communicating with the shipping agents at Plymouth, Queenstown and Falmouth, notifying them not to advance him any money on account of this vessel, and we hope to have secured the services of a competent man to take command after her arrival at the port of discharge.

From the telegram of the Animal Products Co., to their agents at Rio Grande, we consider that the vessel has already been chartered for a return cargo to Pelotas, but we wish it had been otherwise, as we could have secured a good freight for Gibraltar, and worked her in the same manner as our vessels. However, we are bound to carry out the arrangements that have been legally entered into.

We sincerely hope that we shall succeed in getting this unfortunate matter settled without involving you in much expense, as we consider you have been very badly treated from the beginning, and between bad luck and bad management, the vessel has cost you about three times her value.

William Thomas also wrote to the Animal Products Company, confirming that he had accepted the management of the vessel, before going on to say that he wanted to know when it would be convenient for them to transfer the vessel and everything belonging to her into his care. The latter responded without delay, and a further letter was sent to them a week later which exemplified William Thomas's acuity, tact and firmness in matters relating to business:

We beg to own receipt of your favour of the 3rd inst., and carefully note all that you state. You are quite correct in assuming that Dr Macartney has fully acquainted us with his views regarding the matters relating to this vessel, as in addition to the three letters you refer to, we have received other communications from him, also your statements of accounts, and all the vouchers you had forwarded to him. We understand that the Doctor is quite prepared, and even anxious, to liquidate any sum that is properly due to you, and we think that he has made this quite clear in his communications with you, and also to your representatives at Pelotas, and if we can agree upon the amount, we are authorized to settle the whole matter without loss of time, but we wish to state that the points raised by the Doctor are not the only ones that are in dispute, as there are several other items that need adjusting. We, however, are sanguine enough to hope, that if we met and discussed these in a friendly manner, an amicable settlement could be arrived at, as we have no desire to cause any unpleasantness, and for this reason we abstain at present from any reference to other matters which may however, have to be gone into at a later stage. We shall be pleased therefore to know if you are agreeable to go through, and discuss the whole of the accounts with our Senior with this object(ive), and if so, please name a date that will be convenient to you for this purpose. With reference to your statement that you intend taking out further policies of insurance on this vessel until she is transferred from your name, we take this opportunity of notifying you on behalf of Dr Macartney, that you do so on your own responsibility and costs, and that we shall decline to acknowledge any liability for expenditure whatsoever you may incur in this direction, or in any other in connection with this vessel. Further we would point out that according to your accounts, the present policies do not expire until the vessel's safe arrival at a port of discharge in the U.K. or on the Continent, and there is no reason why the whole matter should not be settled before that time.

Copies of all letters concerning the *Balder*, which passed between Amlwch and

Liverpool were sent to Dr Macartney, relating to which, he was asked to note:

the high handed manner they propose to adopt, and this is no doubt with the object of forcing a settlement, but they will find out very soon that they are going the wrong way about it… In the meantime, we trust that you will not make them any payment on account, or admit that there is any sum due to them re Balder.

William Thomas went personally to Liverpool on three occasions to meet officials of the Meat Products Co., to discuss the *Balder's* finances, and following their meeting on the 15th of October, he wrote to them confirming the arrangements under which the vessel would be transferred to him:

1. That we pay you the sum of £50 in full settlement, and discharge of all claims and demands whatsoever you may have against the vessel.

2. We undertake to indemnify you against all claims for which you may become legally liable on account of this vessel, upon the understanding that you adopt the course directed by us, and afford every assistance in the defence of such claims if necessary.

3. We also undertake to relieve you of all claims which the owner of this vessel, or his representatives, may have against you.

4. Upon payment of the above amount, and on receipt of the undertaking, you undertake to send us a properly executed Bill of Sale for the whole vessel, free from all encumbrances, and transfer to us all policies of Insurance and Indemnities, all books, receipts, vouchers and every other article and document in your possession, relating to, and belonging to this vessel.

5. That the amounts charged by you against Captain Potter, shall be accounted for to us, and any balance owing to, or from him, shall be settled by us.

In a second letter sent to them on the same date, William Thomas enclosed a Letter of Indemnity, in which he undertook to indemnify Animal Products against all claims for which they might become legally liable as the registered owners of the barquentine, on the terms stated in his letter of the same date. Included with the letter was a cheque for £50 in full discharge and settlement of their claims and accounts.

For some unknown reason, William Thomas had recently withdrawn all insurance cover on his vessels from the Protection and Collision Club administered by E.R. Evans of London, with whom he had dealt for many years, and his first move as manager of the *Balder,* was to withdraw her from their club as well, and place her cover with Sage & Co., by whom his own vessels were protected.

On the 23rd of October, he was informed by Animal Products that the *Balder* had arrived at Queenstown, and by Registered Post he sent Captain Potter a letter from Dr Macartney, and another from Animal Products, by which he was to understand that William Thomas was now the ship's manager, and that he was not to incur any expenses on the vessel without his authority.

Referring to the *Balder* in his letter to Captain Williams of the *Meyric,* who was without doubt familiar with the vessel and her captain, William Thomas was pleased to state:

that we have knocked off over £350 from the account of the Animal Products Co., and it was only to save going to a law suit that we agreed to settle for this deduction off their account, but we think this a good saving for Dr Macartney and we shall do our best to protect his interests, altho' we must admit that if we knew the amount of work entailed and the worry in connection with it, we would not have accepted the appointment, but having promised, we are bound to do our best. You have no doubt heard that Captain Edwin Hughes is going with her as Master, in place of Potter.

Captain Hughes was master of the schooner *Robert Morris*, then lying at Falmouth.

William Thomas wrote to E.A. Grimm & Co., Ship Brokers of Hamburg, with whom the *Balder* had been placed, expressing the hope that they would be able to inform him as soon as possible, to which port the *Balder* was to proceed from Queenstown. In the event of her port of discharge being on the Elbe, they were asked not to advance Captain Potter any money.

In the meantime, a letter had been received from James Scott & Co., asking if it was all right for them to advance Captain Potter a sum to obtain stores for the vessel. In his reply, William Thomas told them that:

It is of course, quite correct for the captain to obtain what stores are absolutely necessary, but the quantity must be reasonable and not extravagant, and we hope that you will impress this fact upon him, as we wish to do everything that is right and correct, and to have our relations with the Captain as pleasant as possible, and if he studies the ship's interest, we shall deal fairly by him.

As the *Balder* had arrived at Queenstown and not at Plymouth, Captain Hughes was told not to proceed to his new command directly, but to make his way via Amlwch, which would be no inconvenience to him. Despite this, a letter was sent to Captain Potter, who had by then asked to be relieved of his command, telling him that due to the short notice he had given, it would not be possible to find a suitable person to replace him, and he was asked to stay with his vessel. His resulting protest was dismissed summarily when he was reminded that he was not allowed to leave his command at a port of call. Why William Thomas should have done this is explained in a later letter to the owner, and in order to assess the situation for himself, he decided to travel to Queenstown.

Following his return from Ireland, William Thomas wrote a lengthy letter to Dr Macartney regarding the *Balder*, acquainting him of everything that had transpired. As it gives an insight into William Thomas's personality, as well as his business acumen, the somewhat lengthy letter is quoted in its entirety:

Referring to our respects of the 11th inst, I have now pleasure in confirming our cable of the 24th ult., advising you of this vessel's arrival at Queenstown the previous day, also that we had arrived at a satisfactory settlement with the Animal Products Co. Ltd, Liverpool, regarding their claim against you.

As a result of correspondence that had passed between us, I went over to Liverpool on the 10th ult., and remained there for two days to go minutely through the accounts which you had sent us, but we failed to agree with the figures of the Animal Products Co. They however, by this time, had climbed down very much from the stand they had first taken up, so in order to give them an opportunity of considering the various points discussed, and to allow them to prepare an account of payments made by them subsequent to the statement they rendered you for the £372-5-1, it was agreed to adjourn the matter until the following week, and on the 14th ult. I again went over to meet them, and they then presented a statement showing payments of £59-15-3, the bulk of which was quite legitimate. I had noticed however, in going through the papers that you sent us that a second charge for average adjustment had been made against you, and on this account there was a sum of £33-2-10 recoverable from the Underwriters on account of the accident at Cardiff, and whether this would have been disclosed or not, before I mentioned the fact, it is only fair to state that credit was given for this amount, which consequently reduced the sum owing to them to £26-12-5, or a total of £398-17-6.

We again discussed the figures minutely, and at the end of the third day, we arrived at a settlement by inducing them to accept £50 in full discharge of all their claims against you, or in other words, £348-17-6 less than their original claim, and I venture to think that this was a substantial sum to knock off, and I trust you will consider it a favourable settlement under the circumstances, as I constantly kept in mind your desire to avoid the expense, worry and uncertainty of litigation, besides, it is very doubtful if we had commenced an action at law, and had been successful, whether the net result would have been so successful as the one obtained. Further, we are under the disadvantage of being unable to attack the first settlement, and they strenuously maintained that you had accepted their account without a word of objection to a single item charged therein, although you had every opportunity of doing so, and therefore they concluded by your silence, and by the payment made, that all was in order, therefore I did not take the risk of pressing this unduly, but concentrated the attack upon their last statement with the result already stated.

I should state that this settlement did not include the Rs.97.400 charged for Costa's commission, which we agreed to leave out, therefore this sum is due you from the Saladero Trading and Products Co. We discovered that the three waterproof covers value £8 supplied by Frazer &Co., Newport, and charged against the ship were really for the Saladero Products and Trading Co., therefore this amount plus freight is also recoverable from them, and to enable you to collect this sum we enclose the receipted account of Messrs Frazer & Co. I should add that Captain Potter admits that these were delivered to Mr. Skidmore, and we have notified the Animal Products Co. that you will collect the amount on the other side. I would suggest that you should charge at least £3 as freight, which should be added to the cost.

I enclose you an account of the payments made by the Animal Products Co., since they had rendered their account of £372-5-1. Of course, all payments made to Captain Potter have been deducted from his wages, as you will observe from the accompanying account.

I think I have now sufficiently explained the negotiations with the Animal Products Co., and I shall now endeavour to relate my trouble after the vessel's arrival at Queenstown on the 23rd ult.

I was under the impression that the vessel would have called at Plymouth for orders as on previous occasions. In fact, Captain Potter had told Captain Williams of the Meyric that such was his intention, but fortunately we had been in communication with all the agents at Plymouth, Falmouth and Queenstown, and had requested them in the event of the vessel calling at their port to immediately advise us of her arrival, and that on no consideration were they to advance the Captain any money without our instructions. It appears that when Captain Potter called upon our Queenstown Agents, the first thing he did was to make a request for cash, but after explaining to him the new position he became furious, and declined to acknowledge our authority, as he maintained that he had already received orders from you just before sailing from Pelotas, to which he intends to adhere. He also wired to us as per enclosed copy, to which we replied by letter enclosing therewith your letter of authority to us dated 2nd September last, also one obtained from the Animal Products Co., advising him of the transfer of the vessel to us. On receipt of these letters, he changed his tactics, and wired to us that he would not proceed with the vessel, and demanding to be relieved of the command, but as we had not secured the services of a suitable person at that time, and also being anxious to avoid the expense and trouble of making the change at such a distant port, we replied stating that we could not secure a suitable Master at such short notice, and declining to relieve him of the command, hoping thereby that he would reconsider his decision, and continue the voyage to port of discharge, as we knew from experience that a change of Master at a port of call would mean a lot of trouble and expense. We had hardly dispatched our reply when we received a wire from Messrs Scott as per enclosed copy, by which it was quite evident that Potter was determined to cause as much trouble as he could. I therefore had no choice but to hurry away at once to catch the connection for Queenstown, which place I reached on Sunday night, and strange to say, Capt. Potter was staying at the hotel where I put up on my arrival, and although I had never seen the man before, I somehow felt instinctively that he was the master of the Balder. In course of time I got into conversation with him, but taking care not to divulge my identity, but before retiring I told him who I was, and this greatly astonished him, as he had no idea I was expected over there.

At that time he was quite sober, but it was fully evident that he had been indulging in strong drink. However on Monday morning we discussed the whole situation together in a friendly manner, and although he stated that the vessel was no better than a wreck, and not fit to go to sea, he said he would afford me all the assistance he could to get her away without much trouble and expense, and he even requested to be allowed to take her to her destination, but as I had in the meantime secured another Master, I could not agree.

When the weather moderated in the afternoon, we hired a boat and went out to the vessel, as I was anxious to see for myself the state the vessel was in, and I am pleased to state that I was most agreeably surprised to find her so much better than Capt. Potter had described her. There were certainly some things defective, but I was satisfied that there was nothing for which the Board of Trade officials could stop the vessel, and I was congratulating myself that matters were moving more smoothly than I had anticipated, and relying upon Potter's promise of assistance, I advanced him £1, as he stated he was penniless, but as soon as we got ashore he slipped me, went on the drink, so when next I saw him about 11 o'clock that night, he was not in a state to get any reason from him, but as generally happens, persons in that condition state what they would not dream of saying when in their proper senses, and so it happened that I got to know the whole of his intentions, which were that he was going to report the condition of the vessel to the Board of Trade, and that he had persuaded the crew to demand their discharge the next day, and generally to cause all the trouble he possibly could. I however, was satisfied in my mind that the vessel was perfectly seaworthy, but I felt some anxiety about the crew, as, if they had to be paid off, the expense would have been considerable, and that they could not be replaced at Queenstown, so others would have to be obtained elsewhere or runners engaged to take her to her destination, which course would have meant a heavy charge. For all that, I trusted that by the morning, the Captain would be more reasonable, but the following day he eluded me altogether, and when I next saw him at 10 o'clock he was helpless. I therefore took advantage of his condition, and went on board to arrange matters with the crew, and exceeded beyond my most sanguine expectations. I also took possession of the ship's register and took it ashore with me, so practically I was master of the situation, but I wanted the Captain to sign clear of the ship, and this of course he would not do unless I paid him what he demanded, and this was my greatest difficulty; how to get him to sign the ship's articles at the Custom House, but my opportunity came the following day. He was still in a drunken condition, and it was on this account that I discovered he was removing and selling some of the ship's property in order to obtain drink, and when I charged him with this offence, he was staggered and brought to his senses. I gave him the option of signing clear of the vessel, or I should prosecute him for theft, *and I need hardly state that he availed himself of the first, so on Thursday morning we got everything squared up, the new master installed in command, and I got away by the afternoon Mail, and arrived home on Friday morning. I should mention that I advanced Captain Potter £10 to pay his debts at Queenstown and passage home, and as he could not satisfactorily account for money which he had received at different periods, the final settlement was not made until the 7th inst., when we gave him a cheque for £49-17-10 in full discharge.*

I congratulate you on being rid of such a person, as he was not a suitable master for a vessel like the Balder, quite apart from his intemperate habits.

I have now secured a person in whom we have every confidence, and who has had experience of this class of vessel, and with a fair luck she ought to show some return for your capital, although I should state that she will require some outlay before leaving this side. A list of what I observed I enclose herewith, but you can rely that all will be done as economically as possible.

The Lay-days to await for orders expired last Saturday, but no orders have been received yet owing to the depressed condition of the Hide Market. Therefore the vessel is now under demurrage, a very fortunate thing, as she could not sail at present owing to the very severe gales which we are having. As you have not mentioned anything in your letters respecting outward business, I presume that you have not chartered back with salt or other cargo, therefore unless we hear from you by cable, we shall try and fix her up after we know her final port of discharge I must apologise for worrying you with such a long epistle, and also for the delay in not writing to you earlier, but I was called away on very urgent business, hence the reason.

As soon as I collect the freight, and pay all charges, I will render you a full account shewing all receipts and disbursements.

With kind regards,

Wm Thomas

During his brief time on board the *Balder* at Queenstown, William Thomas made what he called 'a rough statement of inspection', which clearly was the outcome of a thoroughly competent assessment of the vessel's general condition he had made and that in a very short time:

Two shrouds of lower fore rigging and fore topmast backstays carried away, also the remaining shrouds of the lower rigging in very poor condition.

Small boat dinghy badly damaged and patched with canvas. This will have to be renewed before leaving England.

Several bulwark stanchions on both sides forward, loose, and will require fastening and caulking.

Will require new Mizen as the one on board is fairly worn, but with some repairs, will be serviceable as a light weather sail.

Several bolts in deadeyes will require renewing, also one main sheet and three or four chain bolts.

The caulking of the upper works appeared slack and may require hardening or recaulking, but this can be better tested after discharging cargo.

Dr Macartney later wrote to William Thomas, enclosing copies of his correspondence with the Saladero Trading Company, which was presumably a Brazilian firm associated with the Animal Products Co. In his reply, Thomas said:

I was sorry to learn of the treatment you received from Mr Skidmore, and if you say that it is worse than the treatment you have suffered in connection with the Balder, I can only say, "God help you". I am however, glad that you are cleared of Potter and your agents at Liverpool, and I consider myself very fortunate in knocking off such a slice from their account.

It was all bunkum of Potter to state that the vessel had come to England to be transferred, this was no doubt said with some object to suit his purpose. Rightly or wrongly, I had no idea that you would wish me to treat Potter severely, hence the reason I let him off so smoothly, altho' he certainly deserved to be punished for his dirty actions.

You may rely that we shall look after the vessel as tho' she belonged entirely to ourselves, and if we have an opportunity of disposing of her, we shall not fail to advise you promptly.

The *Balder* left Queenstown, bound for Altona, on the 16th of December. This was not her first visit to Hamburg, as records show that she was recaulked and resheathed with yellow metal up to 11 feet over patent felt, whilst there in August 1911.

In a letter to Captain Hughes, William Thomas said that the vessel had been offered a cargo of oil cake from Hamburg to an English Channel port, and he saw no objection to such a cargo provided that the hold was properly disinfected and thoroughly washed out after the hide cargo had been discharged. He felt that if the hold were then to be lime washed, the vessel could deliver the cargo in as good a condition as that delivered by iron vessels.

On the 16th of January, 1914 however, the *Balder* was fixed to deliver, not oil cake, but salt, to Poole in Dorset; following which she was to be sailed to Amlwch in order that attention could be given to the defects noted by William Thomas when he inspected her at Queenstown.

This was not be the case however, for having just lost the *Mary Ashburner* and the *Harvest Home,* the last thing William Thomas wanted to hear was that the *Balder* had been towed leaking into Cuxhaven with her pumps choked. Following an inspection, an additional pump had been put on board, and in order to save the expense of discharging and repairing in Germany, it was agreed with the vessel's underwriters that the vessel could be towed to Poole with her cargo, before undergoing whatever repairs were necessary, in a British port.

Having followed her safe progress across a gale swept North Sea, William Thomas was shocked to receive on the 18th of March, a telegram from Captain Hughes which read:

'BALDER SUNK SIX MILES FROM NEEDLES. CREW SAVED. LOST EFFECTS.'

He could barely comprehend how the vessel, having successfully weathered a very rough crossing under tow, could sink within a very short distance of her destination, in what was after all, reasonably fine weather.

His observation that bad luck has unfortunately followed this vessel all along, was something of an understatement, and in his letter to Dr Macartney dated 23rd April, 1914 explaining the circumstances surrounding the loss, he was as usual, thoroughly comprehensive:

Confirming my respects of the 18th ult., I very much regret that I have not been able to write earlier respecting the total loss of this unfortunate vessel, but I had to leave home to attend a Board of Trade inquiry into the loss of one of our own vessels, which was sunk in collision with a steamer during a fog, with the loss of all hands, hence the reason for the delay.

As previously advised you, the Balder sank about six miles from the Needles, Isle of Wight, whilst in tow of a powerful German tug from Cuxhaven to Poole, Dorset, to which port she was bound with a cargo of salt from Hamburg.

I was in great hopes that with a change of master, and the high ruling outward freights, she would eventually yield good interest on your outlay, but somehow, misfortune dogged her footsteps to the last.

As you are aware, she arrived at Queenstown on the 23rd of October last, with 16 lay days (Sundays excepted), to wait for orders, and after the expiration of these days, she was kept a further period of 28 days, which was a very serious loss, as the demurrage of 4d per ton per day was not anything like what she would have earned if she had been permitted to complete the voyage. The total amount of demurrage was only £96-2-8, almost the whole of which had been absorbed by disbursements at Queenstown.

On the 13th December, she got orders to proceed to Altona to discharge, but on account of the boisterous state of the weather, she could not leave port until the 16th of that month when the wind moderated, but after she had been out a couple of days she met with contrary winds of great force, which delayed her arrival until the 27th. The discharging was commenced on the 29th, and completed on the 6th of January, and in the meantime I had been endeavouring to secure a cargo from the Elbe to any convenient port on this side, and after a great deal of trouble I managed to close at 5/9d and 63/- gratuity for a cargo of salt from Hamburg to Poole, Dorset, which was the only cargo offering for a vessel of her size; but even at this low rate, I expected she would have shown some profit, as we were certain of a cargo of clay from Poole to the Mersey at a fair rate, and the vessel would then have been close to us where we could arrange and supervise the necessary repairs. However, after all the arrangements had been completed, very severe frost had set in, and the river was full of ice, which prevented the vessel from shifting to loading berth until the 17th of January, and on the 20th loading was commenced, and completed on the 28th, but the river was strongly impeded by ice which rendered navigation very difficult and dangerous, with the result that she was further delayed until the 3rd of February. She then only managed to get as far as Cuxhaven where she had to anchor until the 9th owing to the very heavy weather which moderated on that day, and she proceeded on her voyage. The wind at that time was moderate but contrary, and little headway was made. On the third day out the wind increased with a heavy sea, causing the vessel to labour heavily and strain, with the result that she commenced to leak. The pumps however were able to keep her free, but later on these became choked, and the water then gained rapidly, and the Captain decided to bear back for safety, and on the 13th of February they reached the Elbe Lightship. By this time the water had gained so much that the vessel was settling down by the head, and fearing she would sink, a tugboat was engaged to tow her into Cuxhaven harbour, and another to pump water out of the hold, until they could get the vessel on the beach. This was eventually done and the leak ceased, proving that the water was coming in from the upper works. Afterwards a survey was held, and it was recommended that either the cargo be discharged and stored and the vessel be towed up to Hamburg to be thoroughly repaired, (as there were no facilities to do the work at Cuxhaven), or that temporary repairs should be executed, an extra pump placed on board, and the vessel towed to destination. This latter course being undoubtedly the most beneficial for the owners of the vessel. We arranged with a German tug company to perform the towage for £100 payable in cash on the vessel's arrival in Poole, but as she did not reach that port, the tug company cannot recover a penny for their service, which I must admit is pretty hard on them after reaching within 16 miles of their destination, but such is the risk of the sea, and of course

I could not make them any allowance at your expense, as the agreement was quite clear at the start.

The cost of putting into Cuxhaven amounted to £71, which apart from the loss of time, was not itself a serious matter, as a great deal of this will be recoverable in General Average from the Underwriters on ship and cargo. I regret to state however that the owners of the two tugs which assisted the vessel into Cuxhaven are claiming salvage remuneration for their services, and before the vessel was allowed to leave Cuxhaven, the sum of £300 had to be deposited with the Secretary of Lloyds, London as security, pending the result of arbitration proceedings that have been instituted to determine what is fair and reasonable amount for such services. We did our utmost to get the matter settled without the expense and trouble of arbitration, but the salvors were evidently under the impression that they would recover more by these means, and they would not listen to anything reasonable, therefore matters must take their course, and I can only hope that the result will be more favourable to us than we anticipate at present.

I cannot but attribute all this misfortune to the long detention at Queenstown, as if the vessel had received orders in a reasonable time after her arrival, she would have escaped all the severe weather that prevailed later on, and the probabilities are that much better cargo would have been available at Hamburg, so this is another instance of the vessel's bad luck.

After completing temporary repairs, she left Cuxhaven in tow on 13th March, and on the second day out she again experienced heavy gales of wind and high seas, which together with the heavy strain of towing, caused her to make a great quantity of water, but the pumps were in good working order, so the crew did not have much difficulty in keeping the vessel free, and she got safely across the North Sea, and had reached St Catherine's Point, Isle of Wight on the 17th when both pumps became choked again, and owing to the heavy seas washing over her, they could not get the additional pump to work, the consequence was that the water gained rapidly, and the vessel settled down by the head. In this condition the Captain signalled to the tug to send a boat to their assistance, which was immediately done, and all hands taken off just as they stood, and in about half an hour after they were got on board the tug, the vessel went down head first in deep water, where she still remains a total loss, and so ends the career of a vessel which I fear has caused you a great deal of worry and expense.

From the foregoing you will observe that no expenditure had been made on repairs, which is the only fortunate circumstance in connection with this unfortunate vessel, our intention having been to do what was necessary on her arrival in the Mersey for reasons already stated. As intimated in my previous letter, the vessel was covered by insurance for £1,500 in a Mutual Insurance Society which undertook the risk at a lower premium than if it had been effected at Lloyds, but under their rules they have six months time in which to pay the claim, but you may rely that as soon as we receive payment, the proceeds will be remitted to you, with a full and complete account of all receipts and payments.

We had no insurance on the freight as we had received M.800 on account at Hamburg before sailing, therefore the amount at risk was so small that I did not consider it worth covering. I shall not fail to advise you the result of the arbitration proceedings, and any further news I may have.

Trusting that I have not bored you too much with this lengthy epistle.

With kind regards, I am, dear Sir,

Yours faithfully,

William Thomas.

William Thomas's later confession that had he been aware beforehand of the problems likely to attend the *Balder*, he would have been very reluctant indeed to assume the mantle of manager, which is a clear indication of the enormous difficulty of the job he had undertaken. However, having informed Dr Macartney at the start of his commission that he would look after the vessel just as if she were his own, he remained steadfastly true to his word. His pursuit of that which was right and best for his client, coupled with his very evident deep understanding of the minutiae and legal implications of ship management, not only gives us a clearer insight into that very exacting business as it was conducted in the early years of the 20th century, but also affords us a glimpse into the very nature of the assiduous professional he undoubtedly was.

CHAPTER 10
LLOYD'S REGISTER AND THE REFINEMENT OF A SUCCESSFUL DESIGN

Many people are more familiar with Lloyd's as an association of insurance underwriters, than they are with *Lloyd's Registry of British and Foreign Shipping*, which is involved in the registration and classification of world shipping. Both organisations originated in the London coffee house owned by Welshman Edward Lloyd in Lower Thames Street; where during the later years of the 18th century, he posted daily news of the arrival and departure of shipping for the benefit of his merchant customers. He then went on to publish *Lloyd's News,* a thrice-weekly journal containing the same information; which with the *London Gazette,* can rightly claim to be one of the oldest newspapers in the world.

In this chapter, the main concern is with the second organisation, *Lloyd's Register,* which gives information regarding the integrity of vessels worldwide for insurance and other purposes. Against each vessel contained in the *Register*, are given details of its official number, tonnage, motive power, owner, classification and equipment. This large book, published annually, is given to all of Lloyd's subscribers, the name of the participating firm heavily embossed in gold on the front cover.

In order to standardise its classification system, Lloyd's set up a committee to lay down rules and standards which could be universally applied, not only by their surveyors, but by constructors as well. Since 1834, the classification of a vessel by Lloyd's involves the use of vowels and numerals. The letter 'A' for example, denotes a vessel of the highest order, whilst the letter 'E' denotes a second class vessel, and the letter 'I', a third, or lowest class vessel, unfit to undertake long voyages or to carry dry or perishable goods. One intermediate category 'Æ', denotes a ship in the second rank of the highest order. The numerals 1 and 2 were added to designate the quality of the vessel's equipment – anchors, cables etc., thus a vessel designated A1 is of very high order in both respects. There are several instances in the Thomas correspondence which refer to some vessels as being classified 'A1 for 8 years' for example, which originally no doubt, meant just what it said: but later classifications often include the term 'A1 for 100 years', which can be confusing, as the figure has no time significance, and is meant for comparison purposes only.

William Thomas's new vessels were invariably built to standards higher than those demanded by Lloyd's; and others which they had acquired were similarly modified to satisfy the same rigorous regulations, all of which operations needed to be inspected and approved by the Lloyd's local surveyor.

At the turn of the century, the local inspector was a Mr Riley, whose office was at Bangor. For reasons which will become apparent, William Thomas and Riley did not hit it off well. Matters came to a head between them when the latter came to classify the schooner *Hodbarrow Miner,* a vessel which had been built in Charnley's Ulverston shipyard in 1871, for the Duddon Shipping Association. In a sharply worded reply dated 29th of March 1902, to a written request by Riley to have additional work carried out on the vessel, beyond that which had been previously asked for and agreed, the owners confessed their great astonishment:

at the contents of your letter dated the 27th inst. Beyond completing the work, we have no intention whatever of doing anything further to this vessel; but under the circumstances, perhaps you will permit us to suggest that you call in another surveyor to assist you in this case, or if you prefer, we will make an application to Head Office. With regard to your statement requesting the Floors etc., we would remind you that after removing the old keelson, and before placing a new one on board, the floors were fully exposed, and you examined them, but you were not then able to find any of them damaged, therefore to suggest now that they are damaged, is beyond our comprehension.

Riley's professional qualifications must have been exemplary to have been given such a responsible position by Lloyd's, and it would seem that much of the annoyance he caused to William Thomas pointed more to his forgetfulness than to anything more serious. A month later, their paths crossed again, and on that occasion, William Thomas was moved to write to the Secretary of Lloyd's, informing him that:

Mr Riley has handed us your letter dated 8th inst., in reference to the freeboard of the schooner Hodbarrow Miner, by which we find that it is one inch more than the freeboard assigned by the Board of Trade when the vessel was not classed. We cannot understand this as we have expended a very large sum in placing this vessel in first class condition, and we fully expected that the freeboard would have been less and not more. We therefore cannot help but think that an error has been made in your (Mr Riley's) calculations. We should be pleased if you could look into the matter again, as we have delayed marking on the vessel's side until we hear from you.

It would appear that their complaint was upheld, for less than a week later, the brothers informed Riley that they had received a letter from Lloyd's Head Office respecting the matter of the *Hodbarrow Miner's* freeboard, and requesting him to come to the yard to verify its painting on the ship's side. A further letter from Riley asking if her hull had been salted, was met with the reply that he had not advised the firm that it was necessary, and pointing out that in any case, the vessel had by then sailed for Caernarfon.

A letter in October 1902, shows that the relationship between the parties had not improved, and indeed had even worsened to the point of bluntness. The problem involved the schooner *Meyric* which represented a stage in William Thomas's planned evolution of a 'super schooner' based on the original *Gelert* design (see Appendix 18), which had by then been languishing on the stocks for 2 years. Two other vessels started after her, the steam lighters *Belfast* and *Walton* had already been completed, and were launched in November 1900 and January 1902 respectively. The firm was very open in its criticism of Riley:

We must confess our great surprise at the contents of your letter, especially after your approval of the manner we propose to connect the main keelson to the after floor, and we cannot but consider this an afterthought on your behalf, to try and hide your other blunders. With regards to connecting the side stringer to the stem plate, we must admit we do not understand your meaning, and we must state that you have never mentioned anything about this to us at any time. We take this opportunity of reminding you that you have already approved of the alterations to the floors forward on account of the additional strength which the keelson gives over the scarph of the keel. When you are next here, we shall take advantage of your visit to discuss all these points with you.

A later complaint made by Riley to his superiors, claimed he had been denied access to the vessel's drawings. This was rebuffed by William Thomas & Sons who replied to their letter, stating:

We are surprised that the Surveyor has made a wrong report to you. We have never withheld the drawings from him, each time he has asked for them, they have been at his disposal. What we have maintained all along is precisely what you now state in your favour (letter), that they are to remain here during the construction of the vessel, and at the completion, that they are to be returned to your office. We cannot understand why Mr Riley should make such an erroneous statement.

January 1904 saw the end of a major slump in the gross tonnage of vessels being built in the United Kingdom. A fall from approximately 1,400,000 tons under construction in January 1902 to 900,000 tons at the end of 1903, resulted in a severe loss of confidence in Iard Newydd, so much so, that the Thomas brothers were minded to sell the business. The letter they wrote to Messrs Yarrow and Co., of London, whom they thought would be interested in buying, gives an insight into the relatively low costs in running the yard at that time:

According to the reports in the daily paper, that you have not yet been suited with a building yard, and therefore perhaps, you will pardon us for drawing attention to our yard which possesses a great many advantages although there are certain drawbacks, but we may mention that the advantages are: the low cost of living, and therefore cheap labour, the Mechanics here get 24 shillings a week, and labourers from 15 shillings to 18 shillings a week. The yard is freehold and of small rateable value, and consequently, the rates are exceedingly low compared with English towns. If you consider that this is worth your consideration, we should be very pleased to furnish you with all particulars you may require.

The steel 3-masted schooner Meyric.

A painting by the well known maritime artist Reuben Chappell, depiciting the Meyric
in foul weather.

The *Meyric* was eventually launched on the 4th of January 1904, and a month later to the day, her Master, Captain Griffiths wrote to the owners from Ymuiden (Ijmuiden), Holland, describing the effects of a hurricane which had overtaken his vessel:

I regret to inform you that I was obliged to put in her for safety of ship, having failed to get round the Texel. The hurricane came down when we were close to the land, and the sea got up like a boiling foam. I never saw the like in my life. I had to keep sail on her to drive her clear of the land, and she was like a duck. Our standing jib and topsails are blown to pieces, also the leach of the mainsail; but worst of all, the band of the foremast that is holding the foreyard worked loose in the heavy sea, and has worked itself deep into the mast. Another night at sea would no doubt have spoilt the mast as we could not do anything to it as she was rolling so much, and so I had to come here, and although the costs will be rather heavy as I have to pay £42 for towage in and out, it will be cheaper than if we had lost the foremast, and perhaps the ship and this valuable cargo.

Shortly after, Captain Lewis Thomas was taken seriously ill, having had what was described by his brother as a severe paralytic stroke. Although he partially recovered from its effects, William was later to claim that he would never be the same again.

Matters generally were to improve a month later, when William Thomas began negotiating with Mr E.O. Roberts of Liverpool, regarding the building of a new three-masted, steel schooner, another step forward in the evolution of the 'super schooner'.

On the 3rd of April, he advised Roberts that they had the half model of the proposed vessel ready, for his comments. Within a matter of days, they had received his observations, to which they replied:

We are pleased that the model has received the approval of your friends. With regard to reducing her forward, we can of course easily do this, but it will certainly affect her carrying capacity to a certain degree. The amount of course, will depend on the quantity we chip off. We observe that you are wishful for Captain Richards to see the model before you decide anything… we hope you will let us have it back as soon as possible to enable us to prepare her laying down.

SPECIFICATION: we observe the alterations which you made.

Hatchways: *we agree with you on the height of the coamings; but the length we fear will interfere with the Registered Tonnage, and this is a matter we have to be careful over, in fact, before we alter the specification and contract, we shall have to estimate roughly what she will register, as we find her gross register will be excessive and we shall either have to reduce her dimensions, or make the vessel finer.*

The caulking of her deck with three threads of Oakum is of course understood. With regard to spare blocks, this is rather a vague term, and may mean a great deal. Our usual practice is to supply the blocks necessary for the usual tackles; but we do not give any spare blocks.

Spare tiller: *it is quite unnecessary to have this specified in the specification as Lloyd's Rules demand that one should be supplied to every new vessel.*

Spare Compass: *this you will no doubt recollect, we pointed out to you, was not to be supplied by us, neither the discharging gaff, nor the stay whips. The hand spikes, we thought we had entered in the specification, and this was entirely an oversight. The one dozen plates, we of course agree to.*

With regard to the keelsons, we have specified these in the manner most beneficial to the owners. We are however, quite prepared to put the bulb in the side keelsons out of the bilge, but our idea was to connect the wash plates with the keelson, and thus make it interact, and the bulb in the keel section is extra beyond the requirements of Lloyd's , so that really you are getting two additions instead of one, and we certainly would advise that our proposal is by far the best. At the same time as we stated before, we are agreeable to alter it if you desire, but you will understand that there will be no bulb placed in the bilge keelson if you desire it to be added on to the side keelson.

Hawse Pipes: *We did not mention these particularly in the specification; but of course it is perfectly understood that all the usual and necessary pipes are to be supplied and fitted. As soon as we have the model back with your remarks, we will at once go into calculations, and then finally arrange the contract.*

A few days later, and in response to a letter received from Roberts, William Thomas noted that:

The model on the whole meets with your approval, but that you require the rize (sic) of the floor altered to 12 inches. We do not exactly understand where you mean the 12 inches to be, as the

present model has a rise of 12 inches at half breadth as shown in the enclosed rough tracing, where you require the 12 inch rise. Of course, you will understand that this will make a difference in her carrying capacity, which we presume you have taken into consideration.
As desired, we will alter the flange of the bulwarks forward, though we have not the same fear as yourself respecting this.

Stern:	*we must confess that we cannot agree with Captain Richards and Mr Toby respecting this, that is, if we properly understand the meaning, therefore we await the promised sketch which Mr Toby is preparing, and we will make any alteration you desire.*
Hatchways:	*we cannot rely on the alteration in the height of the coamings, and therefore we are anxious to make the length as short as possible, combined with utility.*

We shall not fall out about the discharging gaff and the steel runners; but we must state with regard to the spare blocks, we make all the necessary tackles in the first instance, and therefore it is quite unusual to supply these, and with regard to the spare compass, we pointed out to you that in larger vessels than this one, we only supply one compass. We consider that this will be quite sufficient for a vessel (of this size?), so we cannot agree to an extra compass.
 We observe that you are satisfied on our explanation about the keelsons.
 As soon as the model is finally approved, we will prepare a mid-ship section for submission to Lloyd's, and at the same time, we will send you a copy.
 As you make it the absolute condition that this vessel is to be 100 tons g.reg (gross registered tonnage) we think we ought to understand each other clearly in the comment, in case we fail to get her under this tonnage. Of course (you) will understand our object in discussing this matter at the present (time), as it is far better for all concerned that we clearly understand each (other) on this point so as to avoid all possible bother afterwards. Under the present circumstances you might turn round and decline to accept delivery of the vessel at all, and this we would not care about as our ideas of model are quite different. We should therefore be pleased to know how you would propose this matter should be dealt with.

The new owners had their own ideas regarding the design of the vessel, some of which did not exactly accord with what William Thomas believed to be right:
We shall as soon as possible turn to, and make the necessary alterations in the model, and make the rise of the floor 15" instead of 12". We cannot say right off how much it will take off her carrying capacity, but it will not affect it to a great extent. It is also impossible to state exactly right off how much the vessel will carry on the present model. As soon as we have trimmed her down to what we consider are your wishes, we will calculate her register tonnage, but the serious question to be considered is the penalty in the event of her exceeding 100 tons, and the writer will have to consult Captain Thomas before we can go any further in the matter. Of course, we can shape her such that she is bound to be under 100 tons, but we wish her to carry a respectable cargo as well.
 We must say that we cannot agree with Mr Toby's suggestion respecting the rail. We think ourselves that the stern could not be much improved upon, but we confess that we do not clearly follow the tracing which you enclose, as one section shows that the stern would appear just like

a tugboat's, and we are certain that you do not require this association.

Roberts was still pushing his own ideas however, and anxious to cover himself, William Thomas advised him that so long as they understood each other, he would press on with the model until he was satisfied that the full-size vessel would satisfy Roberts' requirements regarding tonnage. He even went as far as to suggest that he would be happy to work to Roberts' own model on condition that the latter took full responsibility for the vessel's tonnage and deadweight.

The offer was very wisely, not taken up, and Roberts was advised that the yard had:

... altered the rise of the floor of the model (ship) to 15" and have cut off a good deal forward and aft, so that in our opinion, she appears to be a very nice model. We shall now proceed to calculate her cubic capacity, and unless it is too large for the 100 tons register, we shall proceed to lay her down... we would like to see you before commencement of work.

The following day, they added:

we have now completed the calculation of the model as amended, and are pleased to state that it works out just to the tonnage we require, therefore we do not anticipate any fear of the vessel exceeding 100 tons register. Our calculations show the under deck tonnage to be 131 tons. To bring her under the 100 tons, we shall have to make a roomy cabin and forecastle. The dimensions of the vessel remain as at first arranged, namely; 95x22x10.3^1/$_2$ moulded, but we have made her finer both forward and aft as you suggested, and also made the rise of the floor 15" at half breadth, and in our opinion, she now looks an exceptionally pretty model.

In a rough calculation, we think that she will carry about 220 tons, but of course you will understand that we do not guarantee this to a ton or so. We now only desire you to see and approve of the model, and we will at once get everything into ship shape.

Unlike the early shipwrights discussed elsewhere, William Thomas was fully acquainted with the technique used to develop ships' lines on a drawing board; and the model referred to in his correspondence would not have been a laminated half model such as that produced for the *Mersey*; but would have been made out of a single block of wood, fashioned simply to illustrate to his client the shape of the hull he was being offered, and upon which he could comment.

All was agreed, and contract documents were sent out for signing 5 days later. In anticipation of the signing, William Thomas & Sons wasted no time in laying down the lines of the *Elizabeth Roberts,* as she was to be known, on the loft floor.

The contract for the *Elizabeth Roberts* had been signed by the 25th of May, 1903, but the yard was unable to make a start on her because the steel they had ordered a fortnight earlier had not arrived. The midship section which had been provisionally approved by Lloyd's, was sent to Mr Roberts, together with a request that he should confirm his stipulation that the depth of the deck coamings was to be 15 inches, which was somewhat less than that normally required by the Lloyd's committee. He was also sent copies of the vessel's mid-ship section, deck, sheer, and sail plans for his final approval.

Mr Riley, the Lloyd's surveyor, made his presence felt at an early stage when he angrily wrote to the builders regarding details of the vessel's construction which deviated from the norm. In their reply, they confessed their surprise:

... at the tone thereof, as we had distinctly called your attention when submitting the plans of

this vessel to two deviations from the rules, namely the height of the deck coamings, and also the floor which showed per plan, the depth at three quarters the half breadth to be 9" instead of 6", and this we placed in order to save turning them up to the two feet at the bilges in the same manner as we have done the Number 29 (Meyric).

The drawings were returned after being approved by your committee without any alteration, and upon these we have been working. We have not received a copy of the reply which you received from London, and which you state you had sent on to us. If the committee insist on the floors being carried to 2 feet above the top of the keel, we claim to reduce the depth to 8" at three quarters the half breadth... let us hear from you as early as possible.

In the meantime, E.O. Roberts had returned the sail plan, with his comments, eliciting a reply which yet again showed William Thomas's thorough grasp of his profession:

We ought to have stated that the sail plan was made for the sailmaker to make the sails by, and which allows a certain percentage for the new sails to stretch out, after which, they will fill their respective places, and we think if you will measure the length of the spars, you will find that we have made the sails very large for a vessel of her size...

... the fore, main and mizzen sails will be as you have shown with lead pencil when they have stretched out, but it will be impossible to get the three sails of the same size as you suggest, as the foresail is altogether a different shaped sail to the other two. The main and mizzen will fit into each other's place as shown on plan. We can however, if you desire it, make the main and mizzen booms exactly the same size. It is always customary to make the foresail shorter than the other two.

We have placed the foremast as forward as we considered it proper to do on account of the fore-hatch, and as you will no doubt have observed, there is only a very small space between the hatch and the post for the fore staysail traveller, and if we put it further forward, we fear it will interfere with the proper working of this sail, however, we are quite prepared to do so if you will take the consequences.

With regard to the topping of the booms, these are quite correct. We have made the allowance on account of the sails stretching, and when they are properly stretched, they will not be more than 6 feet from the deck, which is the usual height in vessels of this class.

We do not think that you need not (sic) have any fear that we shall lose any sail area, of course, the plan as it is, will appear to you in the manner you have pointed out.

With regard to the square sail, we had especially made it of the shape shown in order to save wear and tear of the sail through flapping against the rigging, but we are quite prepared to alter it to the shape you have marked, upon hearing from you. The height of this sail above the deck, will be about 7 feet.

Bowsprit:
We cannot agree with you that this is too long, as we have had experience with a similar vessel, and we had to alter her bowsprit in proportion to the size shown on the tracing.

Jibs:
The same remark applies to this as to the fore and aft sails, namely that we have allowed for stretching, and these will overlap the stays as you desire. The tacks are shown about a foot from the boom because they are secured by a piece of chain about a foot long. This is our usual practice, but if you desire, we will secure them in some other manner, and bring the tacks lower down.

Lower Topsail yard:
if we made this yard 3 feet longer than it is as you suggest, the topside leach would be almost square, and therefore would look very bad. We consider the lengths of the spars to be ample. Of course, the sails will stretch out to the pencil marks which you have placed on the tracing. We have only 9" yard arm on the upper yard, and 1 foot on the lower topsail yard, and we will reduce the fore yard arm if you desire, to 1 foot, but of course, this will not alter the sail in any way.

Fore Topmast:
the drawing shows this to be 9" and not 6" as you state.

William Thomas later added:
We omitted to state in our last letter that the roach in the upper topsail was accounted for by the fact that we are placing the boom jib stay above the lower yard. If you wish, we will bring it down to the same position as the fore stay and standing jib stay, but our experience shows that the sail draws better with the stay in the position we have marked it.

Roberts and his friends were apparently still not satisfied with William Thomas's explanation regarding the positioning of the fore-mast, and by way of further explanation, the latter wrote:
you are quite right in stating that you take the consequences wherever we place the fore-mast, but it is only reasonable that we should exercise all possible foresight before finally deciding the general arrangement. You have not however, read our letter in the manner we intended it. It is not so much the shifting of the fore-mast as the small space that will be between it and the hatch for the working of the fore-staysail. We have however, devoted some time to-day to the matter, and are preparing a tracing showing the utmost extent which the fore-mast can be moved forward, and unless prevented by some unseen circumstance, the writer hopes to call on you on Thursday morning. In the meantime, please keep the sail plan sent you, and we can fully discuss the whole matter, and at the same time, we can explain the difference in the shape of the fore-sail, and the Main-sail and Mizzen, and have no doubt that we shall after talking the matter over, be able to finally agree on the position of the masts, and the size of the sails etc.

A further memorandum from Mr Riley served to ruffle William Thomas's feathers yet again, as is evident from his reply:
We cannot understand your meaning when you state you require pillars fitted at the side of the water tank. This will mean that they will be close to the brackets, and will be of no assistance whatever to the beam itself. We cannot understand why you should insist on these, as in all previous vessels they were never fitted. With regard to the stringer plates on the cabin sole, the rules do not state that these are absolutely necessary, and we thought that the vessel being so shallow that it would not be necessary to fit them – the floors we are making in accordance with approved plans.

Not only was iron ordered for the *Elizabeth Roberts* late in arriving, the quality in some instances fell far short of expectations, as was expressed in a letter to Sir Theodore Fry & Co., of Darlington:

The bars have arrived, but we must confess our disappointment at their appearance, as we fully expected well rolled bars, considering that we are paying you for "Best Best". These we fear will not be passed by Lloyd's surveyor, in which event, we shall have to ask you to supply fresh ones. We therefore impress upon you to send the others of very good quality.

On receipt of the remainder of their order for keel bars, a further letter of complaint was sent to the manufacturers:

...received delivery of the last two keel bars, and very much regret to find that they are even worse than the first two. We commenced working one this morning, when a piece flew out through defective rolling. We are surprised that you should have supplied this quality as we were paying you for "Best Best", and we fear that we shall not be able to work them at all, in which case we shall return them and charge you for this long detention.

In the end, rather than go to the expense which would have ensued, but more importantly, to avoid further delay, which under a penalty clause with the buyer, amounted to £3 per week, William Thomas advised Theodore Fry that they had cut the bad sections from the bars and were welding others in their place; adding that they would charge them for the additional work.

Similarly, the rudder frame and stern post received from Barr Thompson of Kilmarnock, although of excellent quality, was found to be heavier than specified, and as they were required to pay by weight, they wrote to the suppliers expressing their hope that they would not be expected to pay for the additional weight above which they had been quoted.

By August, William Thomas was able to inform Roberts that they were busy raising the frames of his new vessel, and hoped to have her fully framed in a matter of days, adding that they had taken men off their vessel, the *Meyric*, which although launched was still unfinished, in order to press on with his.

When final preparations for the vessel's launch were being made, Mr Riley reappeared at the yard, in order to finally ascertain and verify the actual midship section of her hull as agreed to by Lloyd's. His dismay at finding that his measurements in no way accorded with what they were supposed to be, he wrote to the brothers stating his grave concern. In their warmly articulated reply, the brothers' usual frustration with him appears to have vanished, and they told him that following his letter, they had made enquiries, and that they had discovered that by mistake, he had measured frame number 34, which was considerably abaft of the amidships section he was meant to measure. They then somewhat condescendingly assured him that when he came again to re-measure the section, they would help him!

The launch of the *Elizabeth Roberts* took place on the 4th of April 1904, some 3 months after the launch of the Thomas's own vessel, the three-masted schooner *Meyric*. The photograph of the *E.R* as she would popularly be known, entering the water from the launchway adjacent to the dry dock, is the only known photograph of a vessel being launched at Amlwch.

The launch of the schooner Elizabeth Roberts *in April 1904. This is the only known photograph of a launch at Porth Amlwch.*

Following her launching, the vessel's finishing took a little while longer, and in a letter to her owner a few days later, William Thomas told him that he had men working on every part of her: but that he confidently expected everything to be completed by the following week. He then added that:

the cabin is the chief thing holding us back, and as you very well know, only a certain number of men can work on it – the men will work late on the cabin etc. until she is finished. As regards the manilla, the only thing is, that it has not as much turn in it as we should like, for which reason we have stopped putting it into the E.R. You may depend that everything that we supply to this vessel is of the best, or at least, represented to us as such, and for which we pay (accordingly!).

Within days, William Thomas was able to inform her owner that the vessel had left Amlwch, adding:

The Elizabeth Roberts has commenced her career very fortunately, as she got out of this port just in the nick of time, as it is blowing strong from the north east today, with heavy sea right into the harbour, and it would have been impossible for her to get out. We trust that she arrived safely in Portmadoc (sic), and she secured the Bremen cargo. We are anxiously awaiting a word from the captain with an account of how she acted, as if he had the same breeze last night as we had here, he had every opportunity of testing her qualities.

Writing to Rees Jones, the *E.R.'s* captain, at Porthmadog, William Thomas reminded him of his promise to let him know the quantity of cargo the vessel was able to load: but more importantly, regarding what he as her designer considered to be the acid test – precisely what the people of Porthmadog, a port famous for superb sailing vessels and knowledgeable seamen, thought of his new creation.

The following day he again wrote to E.O. Roberts:

We do not think you have any cause to worry that the vessel missed stays on her passage from here to P'Madoc, as it was only what we anticipated, and explained to the Captain, who quite agreed with us, but he was anxious to get her trimmed by the stern in order to make a good show when entering the port. We shall be greatly disappointed if, when she is in her proper trim, she does not come up to our expectations in every respect, and as you know, those expectations are high ones.

In acknowledging receipt of the last instalment on the *Elizabeth Roberts*, William Thomas was happy to record:

We also desire to tender you our best thanks for your kind appreciation of our efforts to build you a serviceable vessel, and we can only hope that she will turn out fully to our expectations, and that she will have a fortunate career to earn back the capital expended with good interest thereon... our relations have been most happy throughout the whole transaction, and we can only hope that this good fellowship will continue for many years.

A letter received on the 11th of June 1904, from Captain Rees Jones in Bremen, praised the performance of his vessel, and in their reply to him, the brothers wrote:

We need hardly state that we were delighted to receive the report of the ER's good performance, and are extremely pleased at her behaviour during the voyage, and more especially that you are satisfied with her working... We may state that we were particularly pleased to learn that you arrived before the M.A. James, and that the captain of this vessel has such a high opinion of the ER, and we can only hope that we shall shortly have a customer from Portmadoc for the vessel we are now laying down (Cenric).

Captain Jones sent the builders an account of the manner in which the *Elizabeth Roberts* sailed, and how she had kept ahead of a steamer sailing between the Galloper (Galloper sand banks just north of the Thames estuary, and about 300 sea miles from the Elbe) and the Elbe. To have sailed faster than a steamer over that distance was indeed a remarkable feat, and in a letter to her owner William Thomas proudly stated that:

> We received a letter from Captain Rees Jones last week with a most excellent account of the Elizabeth Roberts sailing, and no doubt he has told you that he kept ahead of a steamer from the Galloper to the Elbe. This I consider to be an exceptional thing for such a long distance, and some friends have been urging me to send an account to the Gazette, but being the builders of the vessel, my modesty forbids me doing so.

In a subsequent letter to Roberts, William Thomas, very proud of his achievement, was obviously pleased to elaborate:

> Captain Jones states that the steamer he was in company with, was one of the regular traders between Liverpool and Hamburg, by which we would conclude that she would be of fair speed. If she had only kept ahead of the steamer for a short distance, this would have been nothing extraordinary in the performance, but considering that it was from the Galloper to the Elbe, the old shellbacks here, to whom I narrated the fact, state positively that it was a most exceptional piece of sailing. However, as you state, I agree it would not be wise without minute particulars, to send any account to the papers, but notwithstanding your kind acknowledgement of my extreme modesty, I venture to state that for a vessel of her size, 10 knots on the bowline is a record speed.

As a result of this news, William Thomas was happy to claim that the *Elizabeth Roberts* was then without doubt, the fastest vessel in the 'Three Channels' (The North, St George's and the English Channels).

E.O. Roberts was aware in June 1904 that William Thomas & Sons were laying down another steel schooner slightly larger than the *Elizabeth Roberts*, but on the same model, as a speculative project. According to her designer, she was moulded to carry 225 tons on a nett registered tonnage of 99 tons, and was destined for the British coasting trade.

When the *Cenric's* hull had been substantially completed, the builders wrote to David Hughes of Liverpool, a carver, enclosing a full-size tracing of the stem and lacing of the new vessel, and ordering a male figurehead. As if to satisfy William Thomas's eye for detail, he asked Hughes to throw the figure's head well back so that it would have the appearance of looking straight ahead and not down on to the water.

On the 21st of July 1905, a letter was sent to Johns and Son of Gloucester, who were potential buyers for the new vessel. Apart from illustrating the business methods used by them to persuade people to buy, the letter also gives a clear understanding of the procedure used by the Thomases when they came to launch new vessels:

> The new vessel we have for sale is almost completed, and we are arranging to launch her next springs. The lower masts are already stepped, the rigging set and rattled, all the spars, sails, covers etc., are made, and we have just had delivery of the chains and anchors. There is very little work to be done to complete her ready for sea, as we generally finish them on the stocks before launching; in some cases we even have the sails bent, stores on board, and the vessel leaving here the same tide as she was launched. There are several things we shall require to complete, such as stoves, lamps, hawser, warps, flags, running gear, compass, clocks, barometer, cooking utensils etc. etc., and if any inducement to you, we could arrange for you to supply these.
>
> The vessel is being constructed under the supervision of a Lloyd's surveyor to Class 100 A1 special survey, and as desired, we enclose you a tracing of midship section showing thickness of

scantlings etc., by which you will observe that she has been built considerably in excess of Lloyd's requirements for the purpose of taking the ground to load and discharge.

If you really entertain her purchase, it would be far more satisfactory if you ran over to inspect, as it would give you a far better idea of her value and appearance than it is possible to describe on paper, although we may mention that she has a much finer appearance than even the little vessel (E.R.?) whose photo we sent you the other day, and as a further inducement to buy, we would retain 8 or 10/64ths shares in her. The bedrock price is £2,450, and this only just covers the cost of building, as she has been constructed in the best manner possible and fitted out equally as good, as you would be able to verify if you decided to inspect.

The schooner Cenric *on the yard's northern slipway.*

Writing to Walter Reney, William Thomas took the opportunity to discuss the *Cenric*, describing her as being similar to the *Elizabeth Roberts*, but was generally acknowledged to be a finer looking vessel which could carry between 5 and 7 tons more. As the Johns had not taken up the invitation to the launch on the 2nd of August 1905, and were showing no real interest in purchasing the vessel, William Thomas sought to persuade Walter Reney to buy her himself. His reply, although complimentary, was non-committal: but William Thomas was undeterred, and in a further communication with him, said:

We are pleased to observe the high opinion you have of vessels built by us... altho' freights are so low, a good handy vessel will pay far better interest than you would get from the bank, and you know this as well as anybody, as you have so many vessels. Our price for the new vessel is £2,500 and this figure is only a shade over her prime cost to us... can you not run over here to inspect whilst she is in dock. You can then see exactly the alterations and extras we have supplied to her over the E.R.

Despite his efforts, William Thomas failed to find a buyer for the *Cenric,* and he decided to absorb her into the family fleet. Knowing that Thomas would be needing a master for the new vessel, Captain Tyrran of the *Hodbarrow Miner* wrote to him, expressing great interest in taking command of her. In reply, and knowing perhaps that the Captain, although a dependable and capable master in every way, did not have the wherewithal to invest in the vessel to the extent they expected, they informed him that:

Command of the new vessel will be given to the man who will invest the most money in her… two or three captains have already made enquiries… we shall not forget however, our promise to you in the event of us not arranging to sell sufficient shares.

William Thomas's sons (William and Cecil?) on board the Cenric *when she was being fitted out at Porth Amlwch.*

The one eventually chosen to be her master was Captain Maurice Parry, of Borth y Gest, a single man, who had previously been Master of one of E.O. Roberts's vessels. Under his command the *Cenric* left Porth Amlwch two weeks before Christmas 1905, bound for Porthmadog. On the day he left Amlwch, William Thomas wrote to him at his port of call, informing him that he was anxiously awaiting his report as to how his vessel had behaved on her short maiden voyage, as she appeared to be travelling exceedingly fast through the water.

Captain Parry's encouraging report was received by return of post, to which William Thomas replied:

…pleased to understand that the vessel was admired by those who had seen her, and we can only hope that she will prove as fast in sailing as the Elizabeth Roberts. Judging from the manner she sailed when leaving here, we say that she should prove superior in this respect to the E.R.…indeed, we shall be perfectly satisfied if she does as well as her.

In a mildly provocative manner, William Thomas wrote to E.O. Roberts on the 19th of December 1905 regarding the *Cenric:*

This vessel, as you state, is loading at Portmadoc for Bremen, and like yourself, we hope that she will not have any trouble with the ice when she gets round there. From appearances on shore when she left here on Saturday, we fear that the Elizabeth Roberts will have to yield up the palm for sailing, as no doubt you have heard from your friends that she was going like a greyhound from here on her way to Portmadoc.

I take this opportunity of reminding you of your promise that if we succeeded in building one to beat the E.R., that you would give us an order to build another to beat this one, and we are quite prepared to undertake the commission. Of course, you will understand that the E.R. will not sail any slower because the Cenric beats her.

In a further letter to Roberts regarding the *Cenric's* speed, William Thomas wrote:

…considering that she is now the clipper of the 3 Channels, she ought to arrive before her cancelling date. I might mention that we have had a letter with a full report of her sailing qualities, having been in company with vessels which are considered to be very good sailers, but none of them had a show with her. The only thing now is to get in company with the Elizabeth Roberts, and if she beats her, we may then reasonably expect to be favoured with your promised order for one to beat both… it is quite true that she has not met the Elizabeth Roberts yet; but it is only just a question of time when she will knock smoke out of her, the same as she has done with other vessels, but we have another one building now that is going to eclipse both. .

William Thomas was extremely anxious to break into the Newfoundland fish trade, but brokers generally were unwilling to charter steel vessels for that purpose, fearing that their cargo would be spoilt, and much preferring wooden vessels instead. This reflects earlier fears when the Royal Mail refused to allow letters to be conveyed by iron vessels, and the widely-held belief that tea would be spoilt if conveyed by steamships because of the smell. This did not deter William Thomas however, and his persistence paid off when Messrs Bowring, who were well-established fish brokers, agreed to break with tradition. Writing to Captain Parry, William Thomas said:

… with regard to the fish charter – as the Cenric is the first steel vessel which Messrs Bowring have fixed to carry fish, you can easily understand that it was not without some trouble that they were induced to take her on, and it will depend very much upon the condition which this cargo is carried to market whether they will give another cargo to another steel vessel. As we are extremely anxious to ingratiate steel vessels into charterer's favours, and also to prevent possible claims arising from either short weight or damage by moisture, we trust you will take every precaution when loading to secure the proper weights, and as a precaution against any possible

moisture, we would suggest that you buy some very cheap soft bagging or canvas, say 100 or 150 yards at a price from 2d to 3d per yard, and if something of the nature of tow was put between it, it would help materially to absorb any sweat or moisture dropping off the beams or stringers. The hold stanchions also could be covered over with this, or possibly you could suggest some other manner of protection against the possible chance of damage as we consider it would be to our future advantage if we have to go to a little expense with first cargo.

The *Cenric* arrived safely in Cadiz after an 8-day passage from Cardiff. There, she took on a cargo of 200 tons of salt from the local salinas before sailing for Twillingate, Newfoundland. She arrived there on the 25th of May 1906, having had a fair weather passage until she arrived off the banks of Newfoundland where it was rather rough, with a considerable amount of drift ice.

On the 12th of June, having discharged her cargo of salt, she sailed in ballast for Sydney, Cape Breton, where she was to take on her cargo of fish. Although the passage would normally have taken a week to complete, no news whatsoever had been received of her by the end of July, and William Thomas was very uneasy regarding the long period of silence. However, he remained hopeful that the vessel had been blown out to sea, and that she would soon turn up safe and sound.

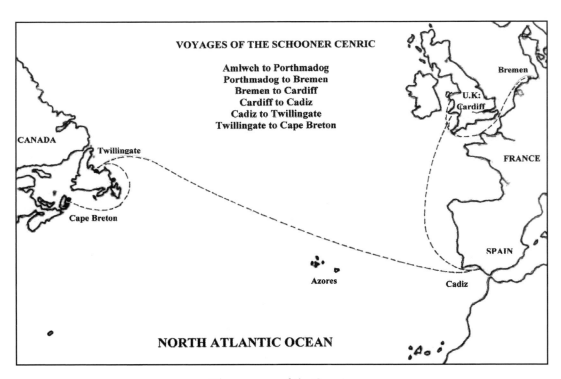

The voyages of the Cenric.

In a letter dated 31st of July to Thomas Canby of Barrow in Furness, Thomas wrote:

This morning we received a letter from a friend of ours in Liverpool, who enclosed us an extract from a letter received by the Liverpool charterers, a copy of which we enclose herein. We also enclose a copy of a report which appeared in the 'Shipping Gazette' on 26th June, and we very much fear that the schooner referred to therein was the Cenric, and we now have no hopes for her safety, as it is now 50 days since she left Twillingate, and we fear there is not the slightest chance of her having been blown out to sea, as the probabilities are that if such had been the case, she would have turned up somewhere by now.

It would appear that the *Cenric* had been seen by another of Bowring's charters in the neighbourhood of Sydney, the day before a very severe storm; and the report in the *Shipping Gazette* referred to by William Thomas, stated that a vessel in distress had been seen off Sydney .

On the 3rd of August, Thomas wrote to the Pritchard brothers of Porthmadog, saying:

we very much fear that something very serious has happened to her, in fact to be candid, we are convinced that she has been lost with all hands, and it is the latter fact which makes it so deplorable, and whilst we naturally feel the deepest sympathy for all members of the crew, we feel extremely so on account of the loss of Captain Parry, to whom we had become very much attached. The writer called with Messrs Bowring Brothers, the charterers, and they showed him a letter they had received from their St Johns house, an extract of which we enclose... the Arietis, the vessel referred to therein, is a Danish vessel which was ready to leave Twillingate for Sydney, the same day as the Cenric, and Captain Parry in his last letter to us stated that he was anxious to get to Sydney to secure his turn to load before she got there. We find that this vessel arrived back at Twillingate from Sydney on the 3rd of July... the sad event following so closely upon the loss of his brother last year will be a terrible blow to the relatives.

In a letter of condolence to the late Captain Parry's sister in Borth y Gest, near Porthmadog, William Thomas wrote:

I cannot express the pain and sorrow which the sad occurrence has caused me, as I had become so attached to your dear brother, who during our short acquaintance I regarded as a personal friend, and with whom I had hoped to enjoy a long and pleasant connection, and it is most sad to think that such a bright and promising career should have been so suddenly cut short. The sadness has cast the greatest gloom over this neighbourhood, as during his short stay here, Captain Parry, by his cheerful and pleasant manner, has endeared himself to all with whom he came in contact... Mrs Thomas particularly desires me to associate her in this expression, as we had the pleasure of your brother's company on one or two occasions, and like ourselves, the children were always particularly pleased to have and enjoy his company, and they often asked when he was coming to Amlwch again.

Thomas was well aware by then, that the days of the wooden sailing ship were numbered, and in reply to an offer made by one of his fellow shareholders in the *County of Cork*, to sell him his shares in the vessel, William Thomas replied:

... we have repeatedly tried to sell this vessel, but unfortunately, we cannot get anybody to entertain her, as this class of vessel is quite obsolete. We ourselves are very anxious to dispose of our interest, and you can rely that at the first opportunity we shall try to dispose of her, but

having so many of this class of vessel on our hands, we would not care to increase our interest, in fact we should be only too pleased to get rid of all the old vessels.

In yet another effort to keep the yard going, Thomas decided at this time to explore a working relationship with the Yorkshire Metal Company, whereby he would break up suitable vessels, and sell the scrap to the company. In this respect however, he had decided that he would not attend further sales of Government vessels, for the simple reason that it was extremely difficult to estimate the amount of metal they contained, and that henceforth he would concentrate on merchant vessels:

We have every advantage to break up, as the labour is very cheap, but our space is rather limited, but no doubt the Harbour Authority would give every encouragement and accommodation in order to attract work to this place, the trade of which has most seriously fallen off lately. With regard to another firm who might take up business with you, we regret we do not know of anyone, as all information respecting these crafts is most jealously guarded by the large ship breaking firms who are also metal merchants themselves as a general rule.

In September 1907, William Thomas & Sons were approached by Stewart and Tyrer of Liverpool, who were exploring the possibility of running a regular steamship service between Liverpool and Amlwch. In his usual measured response William Thomas advised them that:

…there is no regular steam service between Liverpool and here. In our opinion, if a small, handy steamer was placed on the trade, she would give good returns, as we are entirely at the mercy of the L&NW Railway Co., who dictate their own terms, as there is no opposing company. If we can be of assistance to you in promoting a regular service, we shall be very pleased to do what we can.

We cannot give you the exact quantity of the traffic to this port, but the best paying would be general grocery, drapery etc. In the season there is a lot of artificial manure shipped, and we have no doubt but that a great quantity of this could be secured for a regular trader. We should be pleased to introduce you to the shippers when you have further considered the scheme. We do not know the railway rates on groceries, but we know that they are very high, no doubt but that we will be able to get you these rates. We quite agree with you that a small company would be the best, especially if the people interested could be induced to take shares, but they would have to be canvassed before we could form any idea of the support likely to be secured. We ourselves would be very pleased to support it in every manner, and to place all the goods that we shall have coming and going from here. Very often we have a cargo of scrap iron for Connahs Quay or the Mersey.

The vessel William Thomas had in mind was of about 150 tons, on as small a draft as possible: but the response to Stewart and Tyrer's canvassing was far from encouraging however, and although he proposed that he should meet them at their Liverpool office, nothing more was heard of the project.

As he had earlier predicted in a letter to O.E. Roberts, the ultimate refinement in William Thomas's quest for sailing perfection which had begun with the *Gelert*, came to fruition in his design of a three-masted schooner conceived to outperform both the highly successful *Elizabeth Roberts*, and the faster but ill-fated *Cenric*.

Representing as she did, the end of 'real' shipbuilding at Amlwch, the steel, pole masted schooner *Eilian*, as she was ultimately named, came to be what was undoubtedly the best known of Thomas's sailing vessels. Because of her chequered career and extended life span, as well as the fact that she represented all that was finest in the art of schooner building, much has already been written about her (see Appendix 20).

The *Eilian*, like her predecessors, was designed and laid down purely as a sailing vessel: but when Captain David Richardson of Rock Ferry, Cheshire, showed great interest in buying her whilst she was still on the stocks however, William Thomas agreed to alter her structure aft in order to accommodate an auxiliary power unit. This was to be in the form of a twin cylinder, 52 BHP 'Kromhout', paraffin motor of Dutch manufacture, which was to be supplied and delivered to Amlwch, together with two winches capable of lifting half a ton each, at Richardson's cost. In return, William Thomas & Sons consented to invest 24/64ths in the finished vessel, the final price of which was £2,500. As such, she was almost certainly the first ever schooner in the United Kingdom, if not the world, to be expressly designed to make use of auxiliary power.

On the 14th of April 1908, William Thomas had to advise Captain Richardson that work on the vessel was not progressing very well, due to his illness, which had kept him from the yard. It is known that at that time, he was suffering acutely from gallstones, which led him to seek some measure of relief in herbal remedies. In addition to his ill health, pressure resulting from the fact that his brother Lewis's stroke had left him severely disabled, meant that he was having to shoulder the burden of managing the yard, albeit with the assistance of his sons and nephews who had been absorbed into the business.

Captain Lewis Thomas died some 9 days later, on the morning of the 23rd of April, 1908.

As the day of the launching of the new vessel approached, the owner of the steam yacht *Medina* of Caernarfon, offered the services of his vessel as a tugboat to assist with the launch. Although he declined the offer, William Thomas's reply gives some indication of the festivities which were an integral part of a launch day in Amlwch:

> With further reference to your telegram, we thank you very much for your kind offer to attend the launch next Friday; but regret that owing to uncertainty of our getting into communication with you in time, as we did not know your correct address, we took advantage of the services of a small steamer which is now in this port... if in the course of your cruise, you happen to be down this way on Friday, we can promise you a nice sight, as you would be in an exceptional position to witness her launch, and also a share of any good eatables or drinkables that may be knocking about on the day. We greatly appreciate your kind offer, but we fear we cannot now honourably withdraw from the arrangements we have made.

The vessel named *Pioneer*, was launched on the 14th of August 1908. Her name appears to have been suggested by Captain Richardson: but was one which turned out to be unacceptable to the Liverpool Registrar. The second choice, favoured by owner and builder alike, was *Dixie*, but this also turned out to be unacceptable, as Thomas went on to advise his partner in the venture:

> ... you will understand that he declines to register the new vessel under the name Dixie, and that a name should be selected which has not been appropriated by another British ship. We would suggest the name of Eilian, which was the name of a vessel we had some years ago, and which proved to be one of the most fortunate vessels that ever we managed, and there is no question of a duplicate name arising, as there is no other vessel of this name registered. Of course we will agree to any other name you might have in mind, but would suggest that it be a short one.

The method used to appoint the new vessel's master was very similar to that used in the case of the *Cenric*, as was demonstrated in William Thomas's letter to Captain Eben Griffith of the ss *Hopeful*:

The owner of the new vessel was here the other day... we succeeded in persuading him to give you the preference, and he has authorised us to state that you can have command providing you purchase shares to the extent of £300, and subject to your agreeing upon remuneration for your service.

Having purchased the necessary shares, and agreed his salary, Eben Griffith was directly appointed the vessel's first master. After her launch, the *Eilian* was put into the graving dock, so that she could be fitted out with her new motor, supplied through Messrs Perman of London, to whom a letter was sent regarding its installation.

We shall in a few days' time, be in the position to place the motor on board this vessel... pleased if you name a lump sum for the services of your fitter, as this would be more satisfactory than day work, as he would then naturally push on faster with the work and so save the time of the assistants we should have to provide.

The matter of fitting the engine was also discussed with the vessel's owner in a series of letters:

...agree with you that Perman's are asking an unreasonable sum for the services of their fitter. At the same time, we are of the opinion that it would be far better to pay this rather than get an outside man, as eventually, he would take a much longer time to do the work than a man from the works, and then would not probably fit them in their right place... We noticed the report of

The auxiliary schooner Eilian *at anchor in Par.*

the motor schooner in yesterday's *Daily Post* , which proves that somebody is of the same opinion as ourselves that there is money to be made in this class of vessel.

With regard to the installation of the motor, we are pleased to state that good progress is being made, but Jeffereys had a telegram last night instructing him to go to Liverpool. Still we do not think that we shall feel his loss very much. The stern tube and the tail end shaft are in their places, and we have now got the motor engine slung all ready over the bed to be lowered down for the marking of the holding down bolts, and so far, everything has gone satisfactorily. As soon as we are able to release the motor from the present shear legs, we shall be able to ship the three masts, which will allow us to make a more rapid progress towards completion.

We have now got the three masts stepped, and the fitter is making good progress in the installation of the engine. Jeffereys returned this morning from Liverpool and we think that everything will now proceed smoothly. Owing to a new Act which came into force at the beginning of the year, it is necessary to make an application to the Registrar at the port of registry in order that he may decide whether he will allow the proposed name or not. We quite agree with you that we should not be called upon to pay for the whole time that the Dutch fitter is here waiting for the piping from Amsterdam... it is however only fair for us to mention the fact that he has made several alterations on this engine, as he explained that having been built some months ago, it was not of their latest type... the question is, will the alterations that he has made more than repay the outlay on them?

We understand that the engines have to be tried in the harbour for 5 hours continuous running before going out to sea, and for this we are informed by the fitter, that he requires 40 gallons of Russian oil, as the American oil which we stock is not suitable, although we are supplying him with 10 gallons of 'Royal Daylight' to test the small tank and the pumping arrangements.

We have spent almost the whole of the day trying to get the Dan engine to work, but in spite of every effort, she refused to fire the charge... the cause was a leakage from the water jacket into the cylinder and after temporarily stopping this, we got it to work for about a quarter of an hour. Unless this is remedied, we fear that the same defect will occur each time that she is started. The Dutchman thinks that he can remedy the defect...

We acknowledge receipt of your telegram authorising the Dutchman to make the alterations which he considered necessary to the Dan engine.... with regard to the Russian oil, the Dutchman advises that we have at least 120 gallons as he anticipates using a great deal in the trial run whilst in dock. Would it not be better to get a 1 ton lot, as you will gain in the price... Board of Trade surveyor was here yesterday, and finally passed everything.

We had a very successful trial of the new motor schooner yesterday, and obtained an average speed of a shade over 8^1/$_2$ knots, everything working very satisfactorily. We expect that the vessel will be commencing work in a few days.

Eilian's average speed must have pleased William Thomas enormously, for it comfortably exceeded the estimated 5^1/$_2$ to 6 knots recorded on her registration document, which also records the fact that he owned 12/64 ths of her shares. The same amount was held by John Thomas, who was presumably his 28-year-old nephew, who became a junior partner in the firm following his father's death.

The *Eilian* left Amlwch bound for Canning Dock, Liverpool on the 17th of November, 1908.

A dramatic photograph of the auxiliary schooner Eilian *under full sail.*

Her early life was confined to carrying general cargoes, visiting many of the lesser known ports around the coast of the British Isles, and others on the continent of Europe including the Channel Islands. During the First World War, she was, because of her innate strength, commissioned as a 'Q' Ship, a brief account of which appears elsewhere. She entered naval service on the 24th of September 1917, and served until the 1st of February 1919.

In October 1923, she was purchased by the Hartnoll, and then the Newcombe families of Exeter before being sold to a succession of Danish owners, the last being R.B.H. Neilsen of Aalborg, who renamed her *Fjordbo*. 3 years later she was sold to Earl Byron Clarke of Bridgetown, Barbados.

Hopes of returning the vessel to Amlwch where she could have been put on display as part of the town's heritage, were dashed when it was learnt that on the 6th of January 1984, having sailed out of Castries, she began to take in water in Lat. 12.21N; Long. 65.15W. She was last seen in Lat. 13.09 N; Long. 66.43 W. on the 9th of January, after which she was presumed to have sunk, having given 76 years' sterling service to her various owners.

Sailing shipowners and builders alike had been stubborn in their continuing resistance to the introduction of steam power, which was exemplified by William Thomas's own belief in the future of sail as he steadfastly pursued his dream of the ideal – a 'super schooner'. The improvements he instituted in his successive designs in pursuit of this goal, resulted in strikingly beautiful vessels which reflect the engineer's long held belief that "if it looks right, then it is right"! By way of proof, should that be necessary, they were superb sailers as well, more than holding their own and even beating steam-powered vessels when the conditions were right. The use of patent deck gear drastically reduced operating costs, but despite it all, it was impossible to stem the tide of larger, steam-powered vessels as they swept into almost every maritime niche.

As much as they could outperform steamers when the wind was right, even the better schooners were still unable to compete when wind conditions were not favourable. The solution came in the shape of the marine oil engine which had sufficient power to overcome light winds and calm conditions; but which had few of the penalties imposed by steam engines requiring sizeable boilers and large coal bunkering spaces. Even more important was the fact that unlike their steam counterparts, the smaller oil engines required only one engineer to attend them.

Whether or not the idea of building what was probably one of the first, if not the very first auxiliary vessel of its kind, originated with Captain Richardson or with William Thomas, is impossible to say, for as much as the former was clearly well informed, the latter was certainly well abreast of current thinking in every aspect of marine technology. Having said that however, it is possible that William Thomas turned a blind eye to the obvious in his quest for a 'super sailing schooner'.

Although not the ultimate in pure sailing innovation as was originally hoped for by William Thomas, the fact that the *Eilian* in all its guises survived a working life of 76 years, is surely the most telling testimony to his skills as her designer. Having said that however, what should not be overlooked is the very evident level of technical skill possessed by a small force of local artisans employed in what was an out-of-the-way Welsh yard, far from mainstream British shipbuilding, which gave her life.

CHAPTER 11
THE SCHOONER *HODBARROW MINER*
"We have no desire to part with this vessel as she is such profitable property."

The *Hodbarrow Miner*, a 123 ton topsail schooner classed A1 at Lloyds for 8 years, and registered at Barrow-in-Furness, was built by Charnley of Ulverston in 1871. The vessel was especially built for the Hodbarrow Mining Company when Captain William Thomas was in the process of establishing his own shipyard close to the Hodbarrow Mine at Duddon.

Constructed to withstand the rigorous demands of the iron ore trade, the vessel was inherently strong, and for many years it was employed taking iron ore directly to smelters in Wales, or alternatively, to ports from where it could be transhipped by rail to the Midlands.

The vessel had a chequered career, which began on the very day she was launched, when:

> *through both ends of the ship not being started at the same time, the vessel was thrown off her supports, and stuck fast before reaching the water.*

The accident was not as serious as might have seemed at first, for her builders were able to lift her bodily back on to the slipway, thereby allowing her to be launched without incident on the evening tide. The evident ease with which the supposedly unsophisticated artisans of that time were able to quickly overcome problems of this nature, can only incur the professional admiration of modern engineers operating at what is now described as the cutting edge of technology!

The second recorded accident concerning the vessel was when it ran aground near Holyhead in July 1875, where she had to put in for inspection. It is not known what damage she sustained on that occasion: but what is known is that some 4 years later, when she was but 8 years old – a relatively young age for a vessel of her class, she had become so unseaworthy as to be considered unfit for her owners' service, testimony no doubt, to the punishing conditions faced by vessels in the iron ore trade. Faced with losing a great deal of money by selling her in that condition in what was already a depressed market, William Barratt, her manager, decided to have her thoroughly overhauled instead, in the expectation of working her profitably until she could be sold at a reasonable price.

William Thomas's yard at Amlwch was chosen to undertake the work. It comes as no surprise that the vessel's owners should have selected this particular yard, for although the Captain had by then disposed of his interest in the yard at Millom, he was still remembered and personally well respected by John Barratt, who it will be recalled, was one of the two founders of the mining company.

The extensive repairs to the *Hodbarrow Miner* were reflected in the final cost, which amounted to a little over £480. Despite her manager making a £5 call on each of her shares, the vessel still remained over £100 in debt at the end of that year. In the first 6 months of 1881 however, her fortunes improved considerably, and having made three rounds in the Duddon – south Wales – Ireland triangle, each of her shares yielded a dividend of a little over £2.

In 1885 the vessel was bought by William Thomas & Sons. The new owners were rightly known as discerning buyers, and they clearly profited by having first-hand knowledge of the vessel's construction and condition through the extensive repair work they had carried out on her some 6 years previously.

It is clear however, that they did not intend her to remain in the iron ore business, preferring instead to let her join their other vessels in the general coasting trade. As was their custom whenever they bought a second-hand vessel, they gave the *Hodbarrow Miner* a thorough overhaul before putting her to work, and before appointing Captain Richard Griffiths as her new Master.

In March 1889, the *Hodbarrow Miner* was in collision with another vessel, and in a letter to her owners, the Captain informed them that his ship had been arrested. His estimation of the cost of repairing the other vessel amounted to about £75. A few days later, the owners informed the Captain that arrangements were being made to have his vessel released from arrest, at the same time asking him for an explanation as to why a writ of £150 had been served on his ship when his idea of the cost of repairing the damage amounted to only half that amount. This may well have heralded the start of the breakdown in the relationship between Captain Griffiths and his employers, for matters between them steadily worsened from that point on.

As their vessels were by then almost invariably sailed by the shares, William Thomas & Sons required all masters in their employ to write to them every other day whilst in port, and to send them their share of the ship's profits on a regular basis. When this was not done, it was the custom for them to write to the captain concerned to remind him of his duty: but when such letters were ignored, as sometimes happened, they would write to a friend at whatever port the vessel was at, enquiring as to the state of the vessel and the behaviour of the captain. In this way, they wrote on the 19th May 1894, to Mr David Williams, Shipbroker of Portdinorwic, asking if the *Hodbarrow Miner* was loaded, and if so when, and whether she was by then out in the stream, ready to sail.

Following an enquiry from a Mr Swyney of Liverpool, the vessel's owners offered on the 18th August 1894, to sell him the vessel for £900, which was no doubt indicative of their despair with the ongoing situation. The offer was declined; but their continuing dissatisfaction with Captain Griffiths was reflected in the fact that Captain Williams of the schooner *Lady Neave*, then at Wadebridge, was asked if he would care to join the *Hodbarrow Miner*, as there was every likelihood of there being a change of masters. Two days later they acknowledged Williams's telegram in which he stated that he would be pleased to take over her command. This transfer of command however, never came about for some unknown reason.

News of the impending change of masters must have travelled quickly amongst the sailing fraternity however, for in May 1895, Captain Richard Tyrran of the William Thomas built schooner *Mary Catherine*, the first ever iron sailing ship to be built in North Wales, was informed that his application to command the *Hodbarrow Miner* was being seriously considered. No changes were made at that time however, for in July 1895, the owners offered the ship, still under the command of Captain Griffiths, to E.T. Brown & Co. of London for £850, which represented a significant lowering in their former asking price. Despite their latest offer, it was insufficiently tempting, and in August, the owners wrote to Captain Griffiths, who by then had clearly decided to jump before he was pushed, informing him that as it was he who intended to leave the vessel, would he be good enough to let them know when he expected her to be discharged, so that they could send a person to take over her command.

It is very interesting to note that at this time, the firm advised the Dee and Mersey Protection Association, that the value of their 11 coasting vessels, which included the *Hodbarrow Miner,* amounted to no less than £12,225, an appreciable sum by any contemporary standard.

It would appear that despite his earlier wish to command the vessel, Captain Williams, for some unknown reason, did not do so; and this was ultimately given to Captain Richard Tyrran. Although he was always referred to by that name in William Thomas's correspondence, his surname was in fact Tyrer, and why this should have been so, continues to mystify his descendants.

Captain Tyrran was not the luckiest of masters, for on 5th August 1896 the owners wrote to him regretting to hear that his vessel had received damage from a steamer: but as the steamer appeared to be at fault, the owners presumed that his agents had put in claim for damage, towage, detention etc. No blame whatsoever was attributed to Captain Tyrran.

In January 1897, the firm advised John Vickers of the Dee and Mersey Protection Association of Connah's Quay that the *Hodbarrow Miner* was coming out of dock on the following Monday having completed her repairs following an unspecified accident, and that they would be glad to fix her for Leith at 10 shillings a ton, if that was obtainable; or Dover at 8 shillings and sixpence nett.

On the 24th June 1898, the owners wrote to Captain Tyrran advising him that he should try to settle with the owner of a barge for the damage caused to his vessel, provided that he could recover sufficient money to cover his own detention costs and the making good of damage sustained by his vessel. The problems continued, for some three months later, the owners advised their insurers that the consignees of a cargo of clay carried by the *Hodbarrow* Miner from Pentewan in Cornwall, had:

> declined the cargo alleging damage through smell of oil arising from cargo of creosoted sleepers which she delivered last May. The Captain informs us that he has scraped the hold thoroughly and washed it several times since then.

Annoyed by the fact that no surveyor from the Dee Protection Club had been to inspect the vessel, the owners wrote to the Secretary asking him to attend to the matter at once as by acting promptly, the matter could be settled easier than by delay. The matter was not settled as they had hoped however, for on the 29th of September, the owners instructed their business solicitors, Messrs Forshaw and Hawkins to take proceedings to recover the freight money from the consignees on the grounds that despite making exhaustive enquiries, they had clearly failed to inform the vessel's master of the nature of the clay he was loading.

Despite the series of unfortunate accidents involving his vessel, very few of which appear to be directly attributable to him, Captain Tyrran was clearly a very successful master, for in January 1889, the owners refused an offer of £850 for the *Hodbarrow Miner,* declaring that:

> We have no desire to part with this vessel as she is such profitable property, and therefore regret

we cannot accept your offer, but if your friends would care to pay us £950 nett we would let her go.

Bad luck was never far from the vessel however, for in the following September, she had to put into Amlwch for further, more extensive repairs. It would appear that as she was leaving Bangor with a cargo of slates for Galway, she missed stays in the Menai Strait, and went on to a sand bank, where she remained for one tide. A heavy swell which accompanied the flood tide damaged her to such an extent, that when she did eventually refloat, she was making a great deal of water. When her cargo was finally discharged, the owners were dismayed to find that she was so badly damaged that they immediately insured her to the value of £600 for 3 months whilst undergoing repairs in their dry dock at Amlwch. Her damage must have been considerable, for it was not until the 3rd of March 1900, some 6 months later, that the vessel finally left the dry dock, her repairs completed. The work had clearly improved the vessel quite considerably, for a year later, her owners valued her at no less than £1,000. It was not all good news however, for the tax returns relating to the vessel's earnings for 1901 show that although she made an operating profit of £25-2-2 during that year; her value depreciated by £40!

On the 21st of March 1902, the owners wrote to Walter Reney of the Dee and Mersey Protection Association informing him that the *Hodbarrow Miner* was yet again in their dry dock undergoing repairs, and inviting him to send a surveyor down if his Directors needed to have her inspected. At the same time, they asked Mr Riley, the local Lloyd's surveyor at Bangor to attend to carry out his own inspection.

The vessel left the graving dock on the morning of the 6th of April 1902, which allowed a few days clear in which to complete her repairs, bend her sails etc., before she was to sail to Caernarfon to load.

Captain Tyrran continued to be dogged by bad luck, for in September 1902, the owners wrote to him expressing their regret to hear that his cargo of clay had been damaged, and advising him to lodge his protest. A letter to their insurers at about the same time referred to the damage caused by the *Hodbarrow Miner* to the vessel *Gypsy Maid* as a result of the Captain's failure to check his vessel in time, most likely as they entered port.

In August of the same year, William Thomas & Sons were appointed Lloyd's agents for the whole of the north of Anglesey, and in a letter dated 28th of February 1903, the firm advised their London Secretary that:

The schooner Hodbarrow Miner on Thursday night during the height of the gale, drove her anchors in Moelfro roads until she came perilously close to the rocks, signals of distress were exhibited and crew were taken ashore by the lifeboat, but after the gale had moderated yesterday they were again placed on board with assistance and she was eventually brought into safety.

Their letter of the same date addressed to their own insurers concerning the episode was more detailed:

this vessel on Wednesday night drove her anchors in Moelfro Roads and fell foul of the steamer Kilkeel causing some damage to herself, but we do not know what damage if any was caused to the steamer. Again on Thursday night during the height of the gale, she commenced to drive her anchors, and had got into a dangerous position close to Moelfro island, and eventually they showed signals of distress, and the crew were landed by the lifeboat. After the gale moderated yesterday, assistance was placed on board to bring her into safety, and to bring her into Amlwch where she arrived this morning. We shall therefore be pleased if you would send your surveyor here for Tuesday morning to survey the damage.

The vessel's last voyage, under the command of Captain Tyrran began on February 21st 1908 at Runcorn, bound for Truro with a cargo of coal. Second in command of the vessel was 23-year-old Griffith Rowland Owen of Amlwch. Although he had joined the vessel some three months earlier, this was his first ever voyage as mate. The remaining crew members were Walter Moulsdale, an Amlwch man who had joined the vessel during the previous month at Runcorn, and ship's boy, Evan Evans, also of Amlwch, who joined at the same time. The remaining crew member was Joseph Warricker from Falmouth, who had joined the vessel at his home port as a replacement for another seaman who had been discharged at Par.

As the *Hodbarrow Miner* was rounding Land's End in a stiff northerly gale, Captain Tyrran, who was at the wheel, was knocked overboard by the mainsail peak downhaul which had evidently not been properly fastened when sails were shortened.

As is the custom, command of the vessel automatically passed on to the mate, and as the events which followed show, he proved to be exceedingly ill equipped for the task. His experience was clearly very limited, and to exacerbate matters, he was seemingly unable to navigate and had great difficulty in reading charts. From the evidence, it could even be argued that he had little or no idea of the vessel's position when the accident occurred. These factors were to prove significant in the resulting mayhem.

The conditions were without doubt, quite horrendous, and within minutes of having turned back to search for the unfortunate captain, it became very evident to them all that there was no chance whatsoever of finding him, either dead or alive. As it happened, his body was never recovered.

Conditions aboard the vessel were disorganised to say the least, which under the circumstances is quite understandable. What is surprising however, is that despite being told that the vessel was then close to the Longships light, the Mate elected to continue to sail north into the wind instead of running before it around Land's End, where he would have found shelter in Mount's Bay, a relatively short distance away.

According to Warricker, the only crew member to survive the wreck, and the only source of information regarding the sequence of events which overtook the vessel, Owen decided for some incomprehensible reason of his own, to seek shelter in Milford Haven, some 120 miles to the north. Warricker, for equally strange reasons, had then argued that it would be best to head the vessel towards Penarth, which was even further away; where, he claimed, they could beach the vessel safely. Whether it was because of Griffith Owen's lack of experience and confidence, or Warricker's forcefulness that persuaded them to sail for Penarth, will never be known.

Having battled against a headwind throughout the night, the vessel's distress signal was sighted the following morning by a tugboat, which, having stood by them for an hour, eventually made off, much to the consternation of the *Hodbarrow Miner*'s crew. The most likely explanation is that the tug's Master had concluded that they were in control of the situation, and despite their signal, were no longer in need of assistance.

In order to better determine their position, Warricker and Owen went below to consult the ship's charts, and they eventually came to the conclusion that they were not off Lundy Island as they had supposed; but were by then close to Trevose Head, more than a 100 miles to the south of Lundy. The decision was then made to beach the vessel, and they turned about. Despite the nearness of the sandy beach at Constantine Bay, they decided to run before the wind to Mawgan Porth, some 6 miles away to the south. The decision was presumably made for the simple reason that the former was an open beach, whereas the inlet at Mawgan Porth was likely to offer more shelter from northerly winds.

Photographs of the wreck indicate that the vessel had beached close to the mouth of the inlet, suggesting that when they arrived, there was less water than they expected, and they grounded. In fact, conditions in the mouth of the inlet differed little from those at Constantine Bay, and the vessel was left very much exposed to the might of the wind and sea. The moment the vessel grounded, the crew, fearful of the destructive power of the elements, launched the ship's boat, which immediately capsized, throwing them all into the raging sea.

The Hodbarrow Miner *during the storm.*

It is evident that the plight of the vessel had been seen from the shore, and life-saving apparatus was quickly brought down to the beach. It was only at the fourth attempt however, that a rocket line was got on board; but it became clear to the rescuers that the crew had already abandoned the vessel. Griffith Owen, who was not wearing a life-jacket, had disappeared almost immediately, followed by Walter Moulsdale and Evan Evans. Warricker, the fourth member of the crew, was seen struggling in the surf, and brought safely ashore by the rescue party. He was thus able to furnish his rescuers with a first-hand account of the events which led to the loss of the *Hodbarrow Miner.* Two of the rescue party, Sidney W. Matthews, Coastguard and Chief Boatman, and Richard Yelland, his assistant at Mawgan Porth, were rewarded with a sum of 10 shillings over and above their other

The Hodbarrow Miner *aground after the storm.*

allowances for rendering service.

It is evident from photographs taken of the grounded vessel after the gale had abated, that had the crew elected to stay aboard, they would have been spared. The hull itself, built sufficiently strong to withstand the rigours of the iron ore trade, appeared to have survived the onslaught extremely well, despite the loss of part of its bulwarks. The tattered sails and loose rigging however, bore more than ample testimony to the ferocity of the wind which had assailed the unfortunate vessel.

As was the case with all wrecks, the local Lloyd's agent immediately notified the London Secretary of the disaster, and he in turn informed the owners. The local agent, with the aid of an assistant, then put matters in hand to salvage what he could of the vessel. A copy of the salvors' accounts was soon sent to the vessel's insurers, whose manager Walter Reney, then relayed it to the owners for their observations. The latter were particularly incensed by the double expenses claimed by the Lloyd's agent at Padstow for himself and his assistant, particularly as they had initiated the salvage operations before they had been authorised to do so by themselves as owners.

An application by the Superintendent of the Custom House at Padstow to William Thomas & Sons to have the crew's effects identified from his description of them, was met with the response that it would have been better for him to send them up to the Amlwch Custom House at the firm's expense, where they could be positively identified by the families concerned. On the 10th of April, the owners sent to Mr Reney a covering letter enclosing one they had received from Captain Tyrran's widow giving notice of her intention to claim compensation for the loss of her husband. In it they stated that they did not know if the protection club would attempt an amicable settlement or allow matters to take their course, presumably through the Courts. Clearly, they favoured the former option, for they informed him that:

We think ourselves that she should not be unreasonable if approached at once before she gets into Solicitors' hands.

They then went on to say that:

We may state that a relative of the Mate was here today, and gave us to understand that his sister, who was the mother of the Mate, intended also to claim. We told him that we did not think she would be entitled to any compensation as her son was a single man, but we understand that they are going to consult some Solicitor.

For some reason, the owners were clearly in favour of paying compensation to widows, but seemingly, to no one else, because five days later, they sent to Mr Reney a letter they had received from a local solicitor regarding the claim made by the Mate's mother. In it, they suggested that a strong reply would stop all further proceedings.

In a further letter addressed to a Falmouth solicitor acting for John Warricker concerning payment of wages due to his client, the owners advised him that the accounts of the vessel's crew would be paid through the Custom House authorities in the usual manner, and that they were endeavouring to complete them as soon as possible despite being hampered by the absence of relevant papers.

A later letter sent by the owners directly to Warricker at The Well, Falmouth informed him that they had learnt from the authorities that they were permitted to settle directly with him regarding his claim for wages, and were enclosing a postal order for 10 shillings. This they stated, was the balance due to him for one month's service aboard the *Hodbarrow Miner*, less 35 shillings he had already received from Captain Tyrran, and the £1 they had very recently sent him.

At what was already a fraught time for him due to the loss of the vessel, William Thomas, the junior partner in the firm, informed Mr Reney in a letter dated 23rd of April, that Captain Lewis Thomas, his brother and senior partner, had died that morning.

A threatening letter received some days later from Warricker's solicitor regarding what he claimed to be the wrongful deduction of 35 shillings from his client's wages, resulted in the owners telling him that they had earlier received a letter from his client informing them that he had already received the sum from Captain Tyrran, in which case, there were no grounds whatsoever for taking action against them. Despite their explanation, a second letter from the solicitor extracted a further 12 shillings and 6 pence from them in consideration of the fact that Warwicker had lost all his effects aboard the stricken vessel. Why anything should have been lost is a mystery, for a photograph taken when the storm had abated shows the vessel sitting relatively undamaged, on the beach.

On the 16th of May, the owners sent their insurers two County Court summonses they had received relating to claims for compensation made by the families of Griffith Owen and Walter Moulsdale. In a very small community such as Amlwch, there was evidently very little of individual family circumstances that was not widely known to others, as the following reply from the ship's owners to Mr Reney's request for information regarding the Owen and Moulsdale families, clearly shows:

Walter Moulsdale joined the vessel as O.S. on or about 18th February last, so he was only about three weeks on board when the vessel was lost, and therefore his name would not appear on the previous half year's articles. His wages were £3 per month. We do not know what assistance if any, he gave to his parents, but we may state that his father is an able bodied man of about 45 years of age, quite able to work, though not in regular employment, he gets a fair share of labourer's work about the harbour, and other odd jobs. When discharging vessels he makes very good wages, sometimes as much as 6 to 7 shillings a day, a very good rate for a labourer. He has also just come into a legacy of £50 left him by an aunt. He has one son in our employ, but he does not contribute anything to the household as he is living with his grandmother, he has also three daughters in service, and three children at home.

Similarly, with regard to the Mate, G.R. Owen, William Thomas wrote:

He was the Mate, and joined about 11th December last at a monthly wage of £3-15-0. It was the first time he had been Mate, so that his average wages were not so high. He would be earning about £3 or £3-5-0 per month before he joined this vessel. He was the only son of his widow mother, who either keeps house for her brother or boards and lodges him at so much a week, but we are almost certain that she is her brother's housekeeper, as we find that her brother's name appears as the tenant on the list of voters. She has recovered about £110 insurance money on account of her son's death, viz £100 from the ordinary, and about £10 from the industrial branch of the Prudential Assurance Association. She also received a sum of money from the Shipwrecked Mariners and Fishermen's Society, but do not think that this sum exceeded £6, and we have failed to find out whether she has received anything from the Oddfellows Society. Her brother is in regular employment and earns good wages in the tobacco works and is a member of the District Council, so we believe that the claimant is far from being destitute especially considering that both have the means of procuring that which is not considered the absolute necessity of life.

In a letter dated 19th of September confirming their telegram of the previous day to Walter Reney, the owners informed him of:

The names of the vessels Walter Moulsdale served in, in the order that he joined them. He first went to sea in the brigantine Belle of Barrow, afterwards with the Happy Harry, then the Lizzie of Portmadoc, after which he joined the Hodbarrow Miner. We are sorry that we weren't able to obtain any further particulars that might be of assistance at the trial, but we are almost certain that this man had no account at the Savings or any other bank, as it would take all his earnings to keep himself in food and clothing, let alone give anything to his parents. We have however heard that William Moulsdale the father, came into possession of a legacy of £250 during last week, £50 of which we have previously referred to, and £200 further sum left him by another aunt.

The claim, brought under the Workmen's Compensation Act, by Elizabeth Owen, widow and mother of the Mate of the *Hodbarrow Miner,* against the vessel's owners, for the sum of £225-17-6 as compensation for the loss of her son, was first brought before His Honour Judge Moss at Holyhead in June 1908. The legal arguments which ensued, revolved around the definition of a workman in the context of the Act. The question facing the Judge was whether or not the crew were employed by the owners of the vessel, or the Captain who engaged, paid and fed them out of his own pocket.

As was the general custom in the port of Amlwch, the *Hodbarrow Miner* was sailed 'by the halves'. Under this system, the captain was responsible to the owners for the proper sailing and working of the vessel which they provided, insured and maintained in good working order. The captain engaged and discharged his own crew, victualled the ship, and in general, made all the arrangements necessary for the handling of a cargo to a port of his choice.

In such cases, the master, having first deducted owners' expenses such as for minor repairs, and shared expenses such as port dues etc., from the freight money, would send the owners half of the remaining profit. Sometimes however, the master had a share in the vessel, in which case the division of the profits would reflect that fact, allowing him perhaps two thirds of the profit, against the owners' one third.

The argument put forward in Court on behalf of the owners, was that the crew members were employed directly by the master, and not by them, since they had no say at all either in their engagement, their dismissal, or the amount of wages they received.

At the end of the hearing the Judge remarked on the lengthy arguments he had heard from both sides regarding a case he described both as unusual, and quite novel to him. For that reason he proposed to defer judgement until he had had time to fully consider the evidence and the arguments. Referring to the case of the representatives of seaman Walter Moulsdale against the same respondents, the judge proposed to adjourn the hearing, pending his decision on the current case.

By way of better understanding the nature of the problem, it is necessary to explain the commercial arrangements between William Thomas & Sons and their masters. It was a general rule, that on taking command, the captain would be required either to take shares in the vessel, or to lodge a deposit with the owners, as a form of guarantee of his good behaviour. The deposit varied with the vessel and the man, but was generally in the order of £20. If the captain left the vessel on good terms with the owners, that is, having discharged his obligations to them in a satisfactory manner, he would be given his deposit back with interest at the going rate. If, on the other hand, he left owing the owners money for whatever reason, the amount would be withheld from his deposit.

In those cases where the owners had their eye on a pushing, but relatively poor young captain, they would often assist him by lending him the necessary deposit, which they would recover from his earnings. This was a custom first established by Captain William Thomas, and one that was continued by his sons following his death. The fact that the seafaring careers of many of Amlwch's legendary captains were launched in this way says a great deal for the founder's foresight and business acumen.

When it came to the maintenance of their vessels, William Thomas & Sons spared no effort to ensure that all that was needed was executed properly and with the least delay. In those cases where the vessel sustained damage whilst away from her home port, the captain would inform the owners of the circumstances under which the damage occurred, and await their instructions regarding repairs. In most cases where there was damage to the hull or superstructure which was of a relatively minor nature, the captain was empowered to arrange temporary repairs, sufficient only to get him safely back to their yard in Amlwch, where permanent repairs would be effected. If on the other hand, the vessel had been seriously damaged, William Thomas would himself travel to the scene to make whatever arrangements were necessary. In this way, he travelled many miles a year, often to continental ports, where his expertise as a ship builder ensured that only the minimum amount of work commensurate with safety was carried out, before he ordered the vessel back to Amlwch.

The firm had full records of the size of every sail carried by their vessels, and on receipt of a master's notice that any of his sails had been carried away, new ones would immediately be made, and despatched to him within a day or so of receipt of his letter. In those cases where the sail was not vitally important to the running of the ship, they would advise the master that the sail would be sent to await his arrival at his next port of call. In this way, the firm ensured that their vessels were not delayed through any fault of their own.

As William Thomas & Sons required their captains to write to them every other day whilst in port, they more often than not, knew in advance what their intentions were, and although masters 'sailing by the shares' arranged their own charter parties, the owners would, in some cases, object to their taking their vessel to a port considered by them to be unsuitable for any one of a number of reasons. They also felt free to advise their captains of ports likely to have freights offering, as well as the price they could reasonably expect to be paid for each ton of cargo intended for a particular destination.

The judgement on the case brought before His Honour Judge Moss in April was not delivered by him until July 23rd at Menai Bridge. Remarking on the lengthy legal arguments he had heard from both sides, the judge stated that the outcome would be one of great importance to shipowners, insurance societies, as well as the captains and crews which sailed the vessels.

Having defined the arrangements by which vessels were sailed 'by the half', the judge outlined the respondents' argument, that inasmuch as the deceased was the servant of the captain, and not their workman under the meaning of the Act, they were not liable. The applicant's argument on the other hand, was that the arrangement between the captain and the owners did not make the captain an independent contractor as claimed; but was simply a method by which payment was made.

The following summary of the judgement delivered by His Honour Judge Moss was reported at the time:

A compensation case of considerable importance was decided on July 23 at Menai Bridge by Judge Moss. The action, tried at Holyhead some time ago, was brought by Elizabeth Owen, a widow, of Amlwch, to recover compensation from Messrs. William Thomas and Sons, shipowners, Amlwch, for the loss of her son, who was drowned while engaged as mate of the sailing vessel Hodbarrow Miner. Judge Moss, in delivering judgment, said: This is an application under the Workmen's Compensation Act by one Elizabeth Owen, a widow, claiming compensa-tion to the amount of £251-17s- 6d, against the respondents, the owners of the vessel, for the loss of a son. The Hodbarrow Miner was lost off Padstow (Cornwall), on March 6, 1908, and the deceased, with all the crew except one, was drowned. The vessel was "sailed upon shares" as it is termed by the Captain. By this is meant that the Captain is responsible to the owners for the proper sailing and working of the vessel. He engages his own seamen, arranges for the cargo the vessel is to carry, and, subject to a kind of general control by the owners, he chooses his own port. He also victuals the ship. The owners pay for the repairs of the ship, and wear and tear, and insurance. The Captain receives the freight, deducts from it the port dues, then divides it into halves, retaining one-half himself and sending the other to the owners. He pays the sailors, victuals the ship; and makes any other payments which fall to him out of his half of the profits. Any repairs or expenses of the ship itself he deducts from the owners' half. Under these circumstances, the respondents said that they were not liable, inasmuch as the deceased was the servant of the Captain, and not their workman within the meaning of the 'Act The applicant contends that the arrangement between the Captain and owners did not make the Captain an independent contractor, but was simply a method of payment. I come to the conclusion that the deceased was the workman of the employers, and that the respondents are liable. But I do not think that the applicant was wholly dependent upon the deceased, and I think, having regard to the fact that the applicant received assistance from her brother, and only received a part of the deceased's earnings, I shall meet the requirements of the case, and award her compensation proportionate to the injury she received if I award her £150. There will be an award for £150, with costs on scale C.

Having regard to the importance of the case however, the judge said that he would not be dissatisfied if an appeal were entered against his decision.

On the 11th September 1908, William Thomas wrote to Mr Reney regarding Mrs Tyrran's claim:

The writer interviewed this lady today, and we have been able to persuade her to accept your offer; but as the gentleman who has been advising her is away on his holidays, she would not give a definite answer, but on his return about the middle of next week, we will see him and hope to be able to convince him that it will be for the benefit of Mrs Tyrran to settle amicably.

Mrs Tyrran wrote to Walter Reney in September, accepting his offer of £200 compensation for the loss of her husband, and William Thomas & Sons were later informed of the successful County Court judgements against them in the cases brought by the families of Walter Moulsdale and Evan Evans.

Some months later, the owners of the *Hodbarrow Miner* acknowledged receipt of a bill received from Samuel Lobb and Sons of St Mawgan, for Griffith Owen's coffin, adding that they had passed it on to his mother, *as we have nothing to do with this expense, having already paid heavy compensation for the loss of life.* This suggests that the Dee and Mersey Protection Association did not meet the full cost of the judgement, and that the remainder was paid by the owners. What is particularly surprising however, is that in view of the Judge's remarks and the important precedent involved, neither the owners nor the insurers thought it worthwhile to appeal against the judgement.

This chapter contains extracts from: William Thomas & Sons letter books, *The Holyhead & Anglesey Mail* 1907; *Caernarvon and Denbigh Herald* 1908; *Lloyd's Weekly Summary* August 1909.

CHAPTER 12
THE CALM BEFORE THE STORM
"... as one of the selected 500 new Members of the House of Lords..."

Following the launch of the auxiliary schooner *Eilian* in 1908, the yard had no new work in hand, and was having to rely on whatever small scale repair work it could find in order to exist. William Thomas, not one to tolerate idleness, was by then taking a great interest in local politics, and had been elected to both the Amlwch Town Council and the Anglesey County Council.

Little did he expect however, to be told in 1911, that he had been nominated as one of a number of prominent men to whom the King would probably be offering a peerage in the immediate future. The circumstances under which the offer was made, were in some respects, quite bizarre.

Lloyd George, who was then Prime Minister Herbert Asquith's Chancellor of the Exchequer, had earlier proposed a 'People's Budget' which recommended a package of popular reforms which were to provide amongst many other social measures, for a State-provided old age pension. Because of the intention to fund the measures through what the predominantly Tory hereditary peers in the House of Lords saw as an unjust super tax on the landed gentry, they opposed it totally, and rejected the bill out of hand.

In an effort to resolve matters, Asquith, with King George V's reluctant agreement, proposed the creation of some three hundred new Peers of which William Thomas was to be one, with the intention of swamping any opposition to the bill by the House of Lords when it was re-submitted for its consideration. The incumbent Peers held out as long as they were able; but eventually had to capitulate, thereby obviating the need to create new Members of the House.

William Thomas was clearly unaware of this latest development when he wrote in reply to a letter of commiseration from an unnamed friend, who was probably E.O. Roberts of Liverpool, a man unquestionably well informed when it came to most matters of import. The letter reads as follows:

My Dear Friend,

I am much obliged for your letter of the 15th instant; but as one of the selected 500 (sic) new Members of the House of Lords, your sympathy is misplaced, but strange enough you have correctly guessed my Title, and as it has not yet been officially Gazetted, I must ask you to keep it private for the present. Hoping to receive your congratulations when the announcement is made.

I am,

Yours very Truly,

Wm Thomas (For a few days only)

It takes little imagination to guess that had he been elevated to the peerage as he had expected, William Thomas would have included the name 'Eilian' somewhere in his title. His disappointment on learning the truth however, must have been intense, for his daughter Gertrude was surprised to the point of incredulity when told the facts a few years before her death. Either he had made no mention of the matter in family circles in the first place, or as seems more likely, forbade any further reference to it by those he had told in confidence.

A chance sighting at this time by William Thomas, of an advertisement in a local newspaper, inviting tenders for the construction of a hospital ship for the Port of Beaumaris, (as the slate-exporting port of Bangor was then known), prompted him to seek further information.

According to the specification he received, the vessel was to be 81 feet long, 23 feet broad, and 11 feet depth of side, the plating and planking to be additional. Desperate for work for his hard-pressed yard, William Thomas submitted a highly competitive tender, and he was given the contract.

The Port of Beaumaris Hospital Ship Morfudd.

Compared to the beautiful vessels, such as the *Elizabeth Roberts*, the *Cenric*, and the *Eilian*, the slab-sided, flat-iron-shaped *Morfudd* as she was to be called, could have given him no pleasure whatsoever as he watched her taking shape directly under the windows of his office in the yard's counting house. After her launch on Monday 4th of March, 1912, she was towed around to her home port by Bangor Corporation's own vessels *Lady Magdalen* and *Torbay*. According to local legend, she received not one patient during her career as a hospital ship, and she eventually passed into the ownership of Dafydd Cale, a very well-known and respected Bangor sailmaker, who converted her into what was later described by Aled Eames, his son-in-law, as a superb houseboat.

In a letter dated 30th October 1910, William Thomas & Sons, in their capacity as agents, advised Lloyd's of London of the mishap which had befallen ss *Fido* of Hull which had been put into Porth Amlwch, listing badly:

The listing ss Fido *tied up to the Watch House pier.*

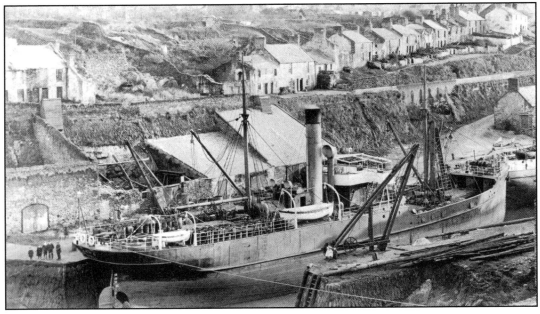

The Fido *being repaired alongside the eastern quay.*

We are now informed that the reason for her putting in here was owing to her leaking badly after striking a rock off Bull Bay at 4 am. The vessel was making so much water that the Master ran her in about 7 o'clock, but at that hour there was not sufficient water for her to enter the inner harbour, and she was therefore moored between the outer piers. By high water, she had become so settled by the head, and could not be moved. Her forward deck being awash, a portion of her deck cargo consisting of empty oil drums was washed away.

The vessel will dry where she lies, at low water, and if the fracture is found to be above the flat of the bottom, it is our intention to patch it up to enable the vessel to be pumped and taken alongside for further examination. Should the damage be located in the bottom, we fear the steamer will have discharged in her present position as her own pumps are insufficient to cope with the leak. The owners' superintendent is expected here tonight.

A week or so later, John H. Farrell, a Marine Surveyor was called in to investigate the accident. By way of adding to their previous letter to Lloyd's William Thomas and Sons, were in a position to report that the vessel's cargo of Melasquit. (regarding which, nothing can be discovered):

…was damaged by sea water, but to what extent, it is at present impossible to estimate. We therefore recommend that such part cargo be re-shipped and taken to destination for the benefit of all, as if offered by auction here, it is doubtful if any reasonable price could be obtained for it.

Within a few days, they were pleased to report that the temporary repairs to the *Fido* were nearly completed, and that they hoped to begin re-loading the cargo on the following day, thereby enabling her to sail on the Wednesday. The vessel sent to take on the cargo of soap was the *Ceres*, and the *Fido's* owners, Thomas Wilson Sons and Co., were advised that all of the discharged cargo had been re-loaded on board their vessel, and as soon as the tides were sufficiently high, she would be free to leave Porth Amlwch. Her progress having left the port, was closely followed by William Thomas, who wrote to Captain Fox, her master after she left Amlwch, saying:

You got away from here in the nick of time, as we had very boisterous weather after you left, with heavy sea from W and NW. We watched all the reports along the coast and were able to follow the vessel's movements as far as Dover, as naturally we were anxious that the temporary work effected here would prove effective until her arrival at her destination.

A fortnight later, the *Fido's* owners were sent an account for £335 - 5 - 0, which included a gift of half a crown to the local policeman, presumably for keeping a watch on the vessel's cargo stored on the quayside.

The *Fido's* master at the time of the accident was a Captain Orme, and by way of illustrating his genuine concern for him, William Thomas wrote to tell him that he was personally:

very pleased to learn that you have been acquitted for all blame for the unfortunate accident to the Fido… I can only hope that the 2nd officer has not been severely treated by your employers, as he appeared to be such a nice young fellow.

CHAPTER 13
THE FIRST WORLD WAR
"the dark clouds gather thicker every day"

As the threat of war continued to gather momentum, the British Government mobilised the Royal Navy on the 2nd of August, 1914, one day before Germany declared war on France. In its response to this, Britain declared war on Germany one day later.

Three days into the hostilities, William Thomas wrote to Captain Williams of the *Meyric*, which was then berthed at Plymouth, informing him that he had no encouraging news to impart:

> *as the dark clouds gather thicker every day, and unless the outlook is brighter next week, we are afraid that you will have to pay off the crew, and lay the vessel up until the English fleet has sunk the Germans, which we hope will be very soon.*

His unwavering faith in the might of the Royal Navy expressed in this and several of his subsequent letters, was soon proved to be little more than wishful thinking.

On the same day as he had written to Captain Williams, he advised the firm's insurers, Messrs L.C. Sage & Co., of London, that he had received their circular dated two days earlier. He went on to seek their permission to allow the schooner *Emily Millington* to sail from King's Lynn to the English Channel, and the *Meyric* to leave Plymouth for either the Bristol Channel or the Mersey. He further sought their reassurance that as the *Kate* and the *Winifred* were already at sea, they would still be covered by insurance until they arrived at their ports of destination.

Immediately he had received their reply to his letters, William Thomas wrote to Captain Williams telling him that based upon private information he had received that morning from his London friends, he feared that there was no chance of him getting his vessel away without tremendous risk to both himself and the vessel. He then went on to describe how the underwriters refused to accept the risk without a prohibitive increase in the premium, before suggesting to him that the only alternative was for him to get the vessel into a place of safety, and then to pay off the crew as soon as he had discharged the inward cargo. It was thought that the (Great Western) Dock would be the best and most convenient place for her, if the Captain could manage to get her towed there. He then advised him that the clay pits of Cornwall and Devon were likely to be closed shortly, adding:

> *the present position is really a terrible one, and calls upon us to make great sacrifices, and we can only hope that the Germans will now get what they richly deserve.*

In the same way, a letter was written to W.R. Smith, Ship Broker of King's Lynn, confirming a telegram sent by them that day to Captain Davies of the *Emily Millington*, in which he was instructed to pay off his crew.

It is evident that the underwriters' concerns were mainly focused on the east coast, for there would appear to have been no corresponding restrictions on vessels serving the western side of the country, and arrangements for fixing the *Eilian* with a cargo of coal for

Penryn in Cornwall continued in the normal way. However, the firm was by now extremely wary when it came to fixing its vessels in the deep-sea trades; and in a letter to Captain Griffiths who had been given command of the *Gaelic* following its former captain's retirement, William Thomas said that it would not be prudent to fix her for anywhere under the existing conditions. He then suggested that matters could well change following the first blow to the German navy.

In his reply, Captain Griffiths sought monthly remuneration whilst his new command, then lying at Runcorn, was awaiting a cargo. The owners, however, refused to be drawn, telling him that he had been given the privilege of sailing the vessel by the shares on the same terms as the previous captain, which was a greater concession than he was obviously able to realise fully if he was dissatisfied with the arrangement, there was nothing more to be said.

From this mild rebuke, it is evident that sailing by the shares was a rewarding profession for those captains who were hard working and who could be left to use their own initiative under difficult circumstances. The advantage to the firm of having such a system, was that a captain who owned shares in his vessel could be relied upon to work it carefully and to the best advantage of its owners at all times. The only drawback to them, if indeed there was one at all, was that they probably made a marginally smaller profit than they might otherwise have done: but apart from that there can be little doubt that for owners, the advantages outweighed the disadvantages.

In the meantime, Captain Davies of the *Emily Millington*, had written seeking permission to leave his vessel at King's Lynn, and in his reply, William Thomas agreed, on condition that the vessel was:

left secure in the hands of a good, trustworthy man at the Captain's expense: as we must all suffer our share of this loss, as you can readily understand that we shall be hit pretty hard by having this and other vessels idle.

Understandably, the Captain was not agreeable to paying a watchman out of his own pocket, and having informed the owners that he could not afford to live on board whilst the vessel was idle, tendered his resignation. William Thomas's reply was equally assertive when he told the Captain that he was clearly not studying his own interests, as the cost of living on board the vessel could not possibly be much greater than if he was living at home. He went on to suggest that in all probability, the voyage could be resumed, with the prospect of greatly advanced freights, in the course of a week or so. However, as the Captain had declined to bear his share of the loss which had occurred through no fault of the owners, he was asked to place the vessel in the charge of a reliable man, and they would arrange to send another captain there to take command as soon as practicable.

This was clearly a bluff; for the firm had, even under normal conditions before the war, already experienced great difficulty in securing the services of suitably-qualified sailing ship captains for the coastal trade.

Captain Williams of the *Meyric* had during this time, been attempting to charter his vessel to either the War Office or the Admiralty, for use as a storage craft. The fact that he had explored this possibility without reference to, and without any subsequent rebuke from the firm, suggests that it was he and not they, who had a controlling share in the vessel. His failure nevertheless came as a great relief, for if the vessel had been accepted, the charter rate was not negotiable under what William Thomas referred to as 'the power of commandeering'.

Informing Captain Gilbert of the schooner *Winifred*, that the *Eilian* had been fixed to take a cargo from Fowey to Runcorn at 4/6d (freight) with 21 shillings (gratuity), William Thomas suggested that were he to have any difficulty in getting a cargo of clay, it would pay him to go to the Mersey in ballast, as freights were advancing so much there. He quite understood the Captain's reluctance to go to the east coast however; but he claimed that there was not the slightest risk if he was to bring his vessel to the Irish channel. Indeed, he went on to say that several vessels had already passed Amlwch that day from the south, amongst them the *Kate*; and as far as any risk was concerned, he suggested that it was no more than before the war began, as unlike the North Sea, no mines had been laid on the western side.

Having closely studied Admiralty reports on the situation on the eastern coastline, William Thomas seemed to be in no way concerned about the possibility of the *Emily Millington* being seized or even torpedoed by the enemy, were she to sail from King's Lynn: but he was nevertheless clearly very fearful of mines. For that reason, he sought reassurances from the vessel's insurers that they were covered against all eventualities by their policy, pointing out:

> that these small vessels make their voyages so near the shores that we hardly think the enemy
> would venture so near our coasts which are so carefully guarded.

No doubt reassured by Lloyd George's declaration in Parliament that in order to keep essential supplies moving, the Government had prepared schemes for a State guarantee against the risks to ships' hulls and cargoes during times of war, William Thomas communicated his ideas to Captain Davies, who, having been told that there had been no real wish on the part of the company to replace him as master of the *Emily Millington*, had by then withdrawn his earlier decision to resign. He was told that contrary to the firm's established practices, the owners were, after all, prepared to pay him a weekly wage to look after the vessel during the time she was laid up, and furthermore, as an inducement aimed at the return of the former crew, they were prepared to pay their railway fares home should they ever be stopped at sea through no fault of their own: pointing out also, that they were at all times fully protected against all claims, including those for compensation.

It would appear however that some of the *Emily Millington's* crew had already left to seek work on board coaling vessels, and Thomas sought to reassure Captain Davies by telling him that the wages on board vessels coaling the navy were very much less than those paid by him, particularly if the great risk they were running was taken into consideration.

The difficulty in finding suitable crew members following the mobilisation of reservists was widespread, for the firm was unable to assist the Master of the *Kate*, who had by then arrived at Runcorn, in his efforts to find a suitable mate for his vessel. In their letter to him, they said:

> that there is not a single person here who would suit you as Mate, in fact, there are no seamen
> of any description available here.

The war brought the firm numerous other problems in its wake, some of greater import than others. In a letter to their Amlwch bank, William Thomas asked if, in view of the prohibition against trading with the enemy, they were compelled to meet a draft for £900 which was owed by them to the firm of Grimm & Co., of Hamburg, following the *Balder* incident. What the bank's advice was, is not known.

Because of the increasing congestion on the railways brought about by the war, delays in the delivery of raw materials necessary for the yard's business caused added complications: but despite that, deep-sea trading continued to occupy William Thomas's thoughts. In a letter to their broker J. W. Petty in Cadiz, where they normally took on salt for delivery to the Rio Grande, they offered both the *Gaelic* and the *Meyric* for the Brazilian hide trade on condition that they were offered good freights, and adding that:

we are quite prepared to take the risk, as no doubt before either of these vessels would be loaded, the high seas will be pretty well cleared of all German destroyers.

This again, was clearly little more than wishful thinking. Despite having informed Captain Griffiths of the *Gaelic*, that they feared that conditions on the east coast were worsening, they received a letter from him on the 18th of September informing them that he had accepted a cargo for Grimsby. As he was one of their most respected captains, their rebuke was relatively mild: but having realised that they had no option but to honour the contract, they reproached him for accepting such a low freight which they considered to be out of all proportion to the risk and distance, particularly as they were getting freights from Charlestown to London for only threepence per ton less. As if to underline their point, they added the following rejoinder:

it is hardly necessary for us to state that we rely you will take all precautions for the safety of the vessel as there is undoubtedly a great risk in going to the Humber as witness the blowing up of the ss Runo, only 25 miles from that estuary, and the fact that the lights of all lightships are extinguished on the east coast. There is no question about this, as the notice has appeared in the daily papers, and it will be quite as well if you apply to the Customs before leaving for the Admiralty's Direction for navigating that part of the coast.

A contemporary report of the incident relates how the *Runo*, a Wilson liner, sank after striking a mine in what was a well-known minefield, following her captain's flagrant disregard of directions issued by the Admiralty who went on to use the incident as an example of the inherent dangers in disregarding their warnings and advice.

In order to emphasise their previously expressed concern, the owners again wrote to Captain Griffiths:

You have no doubt seen in the daily papers an account of the two trawlers blown up at the mouth of the Humber (one yesterday, and the other, the day before), so the risk is greater than we and you realise, especially as we have such a small amount of insurance. If we had not obtained Underwriters' permission for you to sail the day you fixed, the vessel would now be held up, as they decline to allow any vessel to or from ports north of Yarmouth.

The two vessels referred to were the Danish trawler *Skuli Fogete* and the Norwegian vessel *Gottfried*.

The owners' relief on learning that the *Gaelic* had arrived safely at Grimsby was tempered by their receipt of a notice from her insurers informing them that they refused to allow the vessel to leave there for any of the channel ports unless she was first towed as far as Harwich. This presumably, was to ensure that she was confined to lanes which were known to be clear of mines.

In their reply, her owners said that what the insurers were stipulating was out of the question, as the cost of towage would exceed the total freight they could expect, and as they could not agree to hold the vessel at Grimsby indefinitely, they had no option but to transfer the vessel's insurance to another company. Although the new insurers did not insist on towage, they were nevertheless asking 20/- percent for covering the vessel against War Risk.

The firm learnt of the *Gaelic's* arrival in the Downs on the 30th of September, and three days later they wrote to Captain Griffiths, informing him of their relief, as they were naturally anxious about his safety as a result to the many problems facing vessels in the North Sea, which incidentally, had by then been closed to sailing vessels. They also added that their underwriters would not permit another voyage beyond London.

William Thomas's respite from worry was short lived, for on the 6th of January, 1915, he learnt from Captain Davies of the *Emily Millington*, that he had fixed a cargo for London. His barely concealed dismay was evident when he wrote to the Captain, saying:

We were astounded to learn that you had fixed for London without first obtaining our consent, especially after your experience at Kings Lynn, and the instructions we sent you on the 15th August, not to fix to any port eastward of Rye harbour... you appear to ignore us altogether, and we shall have to pay extra insurance for this voyage which will swallow up our share of the freight. We presume you are aware that you will have to take a pilot off St Catherine's which will take you to the Downs, and from there another pilot to the Thames, so the expense on you will be greater than in ordinary times.

Submarines were destined to play a crucial part in German naval strategy during the war, and as it progressed, the losses sustained by the British merchant navy had increased to such an extent that the Admiralty created a fleet of what were known as 'Q Ships', to combat the menace. The ships, later to be dubbed 'Mystery Ships' were armed merchant vessels; which by having their guns cleverly hidden in false deckhouses and elsewhere, gave the impression of being unarmed and vulnerable.

The relative smallness of many of the 'Q Ships' meant that sinking them using expensive and often unreliable torpedoes, was far from being cost effective; and as a consequence, U-boat commanders much preferred to destroy these targets by gunfire. In order to do that, the submarines had to surface, thereby increasing their own vulnerability by bringing them under the guns of what could possibly be decoys.

The Chronicle, an Anglesey newspaper, described the scene at Bangor railway station in August 1914, when a 'merry detachment' of naval reservists drawn from Bangor, Caernarfon, Menai Bridge and Amlwch left for Portsmouth and Devonport with their kitbags slung over their shoulders. Amongst their number may have been William Williams, a young Amlwch man whose later wartime exploits on 'Q Ships' were to win him, amongst other distinguished international awards, the *'Victoria Cross'*, Britain's highest award for valour. According to Peter Williams, the talented Amlwch born maritime artist, his great uncle had been one of the crew members aboard William Thomas's schooner *Cymric* on her maiden voyage to South America.

Vessels designed by William Thomas were all built well in excess of Lloyd's most stringent requirements, and were consequently extremely strong. This was without doubt, one of the most important factors which persuaded the Admiralty to select three of their number to serve as 'Q Ships.' Another consideration which weighed heavily in their favour, was their suitability for conversion into powered auxiliaries if required.

Gaelic, alias Q22, alias *Brig 11*, alias *Gobo*, the first to enter service, was commissioned in the first week of November 1916. The vessel, personally selected for its task by Vice Admiral C.H. Dare, who was in command of the naval base at Milford Haven, was at the time lying at Swansea loaded with 300 tons of coal. She was immediately armed with four twelve-pounder guns, as well as two Lewis guns taken out of the sailing trawlers *Strumble* and *Kemes*, both of which had failed dismally in their own short careers as 'Q Ships'. By that time, no fewer than 47 vessels of various kinds had been absorbed into the decoy fleet.

Unlike some decoys which never encountered a submarine throughout the whole of their service, the *Gaelic's* career turned out to be both long and eventful. Early on in her new role, she engaged an enemy submarine some 50 miles south of the Old Head of Kinsale. In an unremitting exchange of fire, the German vessel succeeded in hitting the barquentine no fewer than six times, resulting in the death of two seamen, and injuring a further four. The vessel's port engine was also put out of action.

A torpedo fired at the stricken vessel from a range of about 4000 yards, was made to miss by some 150 yards when the vessel turned end on to her attacker. In reply, the *Gaelic's* gunners opened fire, and succeeded in hitting the submarine with their fourth shot. Unfortunately when the gunners had the enemy's range and bearing, the gun's firing pin broke, forcing the captain to turn his vessel around to bring his starboard gun to bear on the target. This manoeuvre was itself made more difficult because his remaining engine had been put out of action by water leaking on to it from a fresh water tank pierced during the action.

In a final effort, when each vessel had already fired no fewer than a hundred shells, the *Gaelic's* gunners again struck the submarine, but without causing it sufficient damage to prevent it submerging and making good its escape. Despite having no engines, and with her sails and rigging badly damaged, the *Gaelic*, with the aid of His Majesty's sloop *Bluebell*, managed to limp back to base. After a thorough refit, the vessel was sent to Gibraltar from where she continued her covert operations in the Mediterranean until the end of the war.

The second Thomas vessel to enter service as a 'Q Ship' was the *Cymric*, alias *Olive*. She was commissioned on the 23rd of February 1917; and her armament consisted of one 4-inch gun, one $7^1/_2$-inch gun, two twelve-pounder guns, and a howitzer.

As the war progressed, the traditional use of 'Q Ships' as lone decoys changed when they were put to protecting convoys. By sailing well behind the other vessels, they gave the impression of being stragglers, and by offering themselves as a tempting target to any unsuspecting submarine commander, they also succeeded in drawing hostile attention away from their merchant charges.

Because of the heavy toll exacted on British shipping by U-boats, it was decided that 'Q Ships', instead of sailing uneconomically in ballast as they performed their duties, would carry cargo whenever possible. The resulting change in their trim added greatly to the authenticity of their appearance as working vessels, without in any way reducing their fighting effectiveness. It should be recognised however, that the vessels were, despite carrying cargoes, not armed merchantmen in the accepted sense of the term: but were commissioned warships crewed entirely by naval personnel, albeit dressed in civilian clothing!

On 7th June, 1917, William Williams was serving aboard *HMS Pargust*, a tramp steamer of about 3,000 tons, which had been converted into an armed decoy vessel. Earlier on in his command, the Captain of the vessel had issued what must have surely have been one of the most extraordinary orders ever given by a naval commander to his subordinates:

Should the Officer of the Watch see a torpedo approaching the ship, he is to increase or decrease speed as necessary to ensure it hitting…

Whether the Officer of the Watch saw the torpedo's wake coming towards him when the vessel was out in the Atlantic on submarine patrol that day, may never be known: but she nevertheless took the full force of a German U-boat's torpedo amidships. As the pretend *Panic Party* pulled away from the crippled vessel, leaving its only visible gun unattended, they gave the impression that the entire crew was very hastily abandoning the sinking ship.

Taken in by the ruse, the submarine captain, having first circled the stricken vessel to satisfy himself that the ship had truly been abandoned, and consequently posed no threat to his own vessel, surfaced with the intention of sinking his quarry by gunfire. Unbeknown to him, the Captain of the *Pargust*, together with several of his crew, had remained hidden on board, ready to open fire with their own gun which was concealed inside a false deck house, the sides of which could be dropped to allow an almost unobstructed field of fire.

When the submarine was some 50 yards away from the *Pargust*, and suitably positioned in line with the 'Q Ship's' gun, Commander Campbell ordered the gun to be revealed, and his gunners to open fire. The first shot went straight through the submarine's conning tower, and after a short but savage bombardment, the vessel exploded. As she sank, one of her crew was seen clinging desperately to her bow. Several of the submarine's complement were swept overboard, and these were later rescued by the crew of their intended victim.

The whole engagement could easily have been ruined had the submarine commander suspected for one moment that his adversary was a decoy, and he was not to know that when the *Pargust* was torpedoed, the explosion had freed the releasing weight of the starboard gun port. With great presence of mind, 26-year-old Seaman William Williams supported the whole weight of the port on himself and by so doing, prevented it falling down and prematurely exposing the gun. He remained thus for over half an hour until the order was given to open fire.

For their extremely courageous action, the crew of the *Pargust* were awarded two Victoria Crosses. One went to Lieutenant R.N. Stuart R.N.R., and the other was awarded to Seaman William Williams following a ballot of the ship's lower deck.

William Williams returned to Anglesey after the war, but is known to have suffered acutely from the physical injuries he received as a result of his wartime exploits. He died in 1965, aged 75 at Holyhead, and his Victoria Cross is now in the National Museum of Wales in Cardiff.

William Williams receiving the Victoria Cross from King George V.

Many mistakes are made in the heat of war, and the problems which arose during the First World War, from the inability to identify friend from foe at sea, were often acute. There can be little doubt that no worse tragedy can befall a warship than to be sunk by what is now euphemistically known as 'friendly fire'. Although no details of the event seem to be available, it is known that during the course of her duties on the 5th of October, 1918, the Thomas-built schooner *Cymric* tragically sank the British submarine J6 when she mistook her for an enemy vessel.

The second vessel to be called *Eilian*, and the very last sailing vessel built by William Thomas, became the third of Amlwch-built vessels to serve as a 'Q Ship'. Renamed the *Chromium*, she was commissioned by the Admiralty on the 24th of September, 1917, and armed with two twelve-pounder guns and a Lewis machine gun. Unfortunately, little has been discovered of her subsequent service career.

Back in Amlwch, the needs of the government brought some relief to the hard-pressed

Iard Newydd, when two barges referred to simply as B384 and B499 (Yard Numbers 36 and 37) were constructed. The first, known to have had a draft of 1 ft l0 ins, was launched on 23rd of March 1917, and the second, three months later.

Two other barges (Yard Numbers 38 and 39), known simply as A.C. Barges 1308 and 1309, were laid down on the 25th of May and the 27th of June 1918 respectively. These were subsequently launched at a combined cost of £6,522.

Bearing this figure in mind however, the rudimentary design of the barges, which by their very nature were so simple as to require very few of the skills of the shipwright or his craftsmen in their construction, suggests that the cost of completion charged against the War Office was somewhat high. This, it could well be argued, is supported by the fact that William Thomas had, but a few short years earlier, been more than content to sell larger, brand new steel schooners of a very advanced design, fully equipped and ready for sea, for something in the order of £3,000. In fairness to him however, the situation had more to do with the then current rate of inflation brought about by the exigencies of what was later to be aptly described as *World War One*, than profiteering on the part of a small provincial shipyard.

As many major French coalfields were located in enemy-occupied territory, vast tonnages of British coal had to be shipped across the Channel to satisfy the daily needs of factories which, amongst other commodities, were producing armaments for the war effort. Because of this, vessels of every description were pressed into service to meet the demand, and the gathering of motley collections of coal-laden vessels in Weymouth Bay, in readiness to be escorted across to Cherbourg in convoys, became a very familiar sight. It was undoubtedly for this very reason that two further barges named *Blush* and *Bluster* were laid down in the Thomas yard in the early months of 1918. The fact that they were referred to in the firm's documents as *Admiralty Duffers,* almost certainly meant that they were specifically designed to carry coal slurry, known in the trade as duff. How many of these barges were ordered and built nationwide is not known; but there is no record of either vessel having being launched, and it must therefore be assumed that they were broken up unfinished when hostilities ceased.

A newly discovered leather bound 'Price Book' belonging to William Thomas & Sons, records in William Thomas's handwriting, the average cost in August 7th 1918 of building hulls of steamers constructed of various materials:

Steel Hulls	£35 per ton dw
Wooden Hulls	£30 per ton dw
Concrete Hulls	£25 per ton dw

The book also records an extract from the *Liverpool Daily Post* of the same date, which quoted the average value of Dutch ships recently purchased by the British and American governments:

Vessels up to 10 years old: £75 per gross ton.
Vessels up to 30 years old: £60 per gross ton.
Vessels up to 39 years old: £52-10-00 per gross ton.

Outside his very natural fears regarding the welfare of his sons, who in common with thousands of others, had readily volunteered for war service, and his understandable concerns for the safety of his vessels and their crews, the Great War had very little impact on William Thomas's daily life. The calls on his professional skills in designing and building specialist barges for the war effort were very much run of the mill for him: but one incident brought home to him an aspect of the conflict he had not anticipated. In a tale he often recounted, he described how he and his entire household were rudely awoken at an unusually early hour by heavy banging on the door of *Bryn Eilian*, their elegant home on the outskirts of Porth Amlwch. The caller turned out to be a veterinary surgeon who had been commissioned by the War Office to commandeer horses thought suitable for service on the battlefields of France, and who despite its owner's loud protestations, took William Thomas's favourite steed away with him!

CHAPTER 14
LATER COMPANY-OWNED STEAMSHIPS
"We are getting on famously with the repairs of this vessel."

As has been seen, William Thomas expressed his belief in sailing ships by continually refining the design of his highly successful schooners. Excellent as his vessels may have been however, fewer and fewer buyers were making serious enquiries about them, and quite painfully no doubt, he became more aware of the deep inroads being made by steam power into what had been, but a few years earlier, the seemingly indomitable world of sail. Six years were to elapse between the launching of the *Gaelic* and the *Meyric*, although two iron lighters the *Belfast* and the *Walton*, started after the keel of the *Meyric* had been laid down, were completed before her.

The migration to what quite understandably has been described as more comfortable berths on steamers, resulted in men able to command sailing vessels, and similarly, those prepared to crew them, becoming increasingly difficult to find. According to the Thomas letters, this was true not just of Anglesey; but other places such as Porthmadog and Caernarfon, ports once renowned for their ships and seamen.

Anxious to find work for his men, William Thomas saw a niche market which suited the facilities at Iard Newydd admirably, and an obvious way to keep it going. His idea was to purchase and refurbish old or damaged steamers which were otherwise sound, either for re-sale or for absorption into the Thomas fleet. As it turned out, the move was to prove to be the springboard for the next important phase of the firm's evolution: but the venture could have been still-born had his business acumen been less strong. Efforts to persuade his brother Lewis to join him in a speculative bid to purchase the 281 ton ss *Nar*, an iron, screw steamer which had been damaged in an accident, failed.

In a letter dated 12th of December 1902, to his cousin John Edwards, the Liverpool ship broker, William Thomas said:

I had a long conversation with Lewis respecting the steamer, and having carefully considered the matter overnight, he decided not to purchase… I am going in for her solely on my own account, apart altogether from the firm, but of course if I secure her, she will be brought here to be repaired as though she was the firm's property. When I wired you this morning, I made the stipulation about the engine and boiler. As you are aware there was no opportunity of inspecting them yesterday as the place was locked, and as Mr Williams spoke so confidently of them I thought there would be no objection to (his giving) *a guarantee of their good order. I observe in Lloyd's book that there is a record of 2 D.B., which according to the key, means that she has 2 double ended boilers. Is this correct? I was given to understand that she had only one, and that the firing was done from the after part instead of the fore part, as was the case with the previous boiler. If my offer is likely to be entertained, this matter must be satisfactorily explained before proceeding further…*

The asking price for the vessel was £2,600, but William Thomas was adamant that he would offer no more than £2,500 for her, explaining to his cousin that, as he was going for the vessel purely as a 'spec', he considered that he had offered as much as he could justify under the circumstances, and that a firm decision had to be made by the sellers by one o'clock on the following day. One o'clock came and went, and Thomas was convinced that his offer had been rejected, but a telegram received a little later that day from his cousin, confirmed that his offer had been accepted. Arrangements were made for him to pay the deposit on the following day, and in his communication with Edwards, he asked if the Board of Trade would allow the vessel to bring a cargo of coal to Amlwch, before adding that he hoped that this, his first speculation, would be a profitable one.

A fortnight or so later, even though repairs had not been completed, William Thomas offered the *Nar* for sale through John Edwards's offices. He described her as able to carry 350 – 360 tons on a draft of 10 feet 6 inches, with engines and boiler in first class condition. The asking price was £4,000.

Despite his belief that her machinery was in first class condition, and having had a Board of Trade surveyor on board twice before she sailed, he was a day or so later to write:

When bringing this vessel from Garston Dock last Saturday, the writer had engaged a tug to assist her out until she got fairly under way. Everything proceeded satisfactorily until abreast of Liverpool docks, when the condenser leaked, and the engines had to be stopped, and assistance obtained. The tug towed her to safety, for which they threatened heavy salvage, but through the influence of our Liverpool agents, the tug owners accepted £6 for their services.

It was anticipated that the repairs would take about four weeks. Mr Riley, the Lloyd's surveyor, was again in the line of fire when he wrote to the owner, informing him that he would have to have the *Nar's* engines examined. In his reply, William Thomas wrote:

we shall be pleased to know by what authority you state that the engines of the Nar have to be examined by a Liverpool surveyor, as the engines and boiler suffered no damage when the vessel was ashore.

By mid January 1903, Thomas had revised his estimate of her worth, and was then seeking no less than £4,250 for her, which included all the necessary repairs, and a thorough overhaul of both her hull and machinery. Interest in the vessel was shown by the owners of the ill-fated *Crosby*, which had the previous week been lost off Flamborough Head. As they appeared to name their own price, Thomas was disinclined to do business with them, preferring instead to offer her on a time charter of at least £230 per month, until she could eventually be sold.

Having understood that Messrs De Winton, the Caernarfon engineering firm, had laid men off, William Thomas wrote to them asking if they could recommend a good practical man who could overhaul the engines of the vessel over a period of 2 to 3 weeks. They were unable to help however, and John Edwards was asked to find a qualified man to do the work, on the understanding that he would be offered a job as her chief engineer when the vessel went into service. The engineer he sent was not to William Thomas's immediate liking however; and he told Edwards that the man would be given a week's trial, and in the event of his failing to give satisfaction during that time, he would have to go. It would appear that despite Thomas's earlier misgivings, Mr Robins did give complete satisfaction.

By way of making the vessel more attractive to potential buyers, her owner had altered her interior design in order to reduce her nett registered tonnage to below 100, which had certain advantages where dues were concerned, and he advised John Edwards accordingly:

A rare photograph of a vessel being worked upon in the dry dock – it is believed that the small craft also occupying the dock is the yacht Kathleen.

I am pleased to advise you that the Nett Register Tonnage of the Nar has been reduced to 99 and 49/100 tons, which I trust will be of assistance in selling her... she will look like new when she comes out of dock, she has already improved a great deal, but when she is finished, she will be mistaken for a new vessel.

A week later, he wrote again to Edwards:
We are getting on famously with the repairs of this vessel, we shall complete all the ironwork this week, but on account of the extraordinary bad weather we have been unable to make the same progress with the cleaning and painting. She has turned out to be a far more superior vessel than my most sanguine expectations, and in my estimate, she is far more valuable, therefore your friends' offer of £3,500 will not be entertained for one moment. She is fully worth £4,300 to £4,500. If I do not secure anything in this neighbourhood (around this figure) *I shall work her in the hopes that times will improve, in which event, there would be no difficulty in getting £5,000 for her.*

In a subsequent letter, he added:
Notwithstanding what Messrs Moss, and Messrs McLaren & Co., state, they are not going to get the Nar for the figure which they mention... they have evidently overlooked the fact that the Liverpool estimate to repair was £1,100, this added to the purchase money of £2,500 makes it £3,600 net, without allowing any profit apart from what we have been able to save on repairs. There have been other repairs, alterations and additions made by which we were able to reduce her tonnage below 100, and this we consider of great value, as apart from the Liverpool Pilotage, it will save us 17/6 (17 shillings and 6 pence) lights each trip... it is useless to waste further time with any of these people... I am prepared to fix on time charter at £200 per month.

It did not come to this: but despite his apparent dislike of Messrs McLaren & Co., brokers of Glasgow, it was through them that he eventually sold the vessel to George Webster & Co., for £3,860 less £80 commission.

In a later letter to Mr Robins, William Thomas informed him that the vessel had been sold, and that he would be contacted by the new owners regarding the chief engineer's berth. The command of the vessel was given to a Captain Hughes, who was evidently well known to William Thomas, and probably an Amlwch man, for he described him as being a good, pushing person with a great deal of experience in coasting vessels similar to the *Nar*.

On the assumption that it had cost William Thomas half the amount quoted in Liverpool (£1,100) to repair and refurbish the vessel in his own yard, he had seemingly made £730 profit in a matter of some 3 months on his £2,500 investment, a very substantial return by any standard, amounting to a rate of something like 117% per annum!

Despite the massive profit in his investment in the *Nar* however, it was somewhat marred when William Thomas later received an account from the ubiquitous Mr Riley of Lloyd's, which prompted the following reply:

*I still maintain that your charge of £6 - 19 - 00 for the survey of the damage to the Nar is unreasonable, but so as not to delay the forwarding of your report, I enclose a cheque for that amount which I send **under protest**, and reserve the right of communication with your head office regarding this charge.*

Bearing in mind the profit he had made, and the fact that he was anything but a vindictive man, it is unlikely that, despite his letter, William Thomas had even seriously considered taking the matter further; and indeed, there is nothing in his subsequent correspondence to indicate otherwise.

The realisation that exceptional financial gains could be made through acquiring and refitting relatively old or damaged vessels, which were sound in most other respects, was not lost on Lewis, and was to have a profound effect on the Thomas's subsequent business strategy.

William Thomas received the sad news from Webster & Co., of the loss of the *Nar* on the 16th of December 1904, and of the death of crew members Samuel Pritchard and William Jones, both of Amlwch.

On the 9th of April 1907, William Thomas bought *HMS Wave* from the Lords of the Admiralty at an auction held in Chatham, with a view to stripping her of her machinery and converting her into a schooner. She was then lying in the River Dart, and having had his bid accepted, he was given 6 weeks to take possession of her. Immediately on his return home, he began to make the necessary arrangements to have her towed to Amlwch: but before she was moved however, he offered to sell her through the brokerage business of Brown & Co., of London, for £1,000 to what he called, 'a prompt buyer', after he had first stripped her of her machinery and metals. The *Wave* arrived at Amlwch on the 28th of May 1907.

On the following day, William Thomas wrote to Messrs Fuller, Horsey, Sons and Cassell, the auctioneers involved in the vessel's sale, recording his astonishment at finding:

that the depth (of the vessel) is considerably less than stated in the sale catalogue… we have satisfied ourselves respecting materials, but the error in the dimensions of the vessel is so exceptional and serious to us, that we make this application for an allowance on this account. As you are aware, we paid a very high price for this vessel, relying fully that the dimensions as given, were correct, whereas the depth instead of being 11'-1" from top of keelson to the underside of deck is only 9'-4", a difference which reduces her value considerably to us.

In their reply, the auctioneers claimed that William Thomas should have checked the dimensions for himself before entering the bidding; and in his reply, knowledgeable as usual in matters pertaining to his profession, he said:

We agree that it was unfortunate that we did not measure this vessel's depth at the time of inspection, but we would point out that the measuring of the principal dimensions is never done by intending purchasers, who like ourselves, rely on those stated in the catalogue… which are as a rule, correct, as well as the general descriptions… in this particular instance, there was a difficulty (if we had desired to do so) in checking the depth, as the main keelson was lower than the limber strake, and also as the measurement given in the catalogue was to the top of the keelson, instead of the bottom. We trust you will submit the matter to the consideration of the Admiralty. We can ill afford to bear the loss, but had the difference been only 2 or 3 inches, we would not have troubled you. The loss of stowage space is so great that we sincerely hope that you will at least submit the case to the Admiralty, and we will be quite satisfied on any reasonable sum they might allow.

In a letter to George F. Galbraith of London, William Thomas advised him that :

We have the hull of a special service vessel which we lately bought from the government. She is now fitted with machinery, which we are removing, and have an idea of converting her into either a three masted or an auxiliary schooner. She is extra strongly built, and sheathed with copper up to 11 feet water mark. Her dimensions are 133' x 22'9" x 10' depth of hold. We estimate that as a schooner she would carry from 275 to 300 tons deadweight.

Similarly, he wrote to his cousin John Edwards, describing the vessel:

We have now removed the inside sheathing of this vessel, and we are astonished to find her looking so fresh. In fact, she looks like a new vessel just launched, and although we previously considered her to be a strongly built vessel, she has far exceeded our expectations in this respect, and to give you an idea of her construction, we mention the following facts:
Keel of Elm 11" square outside of garboard strake, so it must be about 17" or 18" overall.
Main Keelson of Teak 13"x 12½"
Rider Keelson of Pitch Pine 11"x 8½"
Outside bottom planking of 3½" American Elm
Top planking of 4" Pitch Pine
The limber strake of Pitch Pine 10½" x 8½"
Ceiling of Pitch pine, 3½" throughout, excepting bilges which are 4" thick
Beams of Pitch Pine 9 x 7¼", each fitted with a strong iron knee
The beams are spaced on average about 2'- 6"
The stringer is of good Pitch Pine, 8" at top tapering to 6" at bottom, and the second stringe 6" at top, tapering to 4" at bottom.
The ceiling as previously stated is 3½'Pitch Pine.

Further, the vessel is diagonally strapped, the strength of which you will appreciate without any remarks from us. The above description will give you a fair idea of her exceptional strength, and we feel sure that if Captain Greaves saw her, he would be delighted with her, as without a word of exaggeration, she is equal to a new vessel. As near as we can estimate, we make her cubical capacity to be about 16,150 feet (cubic), allowing about 16 or 18 feet at each end for cabin aft and chain locker etc., forward, so we have only reckoned on a hold of 90 feet out of about 131 feet.

Captain Greaves arrived in Amlwch to inspect the *Wave* in mid June. Apart from commenting unfavourably on her length, he was suitably impressed by the remainder, and made an offer for her. In letters to John Edwards, they informed him that:

> We cannot accept £850 for this vessel delivered Liverpool... reckoning on Captain Greaves' rough estimate of the cost of alteration to amount to about £250, we consider that she would be a decided bargain at £900 delivered in the harbour here, but to meet them, we will bear the cost and risk of delivering her in Liverpool for the latter figure... we are quite agreeable to the inspection under the boiler as this is only fair, and we have no desire to palm anything on Messrs Rea unless it is satisfactory to them, as we hope this will not be the last transaction with them.
>
> She is not fitted out like ordinary vessels with windlass, pumps etc., which is our misfortune, but we had hoped that the present capstan would have answered the purpose considering it is so seldom that the anchor is used. However, we are wishful to close the matter and therefore agree to £900 delivered Liverpool, altered in accordance with the specification... with regard to caulking, we shall be pleased to do this at 10 shillings per 100 feet... we could give delivery in about 6 weeks, providing the weather would be favourable to tow round.

In terms of scrap, the *Wave* yielded about 6 tons composed of $2\frac{1}{2}$ tons of copper sheathing, the remainder being gunmetal, bearings, flanges, condenser tubes and plates, as well as copper pipes and other metal. What finally became of the vessel is difficult to ascertain. The first of 8 vessels purchased by the firm for total refurbishment as a consequence of the *Nar* experience, was the tug *Briton*, the first reference to which is on the 8th of March 1911, when a letter was sent to Messrs McLaren of Glasgow, enquiring about a small screw tug, presumed to be the *Briton* of Cardiff, which had been seriously damaged in a collision, and which William Thomas suggested was worth no more than £300 to £400 in that condition. Two days later, a letter was sent to Evan Jones & Co., of Cardiff, stating that they had made an offer for her through McLaren, subject to approval on inspection, and enquiring about the condition of her machinery, and whether or not extensive repairs were necessary before she could be brought to Amlwch.

As this was the first damaged vessel which the firm refurbished, the fullest possible details have been included in order to illustrate the extent to which they went in order to carry out a first class job.

The *Briton*, engined by Messrs Cox & Co., of Falmouth in 1880, had at one time been in the ownership of William Williams & Sons of Holyhead, who in 1898 had fitted her with a new boiler manufactured by T. Sumners and Sons of Liverpool. Although used mainly as a tug in the port of Holyhead, the *Briton* was also, according to Amlwch harbour records, an occasional visitor to the port.

On the 3rd of April 1911, William Thomas wrote to McLaren expressing his profound pleasure on learning that his offer for the little vessel had been accepted. As a result he immediately went to Cardiff to carry out his inspection; following which he confirmed his intention to buy. Some 3 weeks later, the *Briton* was being refurbished at Amlwch, a job, which William Thomas hoped would be completed in a matter of 3 or 4 weeks; after which, he estimated her worth would be at least £1,800.

In reply to an enquiry regarding the *Briton* by Sharp Brothers of Newcastle, Thomas wrote:

> We are taking the whole of the machinery of the Briton adrift and cleaning, and any part that requires renewing, we are doing so. The boiler does not require any repairs but we are having it properly cleaned for a thorough examination and testing, but we have not decided whether this will be done by the B.O.T. or by Lloyds' surveyors. We are also gutting out the whole of the after

cabin and cleaning the hull both inside and outside, and when we have finished she will be equal to a new vessel. Of course there are several parts about the deck that have to be renewed. When we are further advanced we should be pleased if your friends would come through and inspect the work we are doing.

It was finally decided that the work would be carried out under Lloyd's supervision, and not under the Board of Trade's own standards, and in a letter dated 29th of June, to Lloyd's Registrar in Liverpool, William Thomas noted that Mr Oxford would be down within a few days in order to survey the vessel, which:

We are pleased to state, that we have now everything ready for his inspection, and we venture to state that he will find the hull and machinery in excellent condition, as in recent years, a considerable amount of money has been expended on her in renewals etc. When the boiler was fitted in 1898, new floors and seatings were then supplied, as well as new bulkheads. The shell plating is also in a very good state… we find that this boat was originally classed by your society, and therefore it is only a question of re-classing.

Mr Oxford was not entirely satisfied however, and insisted that the present rudder arrangement had to be changed, to which William Thomas replied:

With regard to the rudder, we regret to state that it will be impossible to fit crutch pintles on account of the design of the rudder. As you are aware, both the rudder and the sternpost are almost touching each other, and that it will be impossible to port the rudder if we fitted these crutches and we therefore sincerely hope that after consideration you will pass the present ones as they stand as even allowing that we could fit crutch pintles, they will not be near so strong as the present ones.

Unlike the hapless Mr Riley, whose ideas and wishes were so often discredited, Mr Oxford was not for turning, and despite being sent a letter pleading the owners' case, he insisted that he would not approve the rudder as it was. As a result, William Thomas had eventually to concede the point, and had to agree that what the surveyor wanted was practical after all, but somewhat expensive; a factor that was clearly uppermost in his mind when he made his plea to have the existing arrangement accepted.

As a result of what were described as 'Coronation Holidays', goods required for the refurbishment of the *Briton* were seriously delayed: but a further visit by Mr Oxford highlighted a problem which William Thomas had not anticipated. It concerned the working pressure of the boiler, and in a letter to Lloyd's, he said:

We learnt from Mr Oxford yesterday that the working pressure of this vessel's boiler has to be regulated by the size of the crank and tail end shaft, although the boiler itself is capable of withstanding 100 lbs steam pressure. As your rules for regulating this pressure are probably not known generally amongst tug owners, we should feel extremely grateful if you would be kind enough to grant us a special certificate in reference to the boiler only, as this would be of great assistance to us, and would convince any prospective buyer of the good condition of the boiler.

Describing the work he had carried out on the *Briton*, William Thomas listed the following as having been completed:

Fore and after cabins stripped of all woodwork, and the whole of the inside of the vessel from stem to sternpost, including floors, beams etc., chipped, cleaned and painted with three coats of good oil paint.

The two cabins restored, painted and furnished.

The whole of the outside of the vessel from keel to gunwale chipped, cleaned and painted with 3 coats of good oil paint.

Shell plating bored and examined throughout.

New mast supplied.

New daylight fitted on after cabin.

Funnel partly renewed.

Engine taken apart and thoroughly overhauled and machined in shop.

New stokehole plates supplied and fitted.

Bunker floors renewed.

New condenser cover supplied.

Wheelhouse partly renewed.

Rudder fitted with new spindles and gudgeons.

One plate on port side taken out and replaced by a new one.

Five plates renewed on starboard side.

Six new frames supplied and fitted.

About 30 feet of belting renewed.

Bulwark and main rail on starboard side repaired.

The refurbished tugboat **Briton** *with William Thomas Junior on the bridge.*

The Briton *by the dry dock – the dilapidated condition of the yard is very evident by this time.*

When the work on the *Briton* had been finally completed to Lloyd's requirements, the firm agreed to place her sale in the hands of Messrs McLaren. The price they were asking for the refitted vessel was £1,800, to which the brokers were to add their commission. The photograph of the vessel after completion of the work shows that she quite clearly lived up to William Thomas's prediction that when completed, she would be equal to a new vessel, and he was no doubt very proud to have himself photographed standing on the bridge as she was taken stern first from the graving dock to a berth close to the Watch-house.

The first steamships built elsewhere to be refitted with the express intention of absorbing them into the Thomas family fleet were the *Ardgowan* in 1914, the *Black Rock* renamed *Eleth*, in 1913; and the *Maralie* in 1930.

In an effort to keep the yard going during that period, William Thomas & Sons purchased two redundant Admiralty vessels; the Condor class gunboats *Rinaldo* and *Vestal*. The former arrived in Amlwch in tow of the tug *William Poulson* on 8th December 1921, and the latter in tow of the tug *Gladstone* on 15th February 1922. At no time had it been the firm's intention to absorb the naval vessels into the family fleet as had been the case with the merchant steamers, for they were purchased expressly for breaking up, and in this respect, it is interesting to note that they arrived at Amlwch equipped with full armament. A photograph of the yard workers employed in breaking the vessels up is also most interesting inasmuch that it shows a workforce of no fewer than 30 men and boys, some of the latter appearing to be very young indeed for what was recognised to be dangerous work.

The ex-naval gunboats Rinaldo *and* Vestal *at Porth Amlwch for breaking.*

The yard workers employed to break up the gunboats Rinaldo *and* Vestal.

Johnny Thomas the owner, aboard what is believed to be the Rinaldo.

Following William Thomas's death in 1931, the third generation of the Thomas's went on to acquire the *Eilianus*, the *Dunleith*, and the *Ardri*, all in 1936; followed by the *Eilian Hill* in 1955 (see Appendix 12).

The Eilianus *being refurbished alongside the eastern quay.*

Workmen on board the Eilianus *at Porth Amlwch.*

The wreck of the Eilianus.

The steamship Ardri *at Cardiff.*

The ss Eilian Hill.

These vessels have been comprehensively described elsewhere, but there are nevertheless, several incidents relating to the *Eleth* which are not widely known.

Of all of the steamships purchased by William Thomas, the *Black Rock*, or the *Eleth* as she was renamed, had perhaps the most chequered career. Again, the letter books do not cover the period of her purchase; but it is known that she was bought in 1913 by William Thomas after she had been refloated following a collision with the steamship *Balneil* near the Liverpool Bar Light vessel. At the time, she was carrying a cargo of rock salt from Fleetwood to Garston.

The following extract from a national newspaper dated 14th August 1913, refers to her sinking:

> *The bar of the Mersey has once more been the scene of a shipping disaster, the steamer Black Rock foundering after being in collision with the steamer Balniel. The Black Rock began to sink so rapidly that the 13 people on board had little time to save themselves, and two of the crew, James MacMullen and John Lyons were yesterday reported missing. The Captain of the Black Rock, with great bravery, rescued a little girl passenger, carrying her from her bed to the lifeboat.*

According to William Thomas, the vessel was purchased simply as a 'stock job' – a means of keeping the yard workers employed in what were lean times. The severely damaged vessel arrived in Amlwch from Liverpool, on 18th September 1913, towed by the tug *Black Cock*. Apart from cleaning off the mud and debris which resulted from her sinking, there was no hurry to begin work on her restoration as the refurbishment of the *Ardgowan* was then keeping the yard fully occupied. Refurbishment work began in earnest in December 1913, and according to William Thomas at the time, this was not expected to be completed before the end of the following summer, a good indication of the vast

The Thomas steamships Black Rock *and* Ardri *at Porth Amlwch.*

amount of work that needed to be done to restore her to a seaworthy condition.

It is known that the vessel was undergoing repairs in the graving dock in May 1914, and in a letter to her builders a short while later, William Thomas told them that:

we have recently purchased the Black Rock, built by your good firm, and are wishful to renew some portions which were lost at the time of the accident which caused so much damage… please let us have sight of the plans you possess.

As will be seen, *Eleth* and problems were never far removed from each other, and as she sat comfortably on the blocks in the graving dock, a northerly gale, which apparently increased to hurricane force, lashed the entrance to Porth Amlwch, driving high seas over the rocks and into the dry dock. As it filled, the *Eleth* floated off the blocks, and began to surge unrestrained backwards and forwards, until it eventually demolished the dock gates behind it. Driven backwards and outwards from the dock by the wind and the waves, the vessel crashed into the watch house pier, demolishing the little lighthouse in an almost exact repetition of the circumstances and damage caused by the *Emperor* in Captain Thomas's time. Turning broadside across the wind and the waves, she overturned on to her starboard side, and dug her bow into the stonework on the western side of the harbour, closing its entrance completely; the scars of which are evident to this day. The task of righting the vessel was clearly a mammoth undertaking, but somehow, it was achieved using little other than the skills of the workers from the yard using little other than tools and materials which were to hand. By all accounts, the righting and removal of the vessel from the harbour entrance was completed within a matter of days, thus displaying what can only be described as an astonishing degree of engineering skill.

A dramatic photograph of the capsized Black Rock *at the height of the storm.*

The Black Rock *capsized and lying across the harbour entrance. Note the total demolition of the lighthouse and the dry dock gates.*

Despite her innate strength, and her capacity to survive, the vessel had a widespread reputation for being an uncomfortable ship, and for that reason, there were very few men during the Second World War, who were prepared to volunteer to serve aboard her. Indeed, if local legend is to be believed, an attempt was made to hide her identity from mariners who would otherwise have been reluctant to work her, by changing her name to *Empire Lethe*!

Following her return to Thomas management after the war, the *Eleth* was blown on to rocks on Salt Island, Holyhead during a particularly strong north-westerly gale. She was one of nine small coasters which had sought shelter in the port, and under the headline 'Pocket torch SOS saves crew of ten', a report relating to the unfortunate accident appeared in the *Daily Mail*:

The faint glimmer of a pocket torch flashing out an SOS saved the crew of the coaster Eleth, which grounded during heavy seas off Salt Island, near Holyhead, last night. The signal, flashed by one of the crew of ten as the ship was blown on to the rocks, was noticed by the Holyhead Coastguards, who called out the lifeboat. The Eleth (389 tons) owned by William Thomas & Co., of Liverpool, was carrying coal from Preston to Rosslare.

She put into the outer harbour of Holyhead for shelter, but shortly after nine o'clock last night she dragged anchor and blew ashore on to the rocks at the end of Salt Island. The lifeboat was launched, and the life saving crew stood by. Coxswain Richard Jones took the lifeboat between the stricken vessel and the shore, and took off the crew of 10. The Eleth was badly holed, and was taking water into the engine room.

As the lifeboat drew alongside the Eleth, the crew of the coaster leaped into the bobbing lifeboat.

The Eleth *aground in Holyhead harbour.*

Difficulties encountered by small merchant vessels such as the *Eleth*, frequently go unreported, but on the 25th of March 1947, under the banner heading, 'OVERDUE CARGO SHIP', the *Jersey Evening Post* quoted the local shipbroker, Mr John Renouf, as saying that nothing had been heard of the vessel since she left Liverpool 12 days earlier, bound for the island. Under normal conditions, the voyage should have taken about 2 days.

On the following day, the same newspaper quoted a *Press Association* telegram which gave an account of the difficulties the vessel had encountered on her voyage:

Tossed about by heavy seas for 13 days, and twice putting back to Holyhead for shelter and coal, the 369 ton Liverpool steamer Eleth has begun her third attempt to reach the Channel Islands.

The Eleth, owned by the Thomas Company, of Liverpool, and with a crew of 10, left Liverpool with general cargo for Jersey on March 13th. Calling at Holyhead, the steamer left the north Wales coast on March 17th; but after battling with gales for two days she had to return to Holyhead for fuel. The voyage to Jersey normally takes two days.

The following day, undaunted by the weather, the Eleth tried again, but was forced back 24 hours later, and waited at Holyhead over the week-end. Yesterday afternoon, the ship began its third attempt.

The owners said to-day: "She had rather a bad time on the voyage, but has suffered no damage, and is now safely on the way to Jersey."

Mr Renouf, the local agent for the owners of the Eleth said this morning that the vessel was expected here tomorrow morning – weather permitting!

After what can only be described as a very eventful and successful life, the *Eleth* was tragically lost on the 2nd of February 1951, transporting a cargo of coal slurry from Birkenhead to Dundalk. Of her crew of ten, only one man survived the disaster.

The Ministry of Transport investigation into her loss had to consider amongst other things, two matters of great significance; the first being the condition of the vessel itself; and the second, the nature of her cargo, both of which were considered to be possible causes in bringing about her loss. The fact that one man survived, and was able to give evidence, made the task of the enquiry that much easier, for he was able to testify that the hatches were properly fastened, the ventilators were closed, and that there was no water in the machinery space before she sailed. He did say however that the vessel had a very slight list, which was accepted as having no bearing on her loss. Because of the rapidity with which events unfolded however, he was not in a position to express an opinion as to why the vessel had been lost.

It was evident to the Court however, that the *Eleth*, although old, was immensely strong by then current standards, and was very well maintained, having had no fewer than 258 of her plates replaced during her lifetime.

One argument put forward in the enquiry, was that by its very nature, coal slurry was a dangerous cargo, behaving sometimes, particularly when wet, as if it were a liquid. Evidence was given however, that the *Eleth's* slurry cargo was firm enough to stand upon, and had been properly trimmed by skilled trimmers as it was loaded. As the weather was such that it could have had no significant effect on the vessel's stability, it was inferred in the Court that water had somehow entered the hold, and caused the slurry to behave as a liquid, thereby making the vessel unstable. None of these suggestions however, could be proved conclusively.

One outcome of the enquiry resulted from a proposal put forward by Mr P.F. Broadhead who was representing the widow of Captain Alexander Smith, the vessel's master. He had been instructed to ask the Court to recommend in its findings that all commercial vessels travelling out of sight of land should henceforth carry radio telegraphy. The request was apparently acceded to.

EPILOGUE

Running away to sea as he did in 1834, when he was but 12 years of age, William Thomas displayed what has to be described as a daring and adventurous spirit, and despite having experienced the harshness of the north Atlantic, he displayed courage in his unswerving devotion to his chosen career. That gift of tenacity was the very trait which was later to play a prominent role in his business life, making him, despite the shortcomings of his formal education, an extremely successful and wealthy man.

The start of his commercial life at Amlwch had been beset by considerable opposition; and not even his long-established friendship with Nicholas Treweek helped in any practical way, for it will be remembered that the latter chose not to sell him Iard Ochr Draw when he moved his business over to Iard Newydd, preferring instead to sell it to a fellow Cornishman. This was a decision which may have had more to do with the 'Cousin Jack' syndrome, where one Cornishman feels obliged to help another, cousin or not, than with any real opposition, or even indifference, to Thomas's aspirations.

Such was the Captain's business acumen however, that he accumulated wealth readily, which he went on to invest, mostly in shipping, but also in real estate: becoming the owner of several properties in the neighbourhood of his home parish of Llaneilian, and elsewhere on Anglesey. Despite his wealth, he was extremely careful with money, to the point of sending a note to his eldest son Lewis, to whom he had lent a relatively modest sum, reminding him not to allow the debt to 'drift away'; and recording in a little notebook, the gift of one halfpenny to a destitute stranger. This should be seen in the proper light however, for he was unquestionably a very generous person when people were genuinely deserving of help, as was well illustrated when he instituted the tradition of supplying the very many poor people of Amlwch and its hinterland, with loaves at Christmastime. Following his death, this charitable act, however it may be interpreted today, was continued by his sons, and imitated by several other prominent citizens of the town.

The establishment of a new yard at Duddon partially satisfied his aspirations to become a shipbuilder; but his ambition to set up a yard at Amlwch remained very much at the forefront of his mind. The building of the *Holy Wath* and the *Cumberland Lassie* went a long way to satisfying that ambition: but it was only when he was eventually able to purchase Iard Newydd from Nicholas Treweek, that his dreams were finally realised.

There can be little doubt that his sons Lewis and William, whom he had taken into partnership in July 1884, were the mainstays behind the working of the yard, particularly in the later years of the Captain's life, when his health was deteriorating. Lewis had responsibility for the yard and all which that entailed; whilst William was given the task of looking after the counting house, and the design of new vessels. Both sons had been well educated and trained by way of preparation for their eventual assimilation into their father's business, as indeed, had their unfortunate brother John, who although given every opportunity to mend his ways, failed to do so. Whether or not John's misdemeanours had any bearing on his father's withdrawal from the Duddon venture remains an open question.

Captain Thomas's death of a stroke came after many years of ill health, during which he had sought costly relief for his condition at many well-known spas, but without success. As might be expected of one of his calibre, his condition did little to prevent him from attending to business whenever he was able to make the short journey from his home to the yard, right up until the time of his death. The report of his funeral, the largest and best attended ever in Amlwch, is adequate testimony to the esteem in which he was held on the island.

Lewis, nine years older than his brother, assumed the mantle of senior partner; but there is evidence to indicate that there were difficulties in the brothers' working relationship during the early days following the death of their father. William was desperately unhappy with his brother's constant absences from the yard, leaving him to shoulder the responsibility for its efficient running. Despite that, William undoubtedly became the more significant of the two brothers in terms of the yard's continued prosperity, allowing Lewis to indulge his passion for country pursuits.

The demise of Iard Newydd, the 'Commodious Yard', as Captain William Thomas so proudly and aptly described it in his announcement of its purchase in 1872, was a gradual process; and in many respects, appropriately mirrored the founder's own death, by what was referred to at the time as 'creeping paralysis'.

Over the yard's comparatively short lifetime, wooden ship construction had given way, first to iron, and then to steel. Commercial sail had all but finally surrendered to steam; and ships were becoming progressively larger, reflecting the technical developments in metallurgy and motive power. The most successful British shipyards became centred on the great rivers such as the Clyde, the Mersey, the Tyne and the Wear; which were by then quite rightly gaining world-wide recognition as being at the forefront of shipbuilding technology

Because of these far reaching developments in shipbuilding, the end was very much in sight for the tiny Amlwch yard when the auxiliary schooner *Eilian* was launched in 1908. There can be absolutely no doubt that this last sailing vessel to leave Iard Newydd, represented the very pinnacle in the design and construction of medium-sized commercial sailing vessels found anywhere in the world at that time. This success had been achieved over a period of many years, by the systematic refinement of the original outstanding design of the *Gelert,* through to that of the *Elizabeth Roberts*, rightly referred to as, *the fastest vessel in the three channels,* and, its immediate successor, the *Cenric,* to which the *Elizabeth Roberts* reluctantly had to *surrender the palm.* Had the *Cenric* survived the vagaries of the Canadian weather, who knows what tales there would have been to tell, and what further records would have been broken!

The *Eilian's* subsequent long and successful history, especially when she was in the ownership of the Newcombe family of Exeter, is particularly noteworthy. Her life ended in 1984 at the grand old age of 76, when having been successfully converted from an auxiliary schooner to a motor vessel, she sailed out of Castries in St Lucia, and was lost.

The factors which ultimately brought about the closure of Iard Newydd, are somewhat difficult to define: but in common with the great majority of other small yards dotted along the coastline of the British Isles, it had suffered over many years from a lack of new orders. Despite that, repair work had continued to be a regular but ever diminishing source of income, providing some employment at least, for what had become by then, a very much depleted workforce.

There was no apparent lack of foresight or business commitment on the part of the firm in response to the problems which were besetting it. It had tried to diversify within its normal sphere by way of purchasing and refurbishing damaged, but otherwise sound vessels – a strategy which worked well, and one which could perhaps have been profitably extended. Apart from the *Nar*, and the *Briton*, which were sold when their refurbishment was complete, other vessels like the steamers *Eleth, Ardri, and Eilianus,* were absorbed into the Thomas's own fleet. Other ships such as the ex-naval vessels *Rinaldo* and *Vestal*, were purchased simply for breaking, whilst the *Wave* was acquired for conversion from a steam-powered vessel to a schooner.

William Thomas and Sons were no strangers to severe competition, and despite that had been singularly successful, primarily because they benefited from the low wages paid at Amlwch compared to their immediate competitors in Liverpool and elsewhere. The yard had flourished despite its limited resources and numerous drawbacks, another example of triumph over adversity, no doubt. Factors such as its remoteness from sources of raw material, and its reliance on machinery, which although antiquated was still serviceable, made the yard less than efficient, and it fell into terminal decay, no longer able to provide employment to the dozens of shipwrights, carpenters, sailmakers, blacksmiths, blockmakers, riggers, and others, who had once depended upon it for their own existence.

Various half hearted attempts were made in the late 1930s to modernise the yard, but consultants commissioned at that time were so unimpressed by its facilities, that they warned against the folly of spending good money in trying to do so. Later in the 1940s, the firm approached yet more consultants in the hope that by introducing a degree of modernisation, it would benefit from a share of war work by building small craft such as had happened during the First World War. Those consultants too were singularly unimpressed by its potential. As a result, the bending, shearing and punching machines which had been used to build vessels ranging from iron steamers to beautiful three-masted steel schooners, were left to rust in workshops from which the roofs had been stripped by fierce winds such as those which had so beset the small port in the past.

Frank Thomas the founder's grandson surveying the remains of Iard Newydd after its closure.

Although thought of locally as hard and unrelenting employers, who paid minimal wages to their men whilst living in no small degree of affluence themselves, a charge levelled at practically every employer at that time, it is abundantly clear from their correspondence, that there was also a very humane side to Captain Thomas and his descendants. This undoubtedly stemmed from their deep religious convictions, which may also have prompted both Lewis and his brother William to volunteer their services as Town Councillors, and the latter as a County Councillor and Justice of the Peace.

The yard which had given employment and prosperity to the Thomas family over two generations, was subsequently to provide a springboard whereby the third generation became established at both Amlwch and Liverpool, as successful shipbrokers in their own right.

In an epitaph which would have delighted Captain Thomas, and his son Willie particularly, Basil Greenhill in his classic work, *The Merchant Schooners*, was moved to say:
... it was the iron and steel ships produced by this firm that were the best remembered, for most of the few iron and steel schooners built seem to have been of very high standard of design and construction, William Thomas' vessels were considered in their time to be among the finest.

What remains of Iard Newydd today? Not a lot, unfortunately – two of its original chimneys are still standing, thanks to the Isle of Anglesey County Council, who with commendable foresight, have had them consolidated for the benefit of future generations.

The unique dry dock, albeit minus gates, remains as impressive as ever. The yard's sail loft with its sloping upper floor supported by what were once ships' masts, together with its trunnel-holed window lintels salvaged from who knows what ship, survives to tell the tale as a maritime and mining heritage centre: a development which would almost certainly have found favour with Captain William Thomas and his sons.

Following extensive and painstaking restoration by volunteers, some of whom are the descendants of men associated with the *Commodious Yard* in its heyday, the centre is now visited by many thousands of people annually.

APPENDIX 1

An extract from *Enwogion Môn*, an anthology of the notable men of Anglesey

Translation
THOMAS, William, Captain and shipbuilder, was born in Cae Pant, Llaneilian, in June 1822.

He had few of the advantages of education, and in his youth, he worked on the family smallholding, where it was intended that he too, should follow the family into farming. His adventurous spirit proved stronger than the wishes of his father, Lewis Thomas however; for his own sights were firmly set on becoming a mariner, and he left home without their knowledge, to run away to sea. For many years he sent no word of his whereabouts, and there was great concern for his safety.

He happened to be in an American port at the time of the civil war, and as a consequence, he was forced to serve on board one of that country's warships. When he returned home, he was made master of a ship, and in time, he came to acquire his own vessel. He accumulated sufficient wealth to establish himself in business as a shipbuilder in Porth Amlwch, taking advantage of the current opportunities, when the copper mines at Mynydd Parys were flourishing. His business developed quickly, and he went on to employ a great number of workmen, as well as owning many ships. He came to be thought of as one of the business princes of north Wales.

He was endowed with a strong, keen mind, and his accomplishments were characterised by thoroughness and an eye for detail; and he persevered in his diligence until the end of his life. He was foremost in the cause of religion; and in his political life, he supported the Conservatives. He died on the 26th of March 1893, and was buried in the grounds of Llaneilian Church.

(Original version)
THOMAS, William, Capten a llong-adeiladydd, a anwyd yng Nghaepant, Llaneilian, Mehefin, 1822.

Ni chafodd nemawr ddim o fanteision addysg. Gweithiau yn ieuanc ar y tyddyn, ac arfethid iddo ddilyn amaethyddiaeth fel y rhelyw o'i deulu; ond profodd ei ysbryd anteriaethus yn drech na dymuniadau ei dad, Lewis Thomas. Yr oedd ei holl fryd ar fod yn forwr, a gadawodd gartref heb yn wybod i'w deulu. Bu am amryw flwyddi heb anfon gair o'i hanes, ac ofnid yn hir am ei ddiogelwch.

Digwyddodd fod yn un o borthlafoedd yr America adeg y Rhyfel Gartrefol, a gorfodwyd ef i wasanaethu ar fwrdd un o longau rhyfel y wlad honno. Wedi dychwelyd gartref cafodd ofal llestr fel meistr, a daeth I feddiannu llong ei hunan.

Casglodd ddigon o gyfoeth I sefydlu masnach fel llong-adeiladydd ym Mhorth Amlwch, gan fanteisio ar gyfleusderau y cyfnod hwnnw, pryd yr oedd gwaith copr Mynydd Parys yn ei fri.

Dadblygodd ei fasnach yn gyflym; cyflogai nifer mawr o weithwyr, a pherchenogai lu o longau. Daeth I gael ei ystyried yn un o dywysogion masnach Gogledd Cymru. Doniwyd ef a meddwl cryf a chraff, a nodweddid ei holl gyflawniadau gan fanylder a llwyredd. Dyfalbarhaodd yn ei ddiwydrwydd hyd derfyn ei oes. Yr oedd yn wr blaenllaw gydag achos crefydd; ac mewn gwleidyddiaeth ymlynnai wrth y blaid Geidwadol. Bu farw Mawrth 26ain 1893, a chladdwyd ef ym mynwent eglwys Llaneilian.

APPENDIX 2

WILLIAM THOMAS & SONS YARD LISTS

AMLWCH

Yard No.	Vessel	Launch Date	Notes
01	Welsh Girl	March 1869	99T Wooden Schooner
02	Lewis and Mary	2nd Jun 1870	79T Wooden Schooner
03	Holy Wath	9th Mar 1872	119T Wooden Schooner
04	Cumberland Lassie	20th Mar 1874	230T Wooden Brigantine
05	Mersey	6th Apr 1875	79T Wooden Schooner
06	Baron Hill	3rd Jun 1876	224T Wooden Schooner
07	Lady Neave	2nd Nov 1876	99T Wooden Schooner
08	Nantglyn	13th Aug 1877	115T Wooden Schooner
09	Nesta	1st Jan 1878	117T Wooden Schooner
10	Eilian Hill	1st Aug 1878	113T Wooden Schooner
11	Glyndwr	24th Dec 1878	26T Wooden Smack
12	Margaret	14th Nov 1879	83T Wooden Schooner
13	Pearl	22nd Oct 1880	112& Wooden Schooner
14	President Garfield	7th Oct 1881	54T Wooden Schooner
15	W.S. Caine	7th April 1883	155T Iron Steamship
16	Exchange	28th Feb 1884	274T Iron Steamship
17	Anglesea	5th Nov 1884	149T Iron Steamship
18	Elizabeth Peers	10th Sept 1885	183T Iron Schooner
19	Gelert	10th Mar 1887	223T Iron Schooner
20	Eilian (3 m. schooner)	27th Sept 1889	116T Wooden Schooner
21	Prince Ja Ja	21st Mar 1890	294T Steel Steamship
22	Prince George	8th Mar 1890	24T Steel Paddleboat
23	Cygnus	10th Feb 1891	355T Iron Steamship
24	Detlef Wagner	18th Sept 1891	264T Iron Barquentine
25	Maggie Williams	29th Mar 1892	226T Iron Schooner
26	Cymric	20th Mar 1893	226T Iron Barquentine

Yard No.	Vessel	Launch Date	Notes
27	Celtic	27th Oct 1894	226T Iron Barquentine
28	Gaelic	9th Mar 1898	224T Iron Barquentine
29	Meyric	4th Jan 1904	132T Steel Schooner
30	Belfast	23rd Nov 1900	60T Flat
31	Walton	10th Jan 1902	82T Steam Flat
32	Elizabeth Roberts	16th Apr 1904	132T Steel Schooner
33	Cenric	2nd Aug 1905	98T Steel Schooner
34	Eilian (Aux.)	14th Aug 1908	140T Steel Auxiliary Schooner
35	Morfudd	4th Mar 1912	Hospital Ship for the Port of Beaumaris
36	Barge B 384	23rd Mar 1917	
37	Barge B 499	2nd June 1917	
38	A.C. Barge 1308		Ammunition Carrying Barge
39	A.C. Barge 1309		Ammunition Carrying Barge
40	Admiralty Duffer 'Blush'		Coal Carrying barge
41	Admiralty Duffer 'Bluster'		Coal Carrying barge

MILLOM

1	Nellie Bywater	29th Dec. 1873	113T Wooden Schooner
2	Countess of Lonsdale	27th Sept. 1878	199T Wooden Schooner
3	Lady Kate	1st Feb. 1881	139T Wooden Steamship
4	Lady Louisa	18th June 1882	139T Wooden Steamship
5	Lady Bessie	24th June 1884	183T Wooden Steamship
6	Greyhound	October 1886	190T Wooden Schooner

APPENDIX 3

PURCHASE OF IARD NEWYDD

Memorandum of Agreement between Capt. Wm Thomas and Mr Nicholas Treweek.

November 12th 1871
Captain Thomas agrees to purchase, and Mr N. Treweek to sell his Freehold Ship Building Yard and Graving Dock together with Lot 204 of late Bodednyfed Estate opposite the office only partly enclosed – the purchase includes the fixtures of all kinds. Boiler, Circular Saw and bench. Iron Work Machinery, Lathes, Punching and Drilling Machines, Plate Bolters, Plate and Rivett (sic) blocks with Iron Work, Machinery Tools and Smith Tools of great variety as per Inventory annexed, all material being in a working state Some good and some bad.

The amount agreed to be paid for the Said property the sum of – 1450£.

The conditions are that Mr N. Treweek is to hold possession of the same for 6 months in order to dispose of the stock allowing Capt Thomas to commence any Work he may wish to do at the East end of yard East of Smithy in the meantime after the expiration of the 6 Months Say 12 May next Mr N Treweek declines his business as Shipwright, Smith, Blockmaker, Ship Chandler and Sail Maker in favour of Capt Thomas and he engages not to undertake again in Amlwch Such business for Supply of Shipping.

The payment for the Same to come due on the 12th Nov next. On entry the 12th May Capt Thomas to give a 6 Months acceptance of 300£ as deposit (200 pencilled above), or if cash – Interest to be allowed on what paid at 5 per cent to 12th November and the interest charged on the amount that may remain unpaid after that dater, the deeds to be held in Bank untill (sic) payment.

FINANCIAL ARRANGEMENTS

Dr Capt W. Thomas in account with N. Treweek

Cr.

1872					1872				
May 14	To Purchase Shipyard due 14 Nov	1450	-	-	May 13	By bill due Nov 1872	200	-	-
					Nov 28	" -do- Mar 31. 73			
1873					1873				
Mar 31	Interest on 4 months bill 1873	3	16	8	Nov 14	" Cash cheque	200	-	-
Nov 14	-do- on 1050£ @ 5%	52	10	-					
1874					1874				
Mar 4	-do- on 500£	7	12	9	Mar 4	" Deposit note & interest a/c at N.P.Bank	500	14	3
May 5	- do- on 84£ f Nov '73	2	-	-		" Sundry bill 27-7-11 " N.J. bill 6-7-00	21	-	11
					May 5	" Balance due to N.Treweek this date	94	4	3
	£	1515	19	5		£	1515	19	5
						E.E Nicholas Treweek Recd 5 May 1874 Sgd. Nicholas Treweek			

APPENDIX 4

MOVEMENT IN AND OUT OF PORTH AMLWCH OF
VESSELS REFERRED TO AS BELONGING TO CAPTAIN THOMAS
1870 – 1872
(HARBOURMASTER'S DAY BOOK)

In	Vessel	Ton	Cargo	From	Out	Cargo	To
1870							
05/01	CLARA LOUISA	168	COALS	NOT REC.	03/02	BALLAST	BARROW
06/01	LORD MOSTYN	46	COALS	MOSTYN	13/02	COPPER ORE	BARROW
06/01	EUPHEMIA	87	BALLAST	DUBLIN	12/02	BALLAST	RUNCORN
08/03	MARY ANN JANE	56	GUANO	NOT REC.	17/03	GUANO	NOT REC.
06/04	MARY ANN	56	BALLAST	DUBLIN	12/04	BALLAST	DUDDON
06/04	THOMAS	65	BALLAST	DUBLIN	04/05	GUANO	LIVERPOOL
10/04	OCEAN BELLE	73	CORN	LIVERPOOL	19/04	WHEAT	GLO'STER
15/04	MOUNTAIN MAID	53	EMPTY	PT ST MARY	16/04	EMPTY	DUDDON
22/04	MARY ANN	56	IRON ORE	DUDDON	29/04	IRON ORE	SWANSEA
25/04	ELEANOR GRACE	73	BALLAST	DUNCANNON	26/04	BALLAST	DUDDON
11/05	ELIZABETH MARTHA	69	COALS	LIVERPOOL	23/05	EMPTY	DUDDON
23/05	ALBION	95	COALS	LLANELLI	30/05	BALLAST	DUDDON
03/06	LEWIS & MARY	79	NEW SHIP	NOT REC.	09/06	OCHRE	RUNCORN
04/06	MARY ANN JANE	56	COAL	LIVERPOOL	15/06	LIGHT	DUDDON
07/06	LORD MOSTYN	46	LIGHT	BAL'BRIGIN	15/06	COPPER ORE	DUDDON
29/07	MARY ANN	56	COALS	SWANSEA	08/08	PAINT	RUNCORN
07/08	JOHN	38	COALS	LIVERPOOL	09/08	COAL	DUBLIN
19/08	JANE PRINGLE	99	BALLAST	DUBLIN	26/08	BALLAST	DUDDON
31/08	CAROLINE	52	EMPTY	BANGOR	14/10	COPPER ORE	LLANELLI
31/08	OCEAN BELLE	73	SALT	LIVERPOOL	06/09	SALT	LOW'STOFT
02/09	ELIZABETH MARTHA	69	EMPTY	DUBLIN	11/09	EMPTY	DUDDON
07/09	JOHN	38	COALS	LIVERPOOL	21/09	OCHRE	RUNCORN
07/09	MARY ELIZABETH	42	TO REPAIR	BANGOR	??/12	GUANO	DALBEATTIE
02/11	ELEANOR GRACE	73	COALS	MOSTYN	23/11	GUANO	LIVERPOOL
02/11	MOUNTAIN MAID	53	COALS	LIVERPOOL	18/11	OATS	LANCASTER
02/11	? JANE	51	COALS	LIVERPOOL	15/11	BALLAST	BANGOR
27/11	EUPHEMIA	87	STONES	LIVERPOOL	28/12	GUANO	WEXFORD
08/12	THOMAS	65	BALLAST	NEWRY	03/03	GUANO	RUNCORN
16/12	OCEAN BELLE	73	COALS	LLANELLI	17/01	BALLAST	DUDDON
16/12	ALBION	95	COALS	LLANELLI	12/01	BALLAST	DUDDON

In	Vessel	Ton	Cargo	From	Out	Cargo	To
23/12	JANE PRINGLE	99	COALS	LLANELLI	14/01	BALLAST	DUDDON
23/12	LEWIS & MARY	79	PHOSPHATE	BRISTOL	18/01	BALLAST	DUDDON
1871							
04/01	MOUNTAIN MAID	53	SMELT	LIVERPOOL	07/02	COPPER	WOOD END
14/01	CRYSTAL PALACE	90	OLD IRON	LONDON	09/02	COPPER ORE	SWANSEA
22/01	JOHN	38	COALS	GARSTON	01/05	GUANO	DALBEATTIE
25/01	MARY ELIZABETH	42	BALLAST	DALBEATTIE	14/03	GUANO	RUNCORN
25/01	CAROLINE	52	EMPTY	HOLYHEAD	13/02	GUANO	DALBEATTIE
14/02	SARAH	67	EMPTY	HOLYHEAD	24/02	OCHRE	DUBLIN
17/02	LORD MOSTYN	46	NOT REC.	LIVERPOOL	14/03	GUANO	DALBEATTIE
20/02	ALBION	95	CLAY	FOWEY	22/02	CLAY	RUNCORN
03/03	MOUNTAIN MAID	53	EMPTY	HOLYHEAD	14/03	COPPER	WOOD END
18/03	MARY ANN JANE	56	COALS	LIVERPOOL	19/04	GUANO	DALBEATTIE
20/03	MARY ANN	56	TIMBER	LIVERPOOL	13/04	GUANO	WEXFORD
15/04	LORD MOSTYN	46	COALS	MOSTYN	27/04	GUANO	KIRK'BRIGHT
01/05	OCEAN BELLE	73	BALLAST	NEWRY	09/06	COPPER ORE	LLANELLI
13/06	LEWIS & MARY	79	CULM	BRIT FERRY	26/06	BALLAST	DUDDON
13/06	ELEANOR & GRACE	73	CLAY	POOLE	16/06	CLAY	RUNCORN
14/06	SARAH	67	CULM	BRIT FERRY	29/06	EMPTY	DUDDON
16/06	JANE PRINGLE	99	CULM	BRIT FERRY	10/07	BALLAST	DUDDON
29/06	LORD MOSTYN	46	COALS	MOSTYN	12/07	EMPTY	DUDDON
28/07	LORD MOSTYN	46	COALS	MOSTYN	07/08	BALLAST	LIVERPOOL
03/08	EUPHEMIA	87	CULM	BRIT FERRY	21/08	OCHRE	N'WCASTLE
10/08	SARAH	67	COALS	LLANELLI	22/08	EMPTY	DUDDON
10/08	JANE ELIZABETH	60	CULM	BRUT FERRY	24/08	BALLAST	DUDDON
10/08	ALBION	95	COALS	LLANELLI	22/08	BALLAST	DUDDON
10/08	JANE PRINGLE	99	COALS	LLANELLI	22/08	BALLAST	DUDDON
19/08	ELEANOR & GRACE	73	?	BRIT FERRY	29/08	BALLAST	DUDDON
29/08	LORD MOSTYN	46	COALS	LIVERPOOL	??/09	EMPTY	DUDDON
02/10	OCEAN BELLE	73	CLAY	NOT REC.	02/10	CLAY	RUNCORN
06/10	LEWIS & MARY	79	CULM	BRIT FERRY	23/10	BALLAST	DUDDON
10/10	THOMAS	65	SMELT	BRIT FERRY	24/11	OATS	LANCASTER
12/10	ELEANOR & GRACE	73	BALLAST	NEWPORT	13/11	BALLAST	DUDDON
20/10	ALBION	95	BALLAST	DUBLIN	13/10	NOT REC.	DUDDON
01/11	MARY ELIZABETH	42	COALS	PRESTON	02/12	OATS	LANCASTER
14/11	LORD MOSTYN	46	COALS	MOSTYN	11/12	COPPER ORE	WOOD END
25/11	ALBION	95	COALS	LLANELLI	12/01	BALLAST	DUDDON

In	Vessel	Ton	Cargo	From	Out	Cargo	To
10/12	MOUNTAIN MAID	53	COALS	LIVERPOOL	11/01	NOT REC.	DUDDON
10/12	MARY ANN	56	COALS	LIVERPOOL	11/01	NOT REC	DUDDON
11/12	JANE PRINGLE	99	CULM	BRIT FERRY	20/02	NOT REC	DUDDON
13/12	CRYSTAL PALACE	90	BALLAST	DUDDON	11/01	NOT REC.	DUDDON
1872							
01/01	LEWIS & MARY	79	SLATES	BANGOR	10/01	NOT REC.	DUDDON
13/01	LORD MOSTYN	46	OLD TIN	LIVERPOOL	01/05	EMPTY	DUDDON
06/02	EUPHEMIA	87	COALS	LIVERPOOL	28/02	BALLAST	DUDDON
23/02	MARY ANN	56	CULM	BRIT FERRY	27/05	BALLAST	DUDDON
12/03	MOUNTAIN MAID	53	STONES	LIVERPOOL	26/03	GUANO	DUMFRIES
21/03	DALTON	43	EMPTY	KIRK'BRIGHT	05/04	GUANO	KIRK'BRIGHT
29/03	ELIZABETH	97	SALT CAKE	LONDON	11/04	BALLAST	BANGOR
31/03	ALBION	95	COALS	LLANELLI	27/04	BALLAST	DUDDON
31/03	MARY ELIZABETH	42	COALS	MOSTYN	27/04	GUANO	DALBEATTIE
27/04	DALTON	43	NOT REC.	MOSTYN	19/05	GUANO	RAMSEY
02/06	SARAH	67	COALS	LLANELLI	27/06	OCHRE	RUNCORN
13/06	OCEAN BELLE	73	SALT	RUNCORN	17/06	SALT	HAMBURG
15/06	DALTON	43	LIGHT	BARROW	20/06	LIGHT	DULAS
16/06	MARY ELIZABETH	42	COALS	SWANSEA	03/07	BURNT ORE	BRISTOL
02/08	CRYSTAL PALACE	90	LIGHT	DUDDON	09/11	BALLAST	DUDDON
04/09	MOUNTAIN MAID	53	COALS	SWANSEA	16/09	COPPER ORE	WOOD END
06/09	ALBION	95	TIMBER	MILFORD	23/09	COPPER ORE	LLANELLI
14/09	OCEAN BELLE	73	LIGHT	NEWRY	30/09	OCHRE	RUNCORN
07/10	SARAH	67	COALS	SWANSEA	27/10	BALLAST	DUDDON
07/10	ALBION	95	COALS	LLANELLI	27/10	BALLAST	DUDDON
25/10	MARY ANN	56	NOT REC.	NOT REC.	27/10	SULPHUR	LIVERPOOL
02/11	MOUNTAIN MAID	53	SALT	NOT REC.	28/11	OATS	LANCASTER
13/11	ALBION	95	LIGHT	DUDDON	23/06	OCHRE	RUNCORN
19/11	LORD MOSTYN	46	COALS	LIVERPOOL	28/11	OATS	LANCASTER
20/11	SARAH	67	COALS	QU'FERRY	29/11	COALS	DUBLIN
05/12	DALTON	43	GUANO	LIVERPOOL	03/12	OATS	LANCASTER
14/12	ZELINDA	77	COALS	LLANELLI	17/01	BALLAST	BANGOR
20/12	SARAH	67	SLATES	CAERN'FON	18/01	OATS	LANCASTER
22/12	MOUNTAIN MAID	53	COALS	MOSTYN	18/01	OATS	LANCASTER
22/12	LEWIS & MARY	70	NOT REC.	NOT REC.	30/12	CLAY	RUNCORN
30/12	CRYSTAL PALACE	77	BALLAST	DUBLIN	03/01	BALLAST	DUDDON
30/12	THOMAS	65	BALLAST	DUBLIN	25/01	COPPER	NOT REC.

APPENDIX 5

SPECIFICATION OF THE *MERSEY*, LIVERPOOL PILOT BOAT No 11

Specification of a new Schooner Pilot Boat, to be built of wood and the builder's measurement (English) to be of about 110 tons, and to draw about 10 feet of water. The length of keel to be 76 feet, main breadth 19 feet, depth 10 feet. To be classed 12 years at Lloyd's. The whole frame to be of English oak, copper fastened.

Timber and Space, 22 inches.
Keel, sided, $8^{1}/_{2}$ inches; moulded 10 inches.
Stem, sided 9 inches; moulded 10 inches.
Stem Post, sided, 9 inches; moulded 10 inches.
Fore and aft Cants to be let into dead wood.
Floors, sided 7 inches; moulded $7^{1}/_{2}$ inches.
Floors at head; moulded 6 inches.
First futtocks, sided $6^{1}/_{2}$ inches.
Second futtocks, sided 6 inches.
Top timbers, from $5^{1}/_{2}$ to 5 inches; tapered to 4 inches.
Keelson, sided 10 inches, moulded 11 inches, and to be of English Oak or Greenheart.
Deck beams, sided 7 inches, moulded 6 inches.
Two iron hanging knees abreast of each mast, four of a side, the lower leg no less than 3 feet 6 inches. Lodging knees, English Oak.
Outer planking from keel to bilge $2^{3}/_{4}$ inches; bilges $3^{1}/_{2}$ inches; if required, to be tapered to 3 inches.
Inside planking from keelson to bilges, $2^{1}/_{2}$ inches.
Water Ways, the usual size. Also the scuppers.
Deck planking 3 inch pitch pine, 5 inches broad, fastened with copper nails turned and plugged.
Deck beams to be filled with white lead and putty or rosin, to be decided by purchaser.
Fastenings to be coppered up to wales and galvanized bolts of size required by Lloyds rules.
Treenailed with locust treenails in usual way.
Two masts, pitch pine to be found and fixed.
Jib boom, pitch pine.
Main boom and two fore booms, red pine.
Standing rigging, usual size of best hemp, boltrope yarns. Three shrouds of a side set up with lanyards through lignum vitae dead eyes.
Channel plates to be galvanized.
One tackle on each side of foremast, after part of shrouds.
Fore stay, wire 5 inches, charcoal burned with galvanized chain 5 inches through stemhead and set up with lanyards to pawl bit.
Running gear to be of best Manilla and European rope, bolt rope yarns.
Sails, one suit as follows; viz. 1 mainsail, 1 boom foresail, 1 stay foresail, 1 jib 15 cloths, 1 jib 8 cloths, 1 main gaff topsail, 1 main topmast staysail.

Sail coats to cover mainsail, boom and fore staysail.

Quarter and waist cloths, and covers for skylights.

Canvas to be best east Coker (Thompson's), the number of canvas to be decided upon by purchaser.

All the iron about the deck to be galvanized.

Pumps, 2 first class ones to be fixed amidships.

Boats Davits, four, two of a side extra strong with treble and double blocks, falls, guys etc.

Boats, two, each to be 20 feet long of larch, copper fastened; models to be produced by the builder and approved by purchaser.

Oars etc., each boat to have four oars, rudder, tiller, chain on stem for painter same as other Pilot Boats.

Deck chocks and ? (indecipherable) for said boats.

The said Schooner Boat to be coppered with 22 ounce copper, eight inches above the water line sailing trim.

Stem, copper from stem head to fore foot.

Ballast, to be copper dross only; all to be stored below the cabin and forecastle decks leaving headspace of six feet under the beams.

Decks: of cabin and forecastle to be pitch pine, 2 inches full.

Anchors: two, Porter patent, one of $3\frac{1}{2}$ cwt, one of $4\frac{1}{2}$cwt, one kedge $1\frac{1}{2}$ cwt.

Two cables, chain, 65 fathoms each of 13/16 inch, each with shackles, and to bear the Admiralty test.

Anchor davits: to ship on either bow.

Two chain lockers, below, with plenty of space for chains.

Hawse and deck pipes to be galvanized.

Windlass, double patent to be found and fixed, also a purchase mast winch.

Tanks, for water, two strong iron tanks, each to hold no less than 1000 gallons, to be strongly cased over and fitted with pumps; buckets and bucket rack.

Cooking stove: to be first class hold, pans, kettles, boiler and everything necessary to cook for 30 men. To be chosen by purchaser.

Coal lockers: two, below forecastle deck to hold 25 cwt of coal and no less.

Funnel: from stove to deck of strong iron with a drum to admit of cabin funnel to join on deck, to go through a cast plate with elbow similar to those in use in other Pilot Boats.

Locker for potatoes complete.

Locker, paint, with cans and brushes.

A place for large size harness or beef cask.

Tiers, for warps, jibs, fenders, boatswain's locker etc.

Bed berth for cook in forecastle.

Door to go from dining room or cabin into the forecastle, to close with a patent spring, good brass lock and bolts.

Steward's pantry, to be fitted complete with plate shelves, drawers, racks for dishes, cups, saucers, hanging hooks etc.

Filter, first class to be fitted in pantry similar to No 8.

Cabin throughout; to be built of good seasoned pitch pine and French polished.

Dining Tables: mahogany, two similar to No 7's.

Settees and chairs, stuffed with hair and hair covered.

Dining cabin to be of or near the plan of No 7's with alterations as may be suggested.

Stove to be selected by purchaser, to have a copper funnel to lead into forecastle funnel below the deck.

Swinging Lamp, brass mounted to be placed under skylight in dining cabin to be found by builder.

Marine barometer, to be placed under skylight.

Clock, to be placed under skylight.

Globe signal lamp – ditto – ditto.

Sleeping Rooms, not to be less than seven, and each room to have two sleeping berths, built of deal and cedar, and to have three coats of paint.

Dead Lights, patent glass to light said rooms, the number to be decided upon by purchaser.

Rooms, to have each a drawer, locker, candle lamp and perforated zinc ventilators.

Brass locks and bolts to the sliding doors; with handles, locks, bolts and hinges throughout to be of brass.

Wash room with basin and plug, tank and tap underneath same as No 8, to be found and fitted complete.

Coat room, adjoining wash room.

Coat hooks in ditto, substantial for 12 or more.

Sail Room, on starboard side, fitted with lockers, drawers.

Store Room, cupboards, bread bins, locks and hinges similar to No 8 or No 7.

After cabin to be fitted up with two bed berths, table and wash basin, buffet, drawers, one locker on each side with hair stuffed cushions covered with leather or as may be decided upon.

Stove and pipe, first class, copper or brass.

Compass and; lamp in skylight, first class.

Chart boxes, two, in bed berths or elsewhere.

Companion stair rail etc., of mahogany finished with brass and copper.

After skylight guard and all appertaining (indecipherable) to be brass or copper.

Tiller, to be hard wood mounted with brass.

Rudder, to be hung with metal, and that with a rule joint.

Water Closet, patent, complete, to be fitted on starboard side of rudder on deck, similar to 2.

Gratings abaft, and seats to be fitted similar to No 8.

Seats, at side of companion.

Harness or beef cask with brass hoops and fastenings to be placed on fore part of companion similar to No 8.

Taffrail and main rail, to be coppered where required.

Main boom crutch, to be iron, galvanized.

Fore boom crutch – ditto – ditto.

Blocks, of all sizes, sufficient for running gear and other requirements, strapped with best iron and inside bindings on those required, to be well finished.

Main boom, guy and tackle, side tackles for fore boom and stay sail boom, with sheets, (long and short), blocks etc.

Gammoning: on stem head (iron) also main gammoning to be lined with leather, also iron traveller on jib boom.

Rope, jib outhaul, jib pendants and sheets etc.

Jib halliards: of chain galvanized with rope purchase etc.

Warps: 60 fathoms of 5 inch; 75 fathoms 3 inch; 75 fathoms 2½ inch with hauling lines etc.
Side lamps: brass, according to Board of Trade regulations.
Sundries:
1 deep sea lead and line, with reel.
1 hand lead and line.
1 log line and reel, and 2 log glasses.
1 fog horn
1 good-sized brass bell.
1 set of code signal flags and pigeon holes for same inside companion. 1 English ensign, Union Jack, 1 burgee, 1 colour bag.
Hull: to have three coats of paint, colours in conformity with Liverpool pilotage service.
Deck work: 3 coats of paint.
Sky lights, scuttles and companion: polished wood.
The whole of the work as to shipwrights, caulkers, painters, glaziers, blacksmiths, riggers and sail makers to be done in a sound workmanship manner to the fulfilment of this specification, and should any dispute arise, it shall be settled by two arbitrators, one chosen by each party, and if they do not agree, a third to be chosen by the arbitrators, and their decision to be final.
The vessel and boats to be finished and furnished complete for sea according to the above specification, and there should be no extras or bills.
The said vessel when complete to be surveyed by one of Lloyd's surveyors if required by the purchaser, at the expense of the builder.
The said vessel to be ready for delivery not later than in the month of November 1874.
Agreement made and entered into this twenty fifth day of March, one thousand eight hundred and seventy four between William Thomas, shipbuilder of Amlwch, Anglesey, on the one part and Robert Williams for the owners of the new Pilot Boat N 11 of Liverpool in the County of Lancaster on the other part.
The aforesaid William Thomas does agree to lay down, build, launch from his yard a new pilot boat schooner of or about one hundred and ten tons (no less) O.M. of the best materials and workmanship in conformity with the specification above mentioned.
The owners agree to pay to William Thomas the sum of Two Thousand Six Hundred Pounds (£2,600) in the following payments viz: one fourth when the keel is laid; one fourth when in frame; one fourth when the deck is laid, and the remainder when the vessel is finished and ready for sea by a Bill at three months.
A penalty of one Hundred Pounds will be enforced by Robert Williams if the vessel is not ready during the month of November, 1874.
As witness our hands the day and year aforesaid.
Signed:

William Thomas
Robert Williams

Author's note:
Vessels already in the Liverpool Pilotage Service referred to in the specification:

Pilot Boat Number 7 was the Schooner *Lancashire Witch* 56 GT 80.7' x 18' x 9.6' built by Ratsey of W. Cowes . In service 1863 – 1896.

Pilot Boat Number 8 was the Schooner *Pride of Liverpool* 64 GT 80' x 17.6' x 9.7' built by Royden of Liverpool. In service 1861 – 1890.

Pilot Boat Number 2 was the Schooner *Guide* 61 GT 76' x 18.9' x 9.2' built by Harvey of Ipswich. In service 1856 – 1896.

APPENDIX 6

Articles of Agreement between William Thomas and William Doxford & Sons of Sunderland re the building of the BARBARA

Articles of Agreement made and entered into this 7th day of November 1876 between Wm Doxford & Sons of Sunderland, hereafter called the Builders of the one part, and Wm Thomas of Amlwch hereafter called the Owner of the other part.

Now these present witness that the said parties hereby agree as follows:-

First.   That the said Builders will at their own expense, build and furnish for the said Owner, a good and substantial iron ship or vessel, of the best materials and workmanship, and according to the model and lines approved of by the said Owner and the Specification and the Store List hereunto annexed, so far as such specification and Store List set out, and of following dimensions; 219 feet long, per Register, 35 feet breadth, 21 feet depth of hold, and about 1080 tons nett Register tonnage, and completed by the end of April 1877.

Second.   That the said ship or vessel shall be at the expense and risk of the said Builders, and to be launched at the expense and risk of the said Builders, until she is finished and delivered over to the said Owner, and ready to receive in Cargo.

Third.   That at all times during the building, launching and completing of the said vessel, the said Owner and all persons authorized by them shall have free access to the said vessel, to superintend, examine and view the materials and workmanship and progress of same.

Fourth.   That the said Builder shall proceed, continuously the building and completion of the said vessel.

Fifth.   That if any time during the building and completing of the said vessel, or previously to, or after such vessel being ready for sea, any deviation from the said specification or any extra or additional work shall be directed, to be made by the said Owner, such deviation or extra or additional work shall not be begun until the said Owner shall have specified in writing to the said Builders, the precise amount if any, which he will allow for same, and if begun without such authority shall be considered as done gratuitously and solely for the satisfaction of the said Owner.

Sixth.   Any damage which may happen to the said vessel previous to her being delivered to the said Owner, shall be forthwith be made good by and the sole expense of the said Builders, whether such damage be caused by Fire or otherwise.

Seventh. That the said Owner will pay to the said Builder as the price of the said vessel, the sum of Thirteen Pounds, seventeen shillings and sixpence per nett Register ton after deduction of crew's space according to the Board of Trade requirements and payable in manner following:- that is to say the sum of:

£1200 when keel is laid
£2400 when framed
£2400 when plated
£2400 when decked
£2400 when launched

Balance upon completion and delivery, all in cash. Owner to have the option of accepting for the third of the total amount, adding interest to make it equal to cash. The bills to be at six months date, and in case Owner wishes Builders to draw upon him, Owner undertakes to give Builders satisfactory references. Fourteen days notice to be given of each instalment being due.

Eighth.   That the said ship or vessel from the time of the keel being laid down, and all plates planking iron and all materials whatsoever which shall from time to time be designed for, and intended to be fixed on the said vessel, and whether the same shall have been prepared for, or appropriated to the said vessel, or be in a rough or underwrought state, or in course of preparation, shall from the time of the same being brought into the Building Yard, or any premises of the said Builders, be and be deemed, and continue to be in every respect and for every purpose the property of the said Owner.

Nineth.   Penalty for the non delivery of the vessel by the end of April 1877, to be at the
(sic)   rate of One Pound per day, unless the delay is caused by strikes of Workmen, fire, or any other unavoidable causes.

Tenth.   If any dispute or difference shall arise between the said Owner and the said Builders touching the due and fair construction of these presents, or any act to be done in pursuance thereof, such difference of dispute shall be referred to Arbitration under and according to the provisions of the Common Law Procedure Act (1854) of any then existing statutory modification thereof.
          In witness thereof the said Parties have hereunto set their hands the day and year first before written.

APPENDIX 7

NANTGLYN BUILDERS DETAILS 1876/7 (A.R.O. WD2/513)

Date	Description	Sub Item	Acc. Cost
1876			
November 22nd	Keel laid		235-10-7
1877			
January 23rd	In Frame		569-12-6
February 6th	Commenced planking		607-10-6
March 9th	Finished planking	210-11-3 $\frac{1}{2}$	818-1-9$\frac{1}{2}$
Mar 26th	Finished ceiling	105-18-8	924-0-5$\frac{1}{2}$
April 28th	Deck laid	162-6-8	1086-7-1$\frac{1}{2}$
May 22nd	Finished caulking	105-10-2	1191-17-3
June 12th	Launched and named Nantglyn	183-8-7	1375-5-10$\frac{1}{2}$
July 18th	Masts up and rigged	93-0-9$\frac{1}{2}$	1468-6-8
Aug 29th	Sailed for Llanelly	86-12-0	1554-18-8
	Iron knees & Smiths' work	20-4-8$\frac{1}{2}$	1575-3-4$\frac{1}{2}$
	Cost of Hull		£1,575-3-4$\frac{1}{2}$
	Windlass and Winch	9-1-1	
	Iron Work on Masts and Spars	13-7-2	
	Blocks, Sheaves & Water casks etc.	50-7-2	
	Contract for Rigging Vessel	9-10-0	
	Cordage, Rope and Warps etc.	105-6-1$\frac{1}{2}$	
	Cables, Chains and Anchors	67-19-5	
	Castings for Windlass and Pumps etc	15-17-11	
	Lamps & Sundries, Spars and painting cabin	20-10-2$\frac{1}{2}$	
	Boat 17ft	11-9-6	
	Surveyors Fees	17-1-6	
	One suit Sails, Tarpaulings etc.	124-10-0	£445-0-1
	TOTAL COST		£2,020-3-5$\frac{1}{2}$

Multiplier for 2002 values = 46.61

Bowsprit Cap: 2qrs – 12lb   Fore mast Cap: 2qrs – 24lb   Main Mast Cap: 2qr – 15lb

Amlwch Measure 82 feet x 21 feet x10 feet 6inches/94 equals 192 33/94 tons

Draft of water when launched: 5½ forward and 6ft aft

Board of Trade Measure;   88.6 x 21.5 x 10.9/100 =114.67 ons
    deduct lower Forecastle   11.27   9 seamen
    Register Tonnage   103.40

Official number: 63364   Port of Beaumaris No. 4

Gross tonnage in cubic metres   324.51
    less Forecastle   31.89   to accommodate 9 seamen
                                    292.62   cubic metres

Captain Thomas Jones's Certificate No. 84725

Nantglyn classed at Lloyd's A1 for 11 years from June 1877

29th August 1877 sailed for Llanelly with 200 tons Copper Ore
Draft of water 10 feet forward 11 feet aft

Note: A.R.O. – Anglesey Records Office

APPENDIX 8

DRAFT OF PROPOSED MILLOM FLOTATION

The Duddon Shipbuilding Company Limited
Duddon, Millom, Cumberland
Incorporated under the companies acts 1862 to 1880, whereby the liability of
shareholders is limited to the amount of their shares

Capital £10,000 in 1000 shares of £10 each
(the directors and their friends reserve for themselves 300 shares)
Payments will be made as follows viz.,
£3 on application, £3 on allotment, and the balance in four months from date of
allotment, or Allottees can pay up their shares in full on allotment.
Directors
*William Thomas Esq., Ship Builder, Amlwch, Anglesey.
*J. Postlethwaite Esq., Merchant, Millom, Cumberland

Bankers
National Prudential Bank of England Ltd, Amlwch, Anglesey.
Solicitors
Messrs Forshaw and Hawkins, Huntingdon Street, Liverpool.

*Messrs Thomas and Postlethwaite being interested as vendors will not join the board
until after the allotment of shares.

PROSPECTUS

This company has been formed for the purpose of acquiring as from the (blank date) 1882, the valuable shipbuilding and timber yard belonging to Messrs W. Thomas and Company at Dutton, Millom; and of continuing, extending and developing the long established business of shipbuilding, ship preparing, and timber which has been carried on with considerable success by that firm on the about premises.

From long and varied experience of the shipbuilding trade both at Duddon and Amlwch, we consider ourselves fully justified in giving effect to our long contemplated project of converting our yard and works at Duddon into a limited liability company, in order with the introduction of fresh capital to afford due scope and development to this important industry at the above promising seaport and town. Judging from its recent and continuous growth Duddon bids fair to become a second Barrow, and the rich and inexhaustible mining properties of Cumberland converging as they do upon Duddon mark it peculiarly as a commercial centre, and to all appearances, warrant to it an active future of unbroken prosperity. Its commerce being so essentially identical with, representative of, and dependent on shipping, our experience assumes the conviction in a very marked degree that our establishment there must prove remunerative under the fostering guidance of an intelligent Directorate supported by substantial means.

At the last stock taking, the value of stock was £2800 which is proposed to be acquired by the new company as it consists for the greater part of useful modern plant and fixtures in an efficient state of repair: comprising a gridiron, ship chandlery warehouse stocked with great variety, provision shop, sail making and drafting premises, engine and boiler, sawmills, including a large vertical frame, circular and band saws, wood cutting machine, smithy and blast fires with all their requirements in Iron, timber, sail etc. etc.

The area of the yard is about $1\frac{3}{4}$ acres, at an annual rental of £20 upon a lease of which there is 8 years unexpired, after which it can be renewed for 30 years, parallel with a lease of the Hodbarrow Mining Company.

The premises are large and commodious for the storing of timber and other material, and situated within easy access of both water and rail communication.

APPENDIX 9

INSURANCE COMPANIES, ASSOCIATIONS, PROTECTION CLUBS etc. PATRONISED BY WILLIAM THOMAS & SONS

DATE	VESSEL	INSURERS
May 1882 Nov. 1882	Pride of Anglesea Holy Wath Kate Mermaid Zelinda	Bangor Mutual Ship Ins. Soc. Ltd.
May 1882	Barbara Margaret Priscilla	Bangor Freight & Outfit Co. Ltd.
May 1882	Toronto Yuca	Bristol Avon Freight & Outfit Club
May 1882	William Melhuish	The Severn Club Ltd Bristol
May 1882	Barbara William Melhuish	The Bristol Victoria Club Ltd.
May 1882	Barbara	The Bristol Royal Club
July 1882	Barbara	The Liverpool Mutual Marine Ins. Assoc. Ltd., R.N. Leyland, Secretary
July 1882	Toronto Countess of Kintore Juanita	The Pwllheli & Nevin Mutual Mar. Assur. Co.
July 1882 Jan 1883 Mar 1883	Baron Hill Barbara Yuca Toronto Countess of Kintore Countess of Lonsdale Thomas Boustead	Provincial A1 Mutual Marine Ins. Co. Ltd. J.B. Jarrett, Manager

DATE	VESSEL	INSURERS
July 1882 Mar 1883	Toronto Juanita Coila Euphemia President Garfield Lady Neave Margaret Yuca Mary Anne Albion Thomas Boustead	The North Wales Mutual Assurance Assoc. Ltd. Nevin & North Wales Co. Wm Thomas, Manager
July 1882 Oct 1882	Juanita Yuca Toronto Countess of Kintore Barbara	The Cambrian Freight & Outfit Mutual Mar. Ins. Co. Wm Thomas, Manager
Aug 1882	Albion Barbara Baron Hill Caroline Coila Countess of Lonsdale Countess of Kintore Edith Morgan Elizabeth Anne Euphemia Glyndwr Jane Pringle James Reid Lady Neave Lord Mostyn Mountain Maid Mary Ann Margaret Ocean Belle Priscilla Thomas Toronto William Melhuish Welsh Girl Yuca Albion Victoria	The Amlwch Mutual Marine Ins. Co. Ltd.

DATE	VESSEL	INSURERS
Aug 1882 Nov 1883	President Garfield Toronto Yuca Barbara Countess of Kintore Thomas Boustead	The Bristol Protection Club (Bristol Marine Protection Association Ltd?)
Sept 1882	Countess of Kintore Toronto Barbara	The Provincial Shipowners Mutual Mar. Prot. Assoc. Thomas Jarrett, Manager
Dec. 1882 Dec 1883	Albion Mary Ann Jane Pringle Lord Mostyn Euphemia Mountain Maid Caroline Elizabeth Ann James Reid Zelinda Pride of Anglesea Yuca Kate Coila Lady Neave Glyndwr County of Cork Thomas Mermaid Margaret	Bangor & North Wales Mutual Mar. Prot. Assoc. Ltd. R. Hughes, Plas Llwyd, Manager
Dec 1882 July 1884 Dec 1885	Priscilla Countess of Lonsdale Juanita President Garfield Victoria Barbara Hodbarrow Miner	City of Bangor Mutual Mar. Prot. Assoc. Ltd. R. Hughes, Plas Llwyd, Manager
Jan 1883	Lord Mostyn Thomas Caroline James Reid Priscilla	Victoria Mutual Marine Ins. Soc. Ltd. Nevin J. B. Jarrett, Manager

DATE	VESSEL	INSURERS
Jan 1883 Apr 1883	Jane Pringle Victoria County of Cork Elizabeth Ann	
Mar 1883	Thomas Boustead	The North & South Wales Iron Sailing Ships Freight & Outfit Mutual Mar. Ins. Co. Ltd.
Mar 1883	Thomas Boustead	Ancient Briton Iron Sailing Ships and Mutual Mar. Ins. Assoc. Ltd.
Apr 4 1883 May 15 1883 Oct 1883 25 Feb 1884 Nov 1884 Dec 1884 Jan 1885 Sept 1885	No.15 New vessel launching risk. No. 15 trial trip. Thomas Boustead No. 16 New Steamer No. 17 New Steamer Lady Louisa Annie Walker No. 19 New Vessel launching risk.	R. G. Jones, Price & Co., Insurance Brokers, London.
Oct 1883	President Garfield Euphemia Coila Mary Ann Albion Mountain Maid Thomas Boustead Lady Neave Margaret Yuca Juanita	North Wales Mutual Mar. Ins. Co. Ltd. William Thomas, Manager
Oct 1883	Albion Baron Hill Caroline Coila	The Amlwch Mutual Marine Ins. Co. Ltd. Richard Lemin, Secretary, Quay Buildings, Port Amount Insured £350 £800 £266 £660

DATE	VESSEL	INSURERS
		Amount Insured
Oct 1883	Countess of Lonsdale	£1000
	Countess of Kintore	£400
	Elizabeth Ann	£600
	Euphemia	£375
	Glyndwr	£150
	Jane Pringle	£550
	James Reid	£550
	Lady Neave	£1000
	Lord Mostyn	£200
	Mary Ann	£300
	Margaret	£1000
	Mountain Maid	£300
	Ocean Belle	£380
	Priscilla	£1000
	President Garfield	£750
	Thomas	£400
	Toronto	£400
	Victoria	£100
	Welsh Girl	£400
	Yuca	£1000
	Edith Morgan	£1000
	William Melhuish	£800
	Barbara	£800
		A note in William Thomas's hand reads: "This amount is not to be paid the A. M. M. Ins. Co. as it is to be settled in account of claims we have upon the Society and which they refuse paying".
Apr 1884	Annie Walker	Amlwch M.M. Ins. Co.
Jan 1886	See Appendix 16	Eilian (Private) Mutual Marine Ins. Co. Captain William Thomas, Manager
Jan 1886	Hodbarrow Miner	Truro Mutual Mar. Ins. Assoc. Ltd. (Class 2. Total loss only) John Doidge, Secretary
June 1887	Gelert	British Marine Mutual Ins. Assoc. Ltd. E.R. Evans & Co., Managers London
July 1887	Greyhound	North Wales Mutual Mar. Ins. Assoc. Ltd.

DATE	VESSEL	INSURERS
Mar 1890	Greyhound Countess of Lonsdale Thomas Boustead	Barrow in Furness Mutual Ship Ins. Co. Ltd. W.H. Walton, Secretary
Mar 1890	Ref. To Eilian's account	London Mutual Marine Ins. Assoc. Protection Div.
Dec 1889	Mary Catherine	Bangor & North Wales M.M.P.A.Ltd.
Jan 1891	Lady Neave Margaret Greyhound	Dundee Shipping Ins. Assoc. John R. Wilson, Secretary
Jan 1890	Greyhound Lady Neave Ocean Belle President Garfield	Union Association of Underwriters, Dundee Joseph Gibson, Secretary.
Nov 1893	Cymric	Truro Mutual Marine Insurance Association
Jan 1892	Lady Neave	The Dee Ship Owners Mutual Ins. Assoc. Ltd. James Reney, Secretary
Jan 1896 June 1900 Dec 1905 June 1906	Albion County of Cork Euphemia Hodbarrow Miner Jane Pringle Lady Neave Mary Catherine Ocean Belle President Garfield Thomas Pride of Anglesea Eilian Mary Annie Cenric Caledonia Irish Minstrel Emerald	The Dee and Mersey Ship Owners' Assoc. Ltd. W. Reney

APPENDIX 10

List and estimated values of Iard Newydd Fixtures and Machinery at time of Sons' Partnership Agreement

Article	Value £	Article	Value £
Saw Frame as fixed	377	Block making lathe and tools	50
Travelling Bench	150	Nailors Shop and Tools	30
Erecting Machine	50	Hydraulic Lift	20
Steam engine and boilers	350	Punching machine	70
Sail Room, Tools and stock of canvas	300	Steam Hammer	40
Warehouse Fixtures and Stock	500	Pipings	5
Old chains at Tar Shed & Old Boiler	20	Bandsaw	60
2 Cranes	20	Sharpening machine	15
Planing Machine as Fixed	170	Drilling Machine	10
Straps for all the Machines	50	Countersinking machine	10
Old Lever Punching Machine	30	Old Countersinking Machine	5
Small Drilling Machine	5	2 Furnaces	55
Rollers from De Winton	220	Block Bending Machine	70
Small Rollers	20	Garboard Strake Tool	30
Fan in Smithy	20	Old Chains	30
Smithy Cranes & Fixing and Tools	70	Sawing Machine	10
Iron Shipbuilding Tools	100	Stock of Timber	300
Angle Iron Cutter	45	Stock of Slates and Bricks	25

APPENDIX 11 (A.R.O WM/427/73)

No. 3 Steamer *ANGLESEA* of Beaumaris
Official Number 87.233

Builders Measure 95ft x 18ft 6ins x 8 feet 6 inches
Cylinders 14" and 27" x 20"
Horsepower 35 Nominal
Launched November 5th 1884
Christened by Miss C. E. Williams, Parys Farm, Amlwch

SUMMARY ACCOUNT OF BUILDING

Description	£-s-d
Iron (Angles and Plates)	493-10-5
Chains and Anchors	41-15-5
Stern Frame and Keel Bars	49-9-9
Smith Work	140-16-3
Blockmakers' Work	24-10-11½
Timber a/c	169-3-1½
Sawing a/c	16-8½
Rivets and Bolts	53-11-0
Machineries	1295-0-0
Coals for Furnace	40-0-0
Heth Jones Foundry a/c	16-12-0
Boat	14-0-0
R. Williams & Son, London House – suppliers of rivets and bolts say	7-0-0
Henry Williams Cabinet Maker say	10-0-0
Painting and Patent Filling	10-0-0
Chadburn & Co. Opticians – suppliers of Compass	18-4-6
Brass name plate	1-10-0
Patent Windlass and Steering Gear	30-13-0
Steering Wheel	2-10-0
Lloyd's Surveyor's Fees	14-6-6
Use of Machineries	30-0-0

Sail Making	25-3-1½
Warehouse Sundries	131-17-9
Riveters Wages	95-10-6½
Platers, Carpenters etc. Wages	441-5-2
Towage to Carnarvon (£18-00-00) included in Sundries a/c	
William Jones Ironmongery a/c	7-1-6
Samuel Tyzack & Co., Sunderland Iron	8-10-2
H. Watson & Son, Newcastle (Sluice Valves and Pump)	4-16-6
Extras De Winton & Co.	18-4-10
Captain Lewis Thomas expenses to Carnarvon	7-0-0
Hugh Williams Carnarvon Fittings	5-8-5
Sub Total	3223-18-11
Sundry Goods	78-13- 4½
Total	£3302-12-4

Multiplier for 2002 values = 57.88

APPENDIX 12

VOYAGES OF THOMAS-OWNED STEAMSHIPS

Eilian Hill (July 1929 – May 1930)
and
Eilianus (October 1930 – December 1934)

Voyages of the Steamship *EILIAN HILL*						
Date	Tons	Freight £sd/Ton	Cargo	From	To	Profit **Loss** £sd
1929	L.S.F. = Lump Sum Freight					
Jul 8	299	09-06	Oats	Macduff & Aberdeen	London	7-10-00
Jul 15	367	06-06	Railway Chairs	Thames	Havre	55-00-09
Jul 17	338	08-03	Flints	St Valery in Caux	Weston Point	43-03-01
Jul 25	335	06-09	Coal	Garston	Charlestown	**36-05-10**
Jul 31	375	06-09	Clay	Charlestown	Gravesend	18-04-08
Aug 26	380	11-06	Fertilizer	Antwerp	Irvine & Girvan	64-00-01
Sept 4	358	02-06	Coal	Ayr	Belfast	**3-18-09**
Sept 6	349	06-00	Coal	Garston	Cork	**7-12-04**
Sept 12	326	06-03	Coal	Birkenhead	Ballinacurra	11-15-11
Sept 20	L.S.F.	£130	Tin Plates	Swansea	Treport	50-19-10
Sept 27	375	07-00	Cement	Swancombe	Bideford	4-08-11
Oct 4	168	05-06	Coal & Fuel	Cardiff	Brest	10-07-06
	180	06-06				
Oct 11	359	07-03	Clay	Plymouth	Rouen	4-03-10
Oct 15	356	08-06	Flints	Treport	Weston Point	**10-01-05**
Oct 26	360	06-00	Macadam	Trevor	Ramsgate	8-11-04
Nov 5	358	09-00	Whiting	Boulogne	Garston	46-12-03
Nov 15	330	07-00	Coal	Garston	Waterford	5-10-06
Nov 21	250	11-00	Oats	Cork	Poole	**11-01-08**
Dec 2	362	10-00	Clay	Poole	Runcorn	26-08-06
Dec 18	360	07-00	Coal	Birkenhead	Queenstown	**27-11-03**
Dec 27	362	07-00	Coal	Garston	Waterford	24-02-07
1930						
Jan 1	369	07-06	Coal	Lydney	Cork	42-05-06
Jan 6	170	11-00	Timber	Cork	Troon	38-03-06
Jan 13	334	07-09	Coal	Ayr	Fremington	38-18-05
Jan 18	370	10-06	Clay	Fremington	Antwerp	66-09-00

Date	Tons	Freight £sd/Ton	Cargo	From	To	Profit Loss £sd
Jan 27	360	13-00	Fertilizers	Antwerp	Wexford	87-15-11
Feb 8	310	03-06	Stone	Rivals	Liverpool	10-18-05
Feb 10	350	05-03	Coals	Birkenhead	Dublin	**24-07-11**
Feb 14	355	10-00	Rails	Dublin	Newcastle	106-19-08
Feb 22	365	11-06	Wheat	Wisbech	Avonmouth	76-13-04
Mar 4	273	05-06	Coals	Newport	Penzance	12-09-05
Mar 11	L.S.F.	£145	Generals	Llanelli	Middlesborough	45-02-08
Mar 19	346	07-00	Sole Plates	Middlesborough	Dublin	26-10-04
Mar 27	346	05-06	Stones	Carreg y Llan	London	51-09-05
Apr 2	370	04-09	Cement	London	Granton	11-15-09
Apr 10	358	06-06	Coal	Goole	Fowey	5-04-01
Apr 16	384	04-09	Stones	Newlyn	Ramsgate	2-09-08
Apr 25	355	09-06	Coal	Blythe	Portreath	36-10-04
May 1	357	04-03	Coal	Lydney	Rosslare	7-00-10
May 7	365	09-09	Clay	Fremington	Antwerp	36-18-05
May 15	350	05-06	Wheat	Antwerp	London	41-06-04
May 20	380	03-09	Stones	Bruges	London	13-02-06
May 22	280	07-06	Flour	London	Plymouth	54-00-06
May 28	L.S.F.	£95	Potatoes	Roscoff	Cardiff	5-09-06

Voyages of the Steamship *EILIANUS*

Date	Tons	Freight £sd/Ton	Cargo	From	To	Profit Loss £sd
1930						
Oct 7	850	04-00	Wheat	Hull	Thornaby	39-09-05
Oct 16	850	04-03	Salt Cake	Goole	Dunkirk	**15-11-07**
Oct 22	589	07-00	Fertilizer	Antwerp	Milford Haven	57-17-05
Oct 29	766	04-09	Coal	Swansea	Antwerp	**08-01**
Nov 5	L.S.F.	180-00-00	Generals	Antwerp	Cardiff	81-08-05
Nov 12	L.S.F.	180-00-00	Generals	Cardiff & Swansea	Antwerp	**40-16-05**
Nov 24	849	05-03	Grain	Antwerp	Bristol	117-09-08
Dec 3	L.S.F.	210-00-00	Generals	Cardiff & Swansea	Antwerp	26-09-01
Dec 11	L.S.F.	200-00-00	Generals	Antwerp	Cardiff	58-08-04
Dec 23	842	04-06	Coal	Cardiff	Cowes	1-18-03
1931						
Jan 9	649	04-06	Coal	Hartlepool	Caen	**25-10-05**
Jan 13	554	05-00	Scrap	Havre	Briton Ferry	**3-12-02**
Jan 21	704	04-00	Coal	Cardiff	St Malo	**38-04-00**
Feb 6	823	04-00	Coal	Cardiff	Cherbourg	**3-10-10**
Feb 17	797	05-03	Coal	Goole	Fowey	11-00-11

Feb 26	853	03-10½	Coal	Newport	Brest	20-05-04
Mar 6	852	03-10½	Coal	Penarth	Havre	**4-15-09**
Mar 14	856	03-04½	Stones	Antwerp	London	45-02-11
Mar 19	L.S.F.	175-00-00	Valonia	London	Bristol	**48-05-11**
Apr 27	880	03-06	Coal	Swansea	Brest	22-01-11
May 2	839	03-06	Coal	Barry	Poole	**47-15-09**
May 11	867	04-01½	Generals	Antwerp	Cardiff	87-06-11
May 20	830	04-06	Coal	Cardiff	Rouen	23-00-02
May 28	852	03-00	Coal	Newport	Falmouth	**40-09-05**
Jun 4	884	03-06	Coal	Swansea	Brest	15-01-01
Jun 11	816	04-00	Coal	Port Talbot	St Brieux	**8-05-11**
Jun 17	L.S.F.	140-00-00	Potatoes	St Malo	Newcastle	36-03-06
Jun 22	794	04-06	Coal	Blythe	Dublin	31-11-02
Jul 1	699	03-00	Stones	Penmaenmawr	Port Talbot	42-04-09
	201	03-03	Stones			
Jul 3	841	03-07½	Coal	Port Talbot	Trouville	7-12-04
Jul 9	818	05-06	Cement	Newport	Dublin	56-04-08
Jul 24	650	03-09	Coal	Cardiff	Granville	**60-17-01**
Jul 30	812	05-06	Cement	Newport	Dublin	78-01-07
Aug 10	839	03-06	Coal	Cardiff	St Malo	**12-01-03**
Aug 17	711	05-06	Cement	Nieuport	Dublin	39-02-07
Aug 28	864	03-03	Coal	Cardiff	Havre	11-06-03
Sept 4	838	04-01½	Coal	Llanelli	Rouen	28-04-00
Sept 12	739	05-06	Cement	Nieuport	Dublin	50-10-03
Sept 21	834	03-09	Coal	Cardiff	Poole	**16-04-09**
Sept 26	875	03-09	Generals	Antwerp	Cardiff	71-15-06
Oct 6	822	03-09	Coals	Cardiff	St Malo	**14-05-06**
Oct 12	780	05-03	Cement	Nieuport	Dublin	72-11-04
Oct 21	815	04-06	Coals	Penarth	Dieppe	**13-03-06**
Oct 28	851	05-10	Generals	Nieuport	Dublin	90-09-11
Nov 9	820	04-00	Coal	Port Talbot	Granville	12-17-09
Nov 16	864	04-09	Scrap Iron	Cardiff	Briton Ferry	54-06-07
Nov 27	795	04-01½	Coal	Cardiff	Fecamp	**51-01-11**
Dec 2	870	05-10	Cement	Nieuport	Dublin	97-10-00
Dec 14	817	03-09	Coal	Newport	St Malo	**17-10-11**
1932						
Jan 2	820	05-04½	Coal	Newcastle	Dublin	**32-13-06**
Jan 11	828	04-03	Coal	Swansea	Rouen	18-08-09
Jan 18	868	03-00	Steel	Ghent	London	12-15-00
Jan 23	847	03-00	Steel	Ghent	London	**18-17-08**
Feb 18	710	07-09	Fertilizers	Middlesborough	Cork & Waterford	13-03-06
Feb 26	772	02-07½	Coal	Ayr	Llanelli	**7-10-00**

Mar 3	850	04-04	Coal	Llanelli	Rouen	17-04-07
Mar 10	737	07-00	Fertilizers	Middlesborough	Londonderry	108-13-02
Mar 18	782	02-07½	Coal	Ayr	Llanelli	6-03-05
Mar 23	857	04-03	Coal	Swansea	Rouen	**3-16-02**
Apr 1	821	07-00	Coal	Newcastle	Cork & Dublin	57-15-07
Apr 11	839	04-03	Coal	Barry	Rouen	21-11-00
Apr 18	854	03-04½	Dry Slag	Middlesborough	Deptford	11-17-05
Apr 23	767	07-06	Wheat	Antwerp	Ferit	82-01-05
May 7	761	04-04½	Stones	Dinmor	London	**3-06-07**
May 13	852	02-03	Dry Slag	Middlesborough	London	27-10-02
May 19	550	06-00	Scrap	Antwerp	Llanelli	31-13-10
May 31	870	04-06	Stones	Carreg y Llan	Rochester	85-02-02
Jun 6	680	05-01½	Cement	Nieuport	Dublin	**18-02-03**
Jun 18	838	03-10½	Coal	Swansea	Deauville	**2-06-10**
Jun 27	790	04-03	Stones	Carreg y Llan	Barking	74-02-06
Jul 4	869	03-09	Generals	Antwerp	Cardiff	2-05-09
Jul 13	850	04-03	Stones	Carreg y Llan	Barking	23-19-09
Jul 21	798	03-00	Coal	Newcastle	Gravesend	8-16-06
Jul 30	L.S.F.	£225	Generals	Hull & Sunderland	Cork	**23-13-04**
Oct 13	838	04-03	Coal	Barry	Poole	**80-14-04**
Oct 22	827	06-06	Coal	Emden	Dublin	68-02-04
Oct 31	827	04-06	Coal	Port Talbot	Trouville	6-00-04
Nov 8	827	06-06	Coal	Emden	Dublin	56-15-09
Nov 15	814	05-04	Coal	Cardiff	Rouen	35-16-07
Nov 24	827	06-09	Coal	Emden	Dublin	26-10-09
Dec 5	821	05-10½	Coal	Llanelli	Amsterdam	14-15-11
Dec 16	835	06-09	Coal	Emden	Dublin	**9-19-01**
Dec 25	890	04-03	Stones	Carreg y Llan	London	115-05-11
1933						
Jan 2	842	06-06	Coal	Emden	Dublin	**36-11-10**
Jan 12	830	04-06	Stones	Penmon	London	83-08-06
Jan 20	827	07-00	Coal	Emden	Dublin	60-08-09
Jan 30	520	06-06	Burnt Ore	Dublin & Birkenhead	Newcastle	1-18-00
Feb 8	882	02-09	Dry Slag	Middlesborough	Dagenham	9-09-04
Feb 14	874	02-09	Dry Slag	Middlesborough	Rochester	22-05-01
Feb 20	837	06-10½	Coal	Emden	Dublin	55-04-08
Mar 3	L.S.F.	£120	Beet Pulp	Dublin	Aberdeen	29-18-03
Mar 8	869	03-03	Stones	Inverkeithling	London	15-04-07
Mar 17	837	06-09	Coal	Emden	Dublin	38-15-04
Mar 25	887	04-00	Stones	Carreg y Llan	Thames & Rochester	37-19-02
Apr 3	837	06-09	Coal	Emden	Dublin	54-12-08
Apr 11	930	03-09	Stones	Cerrig y Llan	London	61-04-08

Apr 24	788	07-00	Cement	Antwerp	Sligo	31-06-05
May 5	930	03-09	Stones	Cerrig y Llan	Barking	78-14-00
May 12	886	07-00	Cement	Antwerp	Galway	44-19-07
May 25	940	03-09	Stones	Cerrig y Llan	Barking	87-14-01
Jun 2	700	04.00	Generals	Antwerp	Newport	18-12-10
Jun 10	900	03-09	Stones	Cerrig y Llan	London	35-12-02
Jun 16	842	04-06	Coal	Rotterdam	Rosslare	2-08-07
Jun 24	900	03-09	Stones	Cerrig y Llan	Barking	80-10-02
Jul 3	809	02-06	Dry Slag	Stockton	London	25-08-04
Jul 7	895	05-00	Scrap Iron	Silvertown	Llanelli	76-11-01
Jul 21	874	03-09	Stones	Cerrig y Llan	Rochester	85-15-02
Jul 28	891	02-06	Dry Slag	Middlesborough	Rochester	23-02-08
Aug 3	741	04-00	Coal	Blythe	Fowey	28-13-00
Aug 10	588	04-06	Clay	Fowey & Plymouth	Antwerp	54-01-10
Aug 17	597	05-00	Generals	Antwerp	Cardiff	9-01-02
Aug 25	920	03-09	Stones	Cerrig y Llan	London	39-15-07
Sep 2	866	03-08	Stones	Dundee	Newhaven	7-11-01
Sep 30	900	03-08	Stones	Cerrig y Llan	London	73-17-01
Oct 9	761	05-00	Coal	Sunderland	Weymouth	42-08-09
Oct 17	912	03-09	Stones	Cerrig y Llan	Rochester	28-00-00
Oct 28	847	07-00	Coal	Emden	Cork	3-16-09
Nov 9	820	03-09	Stones	Cerrig y Llan	Barking	24-17-05
Nov 17	857	07-00	Coal	Emden	Dublin	**2-09-11**
Nov 23	879	03-09	Stones	Cerrig y Llan	Rochester	32-18-06
Nov 29	774	05-03	Coal	Blythe	Emden	28-09-08
Dec 6	857	07-00	Coal	Emden	Dublin	114-16-07
Dec 14	880	03-09	Stones	Cerrig y Llan	London	15-13-06
Dec 23	806	06-1½	Coal	Blythe	Havre	26-07-02
1934						
Jan 8	798	06-03	Coal	Blythe	Hayle	20-15-01
Jan 20	890	04-00	Stones	Cerrig y Llan	Rochester & London	42-12-06
Jan 29	775	07-00	Sugar	King's Lynn	Bristol, Cardiff & Swansea	18-09-05
Feb 10	900	03-09	Stones	Cerrig y Llan	London	20-07-01
Feb 19	862	04-10½	Scrap Iron	London	Llanelli	78-14-07
Mar 3	880	03-09	Stones	Cerrig y Llan	London	33-05-09
Mar 12	769	05-06	Coal	Blythe	Bremen	35-04-09
Mar 22	798	07-00	Wheat	Amsterdam	Liverpool	45-16-01
Mar 30	880	04-00	Stones	Cerrig y Llan	London	9-11-01
Apr 11	824	06-03	Wheat	Amsterdam	Manchester	44-01-11
Apr 18	860	03-03	Stones	Cerrig y Llan	Rochester	3-16-09
Apr 24	750	04-06	Scrap Iron	London	Llanelli	69-16-07

May 5	935	04-00	Burnt Ore	Birkenhead	Newcastle	7-17-04
May 11	801	04-00	Coal	Blythe	Shoreham	9-19-11
May 19	664	04-09	Cement	Rochester	Guernsey & Jersey	24-15-02
May 26	L.S.F.	£50	Potatoes	Jersey	Portsmouth	44-09-03
May 28	825	02-7½	Stones	Newlyn	Southampton	24-00-01
Jun 1	800	04-06	Scrap	London	Swansea	14-19-06
Oct 12	809	06-00	Generals	Swansea & Newport	London	22-12-04
Oct 22	700	05-03	Scrap	London	Briton Ferry	79-08-01
Oct 31	500	06-00	Generals	Swansea	London	**24-06-01**
Nov 9	L.S.F.	£230	Generals	Antwerp	Guernsey & Cardiff	85-18-07
Nov 29	813	06-00	Coal	Swansea	Amsterdam	3-04-05
Dec 9	847	06-00	Scrap Iron	Hendrik Ido Ambacht	Llanelli	130-06-06
Dec 12	834	06-00	Coal	Llanelli	Rouen	9-09-08
Dec 16	L.S.F.	06-00	Apples	Dieppe	Newport	67-19-04
Dec 19	805	05-06	Coal	Cardiff	Morlaix	41-10-09

BRIEF OPERATIONAL SUMMARY

ss *EILIAN HILL* (July 1929)

44 voyages over 11 months (assume 330 operational days)

Profit-making voyages (37): £1241 – 02 – 04 … 10 carrying coal
1 ....flints
5 ....farm produce
5 ....clay
5 ....stones
4 ....iron products
2 ....fertilizers
2 ....cement
1 ....whiting (chalk)
1 ....timber
1 ....general cargo

Loss-making voyages (7): £ 78 – 10 – 01 … 5 ....coal
1 ....flints
1 ....farm produce

Average days per voyage	7.50
Average profit per voyage	£28.20
Average profit per day	£ 3.76

ss *EILIANUS* (1931)

38 voyages over 12 months (assume 365 operational days)

Profit-making voyages (23): £973 – 00 – 03 ... 9 carrying coal
3 ....general
6 ....cement
2 ....stones
1 ....scrap
1 ....valonia (acorns)
1 ....potatoes

Loss-making voyages (15): £405 – 15 – 01 ... 14 carrying coal
1 ....scrap

Average days per voyage	9.6
Average profit per voyage	£25.60
Average profit per day	£ 2.66

ss *EILIANUS* (1932)

34 voyages over 12 months (assume 365 operational days)

Profit-making voyages (24): £926 – 11 – 02   1 carrying steel
4 .... stones
1 .... general cargo
1 .... wheat
1 .... scrap iron
11 .... coal
2 .... fertilizers
1 .... steel
2 .... dry slag

Loss-making voyages (10): £200 – 19 – 09   6 carrying coal
1 .... steel
1 .... stones
1 .... general cargo
1 .... cement

Average days per voyage   10.7
Average profit per voyage   £ 27.25
Average profit per day   £   2.53

ss *EILIANUS* (1933)

40 voyages over 12 months (assume 365 operational days)

Profit-making voyages (33): £1489 – 10 – 05..........15 carrying stones
                                                                          10................coal
                                                                          3................dry slag
                                                                          1................cement
                                                                          1................general cargo
                                                                          1................clay
                                                                          1................beet pulp
                                                                          1................burnt ore

Loss-making voyages   (7) : £   141 – 03 – 04............3 carrying coal
                                                                          1 ....cement
                                                                          1 ....dry slag
                                                                          1..............stones
                                                                          1 ....general cargo

Average days per voyage   9.1
Average profit per voyage   £37.23
Average profit per day   £   4.08

ss *EILIANUS* (1934)

27 voyages over 12 months (assume 365 operational days)

Profit-making voyages (26): £989 – 02 – 06..............6 carrying coal
                                                                          6..............stones
                                                                          5..............scrap iron
                                                                          2..............general cargo
                                                                          2..............wheat
                                                                          1..............burnt ore
                                                                         1..............cement
                                                                          1..............potatoes
                                                                          1..............sugar
                                                                          1..............apples

Loss-making voyages (1): £ 24 – 06 – 01........1 carrying general cargo

Average days per voyage   13.5
Average profit per voyage   £36.63
Average profit per day   £2.71

Note:
Vessel maintenance and other operational costs have not been included in Profit and Loss accounts.

'Days per voyage' include days loading and discharging; but do not include days laid up for maintenance.

APPENDIX 13

WILLIAM THOMAS & SONS ANNUAL TRADING FIGURES 1923-1924 & 1926-1928

Annual Figures	1923 £	1924 £	1926 £	1927 £	1928 £
Plant & Machinery	436	436	436	436	436
Land & Buildings	470	470	470	470	470
Stock	344	406	416	423	345
Sundry Debtors	163	141	186	287	345
Purchase of HMS *Vestal* & HMS *Rinaldo*	6,730				
Ships' Account	3,483	6,030	7,212	7,475	9,820
Work in Progress		6,729	5,790	5,790	6,250
Scrap Sold					9,238
Turnover	26,840	26,925	26,347	25,950	27,475
Profits to Partners	1,707	3,456	5,959	7,040	8,162
Profits as a ratio of turnover	6.36%	12.8%	22.6%	27.12%	29.71%

Note.
The sale of scrap in 1928 amounting to £9,238, may have resulted from the breaking up of the vessels *Vestal* and *Rinaldo* bought some 5 years earlier. If such was the case, the total profit amounting to £2,508, equates to a gross annual profit of 7.4%.

APPENDIX 14

VESSELS WITH WHICH WILLIAM THOMAS & SONS
WERE ASSOCIATED
AS BUILDERS, OWNERS, SHAREHOLDERS OR MANAGERS

No.	VESSEL	FIRST REC.	REMARKS
1	Abbotsford	18/04/1875	Cpt. W.T. £300 invested in 1875.
2	Ada	03/1874	
3	Adolphe and Laura	1907	T.I.Thomas Master
4	Albion	06/1866	Brigantine owned by Cpt. W.T. 1883
5	Alice Bannister		
6	Alliance	01/1877	
7	Alnwick	09/1876	
8	Amanda	02/1877	W.T. minor shareholder
9	Anglesea Lass	06/1872	
10	Anglesea ss	11/1884	Am. Yard No 17 Cpt. W.T.
11	Ann Crewdson	1878	
12	Ann and Elizabeth	01/78	
13	Ann Mulvey	01/1877	
14	Anne Walker	07/1886	
15	Ardri		
16	Aries	05/1880	Wrecked at Holyhead
17	Arthur Wyatt		Managers
18	Baltic		
19	Barbara	10/1876	W.T. Managing Owner £2,220 share
20	Barge 1308		Am. Yard No 38 Ammunition Carrier
21	Barge 1309		Am. Yard No 39 Ammunition Carrier
22	Barge B499	06/1917	Am. Yard No 37 Ammunition Carrier
23	Barge B384	03/1917	Am. Yard No 36 Ammunition Carrier
24	Baron Hill	06/1876	Am. Yard No 6 W.T.Sen £150 invested
25	Belfast	11/1900	Am. Yard No 30
26	Belle of Barrow		
27	Blush		Am. Yard No 40 Admiralty Duffer
28	Bluster		Am. Yard No. 41 Admiralty Duffer
29	British King	02/1906	
30	Briton		Tug

No.	VESSEL	FIRST REC.	REMARKS
31	Brothers		
32	Caledonia	31/05/1906	Bought for conversion or breaking
33	Caroline	12/1870	Wm Thomas owner
34	Celtic	10/1894	Am. Yard No 27
35	Cenric	08/1905	Am. Yard No 33
36	Charles		
37	Charlotte Maul	06/1880	
38	Christina	c.1888	
39	City of Chester		
40	Clara Louisa	07/1866	
41	Clarence	06/1868	Originally owned by John Thomas
42	Clyde	c.1849	
43	Coila	12/1875	Cpt. W.T. owner
44	Corby Castle	10/1875	
45	Countess of Kintore	07/1879	Cpt. W.T. £300 share in 1879
46	Countess of Lonsdale		Cpt. W.T. £900 invested 1887
47	County of Flint	10/1879	
48	County of Cork	02/1878	Cpt. W.T. owner
49	County of Cardigan	10/1879	
50	Cruizer (sic)	1881	W.T.Jun. Cutter
51	Crystal Palace		
52	Cumberland Lassie	03/1874	Am. Yard No 4 W.T. owner 1876
53	Cygnus	02/1891	Am. Yard No 23
54	Cymric	03/1893	Am. Yard No 26
55	Cymro	06/1863	
56	Dakota	??/1877	Wreck
57	Dalton	03/1871	Smack. Wrecked off Cemlyn
58	Detlef Wagner	09/1891	Am. Yard No 24
59	Dido	1879	Flat-William Pritchard, Master
60	Dinorwic	c. 03/1899	Managers?
61	Dora		
62	Earl of Zetland	1878	
63	Earl of Uxbridge	05/1878	
64	Earl of Chatham		Wreck – salvage 10 / 1899
65	Edith Morgan	08/1875	Wm Thomas owner. Lost Islay
66	Eilian 1	09/1889	Am. Yard No 20

No.	VESSEL	FIRST REC.	REMARKS
67	Eilian 2		
68	Eilian 2	08/1908	Am. Yard No 34
69	Eilian Hill	08/1878	Am. Yard 10 – Schooner
70	Eilianus		
71	Eleanor and Grace	04/1870	
72	Eleth		Formerly Black Rock
73	Eliza	July 1881	Smack-Owen Jones Master
74	Eliza Jane	01/1876	Oct.1894 Reg. No. 47050
75	Eliza Bell	03/1875	Wrecked – Drummore Bay
76	Elizabeth Martha	06/1863	Intermittent Thomas ownership
77	Elizabeth Anne	10/1876	W.T. Sen. £300 invested 1887
78	Elizabeth Peers	09/1885	Am. Yard No. 18 Cpt. WT
79	Elizabeth Roberts	04/1904	Am. Yard No. 32
80	Ellen	01/1877	
81	Emerald		W.T.& S. Managers
82	Emily Millington		
83	Enterprise		
84	Enterprise		W.T.& S. 'Stemar Bach'
85	Equity		
86	Euphemia	06/1866	Cpt. W.T. part owner 1876
87	Eva of Dumfries		
88	Exchange	02/1884	Am. Yard No. 16 Cpt. W.T.
89	Falcon	1888	Yacht. Cpt. W.T. £120 invested 1887
90	Gaelic	03/1898	Am. Yard No. 28
91	Gelert	03/1887	Am. Yard No. 19 Cpt. W.T.
92	George IV	Jan 1879	
93	Glyndwr	12/1878	Am. Yard No 11 Cpt. W.T. owner
94	Grace Evans		Cpt. W.T. part owner
95	Greyhound	07/1887	Mi. Yard No. 6 W.T. Sen.
96	Gwen	01/1877	
97	Haematite		
98	Harvest Home	1911	John Hansen, Master
99	Havelock	07/1878	Shared with W.Thomas L'pool
100	Hodbarrow Miner	12/1874	W.T.& S Lost Mawgan Porth
101	Holy Wath	03/1872	Am. Yard No. 3
102	Irish Minstrel	1906	3M Schooner – Rich. Griffiths, Master

No.	VESSEL	FIRST REC.	REMARKS
103	Isabella	06/1876	
104	J.W. Bebell		
105	James Postlethwaite		W.T.Sen. £500 share in 1878
106	James & Maria	01/1877	James Treweek
107	James Reid	03/1897	Cpt. W.T. £150 share in 1877
108	Jane Pringle	06/1863	Cpt. W.T. £300 invested 1887
109	Jane Gray	03/1877	Built Iard Ochr Draw by Cox Paynter
110	Jane and Ann		
111	Jane Pringle	July 1879	Schooner – John Thomas Master
112	John Stonard		
113	John & Eliza	10/1876	Cpt. W.T.
114	John Nelson	12/1880	Schooner
115	John Bright		Cpt. W.T. half share
116	John	08/1870	
117	Joseph	05/1878	Cpt. W.T. £40 invested 1887
118	Juanita	05/1881	Brigantine
119	Juno	06/1877	John Thomas owner
120	Kate 2		
121	Kate 1	05/1877	
122	Kathleen Steam Yacht		Broken up
123	Kendal Castle		
124	King Ja Ja		
125	Lady Kate		
126	Lady Bessie		
127	Lady Fielding	1887	
128	Lady Louisa		Owned Cpt. W.T.
129	Lady Neave	11/1876	Am.Yard No 7. Wm Thomas owner
130	Lewis & Mary	06/1870	Am. Yard No 2
131	Linda	10/1876	Lost 12/1880
132	Lord Mostyn	06/1863	Cpt. W.T. £200 share 1877.
133	Lord Tredegar		
134	Lord Willoughby		Cpt. W.T. full owner
135	M. A. James		Cpt. W.T. part owner 1876
136	Mabel of Nevin		
137	Maggie Williams	03/1892	Am. Yard No 25
138	Malabar	1881	

No.	VESSEL	FIRST REC.	REMARKS
139	Maralie		
140	Margaret Anne		
141	Margaret Hobley		
142	Margaret	11/1879	Am. Yard No 12. W.T. Sen.
143	Margaret & Elizabeth	08/1877	
144	Marmion	06/1877	Wrecker
145	Marquis of Anglesea	09/1876	
146	Martha	07/1877	
147	Mary Ashburner		
148	Mary Ann Jane	06/1870	Cpt. W.T. £60 share in 1877
149	Mary Emily	02/1877	
150	Mary Emily	02/1877	
151	Mary Ann	05/1900	Cpt. W.T. owner
152	Mary and Elizabeth	09/1870	John Thomas, Master 12/70-12/73
153	Mary (Of Dulas)	10/1876	
154	Mary Catherine	06/1890	
155	Mary Elizabeth	May 1878	Schooner – Hugh Rowlands Master
156	Mary Catherine	1905	Ketch – John Williams Master
157	Mary Ashburner	1909	John Hughes Master
158	Mermaid	05/1880	Cpt. W.T. owner 1881
159	Mersey	04/1875	Am. Yard No 5
160	Messenger	01/1883	
161	Meyric	01/1904	Am. Yard No 29
162	Minnie Coles		
163	Miss Evans		
164	Mona	06/1866	John Thomas owner
165	Morfudd	03/1912	Am. Yard No 35
166	Mountain Maid	04/1870	Wm Thomas owner
167	Nantglyn	08/1877	Am. Yard No 8
168	Nellie Bywater	1882	Mi. Yard No 1
169	Nesta	01/1878	Am. Yard No 9
170	Noah	06/1877	Boiler exploded
171	North Star	1878	Part owned with Wm Thomas Liverpool
172	Nymph	08/1876	
173	Ocean Belle	04/1870	
174	Pacific	04/1878	

No.	VESSEL	FIRST REC.	REMARKS
175	Palendar		Flat – Raynes, L'pool maj. owners
176	Parys Lodge		Cpt. W.T. & W. Cox Paynter shared
177	Pearl	10/1880	Am. Yard No 13 W.T. owner
178	Perseverance	01/1878	James Owen, Master
179	President Garfield	10/1881	Am. Yard No 14. Cpt W.T.
180	Pride of Anglesea	11/1879	Cpt. W.T. £80 share in 1877
181	Prince George	03/1890	Am. Yard No 22
182	Prince Ja Ja	03/1890	Am. Yard No 21
183	Princess of Wales	1879	Schooner
184	Principality		
185	Priscilla	09/1877	Brig. Cpt. W.T. £900 share in 1877.
186	Queens Channel ss		W.T. shareholder
187	Red	12/1870	Cpt WT's first command
188	Renown		Managers? O.G.Owen – owner
189	Rinaldo H.M.S.		Bought for breaking up 1923
190	Rossendale		
191	Sappho	07/1878	Shared ownership with W.T. L'pool
192	Sarah Pringle	Jan 1879	Schooner
193	Sarah Jane		Cpt. W.T. quarter share
194	Sarah	02/1871	
195	Sarah Lloyd		
196	Sarah Ellen		
197	Saucy Arethusa		Private yacht belonging Capt.Thomas
198	Savant	1876	John Thomas Master in 1879
199	Sea Queen		
200	Sluice	04/1877	Flat
201	Stag		
202	Surprise	01/1877	Cpt. W.T £100 share in 1877
203	Syren		Brigantine
204	Temple	05/1883	
205	Thomas Blythe		Cpt. W.T. major owner.
206	Thomas Boustead		Barque c.1888 Cpt. W.T. owner 1883
207	Thomas	04/1870	First owned by Cpt WT and WTJun.
208	Toronto	09/1876	Barque Cpt. W.T. managing owner
209	Tyrol	1879	W.T.Jun. Bark.
210	Unicorn	1881	Schooner

No.	VESSEL	FIRST REC.	REMARKS
211	United Friends	05/1878	
212	Upton	1881	Smack
213	Utopia of Newquay		
214	Velocipede	09/1875	Cpt. W. T. owner. 1875. Broken up.
215	Vestal H.M.S.	1923	Bought for breaking up.
216	Victoria	05/1881	Smack – Wm Thomas owner
217	W..S. Caine	04/1883	Am. Yard No 15 Cpt. W.T.
218	Walton	01/1902	Am. Yard No 31
219	Wave H.M.S.		ex Admiralty vessel – conversion
220	Welsh Girl	03/1869	Am. Yard No 1- Wrecked off Cemlyn
221	Wilhelmina Agata		
222	William Melhuish	10/1876	Part owner with Wm. T. Liverpool
223	William & Jane		Cpt. W.T. major owner.
224	Winifred	1916	Schooner – James Conway, Master
225	Woodman	12/1863	
226	Yuca	10/1876	Part owner with Wm Thomas L'pool
227	Zelinda	12/1871	Schooner – Cpt. W.T. owner 1883

APPENDIX 15

INCOME TAX BOOK (A.R.O. WD2/520)

NAME	TAX YEAR/S	SHARE	NOTES
Albion	79	32/64	
Barbara	77/79	9/64	
Caroline	80	48/64	
Coila	76/79	60/64	
Countess of Kintore	80		
Countess of Lonsdale	81		
County of Cork			
Earl of Zetland			
Edith Morgan	79	25/64	
Elizabeth Anne	75/79	64/64	
Euphemia	79	16/64	
Glyndwr	79/80		
Hodbarrow Miner			
Holy Wath			
James Reid	77/79	19/64	
Jane Pringle	76/79	56/64	
John and Eliza			
Joseph			
Kate			
Lady Neave	76/79	34/64	
Linda	76/79	30/64	
Lord Mostyn	79	20/64	
Mary Anne	79	16/64	
Mermaid			
Mountain Maid	79	40/64	
Pearl			Sold for £2,000 off the blocks.
Pride of Anglesea	81		
Priscilla	77/79	46/64	
Sarah Lloyd			
Savant			
Surprise			
Thomas	79	8/64	
Thomas Boustead	83		
Toronto	75/79	8/64	
William Melhuish	80	32/64	
Yuca	75/79	26/64	

APPENDIX 16

THE EILIAN (PRIVATE) MUTUAL MARINE INS. Co.

Vessels Entered in The Eilian (Private) Mutual Marine Ins. Co. at 12 am on the First Day of Trading 1st January 1886					
Date	Name of Vessel	Port of Registry	Amount (£) insured elsewhere	Amount (£) insured with Eilian MMIC	Valuation £
	Lady Neave	Beaumaris	500 - 0 - 0	300 - 0 - 0	800 - 0 - 0
	County of Cork	Beaumaris		200 - 0 - 0	200 - 0 - 0
	Euphemia	Beaumaris		250 - 0 - 0	250 - 0 - 0
	President Garfield	Beaumaris	300 - 0 - 0	300 - 0 - 0	600 - 0 - 0
	Lord Mostyn	Beaumaris		120 - 0 - 0	120 - 0 - 0
	Thomas	Liverpool		200 - 0 - 0	200 - 0 - 0
	Priscilla	Aberystwyth		400 - 0 - 0	400 - 0 - 0
	Caroline	Beaumaris		200 - 0 - 0	200 - 0 - 0
	Elizabeth Anne	Caernarfon	150 - 0 - 0	250 - 0 - 0	400 - 0 - 0
Lost 3/5/87	Mountain Maid	Beaumaris		200 - 0 - 0	200 - 0 - 0
	Albion	Beaumaris		280 - 0 - 0	280 - 0 - 0
	Mary Ann	Beaumaris		150 - 0 - 0	150 - 0 - 0
	Margaret	Beaumaris	300 - 0 - 0	400 - 0 - 0	700 - 0 - 0
Lost 9/1/86	Glyndwr	Beaumaris		100 - 0 - 0	100 - 0 - 0
	Anne Walker	Runcorn		200 - 0 - 0	200 - 0 - 0
	Hodbarrow Miner	Barrow	600 - 0 - 0	250 - 0 - 0	850 - 0 - 0
	Mermaid	Caernarfon		300 - 0 - 0	300 - 0 - 0
	Yuca	Liverpool	1800 - 0 - 0	150 - 0 - 0	1950 - 0 - 0
	Thomas Boustead	Liverpool	800 - 0 - 0	150 - 0 - 0	950 - 0 - 0
	Jane Pringle		200 - 0 - 0	100 - 0 - 0	300 - 0 - 0
	Pride of Anglesea	Beaumaris		200 - 0 - 0	300 - 0 - 0
	Countess of Lonsdale	Whitehaven	1000 - 0 - 0	250 - 0 - 0	1250 - 0 - 0
	Baron Hill (WT shares)	Whitehaven		200 - 0 - 0	200 - 0 - 0

Additional notes in W.T. & Sons' insurance ledger referring to a few of the vessels insured by the Eilian MMIC:

January 9th 1886:

To total loss of the schooner *Glyndwr* which proceeded from Liverpool for Cemaes, laden with coals. On the evening of the eighth of January 1886, when off Hilbre Island early in the morning of the 9th of January 1886 the vessel missed stays and ran ashore on Hilbre Island. Vessel insured with above club for £100.

May 3rd 1887:

To total loss of the schooner *Mountain Maid*, on Raven Sands off Wexford Harbour this date.

The vessel was loaded with 90 tons of coals at Llanelly (sic) on the 20th April 1887, and was bound for Greencastle in Carlingford Lough, Ireland. Everything went right until the night of the 2nd of May when wind came to the N.E. blowing hard and sea very rough, weather thick and hazy, the Capt. decided to make for Wexford harbour for shelter, but being unable to observe Wexford Lights, he forced the vessel ashore on Raven Sands on the morning of the 3rd of May 1887.

Vessel insured in above club for £200.
Less Proceeds of sale as per account   £32 - 14 - 00
Deduct disbursements as per account £15 - 14 - 00
£183 - 00 - 00

August 9th 1887:

To total loss of schooner *Mermaid*, through collision with the Barque *Minerva*, of Stettin, in the River Thames, near the Nore Lightship, this date. The vessel was loaded with about 135 tons of slates at Bangor, and was bound to Erith. Vessel insured in above club for £300.

APPENDIX 17

VESSELS WORKED ON BY WILLIAM THOMAS & SONS 1890 – 1928

Year	Month	Vessel
1890	October	3–masted Schooner FORD FISHER
1891	September	Schooner PRIDE OF ANGLESEA
1891	October	Schooner ELIZABETH & ELLEN
1891	November	No 26 New Vessel CYMRIC launched 20-3-1893
1891	November	Schooner EUPHEMIA
1891	December	Schooner SILVER LANDS of Plymouth
1891	December	No 27 New Vessel CELTIC launched 27-10-1894
1892	January	Schooner CAROLINE
1892	February	Schooner BALTIC
1892	February	Schooner HODBARROW MINER
1892	February	Schooner BARON HILL
1892	February	Schooner LADY FIELDING
1892	March	Tug ENTERPRISE – sunk at entrance to harbour.
1892	March	Schooner MAGGIE WILLIAMS
1892	March	Schooner MARTHA
1892	March	Schooner EILIAN
1892	March	Schooner COUNTY OF CORK
1892	April	Schooner JANE PRINGLE
1892	April	Steam Yacht SAUCY ARETHUSA
1892	April	Schooner LADY NEAVE
1892	April	ss DINORWIC (contract)
1892	May	Schooner OCEAN BELLE
1892	June	Schooner PRESIDENT GARFIELD
1892	July	Schooner MARY CATHERINE
1892	July	Smack JANE
1892	July	Schooner PEARL
1892	August	Yacht MIRANDA
1892	September	Barque EMILIE DINGLE
1892	September	Schooner MISS EVANS
1892	December	Brigantine ALBION
1893	January	Schooner THOMAS
1893	January	Schooner ELIZABETH & JANE

Year	Month	Vessel
1893	March	Schooner *QUEEN OF THE ISLES*
1893	July	Schooner *EUPHEMIA*
1893	October	Schooner *CWMAVON*
1893	October	Schooner *ELIZA BAIN*
1893	October	Schooner *GLENRAVIL MINER*
1894	January	ss *ENTERPRISE*
1894	April	Barquentine *CYMRIC*
1894	May	Flat *PROVIDENCE*
1894	May	No 28 New Vessel *GAELIC* launched
1894	July	Schooner *MARY ARMISTEAD*
1894	September	Schooner *ELIZA JANE* – T. Williams owner
1894	November	Schooner *OWEN MORRIS* of Portmadoc
1895	January	Schooner *GRIMALDI* of Fowey
1895	January	Schooner *VENERABLE* – John Owen Preswylfa, Moelfro owner.
1895	March	Schooner *DINORWIC*
1895	April	Brigantine *PEARL* of Newquay – owned Arklow – Cpt. Gregory
1895	May	Steam Yacht *KATHLEEN*
1895	June	Schooner *OCEAN MAID* of Arklow – Cpt. William Darragh
1895	October	Schooner *EQUITY*
1896	May	Schooner *ALICE BANNISTER*
1896	July	Schooner *ARTHUR WYATT*
1896	November	Schooner *MERSEY* of Dublin – Cpt. Kavanagh
1897	May	ss *SEA SWALLOW* of Liverpool – Wm Burton & Sons
1897	August	Schooner *SARAH ELLEN*
1898	April	No 29 New Vessel *MEYRIC* launched 4th January 1904
1899	August	Fishing Smack *VIOLET* of Hoylake
1899	August	No 30 New Vessel – Lighter *BELFAST* launched 23rd November 1900
1899	August	Ketch *MYOSOTIS* of Hoylake
1899	October	Schooner *COLORADO* of Dublin – Mr Pim, Wicklow, owner.
1900	February	3-masted Schooner *EDITH CROSSFIELD*
1900	March	Schooner *RETURN* of Greenock
1900	June	3-masted Schooner *IRISH MINSTREL* of Carnarvon
1900	October	Schooner *UNITY*
1901	June	Schooner *ELIZA FRANCIS*
1901	June	No 31 New Vessel Steam Lighter *WALTON* lau. 10th January 1902

Year	Month	Vessel
1901	August	Ketch *CURLEW* of Hoylake
1902	January	Schooner *JOHN NELSON*
1902	April	Schooner *MIRANDA* of Arbroath
1902	May	3-masted Schooner *MARY ANNIE*
1902	November	No 32 New Vessel *ELIZABETH ROBERTS* launched 16 April 1904
1902	December	Schooner *MARY SINCLAIR* of Barrow
1902	December	ss *NAR*
1903	February	Schooner *PRINCE LLEWELYN* of Carnarvon – Cpt. Roberts
1903	March	Schooner *UNITY*
1903	July	Fishing Smack *ASHBY* of Hoylake
1904	March	Barquentine OCEAN SPRAY
1904	April	No 33 New Vessel *CENRIC* launched 2-8-05
1904	May	Schooner *ISLAND MAID* of Belfast
1904	July	Ketch *ANNE MARIA* LL208
1904	July	Brigantine *IMOGENE*
1904	August	Ketch *M.A.G.* FD69
1904	September	Ketch *VIGILANT* of Liverpool LL306
1904	October	3-masted Schooner *HANNAH CROASDELL* (contract)
1905	May	No 34 New Vessel
1905	May	3-masted Schooner *TECWYN*
1905	July	Screw Tug *BRITISH KING*
1905	July	Schooner *ELMA*
1905	September	Schooner *HARRY RUSSELL* of Barrow
1905	October	Schooner *BECCA & MARY*
1905	November	Barge *DORIC* of London
1905	November	Barquentine *EMERALD*
1905	December	3-masted Schooner *CENRIC*
1906	January	Schooner *COUNTY OF CORK*
1906	February	*BRITISH KING*
1906	February	Schooner *UNITY*
1906	March	Schooner *ELIZA FRANCIS*
1906	March	Schooner *CONISTON*
1906	March	Ketch *ELIZA JANE*, owner Mr Jenkins, Pentre Arms, Llangrannog
1906	March	Schooner *LADY NEAVE*
1906	March	Schooner *HODBARROW MINER*

Year	Month	Vessel
1906	April	3-masted Schooner *BRITISH QUEEN*
1906	May	Ketch *CONFIDO* of Dublin
1906	May	3-masted Schooner *DESPATCH*
1906	June	Fishing Smack *FROLIC* LL42
1906	June	No 34 New Vessel launched 14-8-1908 as *PIONEER* – renamed *EILIAN*
1906	July	Barquentine *EMERALD*
1906	July	Fishing Smack *ALICE* DH123
1906	August	Schooner *COUNTY OF CORK*
1906	August	Brigantine *ALBION*
1906	August	Fishing Smack *RELIANCE* LL60
1906	September	Schooner *CALEDONIA*
1906	September	3-masted Schooner *WOOLTON* of Barrow
1906	September	3-masted Schooner *HAPPY HARRY* – owner R. Johnson, Millom – Cpt. William Williams
1906	September	Fishing Smack *VIOLET* DO 73 Cpt. Beck, owner.
1906	October	Barquentine *LUKE BRUCE*
1906	October	3-masted Schooner *MARY MILLER*
1906	October	Fishing Smack *WAVE* CO3 – owners Anderson Bros, Liverpool
1906	November	3-masted Schooner *MEYRIC* – Cpt. Robert Griffiths
1906	November	Barquentine *GAELIC*
1906	November	3-masted Schooner *AGNES MAY* – Cpt. J.H. Lewis – owner E.O. Roberts, Liverpool.
1906	December	Schooner *FRANCIS* of Barrow
1907	January	Schooner *MARY SINCLAIR*
1907	January	Schooner *HODBARROW MINER*
1907	January	3-masted Schooner *IRISH MINSTREL* of Beaumaris – Cpt. Richard Griffiths
1907	March	Barquentine *EMERALD*
1907	March	Smack *PILGRIM*
1907	May	Steam Yacht *WAVE*
1907	May	*MAGGIE BROCKLEBANK* – (Used old, and second hand materials)
1907	May	Schooner *ELIZA FRANCIS*
1907	June	Removing Semaphore at Point Lynas
1907	June	Schooner *ALICE & ELIZA*

Year	Month	Vessel
1907	August	Schooner *NANNY WIGNALL* of Fleetwood
1908	February	ss *LINCOLNSHIRE*
1908	April	*MAGGIE A* of Poole
1908	May	3-masted Schooner *EDWARD* of Dublin
1908	June	Smack *RELIANCE* – owner, Mrs Rutter
1908	July	ss *OLIVE*
1908	August	No 35 New Vessel (Motor Schooner – project abandoned)
1908	August	Brigantine *ADOLPHE & LAURA*
1908	November	Schooner *MARY ASHBURNER*
1909	January	3-masted Schooner *MEYRIC*
1909	June	Schooner *SPARLING* of Chester
1909	July	Motor Schooner *EILIAN*
1910	January	Barquentine *GAELIC* – Damage repairs Total cost £634-18-6
1910	July	3-masted Schooner *HARVEST HOME*
1911	April	Screw Tug *BRITON*
1911	June	No 35 New Vessel floating hospital *(MORFUDD)* launched 4th March 1912
1911	June	Schooner *EMILY MILLINGTON*
1911	Aug	Fishing Smack *LILY* LL133
1911	November	ss *BRITON* of Glasgow
1911	December	Schooner *KATE*
1912	April	ss *OSPREY* of Waterford – Mortgage I. Mackie
1912	July	Fishing Boat *CONQUEROR* DH321
1912	August	Fishing Boat *SUNBEAM*
1912	August	Ketch *MARY CATHERINE*
1913	February	W.C. Paynter – supplies to *FALCON*; *CAMBORNE*; *EMILY MILLINGTON*; *CERES*; *AGRICOLA*; *ELIZABETH CHARLOTTE*
1913	June	Schooner *WINIFRED* of Inverness
1913	September	ss *BLACK ROCK* arrived in tow of *BLACK COCK*. 18-9-1913 ex Liverpool
1913	September	Sale of scrap metal ex *WAVE* to Wolverhampton Metal Co.
1913	September	ss *ARDGOWAN*
1913	October	ss *FIDO* of Hull
1914	April	Ketch *CERES*
1914	August	ss *HEMPOCK*
1915	June	ss *BLACK ROCK* – floated 1-7-15 - got into harbour 2-7-1915 at 1 am

Year	Month	Vessel
1915	October	Fishing Ketch *MABEL* of Liverpool LL300. William Davies, Owner and Master
1915	November	*MARY CATHERINE* Altering into Barge
1916	March	Ketch *MARY CATHERINE* – Standard Lighterage Co, Liverpool
1916	October	Nos 36 and 37 New Vessels (W.O.Barges 70x10x6) 384 launched 23-3-1917 Draft 1ft-10ins
1917	January	Paddle Steamer *PANSY* of Liverpool – ashore at Bull Bay
1917	July	Motor Schooner *CLAGGAN* ashore on Dulas Island
1917	November	Nos 38 and 39 New Vessels – A(mmunition?)C(arrying?) Barges 1308 and 1309
1917	December	Schooner *KATE*
1918	May	ss *BLACK ROCK* sailed from Amlwch to Garston 7-5-1918
1918	May	*ELETH* ex *BLACK ROCK*
1918	July	No *38* New Vessel. Keel laid 25-5-1918 No 39 New Vessel Keel laid 27-6-1918
1918	August	ss *SIRDAR* of Exeter
1918	September	Nos 40 and 41 New Vessels. Admiralty Duffers *BLUSH* and *BLUSTER*
1919	February	Motor Schooner *EILIAN* arrived Amlwch in tow of Tug *DREADFUL* from Devonport via Holyhead
1919	March	Barquentine *GAELIC* – reconditioning account.
1919	September	ss *PIONEER* of Conway.
1920	March	Painting etc. A.C. Barges
1920	June	Motor Barquentine *GAELIC*
1920	September	ss *DUNLEITH* – Arrived Amlwch from Aberdeen via Caledonian Canal in tow of Tug *NESTOR*
1921	May	*ELETH* and *DUNLEITH* at Amlwch
1921	November	ex HMS *RINALDO* arrived Amlwch in tow of Tug *WILLIAM POULSON* December. 8th 1921
1922	February	ex *HMS VESTAL* arrived Amlwch in tow of Tug *GLADSTONE* February 15th 1922.
1923	October	ss *ARDRI* arrived Amlwch ex Dublin in tow of Tug *HARRINGTON* October 18th 1923
1923	November	Motor Schooner *CREMYLL* at Beaumaris – salvage.
1924	January	*ARDI* and *DUNLEITH* at Amlwch
1927	December	ss *GERTIE* of Liverpool – Mr Bradburn Owner
1928	September	ss *MARALIE* purchased Cardiff September 19th 1928 arrived Amlwch Bay September 20th – 23 hours passage.

APPENDIX 18

IRON AND STEEL SAILING VESSELS DEVELOPED FROM
THE *GELERT* MODEL

Vessel	Built	Type	Tonnage	Length	Breadth	Depth
Gelert	1887	I Sch	222.9	124	24	10.9
Detlef Wagner	1891	I Bqn	225	127	24	10.8
Maggie Williams	1892	I Sch	226	123	24	10.8
Cymric	1893	I Bqn	226	123	24	10.8
Celtic	1894	I Scr	224	123	24	10.6
Gaelic	1898	I Bqn	224	126.8	24	10.8
Meyric	1904	S Sch	253	129.7	24.8	11.5
Elizabeth Roberts	1904	S Sch	134	102	22.1	9.4
Cenric	1905	S Sch	225	102	22.1	10.3
Eilian	1908	S Sch	140	102.6	21.9	9.4

I – Iron   S – Steel   Sch – Schooner   Bqn – Barquentine

APPENDIX 19

Number 20 New Vessel *(Eilian 1)* launched 27th September 1889

Breakdown of Building Costs

Cost of frame	£150-00-00
Cost of Planking	£ 120-00-00
Second Hand Timber	£ 50-00-00
Sawing	£ 50-00-00
Labour in all	£ 300-00-00
Iron Work	£ 80-00-00
Spars	£ 50-00-00
Rigging	£ 25-00-00
Chains Small	£ 20-00-00
Chains and Anchors	£ 40-00-00
Water Ropes	£ 60-00-00
Paints and Oils	£ 15-00-00
1 Boat	£ 15-00-00
Sails and Covers	£ 75-00-00
Copper Bolts	£ 50-00-00
Block	£ 20-00-00
Total	£ 1120-00-00
Profit	£ 100-00-00

APPENDIX 20

AUXILIARY SCHOONER *EILIAN* PURCHASING AGREEMENT

Amlwch Port
23rd October 1907

IT IS THIS DAY MUTUALLY AGREED BETWEEN CAPTAIN D. RICHARDSON OF 27 ROCK PARK, ROCK FERRY, CHESHIRE, hereinafter styled the PURCHASER, and WILLIAM THOMAS & SONS, SHIPBUILDERS, OF AMLWCH PORT, ANGLESEY, herein after styled the BUILDERS, as follows:

The said BUILDERS will as expeditiously as possible at their own cost and charge build, launch, and complete as a three-masted fore and aft schooner with three patent reefing gears, the steel vessel now in course of construction at their building yard, and designated by them number 34, but altered aft in a suitable and approved manner to receive a 50 hp motor engine a property of the PURCHASER.

The vessel to be delivered at Amlwch Port, and Lloyd's Certificate of Classification for 100 A.1. (Special Survey). Certificates of Freeboard, and chains and anchors, and Builders' Certificate, furnished at Builders' expense, and all requirements of the Board of Trade Regulations for the Coasting Trade complied with.

The said PURCHASER will pay to the BUILDERS as the contract price of the said vessel, the sum of TWO THOUSAND FIVE HUNDRED POUNDS, (£2,500) but the BUILDERS agree to accept as part payment of this sum, such number of shares in the vessel when fitted and completed with motor engine, outfit, and winches, of the total value of TWELVE HUNDRED POUNDS (£1,200), or 24/64th shares.

The PURCHASER shall supply, and deliver to Amlwch Port a 50 hp Kromhout motor engine, outfit, and two motor winches, each capable of lifting 10 hundredweights. The cost of such motor, outfit, carriage and expense of fitting on board to be added to the above contract price, and the total to be the capital value of vessel ready for sea (exclusive of consumable stores), and the amount of such costs to be deducted out of PURCHASER'S portion of the capital, the balance or difference of such value to be paid to the Builders on or before JANUARY 15th 1908

In the event of the PURCHASER not being able to sell or otherwise dispose of 15/64th shares of the vessel, the Builders agree that the value of such unsold or undisposed shares shall be raised by Mortgage, Bankers Overdraft, or other means to be hereafter mutually agreed upon in which event such charge to be paid off out of the vessel's earnings, after providing the necessary working capital.

Signed: William Thomas & Sons
      D. Richardson

Witness: R. Jones, 11 Parys Lodge Square, Amlwch
Witness: Alf. B. Toms, 22 Brown's B'dgs, Liverpool

APPENDIX 21

CREW'S RATIONS ABOARD THE SCHOONER *KATE*

During the course of his research, the author was given a copy of the following table detailing what would appear to be remarkably generous daily rations applicable to the crew of the Schooner *Kate* when she was in Manx ownership. How they compare with those applying when the vessel was in Thomas ownership is not known; but it is thought that they would have been comparable (with thanks to Wynne Lewis) .

	Bread lb	Beef lb	Pork lb	Flour oz	Peas pint	Rice oz	Tea oz	Coffee oz	Sugar oz	Water quarts
Sun.	1	$1\frac{1}{2}$	-	$\frac{1}{2}$	-	$\frac{1}{2}$	$\frac{1}{8}$	$\frac{1}{8}$	2	3
Mon.	1	-	$1\frac{1}{4}$	-	$\frac{1}{8}$	$\frac{1}{2}$	$\frac{1}{8}$	$\frac{1}{8}$	2	3
Tue.	1	$1\frac{1}{2}$	-	$\frac{1}{2}$	-	$\frac{1}{2}$	$\frac{1}{8}$	$\frac{1}{8}$	2	3
Wed.	1	-	$1\frac{1}{4}$	-	$\frac{1}{3}$	$\frac{1}{2}$	$\frac{1}{8}$	$\frac{1}{8}$	2	3
Thur.	1	$1\frac{1}{2}$	-	$\frac{1}{2}$	-	$\frac{1}{2}$	$\frac{1}{8}$	$\frac{1}{8}$	2	3
Fri.	1	-	$1\frac{1}{4}$	-	$\frac{1}{3}$	$\frac{1}{2}$	$\frac{1}{8}$	$\frac{1}{8}$	2	3
Sat.	1	$1\frac{1}{2}$	-	$\frac{1}{2}$	-	$\frac{1}{2}$	$\frac{1}{8}$	$\frac{1}{8}$	2	3

NOTE: 2 oz butter may be given in lieu of $\frac{1}{2}$ lb of Beef or Pork daily.

1 lb = 450 grms
1 oz = 28.35 grms
1 pint = 0.568 litres
1 quart = 1.136 litres

APPENDIX 22

MISCELLANEOUS LETTERS

Within the Thomas copy books, there are several letters which do not readily fit into the narrative, but which, because of their content, are nevertheless interesting and worthy of quoting. They are presented in date order.

Letter 1

Following his arrival in Canada on board the ss *Laurentian* in 1894, John Thomas wrote the following letter to his brothers Lewis and William, asking for money to enable him to go to British Columbia:

100 Delorimier Avenue
Montreal
Canada

January 9th 1895

My dear Brothers,

In my last letter I omitted to enclose you a letter from a young man that came out with me on the Laurentian last year – he is an engineer and his brother is manager of the Hall Mines Co., Nelson, B.C. You can see that he promises me a job of some kind if I go out there. I am willing to do anything at all, even working in the mines, but how can I get out there, as I told you before, I am stranded and have not a cent.

I have not got anything to do, and its useless looking for anything to do here business is very dull, and since the snow and cold weather has set in – business is almost entirely suspended. I do hope and trust that you will send the money I asked you viz. £25 to enable me to get out to B.C. and do something for myself. I have left no stone unturned to try and get something here, but it is simply impossible to get anything even if you gave your services free. I am simply sick of Montreal, once I get away from here, I would not return in a hurry. You have no idea what hardships I am suffering here, and if you do not send me the money, God only knows what will become of me, but I have every faith that after giving my case your consideration you will consent to enable me to get out to B.C. as I stated in my last, I would be willing to allow 1 year's annuity for the advance.

My face and arms are all covered with scales after the boils that broke out. I am a pitiful sight, and last week I had one of my ears frostbitten with the cold – the pain is intense. I never experienced anything like it before. If you knew half of the suffering I have endured here I am sure you would never tolerate it. It will cost nearly £20 to get out to Nelson and if you send £25 I will have a little in my pocket for meals on the train. As you know, I would have to buy my own meals. It takes 8 days to get out there.

I do hope you will remit as soon as you get this, unless you have already done so.

> *My fond love to all,*
> *I am, your loving brother,*
> *John*

Letter 2

There are several instances, where because of their higher standard of education, as well as their fluency in both English and Welsh languages, the Thomas brothers were often asked to write letters on behalf of others less well able to express themselves.

In one such letter dated March 1907, signed by Captain Owen Jones of Olinda Villa, Porth Amlwch, but composed and personally written by William Thomas, was addressed to the Member of Parliament, Mr E. J. Griffith. The letter illustrates the sheer and utter callousness which often attended the life of a British seaman at the beginning of the 20th century:

Dear Sir,

I trust you will pardon me for taking the liberty of writing to you, but as the matter is so deserving of attention, I hope you will give it your earnest consideration.

I have been advised to state to you the facts in connection with an accident which happened to Richard Thomas, a mariner of this port, with a view to bringing the case before the House of Commons or the Board of Trade.

The said Richard Thomas, who is 49 years of age, was employed as an able seaman on board the ss Isle of Anglesey, and whilst she was leaving Maryport bound for Swansea, at about one o'clock in the morning of the 2nd December last, he was engaged attending to the steam winch forward, to which were attached two ropes – one on the port, and one on the starboard bow, for the purpose of hauling the vessel out of dock. Whilst thus engaged, he was ordered to take a 'kink' out of one of the ropes, and in doing so, the slack of the other rope got round his leg, with the result that he was carried to the top of the forecastle head against the bitts, and had his leg crushed. As the pilot boat was in attendance, he requested to be taken ashore by the pilot, but met with a refusal. On approaching Holyhead, he again applied to be put ashore there, but was again refused. As the voyage occupied about 60 hours, he suffered great agony, his leg bleeding profusely, and by the time he reached Swansea, he was in a serious state. On taking him to the hospital, it was found that blood poisoning had set in, and they therefore had to amputate his leg below the knee, but unfortunately it became necessary to make another amputation above the knee. The medical gentleman at Swansea informed him that had he been put ashore at Maryport immediately the accident took place, an amputation would have been unnecessary as they would have been in time to prevent blood poisoning.

I understand that Richard Thomas has written to the owners of the steamer with the object of receiving some compensation, but they replied that they were not prepared to compensate him, and that they would defend any action that might be taken against them, but as Richard Thomas is in very strait circumstances, it is impossible for him to do anything, as he has a large family depending on his earnings.

I should therefore, esteem it a great favour if you would be so kind as to take some steps that would ensure for him, some compensation for his loss, as it is palpable that he has lost his limb through the most cruel negligence.

Thanking you in anticipation, I am, dear Sir,
Yours respectfully,

Owen Jones, Master Mariner

Letter 3

John Thomas's last known letter was addressed to his brother William. Whether or not it was yet another example of similarly couched letters which were intended to part his family from their money, will perhaps never be known.

Despite claiming to be so weak as to be unable to write, his handwriting is nevertheless seen to be as firm as it always was, and not what might have been expected from a man claiming to be so weak as to be unable to write. Yet, for some reason, the letter has the ring of truth about it!

1439 18th Avenue South,
San Francisco,
California

September 11th, 1911

My dear Brother,

Just a line to tell you that I am very seriously ill, and am going to the hospital today. I am given up by three doctors, and they recommend the hospital as a last resource. Where there is life there is hope of course; but I am afraid I shall never get better, and this my last request. I want you to help my wife and little boy, they have nothing to fall back on when I go – I have been sick so long that we could not save a cent, so I beg of you to be good to them, and send them some money to live on whilst I am in the hospital. I am sorry having to ask you but under the circumstances, it cannot be helped. Please notice change of address – excuse brevity, but I am so weak I cannot write.

Your affectionate Brother,
John.

Letter 4

William Thomas's keen sense of recognition of others' achievements, came to the fore when he learnt of a French seaman's bravery in attempting to rescue a drowning child from the waters of Porth Amlwch.

In similar letters addressed to the Secretary of the Royal Humane Society, and to the Foreign Office in Downing Street, London, he respectfully desired:

… to bring to your notice, the gallantry displayed by a French subject of the name of Jean Jaffray (sic), *a fireman on board the ss Olive lying at this port. Last evening, a little boy was perceived to be drowning at the entrance of this harbour, and before assistance could reach him, he had disappeared. Jaffray, as soon as he arrived at the spot, without divesting himself of clothing, and at great risk to himself, dived into the water amongst sunken rocks, and after several attempts, and by untiring efforts, he ultimately was able to recover the body, but unfortunately in spite of immediate application of artificial means of restoring respiration, the lad did not survive the effects of immersion. We respectfully submit this case to the kind consideration of H.M. Government as being in our opinion, very worthy of their recognition, and we hope they will see their way clear to acknowledge this brave deed.*

The *ss Olive* was at that time being worked upon in Iard Newydd, and in a further letter to the Secretary of the Royal Humane Society, William Thomas enclosed the reply he had received from an Under Secretary at the Foreign Office, before adding:

… trusting that your Society will recognise the services of this man, who in addition to being a stranger, owing to him being a monoglot Frenchman, no one could clearly communicate with him.

Soon after, as a result of William Thomas's intercession, Jaffré, as his surname turned out to be, received the Bronze Medal of the Royal Humane Society for his great courage in attempting to save the life of a local lad called Hugh Owen, albeit unsuccessfully.

Letter 5

An undated letter (probably from the middle 1930's) intended for a newspaper or maritime journal, was written by William Thomas Junior's son John. In it, he addresses what he described as:

The Plight of the Coasting Boats

We do not wonder at the state of affairs in all British seaports. Unemployment among our sailors is rife, and things seem to be getting from bad to worse. The reason for this is that the British Coaster is being driven into dock, through the unfair competition of the foreigner. The foreigner is being granted a subsidy by his respective government, and can therefore afford to quote lower freight. Of course, they are paid a good freight for their cargoes from their own seaports, and an equal freight for what they carry back; but when in our waters, they accept a much lower rate in order to work their way towards their home ports, and by doing so, unremunerative rates are established.

For instance, the writer, a few days ago, was at a Cornish port, and saw for himself no less than five foreign coasters arriving there from the Bristol Channel at a rate which any British boat would not consider. The vessels were again loaded with cargoes for the English Channel and the east coast, at very low rates. Some few days ago, a small foreign coaster came from Spain, light, to one of the north Wales quarries to load stone for London, at 6d per ton lower than any previous rate paid to any British boat. This is the rate which is now offered to a British boat.

The transport workers have jibbed at trifling matters in the past, and have struck work in sympathy with their fellow workmen, and yet they work at something which has a vital consequence on the employment of the British sailor. It is the duty of every transport worker to stand by his brother the sailor, and refuse to handle any cargo which is brought into our ports by the foreigner who cuts the freights. We stand by and allow him to take away the bread of our children.

It is high time that drastic action should be taken to compel His Majesty's Government to act before the last straw of hope has been captured by the foreigner by his unfair competition. We have no objection to them bringing their cargoes to our ports, or taking cargoes to their own ports; but to allow them to trade on our coast at reduced rates is absolutely absurd.

J.T. Amlwch

Letter 6

Following the death of William Thomas Junior, his successors were minded to modernise the yard and continue its shipbuilding tradition. In this respect they engaged several consultants to investigate the feasibility of doing so. One such was A.D.R. Kelly of Glasgow who reported back to the firm in December 1938.

Dear Sirs,

Ship Yard

I am very much obliged for your favour of yesterday's date, enclosing a sketch of the yard, and at the same time, I must thank you for the courtesy and information which your mr Thomas gave me on my call at Amlwch.

I have considered the matter carefully, and find, that to modernise the yard sufficiently to build say, three vessels per annum, two of which would be in the larger berth, which is about 70 ft wide, and one in the smaller berth, a sum of round about £6,000 would be necessary, this would include the following:-

(Shed) Shell, Decks etc.
One punch and shear.
One plate planing machine.
One set of plate rolls, up to about 22 ft, with a slot cut in one of the rolls for flanging purposes.
Two C.S. verticals.

(Shed) Frames, Beams and other bars.
One combined fired bar and plate furnace to take bars up to 35 ft, and plates up to 12 ft long.
One angle punch and bar shear.
One beam setter and bar shear.
One horizontal bar punch.
One punching, shearing, and limbering punch.
One hydraulic M.H. punch.

I have also included for a hydraulic pump and accumulator to give power for rivetting frames, floors etc., also for a M.H. punch, and for a hydraulic frame bender.

This price also covers for a few sundry machines, for a Machine shop, Carpenters shop, and Smithy etc., a welders plant, and also for Electric installation, and sheds, and wages spent in the layout of the yard.

After you have considered the foregoing, perhaps you will let me have your opinion on same. Might I venture however, to state that in my view, the yard is not in a very good position from the point of view of obtaining new work or repair work.

The small yard which I mentioned to Mr Thomas I had looked into, is in a much more convenient place on the west coast, (although not in the Liverpool district) the ground is nearly square, and is not of a hilly or rocky nature, as the yard is at Amlwch.

The railway is presently run up to the gate, and the yard can be obtained on a lease at a very moderate rent, of round about £200 with the benefits of derating and a reduction in, rates, taxes and Income Tax, and N.D.C. for a period of years.

This proposition seems to me much better if the necessary capital can be obtained, also the port is getting busier, and vessels with Diesel engines could be fitted out complete, as there is a

15 ton crane in the harbour.

    Also small vessels could be beached for breaking, and the steel works are quite adjacent to take the scrap.

    There are also the foundations ready for a patent slip, and the matter of any skilled nature, which would be required, could be got over quite easily.

    In this yard, four to five coasting vessels could easily be turned out per annum with the yard fully equipped as I am proposing.

           Yours faithfully etc.,

Letter 7

It is apparent that nothing was done to modernise the yard; but possibly in the hope that they might benefit from the requirements of the Second World War, as had happened during the First World War, the Thomas family again addressed the deficiencies of Iard Newydd, and on the 15th of February 1943, they wrote in reply to a letter received from Dowsett Engineering of Colwall, Worcestershire, as follows:

Dear Sirs,

           Shipyard, Amlwch Port

We thank you for your favours of the 8th and 9th instant covering your Mr H.L.Dowsett's report in respect of his recent visit to the above yard, and conclude therefrom that he was not too favourably impressed with the property – which we regret.

    In reply to your various observations:-

1. The question of time to get the yard into working condition would depend entirely on the labour available, and would in our opinion not present serious difficulties which we venture to suggest could be overcome by your firm, being engaged as you are on government work which should materially assist in obtaining the Ministry of Labour support for the transfer of the requisite labour from one district to another, especially in this case which would be of a priority nature. (vide "Essential Works Order")

2 As regards power, the North Wales Power company have mains laid to within a few hundred yards from the site, and having regard to the work undertaken in the past, our friends consider that a Diesel engine would prove to be more economical in comparison with electric power.

3. "Machine Tools" – Although not modern, they are in working condition, and in fact, the Admiralty offered to purchase same some time ago. As mentioned in our previous letter, the Admiralty have the yard presently under review, and their decision is expected shortly.

4. We are at a loss to understand your remarks regarding the slipways being unsatisfactory, and for your guidance, numerous vessels have been constructed in the past, the largest being a 450 tons deadweight iron streamer. Our friends would not have any hesitation in laying a keel again for a 750 tonner on the larger slipway with hardly any alteration to the berth. In view of the depth of water at this slipway viz.:- 20 to 25 feet, it is considered that with certain modern improvements the works would be able to build two vessels of 1000/1200 tons or alternatively one 2000 tonner at a reasonable outlay to the existing berth.

As regards disposal, we will communicate with you when the Admiralty have made their decision, meantime we shall be glad if you will give us some indication of your idea of price.

        Signed WT

APPENDIX 23

CAPTAIN WILLIAM THOMAS'S OWN ESTIMATES OF HIS ASSETS
IN 1882
10 years after the purchase of Iard Newydd

PROPERTY	1882 VALUE £	2002 VALUE £
Yuca (vessel)	1000	54340
Toronto (vessel)	500	27170
Countess of Lonsdale (vessel)	2250	122265
Countess of Kintore (vessel)	400	21736
Lady Neave (vessel)	700	38038
Margaret (vessel)	1200	65208
President Garfield (vessel)	1000	54340
Eilian Hill (vessel)	400	21736
Juanita (vessel)	650	35321
Coila (vessel)	600	32604
Thomas (vessel)	350	19019
Elizabeth Ann (vessel)	500	27170
Jane Pringle (vessel)	500	27170
Caroline (vessel)	250	13585
Mountain Maid (vessel)	250	13585
Welsh Girl (vessel)	550	29887
Pride of Anglesea (vessel)	300	16302
Mary Ann (vessel)	300	16302
Albion (vessel)	250	13585
Glyndwr (vessel)	200	10868
Victoria (vessel)	120	6520
Lord Mostyn (vessel)	200	10868
Priscilla (vessel)	600	32604
James Reid (vessel)	180	9781
Baron Hill (vessel)	400	21736
Cumberland Lassie (vessel)	150	8151
Ocean Belle (vessel)	100	5434

PROPERTY	1882 VALUE £	2002 VALUE £
Alnwick (vessel)	100	5434
Amanda (vessel)	55	2988
Total	14055	763748
Insurances	1500	81510
In Bank	1000	54340
to (indecipherable) William Melhuish	1500	81510
Duddon .... (indecipherable)	600	32604
Cash in my hand	270	14671
Duddon Yard	1000	54340
Sub Total	19920	1082724
Yard at Amlwch	2500	135850
Mazinerys (sic) at low estimate	1500	81510
Stock in wherhouse (sic)	500	27170
ditto in Sail Room	500	27170
Stock in yard in all	500	27170
Improvement N yard	150	8151
New House – Bryn Eilian	1500	81510
Penysarn Houses	250	13585
Port Houses	500	27170
Stock Dairy (?) Cattle	200	10868
Furniture (in) House	400	21736
Land Bodednyfed	1500	81510
Land Towyn Trewan	140	7607
Sub Total	30060	1633732
Cae Pant (Family Smallholding)	1650	89661
Ponc Taldrwst (property)	1650	89661
Donan Lâs (property)	1100	59774
Tyddyn Sara (property)	1100	59774
Pensglaets (property)	680	36951
Bryn Eilian (property)	1050	57057
Sub Total	37290	2026610
Less Mortgage	5000	271700
TOTAL	32290	1754910

APPENDIX 24

TABLE TO CONVERT THE PURCHASING POWER OF EARLIER POUNDS (UK) TO 2002 VALUES

For example: £1 in 1858 had the same purchasing power as £52.06 in year 2002

Year	Multiplier	Year	Multiplier
1858	52.06	1889	65.42
1859	51.05	1890	65.42
1860	47.17	1891	62.07
1861	47.60	1892	62.23
1862	48.03	1893	67.77
1863	54.16	1894	63.15
1864	51.66	1895	64.00
1865	50.07	1896	65.42
1866	47.84	1897	64.35
1867	46.06	1898	63.15
1868	48.03	1899	65.24
1869	49.81	1900	62.39
1870	49.97	1901	62.89
1871	46.94	1902	64.35
1872	44.97	1903	61.74
1873	43.12	1904	62.89
1874	43.55	1905	62.64
1875	47.31	1906	61.02
1876	45.23	1907	60.09
1877	46.61	1908	59.41
1878	48.38	1909	58.60
1879	51.22	1910	62.39
1880	52.82	1911	62.98
1881	51.11	1912	62.07
1882	54.34	1913	60.71
1883	52.41	1914	54.03
1884	57.88	1915	47.08
1885	60.40	1916	37.26
1886	66.53	1917	31.55
1887	64.88	1918	24.83
1888	65.24	1919	27.50

Source: John J Mc Cusker: "Comparing the Purchasing Power of Money in Great Britain 1264-2002"
Economic History Services Miami University / EHNet / Wake Forest University

INDEXES

SHIPS

PEOPLE

BIBLIOGRAPHY

Bennet, Douglas
   Schooner Sunset, Rochester, 2001
Cunliffe, Tom (Ed.)
   Pilots, Douarnenez, France 2001
Eames, Aled
   Ships and Seamen of Anglesey, Llangefni,1973
   Ventures in Sail, Caernarfon 1987
Fenton, Roy
   Cambrian Coasters, World Ship Society, 1989
Greenhill, Basil
   The Merchant Schooners, London, 1988
Greenhill, B and Manning, S
   The Evolution of the Wooden Ship, London 1988
Harris, John R
   The Copper King, Liverpool 1964
Hasslöf, Olof, et al.
   Problems of Ship Management and Operation 1870-1900,
   National Maritime Museum, Greenwich 1972
Hollett, David
   The Alabama Affair, Wilmslow 1993
Hope, Bryan D
   A Curious Place, Wrexham 1993, and Moelfre 1997
   The Mersey, Liverpool Pilot Boat 11, Volume 11, Maritime Wales, Caernarfon, 1987
Mannering, J (Ed.)
   Inshore Craft, London 1997
Morgan, Trevor
   The Cumberland Connection, Volume 7, Maritime Wales, Caernarfon 1983